Memoirs of the Museum of Anthropology
University of Michigan
Number 57

Caribou Hunting in the Upper Great Lakes

Archaeological, Ethnographic, and Paleoenvironmental Perspectives

---

edited by

Elizabeth Sonnenburg

Ashley K. Lemke

John M. O'Shea

Ann Arbor, Michigan
2015

Printed in the United States of America
ISBN 978-0-915703-85-2

Cover design by Katherine Clahassey

The Museum currently publishes two monograph series: Anthropological Papers and Memoirs.
For permissions, questions, or catalogs, contact Museum publications at
1109 Geddes Avenue, Ann Arbor, Michigan 48109-1079;
umma-pubs@umich.edu; www.lsa.umich.edu/ummaa/publications

Library of Congress Cataloging-in-Publication Data

Caribou hunting in the upper Great Lakes : archaeological, ethnographic, and paleoenvironmental perspectives / edited by Elizabeth Sonnenburg, Ashley K. Lemke, John M. O'Shea.
pages cm. -- (Memoirs of the Museum of Anthropology, University of Michigan ; number 57)
Includes bibliographical references.
ISBN 978-0-915703-85-2 (alk. paper)
1. Indians of North America--Hunting--Huron, Lake Region (Mich. and Ont.) 2. Indians of North America--Huron, Lake Region (Mich. and Ont.)--Antiquities. 3. Indians of North America--Great Lakes Region (North America)--Antiquities. 4. Hunting, Prehistoric--Huron, Lake Region (Mich. and Ont.) 5. Hunting, Prehistoric--Great Lakes Region (North America) 6. Caribou hunting--Huron, Lake Region (Mich. and Ont.)--History. 7. Caribou hunting--Great Lakes Region (North America)--History. 8. Underwater archaeology--Huron, Lake (Mich. and Ont.) 9. Huron, Lake Region (Mich. and Ont.)--Antiquities. 10. Great Lakes Region (North America)--Antiquities. I. Sonnenburg, Elizabeth, 1974- editor, author. II. Lemke, Ashley K., 1985- editor, author. III. O'Shea, John M., editor, author.
E98.H8C37 2015
977.004'97--dc23

2014044938

The paper used in this publication meets the requirements of the ANSI Standard Z39.48-1984 (Permanence of Paper).

Contents

Contributors

Peter J. Barnett
Department of Earth Sciences
Laurentian University, Sudbury, Ontario

Gregory Beaton
Archaeological Survey of Laurentian University
Laurentian University, Sudbury, Ontario

D. Brian Deller
Department of Anthropology
University of Western Ontario, London

Christopher J. Ellis
Department of Anthropology
University of Western Ontario, London

James Fogarty
Department of Computer Science
Wayne State University, Detroit, Michigan

William A. Fox
Archaeological Services
Parks Canada and Trent University Archaeological Research Center, Peterborough, Ontario

Patrick J. Julig
Department of Anthropology
Laurentian University, Sudbury, Ontario

Ashley K. Lemke
Museum of Anthropological Archaeology
University of Michigan, Ann Arbor

John H. McAndrews
Department of Earth Sciences
University of Toronto, Ontario

Francine M. G. McCarthy
Department of Earth Sciences
Brock University, St. Catharines, Ontario

John M. O'Shea
Museum of Anthropological Archaeology
University of Michigan, Ann Arbor

Thomas Palazzolo
Department of Computer Science
Wayne State University, Detroit, Michigan

Elli Papangelakis
Department of Geography
University of British Columbia, Vancouver

Robert G. Reynolds
Department of Computer Science
Wayne State University, Detroit, Michigan

Areej Salaymeh
Department of Computer Science
Wayne State University, Detroit, Michigan

Elizabeth Sonnenburg
Museum of Anthropological Archaeology
University of Michigan, Ann Arbor

Andrew M. Stewart
Strata Consulting, Inc.
Toronto, Ontario

Illustrations

Color Plates

Tables

Foreword: **Below the Waves of Time**

by Henry T. Wright

When archaeologists, during the period between the two World Wars, first recognized the distinctive technologies of Late Glacial hunters on the Great Plains of North America, there seemed little relation with the flaked stone technologies of later Native American peoples. During the 1950s, research gave archaeologists some understanding of cultural developments from late Paleoindian to earlier Archaic technologies. In the southeast, Joffre Coe (1960, 1964) provided the first evidence of a transition from Late Paleoindian Dalton points to Early Archaic Kirk points. Subsequent research showed parallel technological developments from the Florida Peninsula to the Mississippi Valley. To the north, however, progress has been much slower. In the central Great Lakes region, Late Paleoindian industries were documented by the exemplary work at the Holcombe sites (Fitting, DeVisscher, and Wahla 1966); a few tiny calcined bones from a single feature were identified as *Rangifer*, indicating that seasonal caribou hunting was practiced by Holcombe hunters (Cleland 1965). It was, however, a quarter of a century before an Early Archaic assemblage in the region was retrieved and fully described (Ellis, Wortner, and Fox 1991), although this excellent study produced no direct evidence of the date or subsistence pursuits of the Early Archaic people. Where could well-preserved evidence of the transition from Paleoindian to Early Archaic lifeways in the Great Lakes region be found? As demonstrated by this volume, the answer lies under the waters of the Great Lakes.

It was little more than a year after Michigan geologist George M. Stanley published the first evidence of postglacial low-water stages in the central Great Lakes (1936) that he visited the George Lake area with Emerson Greenman (Stanley 1937; Greenman and Stanley 1940) and realized that early Native American foragers would have lived along the shores of these lower lakes. It was, however, only when Illinois geologist Jack L. Hough recognized and dated the deeply submerged traces of Lake Chippewa in the Lake Michigan basin (1955) and deduced the implications of this discovery for an even lower lake in the Huron basin—one that he termed "Lake Stanley" (Hough 1958)—that the scope of the possibilities became evident. Hough's redating of pro-glacial Lake Algonquin (Hough 1963) indicated that perhaps five millennia of lakeside and river mouth sites were hidden below modern Lakes Michigan and Huron, a deduction that was soon noted by archaeologists (Fitting 1970:57). Fifty years ago, however, it seemed likely that archaeologists would have evidence available only from peripheral sites in the headwaters of rivers from this long period.

In fact, the solution to this problem was at hand. Scuba gear (Ellis et al. 1979) and submersibles (Somers, Tetzloff, and Anderson 1968) had been used on the Great Lakes by researchers and avocational divers since the1960s. If these endeavours had any archaeological intent, it was to examine the many well-preserved shipwrecks, most from the past two centuries (Halsey and Lusardi 2008; O'Shea 2004). However, this work prepared Great Lakes scientists to undertake the innovative research extensively presented for the first time in this volume. John O'Shea has melded his long-standing interests in complex hunter-gatherers and intensive food gathering economies in general, and in early Great Lakes peoples in particular, with skills in remote sensing, underwater diving technologies, and the integration of diverse digital data sets. However, beyond the fusing of a theoretical anthropological toolbox with cutting edge technology, O'Shea was able to bring together a very diverse group of experts and infuse them with a vision of a lost world of ancient hunters, the traces of which must be preserved below the waters of modern-day Lake Huron. For this, he merits the thanks of all concerned.

This book is an interim report on the research to date on the archaeology, geology, and paleoecology of the Lake Huron basin with a special focus on the Alpena-Amberley Ridge. This cuesta of dolomite, exposed and sculpted by moving glacial ice, connected the northern lower peninsula of Michigan to southern Ontario in times of lowered lake level. The volume is not simply the product of a single research symposium. Rather, it is a series of studies based on many smaller meetings, site visits, collegial discussions, and workshops, with many different funding sources, all duly acknowledged in the individual papers.

Part I begins with the general geological background of the Great Lakes, focusing on evidence for changing advances and retreat of the Laurentide ice mass, the depression and rebound of the earth's surface in response to the weight of the ice, and the exposure and closing of different passages through which water could flow out of the different lake basins. The contributors are largely Canadian, reflecting the fact that most recent research has been done in Canada. They do not cite interesting discussions by U.S. geologists (Larsen 1987, 1999), but they do synthesize very important recent Canadian research (Barnett and Delorme 2007; McAndrews 1994; McCarthy et al. 2012; Karrow 2004) of which most U.S. scholars—and certainly most U.S. archaeologists—are unaware. Their contributions are most welcome. This part ends with something quite different, rarely seen in archaeological studies, but certain to be of increasing utility in future studies of foraging societies, particularly those of Pleistocene hunters. This is the presentation by Robert Reynolds' team from Wayne State University of an agent-based simulation model of prey behavior (in this case, caribou) upon a detailed digital representation of parts of the actual landscape of the Alpena-Amberley Ridge. This simulation, built on an successful pioneering model of plant gathering (Reynolds 1986), is only an initial presentation. The covering of larger areas, improved knowledge of the vegetation, and incorporation of other types of agents such as wolves and people, with more adaptive learning among all agents, will make this a more powerful tool, both for defining the research problem and for creating contexts for testing propositions about hunting using the archaeological data from the lake floor. Nonetheless, this first approximation is indeed promising.

Part II presents important background cultural studies, without which the archaeological work under Lake Huron would be difficult. The limited prior knowledge of the forager cultures of the ninth millennium BCE (primarily that gleaned from terrestrial sites on beaches of some of the low-stage lakes in Canada on the north and west of the Huron basin) gives archaeologists an idea of what kind of stone tool industries might have been used on the ridge, and is summarized by Canadian archaeologists Patrick Julig and Gregory Beaton, who themselves have made many key contributions (Julig 1994, 2002). The raw material used for such in Late Glacial and early Post-glacial times are detailed by William Fox, Brian Deller, and Christopher Ellis, Canadian researchers who have spent decades studying the issue (Deller 1989; Ellis 1989; Ellis, Wortner, and Fox 1991). The work of anthropologists and archaeologists on the use of structures by hunters to guide herbivores into traps in many parts of the world is presented by Ashley Lemke, a member of the Ann Arbor team. The use of such structures specifically for taking caribou in northern Canada, an extant environment similar to that more than ten millennia ago in the Huron basin, backed up with spectacular photographic images and interviews with the actual hunters, is presented by Andrew Stewart, who has done both archaeology and ethnography in these high latitudes (Stewart et al. 2000; Stewart, Keith, and Scottie 2004).

Part III presents overviews of the actual research on the Alpena-Amberley Ridge by the team's principal archaeologists and geologist, who were based in Ann Arbor through much of this research. It starts with a useful account by John O'Shea of lessons learned as the project developed, with an emphasis on the successes and limitations of different equipment and techniques. This is followed by his detailed description accompanied by copious images of apparent constructed features found in the three different intensive survey areas on the ridge using both sonar and direct study by divers. Lemke discusses the cultural nature of these features that is verified by the distribution of small stone flakes from the retouching of tools, some of raw materials known to have been used by eighth-millennium BCE foragers on terrestrial sites around the central Great Lakes. Ending this part is Sonnenburg's detailed presentation of the present state of paleoecological knowledge of each studied locality of the Alpena-Amberley Ridge.

In **Part IV**, the Ann Arbor team summarizes the work, in places moving beyond the available evidence to propose ideas about paleoenvironment, seasonality, and social organization. These conjectures stand as provocative proposals to be tested in future research. If the project's specific accomplishments are impressive and convincing, the volume provides a broader model for how prehistoric archaeology underwater can be conducted. It moves beyond the study of chance finds, to place underwater archaeology firmly in the same framework of research design, excavation and recovery, and analysis to evaluate the propositions defined in the research design that is found in the best of terrestrial archaeology. The development of such an integrated approach in the context of the Great Lakes will help equip archaeologists to face the challenges posed by global sea level change.

The volume also clearly demonstrates that much remains to be done in the Great Lakes and that the team is on the verge of further exciting results. Though they have evidence of features, flaked stone tools and debris, dated wooden objects, and micro-remains such as pollen and diatoms, there is—thanks to the ravages of the zebra mussels—only one definite macro-fragment of a cervid, not definitely *Rangifer*, the likely principal prey. More evidence of the prey of early hunters, as well as the actual ninth-millennium vegetation of the ridge, must be sought. They will be found, perhaps in the sediments of one of the small ponds on the ridge, located but not yet tested, if the funds and courageous researchers can be brought together to continue this difficult and dangerous work.

Acknowledgments

This monograph is dedicated to the memory of Gerald Larson, who was instrumental in creating the initial computer simulation modeling for the Alpena-Amberley Ridge.

This monograph would not be possible without the excellent discussion and presentations from the original symposium held in Ann Arbor, Michigan, in February of 2013. We would like to thank the many people involved in the data collection and analyses of material from the Alpena-Amberley Ridge, especially Guy Meadows, Lee Newsom, Eduard Reinhardt, Elizabeth Callison, Luke Toebler, and Jessica Tangert. We especially thank the ProCom dive team members Tyler Schultz, Michael Courvoisier, Annie Davidson, Chris Gula, Derek King, and Betsy Campbell. We would also like to thank the Great Lakes Shipwreck Festival for inviting us to share our research over the past few years. Institutionally, we would also acknowledge the support of the Museum of Anthropological Archaeology, University of Michigan; the Department of Computer Science, Wayne State University; and the Thunder Bay National Marine Sanctuary. This research was supported in part by grants from the National Science Foundation, award numbers BCS0829324 and BCS0964424, and by NOAA's Ocean Exploration–Marine Archaeology program award number NA10OAR0110187. We would also like to thank Katherine Clahassey for her work on the cover and many of the interior illustrations and images. Finally, a very large thank you to Jill Rheinheimer, whose editorial skills ensured this book became a reality.

1 Introduction to Lake Stanley Archaeology in the Lake Huron Basin

by John M. O'Shea and Elizabeth Sonnenburg

The renewed archaeological interest in the Lake Stanley-era lakes of the Lake Huron basin, which was the impetus for this volume, has grown out of the convergence of recent new bathymetric mapping in the Great Lakes, new environmental data including the discovery of preserved ancient trees in the Lake Huron near shore, and accumulating ethnographic and historic literature on the hunting and herding of caribou.

Since the first recognition of the existence of one or more low-water stands in the Great Lakes, the possibility that archaeological sites representing the Late Paleoindian and earlier Archaic periods might be preserved has tantalized archaeologists (Lovis et al. 1994; Jackson et al. 2000). It has become commonplace to associate and date early sites in the Great Lakes region with the relict shores of the high-water stands, such as Lake Algonquin and Lake Nipissing, although it is now recognized that these preserved lakeshores may represent much more complex processes than originally thought (Jackson 2004; Karrow 2004). Since these relict shores are now on dry land, they are directly accessible to geologists and figure prominently in models for the gradual evolution of the modern Great Lakes. The low-water stand represented by the Lake Stanley stage is less well known and our knowledge of it is derived from cores of presumed contemporary features on dry land, or from deep lake deposits (Lewis and Anderson 2012; Dryzyga, Shortridge, and Schaetzl 2012). As such, the sequence of formation and disappearance, the actual elevations maintained, and the dating are not as well established as the transgressive events of glacial Lake Algonquin (GLA) and Nipissing.

What is not speculative is the immense impact the lower lake level would have had on resident human communities and their environment. Using a plausible mean average of 140 meters above sea level (masl), an incredible 250,000 hectares of land—prime habitat for hunters and gatherers—would have been available and then lost to occupation within the Lake Huron basin (Lewis, Blasco, and Gareau 2005). The shape and extent of the Lake Stanley lakes within the modern Lake Huron basin have varied over time (see Chapters 2, 3, 12) and may, at various times, have been composed of as many as three distinct lakes. The most marked features of these ancient lakes would have been the radically altered shorelines in which Saginaw Bay and the North Channel would have been entirely dry, and two arching landforms—one the extension of the Bruce Peninsula/Manitoulin Island, and the second a high rocky ridge, in the center of the Lake Huron basin, extending from Presque Isle in Michigan to the Point Clark area of southwestern Ontario. On nautical charts, this latter feature is designated Six Fathom Shoal, due to its shallow depth. In the most recent bathymetric mapping of Lake Huron, the feature is termed the Alpena-Amberley Ridge.

The Alpena-Amberley Ridge (AAR) is formed from the resistant limestones and dolomites of the Traverse/Onondaga formation, and it divided the Lake Huron basin into two distinct Stanley-era lakes: a deep cold lake to the east, and a shallower, brackish lake to the west (see Chapter 3). The feature was well known but what the new bathymetric mapping revealed was that it was continuous, and it would have formed an unbroken link across the lake basin. This has major implications for its potential role as a migration route for caribou and as a focus for human hunting.

The idea that the submerged lakeshores of the Lake Stanley stage might preserve evidence of early human occupation has been around since the 1960s (Quimby 1963). Between 1993 and 1995, the Ontario Marine Heritage Committee, the Geological Survey of Canada, and Parks Canada conducted surveys of the submerged gaps in the Bruce Peninsula-Manitoulin Island features, which revealed rooted trees and other features associated with the low-water stand. This work also began to circumscribe the actual levels of lake waters associated with the Lake Stanley stage, and suggested the possible isolation of Georgian Bay from the rest of the Lake Huron basin during a portion of the low-water stand (Janusas et al. 2004).

Preserved trees, some rooted, were also discovered in 18 m of water offshore from the "thumb" of Michigan (Hunter et al. 2006). This preserved forest yielded radiocarbon dates in the range of 7180 to 7920 cal BP, suggesting that it was inundated by the rising water after the end of the Lake Stanley stage. Preserved wood of a similar date has subsequently been discovered in 6 m of water within the Thunder Bay National Marine Sanctuary at Alpena, Michigan.

Archaeologists have long been aware that sites of the relatively poorly known Early and Middle Archaic age might be concentrated beneath the modern Great Lakes (cf. Shott and Wright 1999). There was relatively little effort, however, directed at locating and investigating such sites. One approach was to test deeply buried sites in alluvial environments that might be associated with the low-water stands in the Grand River and Saginaw River valleys. There were also tentative efforts to identify possible settlements near the mouth of Saginaw Bay, with the idea that the exposed chert at locations such as Charity Island might have attracted Archaic-era hunters (cf. Monaghan and Lovis 2005).

The new bathymetry showed that the AAR could have provided a dry land corridor between northern Michigan and southwest Ontario. The questions that remained were: (1) what might attract human occupation on the AAR, and (2) assuming there was human use of this feature, how would archaeologists be able to discover and recognize the sites?

The key to answering the first question is to understand the general character of the environment during the Lake Stanley phase, and more specifically to document in detail the local conditions, such as climate, vegetation cover, and hydrology. The first step in this process is determining the timing and character of major changes in the Lake Stanley water levels. Such environmental documentation would, in turn, allow the resource potentials of the AAR for hunter-gatherer exploitation to be modeled and simulated. To approach the second question, we turn to the rich historical and ethnographic record of recent caribou hunters in more northerly regions, and an equally rich archaeological record of global caribou exploitation, and to later Paleoindian and earlier Archaic occupations of the Great Lakes region.

The desire to answer these questions and to understand the early Holocene Great Lakes region brought the contributors to this volume together, and, consequently, Part 1 considers the character and modeling of the past environment, Part 2 describes the multiple lines of cultural evidence, and Part 3 provides a preliminary description of the initial results from new archaeological research on the AAR. Unless otherwise stated, all dates will be reported as either uncalibrated radiocarbon years BP, and/or as calibrated dates reported as cal BP.

The monograph begins with Peter Barnett's discussion of the geological processes that show how areas like the Alpena-Amberley Ridge have been submerged and preserved, and where other potential sites from this time period may be located. Francine McCarthy and her colleagues provide an overview of the paleoenvironmental context of Lake Huron during the Lake Stanley lowstand phase. Finally, James Fogarty and his colleagues describe the use of cultural algorithms to build a simulation model of caribou behavior, and, using data from the ridge, provide a window on how caribou may have migrated through the landscape.

Part 2, which describes cultural evidence, opens with Pat Julig and Gregory Beaton's discussion of the terrestrial archaeological record of Late Paleoindian and Early Archaic sites in the upper Great Lakes. Bill Fox and his colleagues provide an overview of chert sources that would have been utilized by Late Paleoindian/Early Archaic peoples in the upper Great Lakes. Ashley Lemke introduces the different types of ungulate hunting structures that are found archaeologically worldwide in order to create an understanding of how the structures found on the AAR may have been utilized, and the kind of additional archaeological sites and artifacts that may (or may not) be found. Finally, Andrew Stewart looks at caribou hunting structures in the Arctic and considers how these can be compared to structures that may have been utilized in Ontario during the Paleoindian period.

Part 3 focuses on finds specific to the Alpena-Amberley Ridge. John O'Shea first outlines the research strategy employed to locate hunting structures on the ridge, and subsequently provides detailed analysis of the currently known hunting structures on the ridge and how they may have been utilized. Ashley Lemke then describes and analyzes the lithic artifacts recovered near submerged archaeological sites. Lastly, Elizabeth Sonnenburg describes the AAR paleoenvironment during this time period and the potential for preservation of additional archaeological materials.

In the final conclusive discussion (Part 4), Sonnenburg, Lemke, and O'Shea summarize the findings of the Alpena-Amberley Ridge, creating a picture of the landscape and how ancient peoples would have utilized it during the Lake Stanley lowstand.

Informed by these various lines of investigation, the results of current archaeological research on the AAR can be evaluated and compared. While the conduct of archaeological research beneath 18–40 m of water and 80 km offshore presents technical and practical challenges, the potential payoff of such work is considerable. It could be argued that the AAR provides the only opportunity for archaeologists working outside the Arctic North to recover an entire ancient human landscape intact, with minimal disturbance from subsequent occupation or development.

PART I

Past Environments of the Upper Great Lakes

2 | Potential for Deeply Buried Archaeological Sites in Ontario Based on Glacial History

by Peter J. Barnett

During deglaciation of the Great Lakes region, events occurred that may have resulted in the burial of archaeological sites. Such events include oscillations of the ice margin that could have resulted in the direct burial of archaeological sites by till, or blocking of meltwater drainage passageways at lower elevations, resulting in the flooding of former land surfaces in front of the glacier and possibly the deposition of lake sediments on abandoned archaeological sites. Changes in the routing of glacier meltwater as the ice margin receded—combined with glacial isostatic adjustment and climatic change—created situations where former land surfaces became inundated and, with sediment deposition, possible burial of archaeological sites.

Examples of these various types of events are described, including the Arkona-Whittlesey (ice advance and blockage of outlets at lower elevations), Kirkfield-Main Algonquin and the Nipissing Great Lakes transgressions (glacial isostatic adjustment), and the glacier re-advance to the Marks and Dog Lake moraines (Marquette advance), an example where there is a possibility that a habitable preexisting landscape was overridden and covered with till, and areas immediately in front of the ice were rapidly flooded by ponded meltwater. Climatic change and the glacial meltwater bypassing of the Great Lakes may have combined to form closed-basin lakes within the basins of the Great Lakes, and concurrent and subsequent glacial isostatic adjustment resulted in the eventual flooding of once exposed forest beds and potential archaeological sites on the floors of the present-day Great Lakes.

Preamble

Events during the deglaciation of the Great Lakes region may have resulted in the burial of landscapes that were potentially sites of human occupation. These events include re-advance of the ice margin that either buried preexisting landscapes directly or blocked glacial lake drainage ways, raising water levels and flooding areas that were once exposed land. Changes in the routing of glacier meltwater related to ice marginal recession and glacial isostatic adjustment have also produced conditions that have resulted in the potential burial of archaeological sites, either by sediments or by lake water (flooding).

Karrow and Warner (1990) and Karrow (2004) have provided excellent summaries of the overall patterns of deglaciation with comments concerning associated vegetation changes and human occupation in the Great Lakes region. Several other summary papers have been written about the Quaternary history (Prest 1970; Shilts et al. 1987; Fulton and Andrews 1987; Dredge and Cowan 1989; Fulton 1989; Barnett 1992). These papers not only provide an overview of the glacial history of the Great Lakes region but also introduce the reader to some of the different interpretations and views on this subject. Many of the articles in the book *The Late Palaeo-Indian Great Lakes: Geological and Archaeological Investigations of Late Pleistocene and Early Holocene Environments* (Jackson and Hinshelwood 2004) present alternative interpretations on various events that occurred as the exposed landscape became available for human occupation.

All these summaries are not without contradiction or controversy. Disagreements arise from several events and their consequences and significance. Some key events that may be of interest to Paleoindian researchers include: glacial Lake Algonquin, glacial Lake Agassiz and discharge events, and the Nipissing Great Lakes transgression.

This chapter will not summarize deglaciation, as many of the above cited papers have, but it will attempt both to highlight the events that could lead to deeply buried archaeological sites and to touch on some of the more controversial or conflicting ideas associated with deglaciation and glacial lake history in Ontario. Timing of events will be given in both ^{14}C yr BP and calendar years (cal yr BP), following the conversion table suggested by Reimer et al. (2004).

Events That May Have Led to Burial of Archaeological Sites

Glacial Re-advance

There are several events that could have led to the burial of cultural occupation sites within the Great Lakes region. Table 2.1 summarizes the glacial events, resultant lake level changes, and approximate ages. A discussion of transgressive events associated with glacier re-advance is presented first, followed by transgressions associated primarily with glacial isostatic adjustment.

Port Huron Phase

The first event to be considered is the Port Huron advance to the Wyoming-Port Huron moraines along Lake Huron; the Banks and Waterdown moraines roughly delineate the extent of this advance. This advance—approximately 13,000 ^{14}C yr BP (15,340 cal yr BP)—raised water levels, some 60 m, from Lake Ypsilanti, a low-water stage in the Erie basin, to that of glacial Lake Whittlesey (Eschman and Karrow 1985). A low-water stage was postulated to exist in the Michigan and Huron basins, and drainage for this low-level lake has been suggested as eastward via the Trent River (Evenson and Dreimanis 1976; Eschman and Karrow 1985).

"Ontario Island" would have been available for Paleoindian occupation during both lake levels but a large area surrounding Lake Erie became flooded during the transgression to the Lake Whittlesey level. It has been suggested that periglacial conditions occurred on "Ontario Island" during the Port Huron phase (Morgan 1972; Gao 2005). The question remains, however, whether Paleoindians were present in the Great Lakes region at this time.

Two Rivers Phase

The next major glacial re-advance resulted in the deposition of the Two Rivers till over the Two Creeks forest bed in Wisconsin. Well dated (Broeker and Farrand 1963; Larson, Lowell, and Ostrom 1994) at approximately 11,850 ^{14}C yr BP (~13,730 cal yr BP), the extent of this advance is not well marked by end moraines in Wisconsin or Michigan, and, to date, there are no equivalent moraines identified or dated in Ontario. The advance may well have occurred only in the Lake Michigan basin, raising water levels to that of the Calumet level (Hansel et al. 1985). It has been postulated that the Trent River was the outlet for the low-level lake that allowed the landscape at Two Creeks to become forested, and that water levels in the Huron basin began rising to that of Main Algonquin while the Calumet level existed within the Lake Michigan basin (Hansel et al. 1985). Hansel et al. (1985) also suggest that the Chicago outlet was not used again until the Nipissing transgression or from a period between ~11,200 ^{14}C yr BP (13,100 cal yr BP) and ~5500 ^{14}C yr BP (6290 cal yr BP; Hansel et al. 1985). If this is the case, then the outlets in the North Bay area must have began operating shortly after 11,000 ^{14}C yr BP (12,900 cal yr BP) because there is apparently no evidence of lakes existing at 184 masl, or the level of Main Lake Algonquin, after this time.

Therefore, in summary, the Kirkfield outlet was in operation during Two Creeks or by 11,850 ^{14}C yr BP (13,730 cal yr BP) and closed well before 11,000 ^{14}C yr BP (12,900 cal yr BP), when outlets in the North Bay area began to open. Ice advance in the Michigan basin (Two Rivers till) separated the lake histories in the Michigan basin from the sequence of lakes that were occurring in the Huron and Georgian Bay basins. Apparently, only

Table 2.1. Summary of glacial advance events that may have led to burial of archaeological sites.

Glacial Event	Lake Fluctuations	Estimated Age ^{14}C yr BP (cal yr BP)
Port Huron advance	Ypsilanti – Arkona – Whittlesey	13,000 (15,340)
Two Rivers advance	Kirkfield – Calumet (Michigan basin)	11,850 (13,730)
isostatic rebound	Kirkfield – Main Algonquin transgression	11,850 (13,730)
Marquette advance	Early Minong – Duluth	10,000 (11,400)
	Moorhead – Emerson? (Agassiz basin)	
Nakina II advance	Low stage – Minong? (Nipigon basin)	8300 (9300)
Cochrane advance(s)	Ojibway	
isostatic rebound	Nipissing transgression	6200 (7160)

Various sources.

after the opening of the southern North Bay area outlets—and water levels began to fall from the level of Main Algonquin down to the Chippewa, Hough, and Stanley levels—did these lake basins share the same histories. Discussions of the changes in glacial Lake Algonquin water planes are presented below (see glacial Lake Algonquin).

Marquette Advance

The third re-advance that may have resulted in the burial of archaeological sites is that of the Marquette advance to the Grand Marais moraines in the Upper Peninsula of Michigan and in Wisconsin. This event occurred about 10,000 ^{14}C yr BP (11,400 cal yr BP), based on the burial of organic-bearing sediment by proglacial outwash deposits originating from the ice margin as it was building the Grand Marais moraines. This advance directly affected the Lake Superior basin and may have indirectly affected water levels in the glacial Lake Agassiz basin. The glacier in the Superior basin overrode a landscape that could have contained evidence of human occupation and possibly a spillway system that might have drained a large quantity of water from glacial Lake Agassiz eastward to the Superior and possibly the other Great Lake basins.

The Marks and Dog Lake moraines mark the extent of this advance in northwestern Ontario. Deltas built along these moraines indicate a substantial ice-contact glacier-fed lake flooded the low-lying terrain along the Kaministikwia River valley to the west. Glacial Lake Duluth likely formed at the southwestern end of the Lake Superior basin at this time. During ice-marginal recession following the Marquette advance, waters fell in the Superior basin to that of the Main Minong. Paleoindian occupational sites occur along Minong shoreline features in the Thunder Bay area (Julig 1994; Phillips and Hill 2004). Prior to the Marquette advance, Farrand (1988) suggests that early Lake Minong existed along the ice sheet margin, and Phillips and Hill (2004) indicate that even lower water levels may have existed. Thus, there is high potential for buried Paleoindian sites in the region along the west shore of Lake Superior because of the timing of the event; Paleoindians were within the Great Lakes region by then, and palaeo-Minong levels or lower existed within the Superior basin prior to the Marquette re-advance (Fig. 2.1).

This re-advance in the Superior basin has been suggested as the mechanism to close off eastward outlets of Agassiz, resulting in the raising of water levels within the glacial Lake Agassiz basin from the Moorhead low to the Lockhart level. Glacial Lake Agassiz used a number of outlets during its long history. Table 2.2 summarizes the history of glacial Lake Agassiz's outlet use. The transgression from Moorhead low to Lockhart inundated a fairly large area in northwestern Ontario, Manitoba, and adjoining states, an area where there is a possibility for the occurrence of deeply buried archaeological sites.

Recent work by Fisher (Fisher and Smith 1994; Fisher 2003; Lowell et al. 2005) is beginning to question the use of the eastern outlets during the Moorhead lowstand of glacial Lake Agassiz, and based on paleoclimate reconstruction during this interval, Yansa and Fisher (2007) hint that there were possibly no outlets for the Moorhead lowstand (Table 2.2).

Nakina II Advance

Recent mapping in the Lake Nipigon basin has identified a lowstand lake that occurred between two high-water lake levels in the Lake Nipigon basin (Barnett and Delorme 2007). Based on stratigraphic sections along the Little Jackfish River, fossiliferous shallow water sandy sediments and marl containing *Chara* oogoniums and casts occur between deep-water rhythmically bedded silts and clays. The assemblages of ostracodes and the distribution of *Chara* indicate that a shallow lake or permanent pond with occasional incursions of a stream existed within the sediment interval sampled. The assemblages below the marl indicate a littoral part of a lake with water depths estimated at being 0.6 and 1.5 m + 2 standard deviations of 5.2 m. Water depths during the growth of the algae *Chara* were likely less than a meter, and the return of *Cytherissa lacustris* indicates that the water levels increased following the deposition of the marl (Barnett and Delorme 2007). Drainage of glacial Lake Agassiz to glacial Lake Ojibway bypassed the Nipigon and Superior basins at this time as it flowed down the Whiteclay Lake-Mojikit spillway, a previously unconsidered pathway for Agassiz drainage (Barnett and Delorme 2007).

The sediments have not yet been dated because of the high carbonate content of the fossils; however, the advance to the Nakina moraines is thought to have occurred before 8000 ^{14}C yr BP (~8860 cal yr BP). Re-advance to the Nakina II moraine increased water levels in the Nipigon basin by some 50 m and flooded a large part of the shore area of Lake Nipigon, now areas of potential deeply buried archaeological sites. This re-advance has been suggested to have occurred at about 8300 ^{14}C years ago based on a thickening of rhythmites, assumed to have been the result of this re-advance, in a sequence of rhythmically bedded sediments deposited in a lake basin that was not in contact with the moraine and counting from an estimated timing for the glacier to leave the north shore of Lake Superior (Thorleifson and Kristjansson 1993; Lewis et al. 1994). The event would have reintroduced glacial meltwater into the Lake Superior and Lake Huron basins, as indicated by the abrupt decrease in the $\delta^{18}O$ composition of benthic ostracodes (Rea et al. 1994) that occurred between 8100 and 8400 ^{14}C years ago (Breckenridge and Johnson 2009). It is quite possible that the re-advance to the Nakina moraine not only raised water levels in the Lake Nipigon basin, but also in the Lake Superior basin, from the Houghton lowstand up to that of the Dorian level as defined by Farrand (1988), burying the existing landscape between, by water and sediments. Dates on detrital organic material within deltaic sediments deposited along the Black River in Ontario (Bajc, Morgan, and Warner 1997) lend further support for this suggestion (8310 ± 100 ^{14}C yr BP, Wat-1508; 8070 ± 180 ^{14}C yr BP, Wat-1623). Upon recession of the Laurentide Ice Sheet

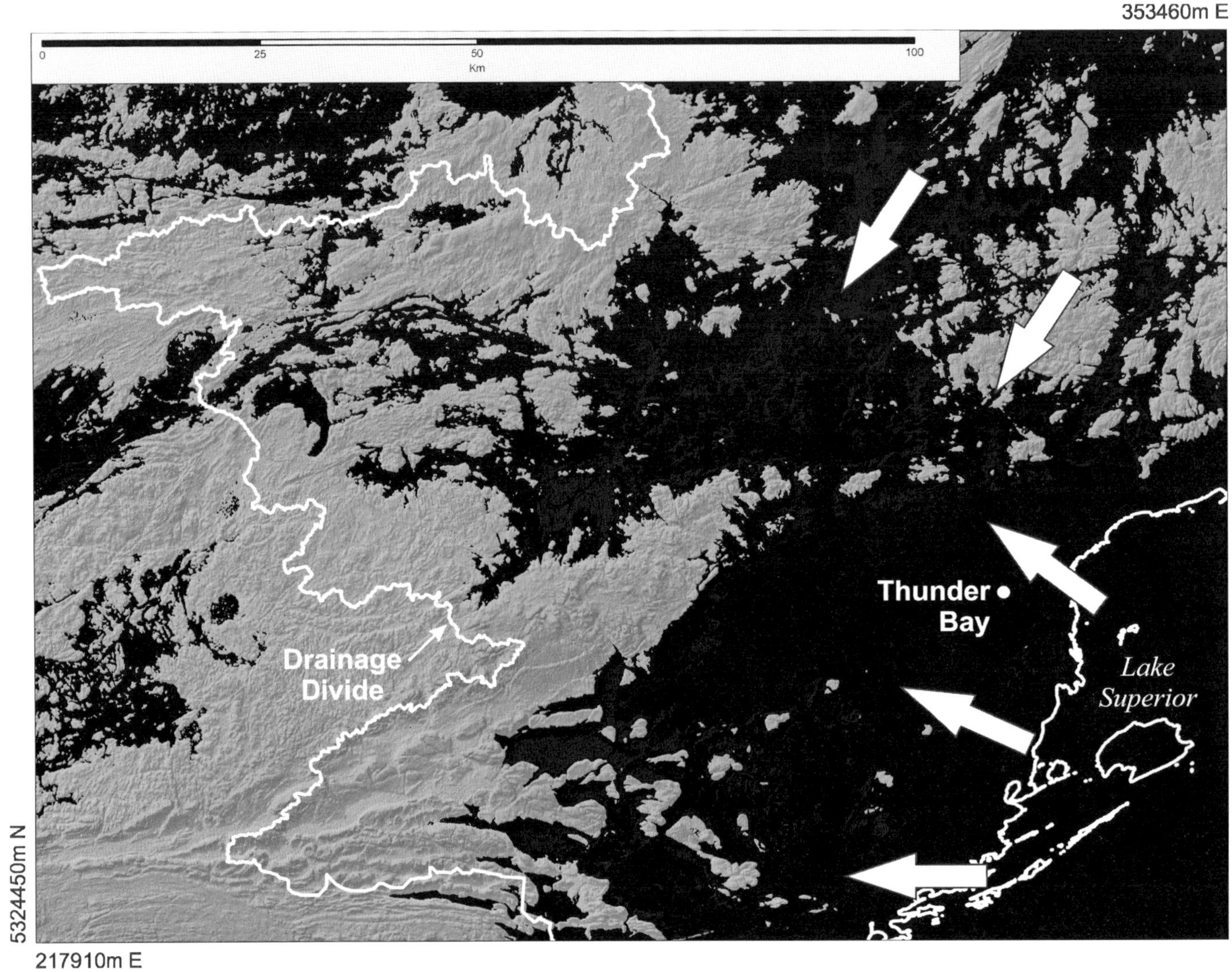

Figure 2.1. Hillshaded digital elevation model of the Thunder Bay, Ontario, area. Areas of possible deeply buried archaeological sites (in black) as a result of the Marquette advance (to tips of white arrows) approximately 10,000 ^{14}C yr BP (11,400 cal yr BP).

Table 2.2. History of outlet use of glacial Lake Agassiz.

Phase of Glacial Lake Agassiz	Outlet	Estimated Age ^{14}C yr BP (cal yr BP)
Cass phase	southern outlet	12,000–11,800 (13,840–13,690)
Lockhart phase	southern outlet	11,800–10,650 (13,690–12,760)
Moorhead phase	eastern outlets (?)	10,650–9700 (12,760–11,175)
Emerson phase	northwest outlet	9700–9400 (11,175–10,620)
Late Emerson phase	southern outlets	9400–9350 (10,620–10,570)
Morris phase	eastern outlets	9350–8100 (10,570–9015)

After Yansa and Fisher 2007.

north of the Continental Divide, meltwater then bypassed the Great Lakes basins, and the closed-basin lake (Houghton) in the Superior basin could be reestablished.

Burial of a forest bed by silt-clay rhythmites in the Thunder Bay area (Loope 2006; Boyd et al. 2010) may have occurred as the result of the Nipissing transgression. The buried forest exposed at the Boyd River cut in the Thunder Bay area is dated about 8000 ^{14}C yr BP (~8900 cal yr BP), and could possibly date the reestablishment of the Houghton lowstand following the deposition of the buried marl bed in the Lake Nipigon basin and the re-advance to the Nakina II moraine. Boyd et al. (2010) estimated forest burial at 7970 ± 30 ^{14}C yr BP (~8851 ± 94 cal yr BP) related to Agassiz floods; however, it is also possible that the burial of the forest occurred later, during the Nipissing transgression after 6420 ± 20 ^{14}C yr BP (7400 cal yr BP), as uplift of the North Bay outlet rose above the level of the outlet at the St. Marys River, raising water levels to that of the Nipissing Great Lakes (see below).

Cochrane Advances

The fifth set of re-advances is related to the Cochrane till in northern and northeastern Ontario. Although it is debated whether or not the Cochrane till was deposited in one or two major re-advances (Prest 1970) or surges or as multiple small-scale surges (Dredge and Cowan 1989), it does not really matter in the context of potential deeply buried archaeological sites. The advances or surges occurred within a large ice-marginal lake (glacial Lake Barlow-Ojibway), not over exposed land, and do not appear to have affected water levels of the ice-marginal lake.

Glacial Isostatic Adjustment

Other events that may have caused deep burial of archaeological sites in the Great Lakes region are associated with the opening of a series of lower outlets as the ice-margin of the Laurentide Ice Sheet receded and with the subsequent closure of these outlets by isostatic rebound. This relates to the entire glacial Lake Algonquin history, lowstands, and the formation of the Nipissing Great Lakes (Nipissing transgression).

Glacial Lake Algonquin

Early Lake Algonquin appears to be a forgotten stage in the archaeology literature. Although originally suggested as a necessary hypothetical stage, there is good evidence of shoreline features along the margins of Lake Huron and Georgian Bay above shoreline features attributed to the level of Main Lake Algonquin. Some of these shorelines may be associated with various levels of the Schomberg Ponds, particularly those that occur along the northern flank of the Oak Ridges moraine (Barnett et al. 1999); however, shoreline features that occur above Main Algonquin shoreline features north of Lake Simcoe are likely the product of this "hypothetical" lake stage. Therefore, shoreline features at the southern end of the lake are likely Early Lake Algonquin shorelines and possibly indicate an older time of occupation, if the human occupation is coincident with the shore deposits.

The distribution of Paleoindian sites in relation to shoreline features around the Thetford embayment is interesting. Most of the sites occur along tributary streams or elevated above the level of Early Lake Algonquin and cannot be associated with this lake; however, two sites are of interest. One site occurs adjacent to and just above the level of the Algonquin shoreline. There appears to be very little reason to be located here without the shoreline being active at the time. Artifacts collected at this site are of the Early Paleoindian Gainey culture. In contrast, the second site lies within the area flooded by Early Lake Algonquin but above the Nipissing transgression, and contains the Late Paleoindian Holcombe cultural assemblage of artifacts.

Lake level dropped from Early Lake Algonquin to the Kirkfield phase of Lake Algonquin as the ice uncovered the Fenelon Falls outlet. The drop to the Kirkfield phase and subsequent rise to the Main Algonquin phase is thought to be substantial by some (Stanley 1938a; Deane 1950; Lewis et al. 1994). The drop to the Kirkfield phase of Lake Algonquin was substantial (~30 m); however, the subsequent rise to the Main Algonquin level may not have been. There are three main controversies associated with this chain of events: (1) whether the outlet was closed by a re-advance or by isostatic rebound; (2) the amount of tilt of the main Algonquin shoreline and whether the lake's southern shore was at 184 m or below present-day Lake Huron; and (3) how much the water level changed during this sequence of events.

The outlet probably closed as a result of isostatic rebound. The Lake Simcoe moraine—the ice-marginal position that some suggest marks the re-advance that closed this outlet—is truncated by the outlet and therefore must predate the erosion that occurred associated with its formation. In addition, a delta built along the moraine, south of the outlet, is at a level high—above the Main Algonquin level in this area and most likely formed along with the moraine in contact with glacial Early Lake Algonquin.

Kaszycki (1985) suggested that glacial Lake Main Algonquin's southern shoreline is below the level of Lake Huron and that this lake did not drain through Port Huron or flood the Thetford embayment. It is debatable whether the waters of Lake Algonquin ever entered the Gull River valley to the extent suggested by Kaszycki (1985). The amount of tilt, or slope, indicated on her Algonquin "shoreline" is about 5.8 feet per mile—almost double that suggested by Deane (1950; 3 ft/mi) on shoreline features along the main body of the lake, high compared to the estimates of Finamore (1985; 3.5 ft/mi), and high compared to other ice-marginal lakes (e.g., glacial Lake Whittlesey; Barnett 1979). The terraces that were described and measured by Kaszycki (1985) are probably fluvial terraces. Local ponding behind bedrock sills along the Gull River valley resulted in the formation of deltaic deposits that are well documented in her paper. These deltas, however, probably do not reflect the level of glacial Lake Algonquin. The projection of river terraces to lake levels is difficult at the best of times. The slope of the terraces along the Gull River does not represent the slope of glacial

Lake Main Algonquin shoreline features. And the projection of the slope of the Gull River terraces southward has resulted in an overestimation of the slope of this paleolake and the location of its southern shore.

What was the change in water level from the Kirkfield lowstand to the level of Main Algonquin? Deane (1950), based on the examination of sediments exposed near Allison, Ontario, suggested the rise in water level was in the order of 50 feet or more (>15.5 m). Stanley (1938a) had also suggested a substantial rise of approximately 50 feet. Reexamination of the Allison site indicated that the underlying non-fossiliferous sediments are likely much older than the fossiliferous sediments of Lake Algonquin and are likely exhumed, erosional remnants of the upland sediments that occur to the east. Therefore, they do not indicate the change in water level associated with this transgression as suggested by Deane (1950).

There are also possible alternative interpretations of Stanley's (1938a) impounded shorelines at Sucker Creek, Ontario. Sucker Creek is located in an interesting channel carved into bedrock at the base of the Niagara Escarpment. This channel, for much of its length, is filled with sediments up to an elevation of 770–775 feet (234–236 m). Photographs in Stanley (1938a) show imbricate gravels that are more likely fluvial or glaciofluvial deposits associated with the channel rather than shoreline deposits. It is possible that the impounded beaches are spits that formed during the initial stages of bay-mouth bar formation, and that the change in water depths suggested by Stanley (1938a) is greatly overestimated.

It appears that the tilt of Main Algonquin shoreline features has been overestimated by Kaszycki (1985) and that the amount of water level change between the Kirkfield low stage and Main Algonquin has likely been overestimated. The time necessary for transgression and the amount of transgression could be much less, and therefore the impounded bay-mouth bar in the Thetford embayment may relate to glacial Lake Main Algonquin. In addition, it should be noted that, by definition, shoreline features built during the transgression from the Kirkfield level are of glacial Lake Main Algonquin, not Ardtrea as recently suggested by several workers (e.g., Jackson 2004); similarly, shoreline features of the Nipissing Great Lakes are time transgressive.

Low-water Levels in the Great Lakes and the Nipissing Great Lakes Transgression

With ice marginal recession to the North Bay area, lower outlets across Algonquin Park were opened to create a series of falling water levels in the lower Great Lakes basins. Upper Great Lakes drainage to the Erie and Ontario basins ceased and low-water stages began to develop. About 8000 ^{14}C yr BP (8985 cal yr BP), waters of glacial Lakes Agassiz and Ojibway combined, and meltwater draining from this lake is said to have changed from draining into the Lake Superior basin to draining down the Ottawa River valley, thus bypassing the Great Lakes basins (Teller and Leverington 2004; Lewis, King, et al. 2008). As suggested above, it is also possible that meltwater drainage bypassed the Great Lakes basins earlier, between the deposition of the Nakina I and Nakina II moraines between 8900 and 8400 ^{14}C yr BP. In addition, or in part as a result of this drainage rerouting, climatic conditions in the Great Lakes region changed from cold and dry to warm and dry (Edwards, Wolfe, and MacDonald 1996), conditions that would promote evaporation (Lewis et al. 2007). Lewis and Blasco (2001) suggest that these events caused a lowering of lake levels in the Great Lakes basins such that lake levels were no longer controlled by outlets.

Following the deglaciation of the outlet at North Bay, Ontario, and the end of the ice-contact proglacial Lake Algonquin, about 10,000 years ago, water levels in the basins of Lakes Michigan and Huron fell by 100 m or more (Karrow, Appleyard, and Endres 2007). This resulted in the establishment of "low water, river-linked lakes Chippewa, Stanley, and Hough, low stands in the basins of lakes Michigan, Huron, and Georgian Bay respectively" (Karrow et al. 2007:419). The gradual rise of water level as the North Bay outlet rose, due to glacial isostatic adjustment, is referred to as the Nipissing transgression (Karrow 1980). During the transgression, water levels rose and peaked at approximately 6 m above the present-day level of Lakes Huron and Michigan until water flowed southward via channels at Chicago and Port Huron-St. Clair. This transgression occurred between 10,000 ^{14}C yr BP (ca. 11,470 cal yr BP) and 5000 ^{14}C yr BP (ca. 5760 cal yr BP; Karrow, Appleyard, and Endres 2007).

However, during this overall transgression, several extreme lake levels have been proposed in the basins of Lakes Huron, Michigan, and Superior. Lewis and others (Lewis and Anderson 1989; Lewis et al. 1994; Lewis, Blasco, and Gareau 2005; Lewis et al. 2007; Lewis, Karrow, et al. 2008) suggest that between approximately 10,000 ^{14}C yr BP (ca. 11,470 cal yr BP) and 7500 ^{14}C yr BP (ca. 8300 cal yr BP), "lake levels fluctuated dramatically through a possible range up to 60 m" and water "levels rose 40 to 60 m above the North Bay outlet about three times for short periods to Mattawa high stands . . . which are thought to have been held up by constriction of the large outflows in the Mattawa and Ottawa valleys" (Lewis, Karrow, et al. 2008:132). They suggest that the Mattawa highstands were caused by overflows of lake waters from glacial Lake Agassiz (Teller, Leverington, and Mann 2002) or from subglacial outburst floods (Breckenridge et al. 2004; Breckenridge 2007).

Several authors (Lewis et al. 1994; Blasco 2000; Blasco et al. 2001; Lewis and Blasco 2001, 2002; Anderson and Lewis 2002; Blasco and McCarthy 2004; Lewis, Blasco, and Gareau 2005; Lewis, Karrow, et al. 2008; Lewis, King, et al. 2008) have also suggested that water levels in the Huron and Michigan basins fell even further below that of Lakes Chippewa, Stanley, and Hough, and that hydraulic closure occurred and low-level, closed-basin (evaporitic) lakes formed. They (Lewis, Karrow, et al. 2008; Lewis, King, et al. 2008) suggest that this occurred following 8000 ^{14}C yr BP (ca. 8890 cal yr BP), when glacial meltwater was channeled directly down the Ottawa River system, thus bypassing

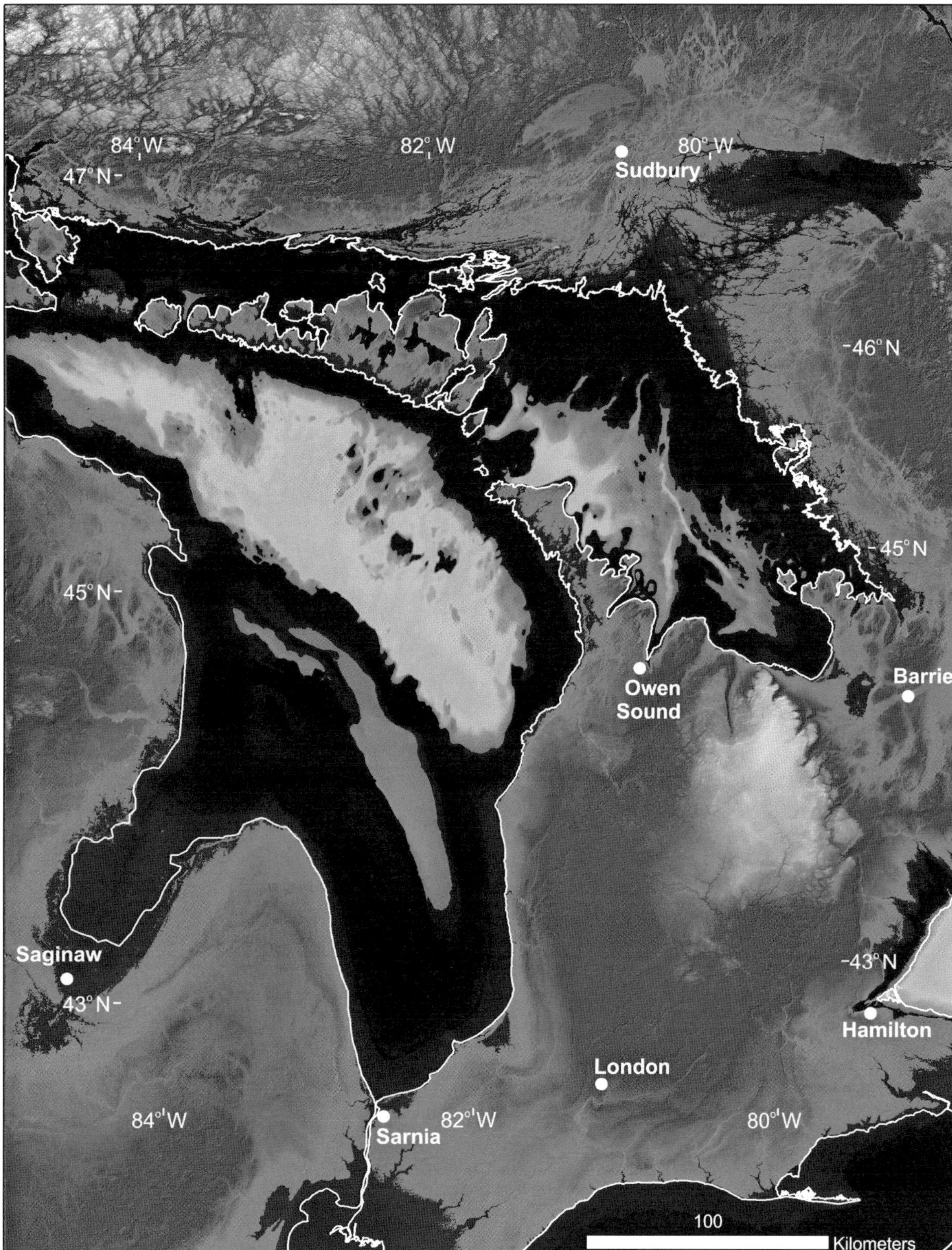

Figure 2.2. Hillshaded digital surface model of the Lake Huron and Georgian Bay area. Potential buried archaeological sites areas affected by the Nipissing transgression within the Georgian Bay and Lake Huron basins are shown in black. Figure based on rebound curve of Lewis et al. 2007, and rebound grid produced by Frank J. Krist Jr. (pers. comm., 2014).

the Great Lakes basins. They ended as increasing precipitation and water supply caused the Huron water body again to overflow the North Bay outlet at about 7500 ^{14}C yr BP (ca. 8300 cal yr BP; Lewis, Karrow, et al. 2008:132). Sarvis, McCarthy, and Blasco (1999) suggested that slightly brackish conditions existed between 9000 ^{14}C yr BP (ca. 10, 210 cal yr BP) and 7000 ^{14}C yr BP (ca. 7845 cal yr BP), based on thecamoebian successions in a sediment core taken from the floor of Georgian Bay beneath about 120 m of water, apparently supporting a closed-basin evaporitic lake.

During the existence of the low-water stages, the land above the lakes became dissected by streams, and the interfluves, forested (Karrow, Appleyard, and Endres 2007). The Nipissing transgression raised the water level above the present level, submerging the forests and infilling the valley systems. Karrow and others (2007) describe the sediment and age of four infilled valley systems in Ontario, and Hunter et al. (2006) describe the composition and age of submerged forests found in the vicinity of Lake Michigan.

With continued glacial isostatic adjustment and differential uplift in the North Bay area, drainage shifted to more southerly outlets once again. The Nipissing transgression occurred, slowly rising water levels in the lower Great Lakes basins (Fig. 2.2). Several researchers suggest that this was a rapidly occurring event, but this is highly unlikely. Water levels rose to create the Nipissing Great Lakes. In the Lake Erie basin, water levels rose to about 5 m above the present-day lake level during this return of upper Great Lakes waters, and then fell from there once the moraine dam at Fort Erie was removed as a result of the increase in water flowing through the Erie basin (Barnett 1985).

Agassiz Flood

Drainage events associated with the opening of eastern outlets for glacial Lake Agassiz have been suggested to have happened several times during deglaciation. Some very elaborate schemes have been suggested based on the interpretation of digital elevation modeling (Teller and Leverington 2004) but many of the scenarios suggested lack evidence on the ground, particularly in the pivotal area, Lake Nipigon basin. The timing of these events is currently being questioned, as should the evidence for suggested transgressive events being attributed to Agassiz floods all around the Great Lakes. These floods are sometimes referred to as Mattawa highstands based on pioneering work in the North Bay area (Lewis and Anderson 1989).

Dates of possible floods, based on the study of glacial Lake Agassiz history, occur between 10,650 and 9700 ^{14}C yr BP (12,760–11,175 cal yr BP) and 9700 and 9400 ^{14}C yr BP (11,175–10,620 cal yr BP) and after 9350 ^{14}C yr BP (10,570 cal yr BP; Table 2.2; Yansa and Fisher 2007). Suggested timing of these events from evidence in the Lakes Huron and Michigan basins—9600 to 9500 ^{14}C yr BP (11,075–10,740 cal yr BP) for the early Mattawa flood and 9000 to 8000 ^{14}C yr BP (10,200–8985 cal yr BP) for "Main Lake Mattawa" (Lewis et al. 1994)—is not entirely the same and indicates that there are some problems with this proposed timing.

Water levels in the Huron basin have been suggested to rise rapidly some 30 m during the Mattawa events due to hydraulic damming at the outlets. Water levels in the Lake Huron and Georgian Bay basins during these events rose to elevations between 140 and 160 masl (see Lewis, Blasco, and Gareau 2005: fig. 10). These events would not be high enough to flood into the Lake Erie basin and affect water levels there, as has been suggested (e.g., Pengelly and Tinkler 2004).

The effects of the suggested magnitude of these floods on human occupation of the area transgressed by the Nipissing Great Lakes would be great (Fig. 2.2). However, with the occurrence and preservation of now-flooded forests (i.e., below the present Georgian Bay and southern Lake Michigan) on this transgressed landscape (Janusas et al. 2004; Hunter et al. 2006; Leavitt et al. 2006; Panyushkina and Leavitt 2007; Lewis, King, et al. 2008), there remains potential for the preservation of archaeological sites.

Conclusions

There are several events that could have led to the burial of cultural occupation sites within the Great Lakes region. Both transgressive events associated with glacier re-advance and transgressive events associated primarily with glacial isostatic adjustment could have created areas where landscapes once exposed to human occupation have now been buried beneath till, proglacial lake or fluvial sediments, or the waters of the Great Lakes themselves. However, locating these potential deeply buried occupational sites may prove to be difficult. The investigation of sites presently located below the waters of Lake Huron are the subject of the remaining chapters in this volume.

3 | Paleoenvironmental Context for Early Holocene Caribou Migration on the Alpena-Amberley Ridge

by Francine M. G. McCarthy, John H. McAndrews, and Elli Papangelakis

The hydrologically closed Lake Stanley occupied the deepest part of the Huron basin during the arid early Holocene except for brief intervals of meltwater incursion—the Mattawa highstands. Lake Stanley had two subbasins—the larger, deeper Manitoulin basin and the smaller, shallower Goderich basin—separated by the Alpena-Amberley Ridge that extended from Presque Isle, Michigan, to Point Clark, Ontario, during the late Lake Stanley lowstand, ~7.9 ±0.3 ka BP/8464 ±353 cal BP. The boreal woodland that this windswept ridge supported would have been a hospitable environment for caribou until sudden warming and increased precipitation caused succession to dense mixed forest and the inundation of the Lake Huron basin. The stone structure artifacts on this causeway associated with caribou hunting are consistent with the paleovegetation reconstruction. The negative water budget calculated using pollen-derived transfer functions combined with inflow of saline groundwater from outcrops of evaporitic strata of middle Paleozoic age produced brackish waters in the Manitoulin and Goderich basins of Lake Stanley that could have been used to preserve caribou meat.

Lake Huron during the Early Holocene

After meltwater from the Laurentide Ice Sheet was diverted north of the upper Great Lakes, ~8.8 BP/~10,000 cal BP (Lewis et al. 1994), hydrologically closed lowstand Lakes Stanley and Hough developed in the Lake Huron and Georgian Bay basins (Lewis et al. 2007; McCarthy and McAndrews 2012) (except for short-lived Mattawa highstands from meltwater diversions into the basin [Lewis, Karrow, et al. 2008; Lewis and Anderson 2012]) (Fig. 3.1). The negative water budget is primarily due to early Holocene aridity throughout mid-latitude eastern North America (Newby et al. 2000; Webb, Shuman, and Williams 2004). This aridity—attributed to stronger, more prevalent Pacific and Arctic air masses in the Great Lakes basin—is linked to the retreat of the Laurentide Ice Sheet during the early Holocene (Shuman, Bartlein, et al. 2002), which led to slightly brackish waters in late Lake Hough (Sarvis, McCarthy, and Blasco 1999; McCarthy et al. 2012); this was primarily due to the hydrologic isolation of Lake Superior that cut off the main inflow to Lake Huron (currently 2140 m^3/s) at Sault Ste. Marie (McCarthy and McAndrews 2012). It also allowed boreal woodland vegetation to spread southeast of its current biogeographic range, as far as the Georgian Bay drainage basin (McCarthy et al. 2012; McCarthy and McAndrews 2012).

The late Lake Stanley lowstand (Croley and Lewis 2006; Lewis et al. 2007) was the lowest (and last) of the early Holocene lowstand phases in the main Lake Huron basin, and the resulting erosional unconformity is represented by seismic reflection light blue (Rea et al. 1994; Moore et al. 1994; Dobson, Moore, and Rea 1995). Based on this sedimentological/geomorphological evidence, Lewis et al. (2007) inferred the late Stanley lowstand to be ~50 m below present in northwestern Lake Huron, far below the elevation of the controlling North Bay outlet or any of the sills in the main basin of Lake Huron. They estimated the age of this late Lake Stanley unconformity as ~7.9 ± 0.3 ka BP (8464 ± 353 cal BP). This interpretation parallels the pollen chronology in the Flowerpot Beach core (McCarthy et al. 2011), where the coeval late Lake Hough lowstand (53 m below modern lake level) occurs in sediments assigned to pollen zone 2b of McAndrews (1994)—the white pine zone.

Land bridges were exposed throughout the Huron basin during the early Holocene by this decline in water levels. The

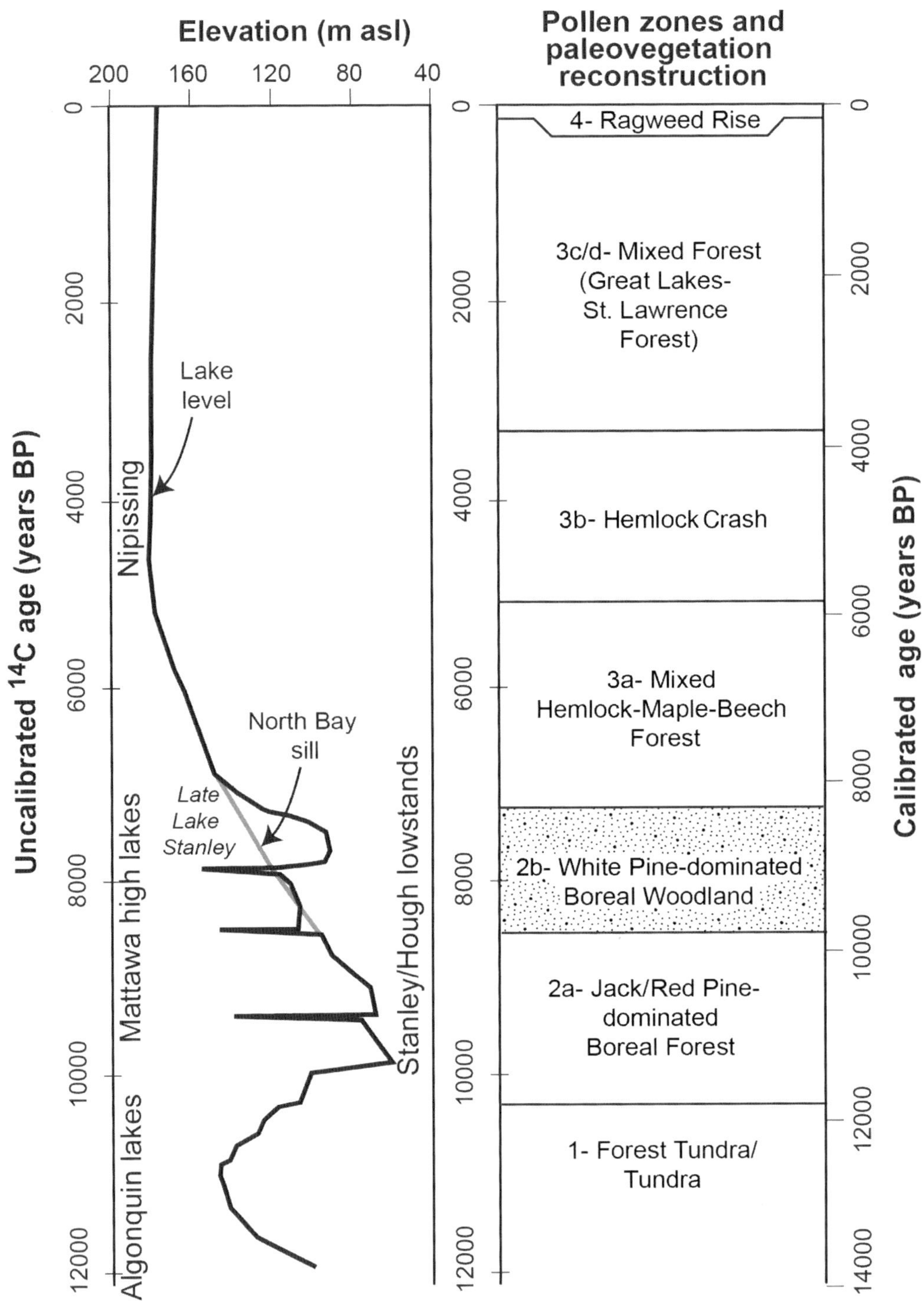

Figure 3.1. Following the diversion of the Laurentide Ice Sheet from the Great Lakes circa 8.8 ka BP/10,000 cal BP, lake levels in the Lake Huron basin were controlled by isostatic uplift of the North Bay sill except (1) when negative water budgets caused water levels to fall below the sill, producing the Lake Stanley/Hough lowstands in the main and Georgian Bay basins, respectively, or (2) when ice damming produced short-lived Mattawa highstands punctuating these. There is evidence that slightly brackish conditions developed in the closed basin of late Lake Hough (McCarthy et al. 2012). The white pine-dominated boreal woodland represented by pollen subzone 2b of McAndrews (1994; *stippled*) records aridity sufficient to have driven Lake Hough to closed-basin status (McCarthy and McAndrews 2012). Lake levels rose quickly in response to the climate change that established the mixed hemlock-maple-beech forest (pollen subzone 3a).

emergence of a land bridge across the Main Channel linking the main basin of Lake Huron with Georgian Bay produced a causeway between the Bruce Peninsula and Manitoulin Island known from the oral traditions of the Ojibway (L. Keeshig-Tobias, pers. comm.). This chapter examines pollen data from lakes in the drainage basin of the main basin of Lake Huron to reconstruct the paleovegetation and paleoclimate on and around that causeway, or the Alpena-Amberley Ridge. This quantitative reconstruction of paleoclimate uses transfer functions to obtain estimates for mean annual precipitation, mean July temperature, and mean January temperature. These paleoclimate values also allow the creation of a water budget for late Lake Stanley and insights into the paleolimnology of the Manitoulin and Goderich subbasins. We then assess archeological evidence of hunting woodland caribou on this causeway (O'Shea and Meadows 2009; O'Shea, Lemke, and Reynolds 2013) in light of the vegetation and limnology of the early Holocene.

Early Holocene Paleoenvironmental Reconstruction, Amberley Region

Shouldice Lake, Edward Lake, Pike Lake, and Wylde Lake (Fig. 3.2) are in subzone L.1 (Huron-Ontario) of the Great Lakes-St. Lawrence forest, which is rich in sugar maple and beech, together with basswood, ash, yellow birch, red maple, and white, red, and bur oaks (Rowe 1972). The only common conifers are hemlock and white pine. Pollen data from these (Figs. 3.3–3.6) and other sites were plotted using CANPLOT (Campbell and McAndrews 1992) against calendar ages, with calibrations performed using CALIB 6.0.[1] Because the abundance of pollen of various taxa is not uniformly related to the tree species biomass (Bradshaw 1981), *r*-value corrections (Delcourt, Delcourt, and Webb 1984) were applied to the pollen data using CANPLOT. Figures 3.3–3.6 thus illustrate changes in tree biomass since deglaciation.

The diagrams illustrate the standard well-dated pollen succession in southern Ontario (McAndrews 1994); this records the establishment of tundra (sedges, other nonarboreal pollen, and spruce woodland) following the retreat of ice sheets through to the expansion of weeds (notably ragweed) accompanying Canadian land clearing in the mid-nineteenth century in southern Ontario. The pollen zonation provided additional chronological control to supplement multiple radiocarbon dates from each core.[2] The ages of the boundaries between pollen zones 1 and 2a, 2a and 2b, and 2b and 3a are diachronous across latitude in Ontario, whereas the boundaries between the subzones of zone 3 (3a and 3b, 3b and 3c, 3c and 3d) and between subzone 3d and zone 4 appear to be synchronous from 41° to 49° latitude. The results shown in Figure 3.7 were used to place the ages of the zone boundaries in all four diagrams, assisting in the comparison across all sites.

Early Holocene Paleovegetation and Paleoclimate

Aridity is recorded in subzone 2b (10,000–8200 cal BP) by the dominance of pine pollen (~60% of the assemblage in Shouldice Lake, Edward Lake, Pike Lake, and Wylde Lake; Figs. 3.3–3.6). Although pine pollen is vastly overrepresented relative to biomass (Delcourt et al. 1984), this drought-tolerant genus was a major component of the vegetation in this region during the early Holocene, together with birch. Because we have accounted for *r*-values in our plots (Figs. 3.3–3.6), it is evident that oak, elm, maple, and spruce were also common components of the vegetation, as they were in the early Holocene aspen parkland reconstructed for Porqui Pond (Fig. 3.2) in the Georgian Bay watershed (McCarthy and McAndrews 2012).

Paleoclimatic values were reconstructed from pollen diagrams (Figs. 3.3–3.6) using the transfer functions for region G of Bartlein and Webb (1985) and Bartlein and Whitlock (1993). Pollen-derived mean annual precipitation values as well as mean January and July temperatures for each lake were compared against modern data from nearby climate stations.[3] Mean annual precipitation during pollen zone 2b at these locations varied between 59 and 67% of modern values in the Lake Huron drainage basin (Fig. 3.8). These values are similar to the reconstructions for pollen zone 2b in the Georgian Bay catchment, where the range was 66 to 81% of modern values (McCarthy and McAndrews 2012), but represent slightly greater aridity. The similar values of mean annual precipitation since deglaciation at all four sites also suggest that our paleoclimatic inferences are quite robust.

As elsewhere in mid-latitude eastern North America (e.g., Webb, Shuman, and Williams 2004), transfer functions record a rapid increase in mean annual precipitation around 8000 cal BP at all four sites in this study. Reconstructions of mean annual precipitation reached values as high as 110 cm in pollen zone 3a at Wylde Lake and Edward Lake—values comparable with modern values at climate stations (and from a low of ~70 cm circa 8300 years ago; Table 3.1).This sudden (century scale) climate change subsequently allowed mesic taxa like hemlock, sugar maple, and beech to become dominant, and boreal conifers (pine, spruce, balsam fir) to become rare (Figs. 3.3–3.6). The boundary between pollen zones 2 and 3 of McAndrews (1994) has been dated between ~8200 and 7500 cal BP between ~41° and 49° north latitude in southern Ontario (Fig. 3.7), reflecting the succession to the Great Lakes-St. Lawrence forest of Rowe (1972) as hemlock, maple, and beech migrated northward, replacing the boreal forest/boreal woodland of the early Holocene (McCarthy and McAndrews 2012).

1. Calib. ^{14}CHRONO Centre, Queens University Belfast. http://calib.qub.ac.uk/calib/calmenu.cgi?datamenu.
2. North American Pollen Database, Springfield, Illinois. National Climatic Data Center, National Oceanic and Atmospheric Administration. http://www.ncdc.noaa.gov/paleo/napd.html.
3. Canadian Climate Normals. National Climate Archive. Environment Canada, Government of Canada. http://climate.weatheroffice.gc.ca/climate_normals/index_e.html.

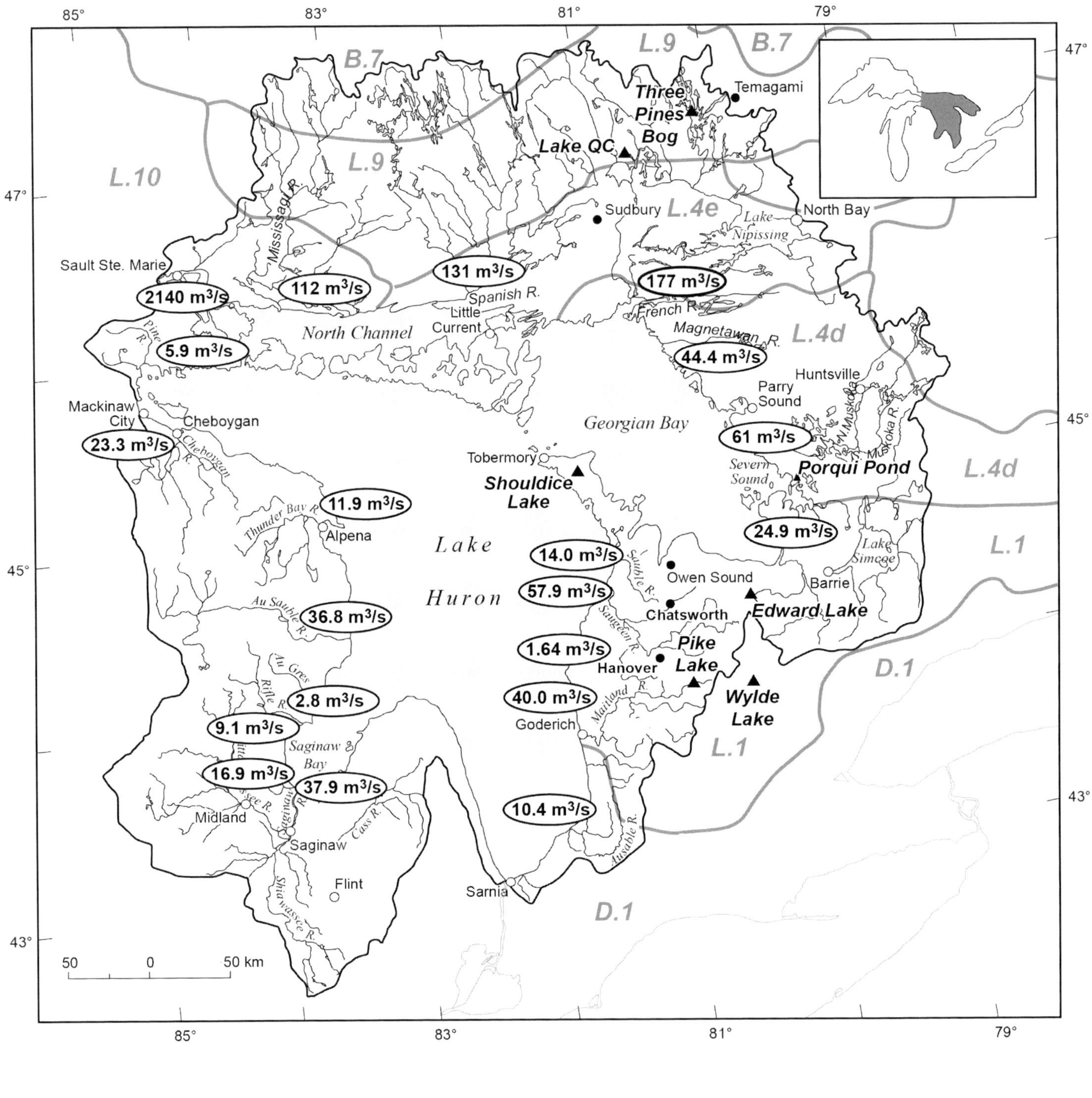

Figure 3.2. The Lake Huron drainage basin, identifying the streams flowing into the main basin and their discharge, the pollen diagrams referred to in the text (*triangles*), climate stations in the vicinity of our core sites (*filled circles*), and major cities/towns (*open circles*). Vegetation zones are from Rowe (1972); all the sites in this study are from vegetation subzone L.1: Huron-Ontario, of the Great Lakes-St. Lawrence forest. Excepting the dominant inflow from Lake Superior into the North Channel (discharge in the St. Marys River at Sault Ste. Marie is ~2140 m^3/s), nearly two-thirds of the total discharge (277.5 m^3/s) into the main basin is from the four largest streams: Saugeen and Maitland Rivers (Ontario) and Saginaw and Au Sable Rivers (Michigan) (discharge shown in ovals for each stream).

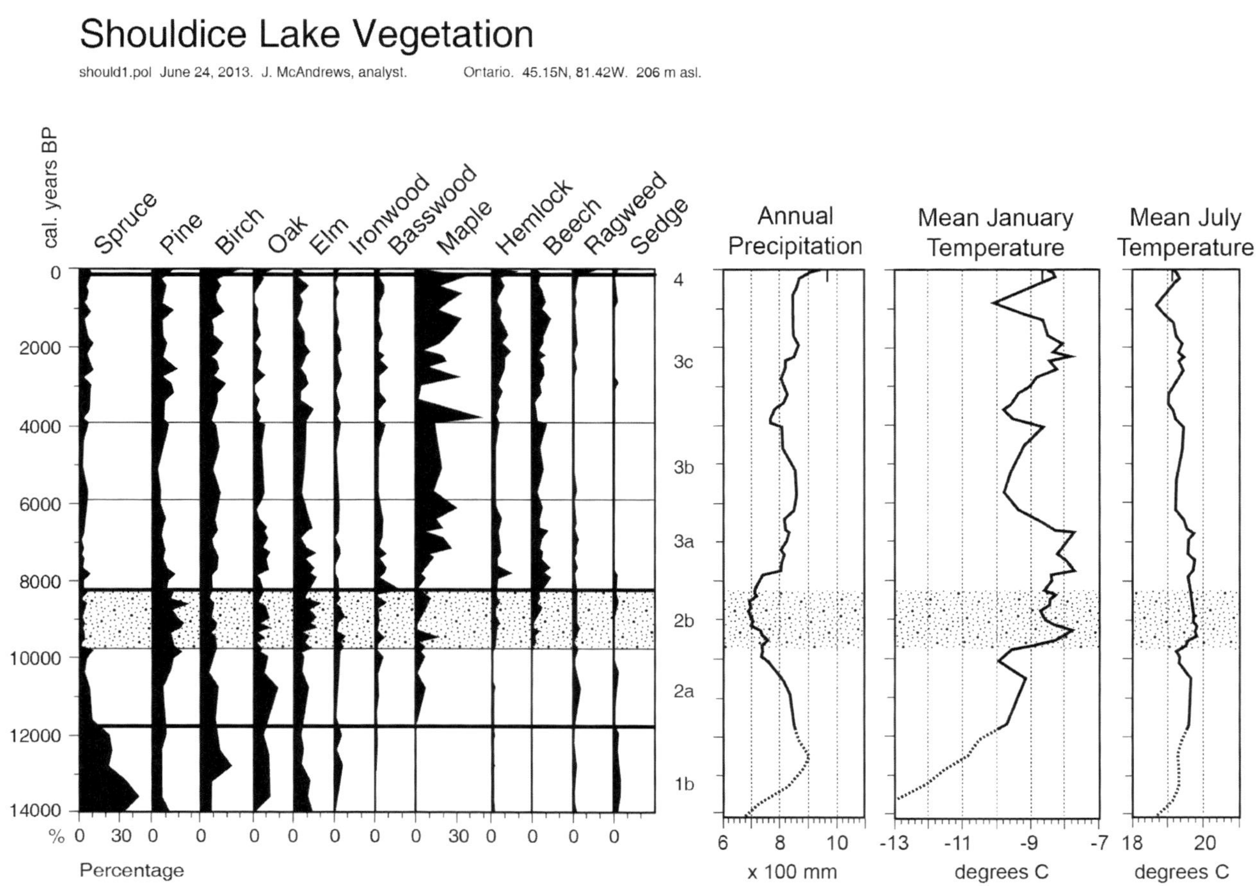

Figure 3.3. Reconstruction of vegetation based on pollen analyzed from a Livingstone core from Shouldice Lake. Stippling identifies pollen subzone 2b of McAndrews (1994), ~8500–7800 cal BP, the most arid part of the Holocene recorded in most pollen records from eastern North America. Mean annual precipitation is reconstructed ~70 cm/y using transfer functions for area G of Bartlein and Whitlock (1993), which is only 64% of the modern measured value in nearby Owen Sound (Table 3.1). Rapid amelioration of mean January temperatures followed by a sharp increase in mean annual precipitation allowed the boreal woodland to be succeeded by a mixed forest similar to subzone L.1 (Huron-Ontario) of the Great Lakes-St. Lawrence forest of Rowe (1972). There is relatively little hemlock, sugar maple, or beech at this site in zone 3, due to its northern setting on the thin, limestone soils of the Bruce Peninsula. Note: paleoclimatic reconstructions using the transfer function for area G are considered unreliable for zone 1, and are thus shown as fine dashes.

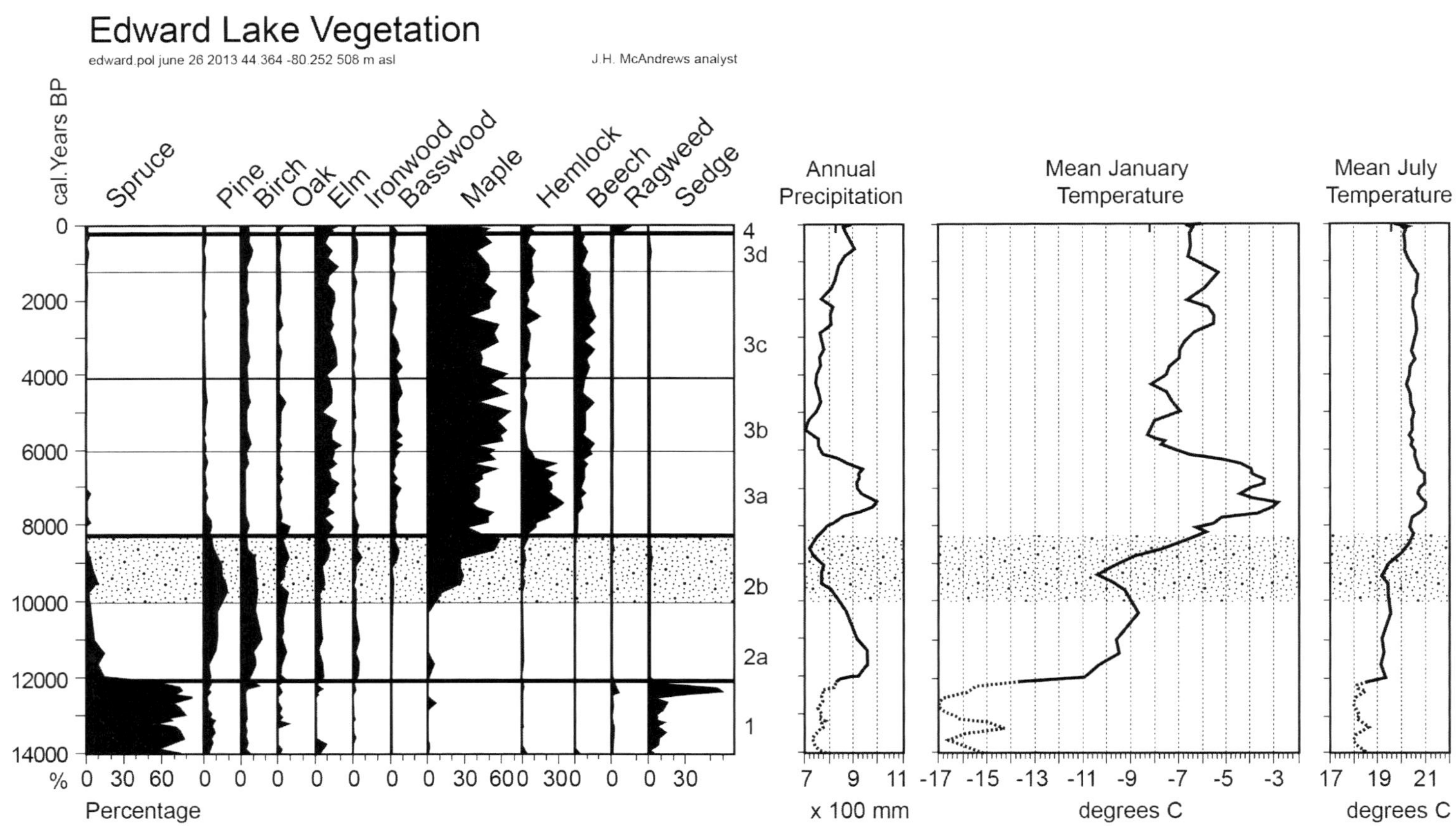

Figure 3.4. Reconstruction of vegetation based on pollen analyzed from a Livingstone core from Edward Lake. Stippling identifies pollen subzone 2b of McAndrews (1994). Transfer functions for area G of Bartlein and Whitlock (1993) reconstruct a sharp increase in annual precipitation around 7500 cal BP following a sharp increase in mean January temperature ~8000 cal BP that led to the succession of the boreal woodland (subzone 2b) by the hemlock-maple-beech mixed forest (subzone 3a). Mean annual precipitation during the driest part of the early Holocene drought, ~8200 cal BP in subzone 2b, is reconstructed ~72 cm/y, which is only ~62% of the modern measured value in nearby Chatsworth (Table 3.1).

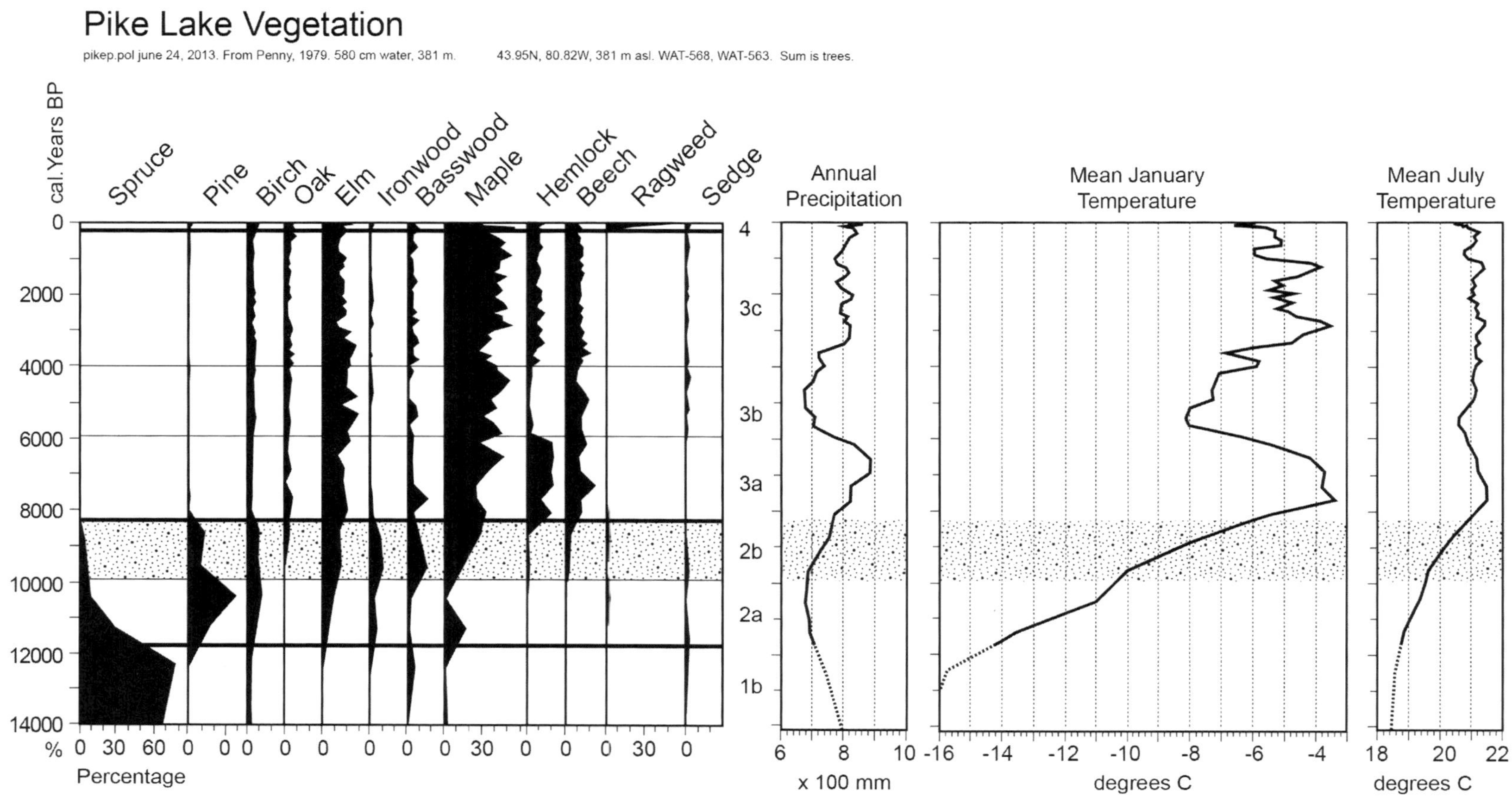

Figure 3.5. Reconstruction of vegetation based on pollen analyzed from a Livingstone core from Pike Lake. Stippling identifies pollen subzone 2b of McAndrews (1994). The vegetation reconstruction is very similar to that in Edward Lake, with a hemlock-maple-beech mixed forest succeeding boreal woodland in response to an increase in winter temperature followed by an increase in mean annual precipitation. During the driest part of the early Holocene drought in subzone 2b, mean annual precipitation is reconstructed ~69 cm/y, which is only ~62% of the modern measured value in nearby Hanover (Table 3.1).

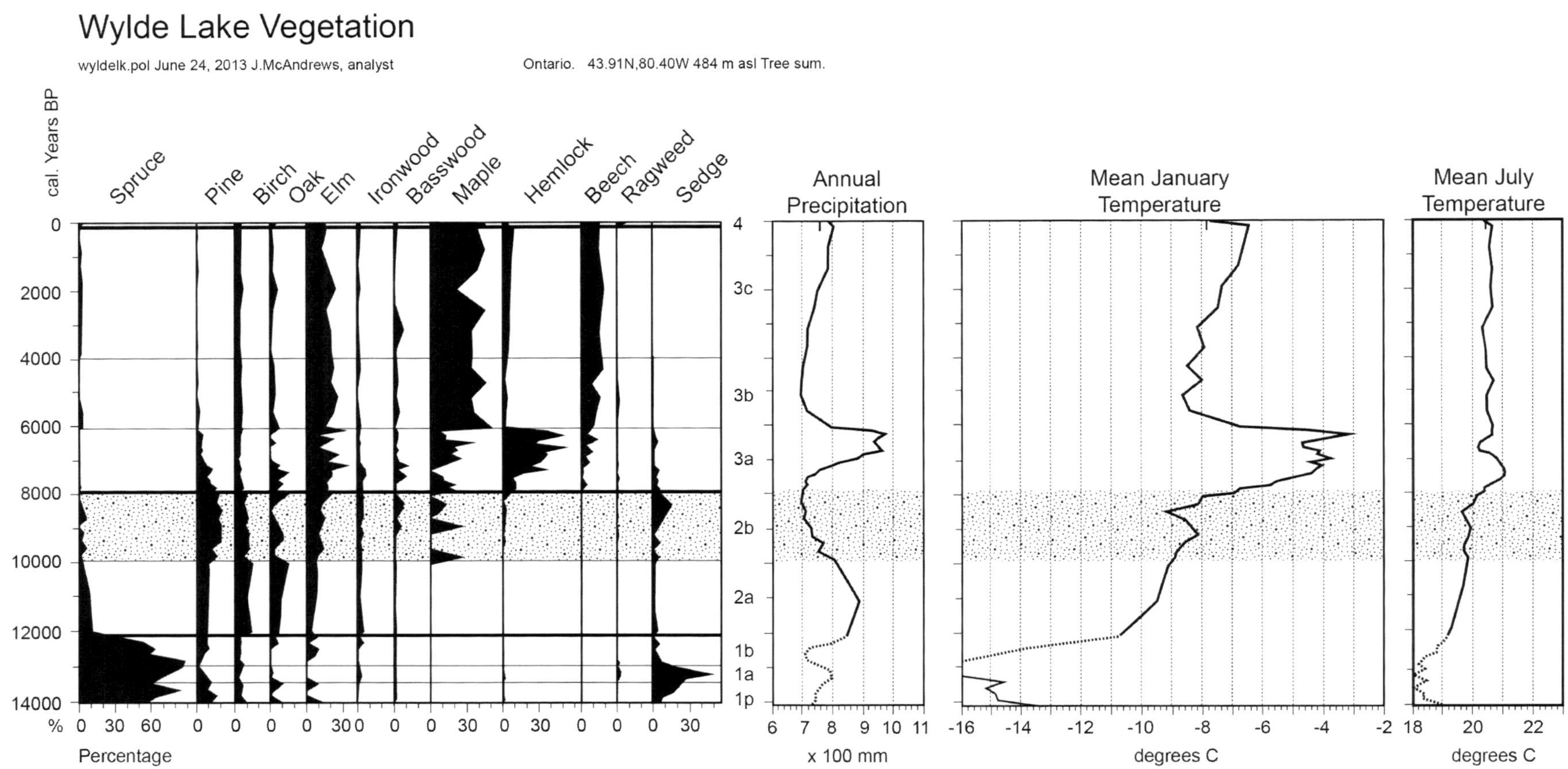

Figure 3.6. Reconstruction of vegetation based on pollen analyzed from a Livingstone core from Wylde Lake. Stippling identifies pollen subzone 2 of McAndrews (1994). The vegetation reconstruction is very similar to that in Edward Lake, but transfer functions reconstruct the sharp rise in mean January temperature early in subzone 3a, immediately preceding the rise in mean annual precipitation. During the driest part of the early Holocene drought in subzone 2b, mean annual precipitation is reconstructed ~70 cm/y, which is only ~69% of the modern measured value in nearby Hanover (Table 3.1).

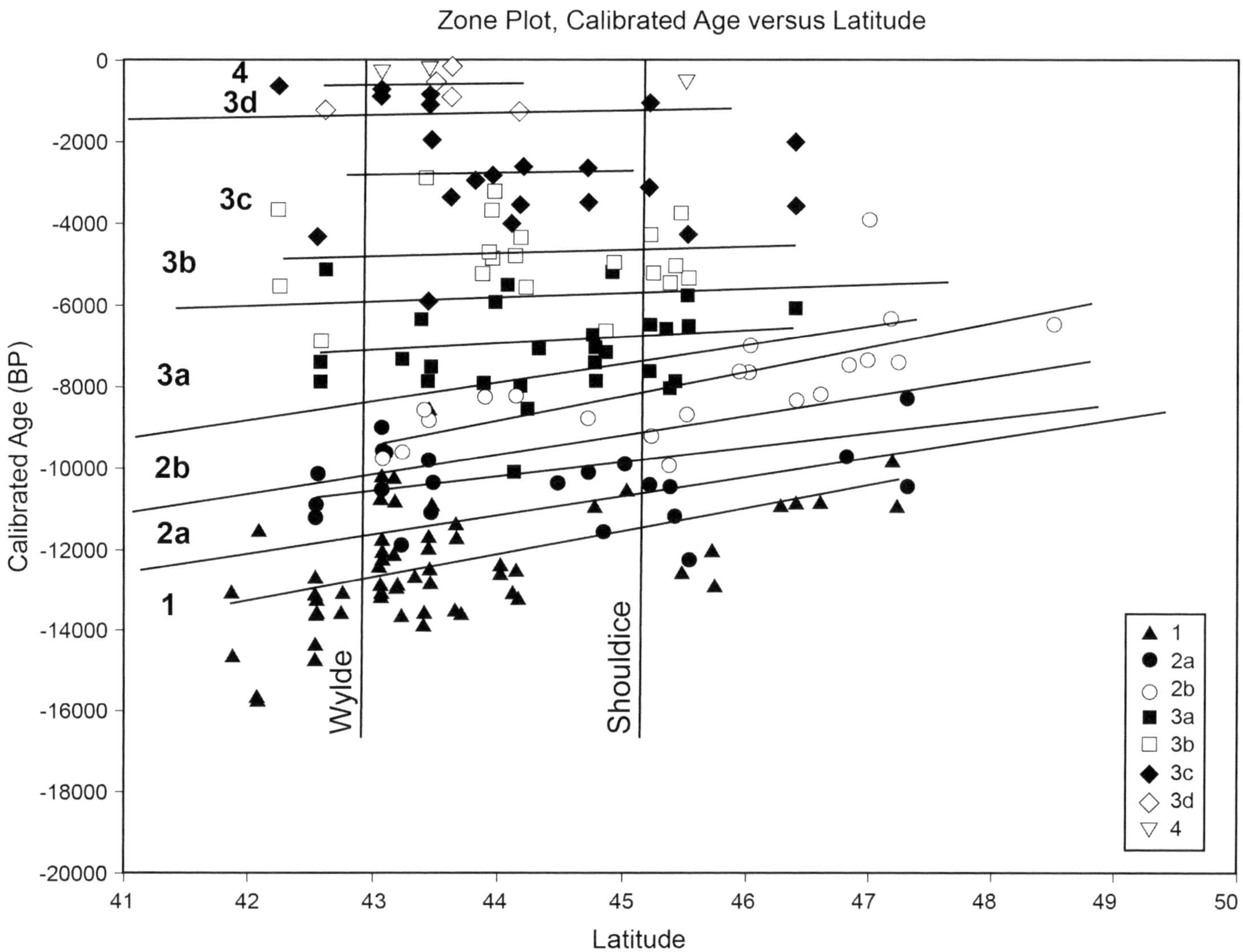

Figure 3.7. Calibrated ages of the pollen zones of McAndrews (1994) between 41° and 49° latitude. These ages were used to supplement radiocarbon dates available at the four sites studied (the southernmost and northernmost sites, Wylde Lake and Shouldice Lake, are illustrated). The greater latitudinal diachroneity in zones 1 and 2 records a steeper climate gradient during the late glacial–early Holocene.

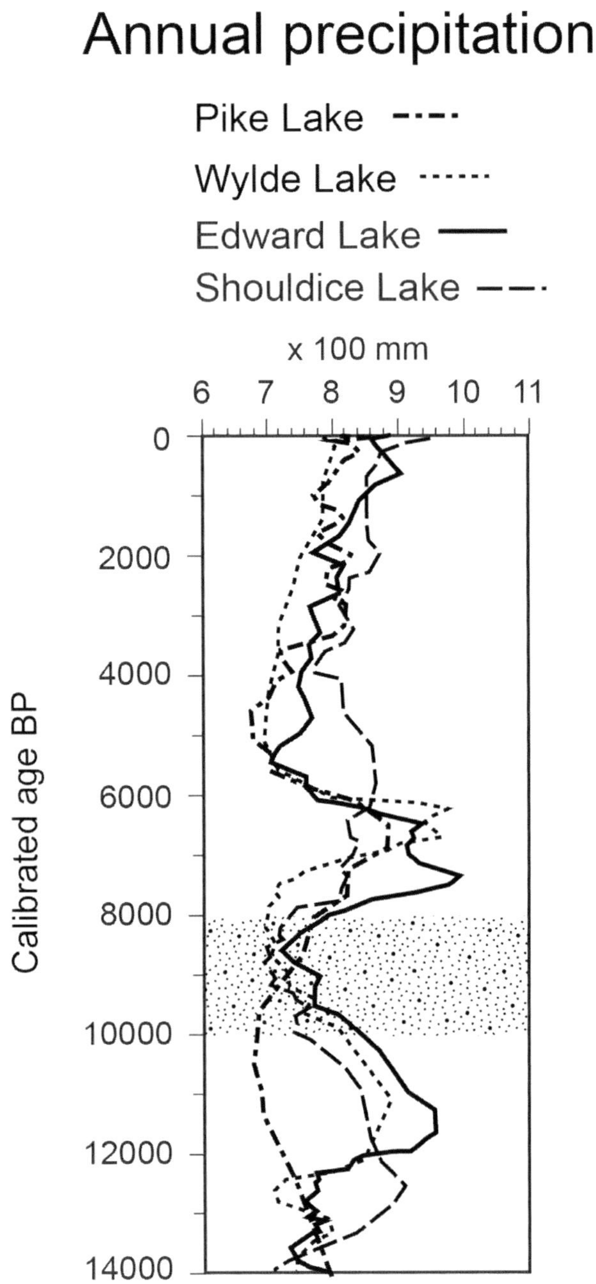

Figure 3.8. The similarity in transfer function reconstructions of mean annual precipitation in the four lakes studied implies a robust response to climate change. Early Holocene aridity promoted the southeastward migration of boreal forest and boreal woodland vegetation in the Great Lakes region. The boreal woodland vegetation dominated by white pine and birch (pollen subzone 2b; *stippled*) would have provided ideal foraging for woodland caribou that rely on lichens adapted to taiga.

Paleohydrology of the Goderich and Manitoulin Basins

Several streams flow into the main basin of Lake Huron from the State of Michigan and the Province of Ontario (Table 3.2); surface water can also enter the main basin from the North Channel and from Georgian Bay (Fig. 3.2). During the early Holocene, however, isostatic depression of the northeastern part of the basin (Lewis, Blasco, and Gareau 2005), combined with the end of discharge at Sault Ste. Marie (currently 2140 m^3/s) due to the hydrologic closure of Lake Superior, produced a negative water budget throughout the Lake Huron basin. In the main basin, two subbasins were isolated from each other (by the Alpena-Amberley Ridge) and from Lake Hough in the deepest part of the Georgian Bay basin (Fig. 3.9). The larger northern (Manitoulin) basin and the smaller southern (Goderich) basin received ~69.9 and 71.7 m^3/s respectively from a subset of the streams that now discharge into the main basin of Lake Huron (compare Figs. 3.2 and 3.9). Paleostream flow into these subbasins was estimated from a bathymetric map of the Lake Huron basin (Fig. 3.9) and by reducing the discharge for those streams flowing into the Manitoulin and Goderich basins during the late Lake Stanley lowstand to ~63% of modern values, accounting for the decrease in mean annual precipitation estimated from the transfer functions (Table 3.1). There was no discharge into Lake Stanley through the North Channel or the Main Channel separating Georgian Bay from the main basin at this time (Table 3.3). Comparison of these values with modern discharge (277.5 m^3/s plus the 1240 m^3/s from Lake Superior via the St. Marys River, 1517.5 m^3/s) illustrates that the subbasins of late Lake Stanley received less than 5% of the modern discharge.

The volume of the two late Lake Stanley basins (regardless of water level) was calculated using a contour map in ArcMap by adding the volumes of consecutive frustums, with each frustum having a volume (V) of:

$$V = \frac{1}{3} H \left(A_1 + A_2 + \sqrt{A_1 A_2}\right)$$

where H is the difference in elevation between chosen contours, A_1 is the area of the lake at the outer contour, and A_2 is the area of the lake at the inner contour. Contour depth values were read off the contour map, while areas were estimated using ArcGIS. Three frustum volumes were calculated and summed for the Manitoulin basin, and two for the Goderich basin. The Manitoulin and Goderich basins have volumes of about 1824 km^3 and 129 km^3, respectively. In addition to the decrease in stream discharge and precipitation onto the surface of each subbasin, evaporation rates were higher during the early Holocene. Evaporation (E) was estimated for each basin during the peak of late Lake Stanley using the Penman formula simplification outlined in Linacre (1977):

$$E_0 = \frac{700\,(T+0.006\,h)/(100-A) + 15(T - T_d)}{(80 - T)} \quad \text{[mm/day]}$$

Table 3.1. Precipitation and temperature means derived from pollen subzone 2b and measured at climate stations (1971–2000). Reconstructions of precipitation during the peak early Holocene drought range between 59 and 67% of normal values.

Climate Station	Lake	Precipitation (cm/yr)		Temperature (°C)			
		modern	past	modern Jan.	past Jan.	modern July	past July
Owen Sound	Shouldice	110.0	70.0	-5.8	-8.6	19.7	19.6
Chatsworth	Edward	115.3	73.0	-7.4	-8.0	18.9	20.0
Hanover	Wylde	104.5	70.0	-7.1	-8.9	19.5	19.8
Hanover	Pike	104.5	62.0	-7.1	-8.0	19.5	20.2

Table 3.2. Modern mean discharge data of streams flowing into the main basin of Lake Huron.

River	Location	Gross Drainage Area (km^2)	Present Discharge (m^3/s)
Penetangore	Ontario	100.0	1.64
Sauble	Ontario	913.5	14.0
Saugeen	Ontario	3953.5	57.9
Cheboygan	Michigan	2302.5	23.3
Pine	Michigan	523.2	5.9
Ausable	Ontario	865.4	10.4
Bayfield	Ontario	460.4	6.27
Maitland	Ontario	2544.8	40.0
Au Sable	Michigan	4504.0	36.8
Thunder Bay	Michigan	3206.4	11.9
Saginaw	Michigan	22260	37.9
Au Gres	Michigan	398.9	2.8
Rifle	Michigan	828.8	9.1
Kawkawling	Michigan	261.6	16.9

Compiled from Environment Canada's Water Survey of Canada (http://wsc.ec.gc.ca/applications/H2O/index-eng.cfm) for Canadian streams, and from the USGS Surface-Water Annual Statistics (http://waterdata.usgs.gov/nwis/annual) for streams located in the USA. Mean discharge values are obtained from data collected over at least 20 years.

Table 3.3. Stream flow input data for the Manitoulin and Goderich subbasins of late Lake Stanley.

River	Present Discharge (m^3/s)	Past Basin	Past Discharge* (m^3/s)
Penetangore	1.64	Manitoulin	1.0
Sauble	14.0	Manitoulin	8.8
Saugeen	57.9	Manitoulin	36.5
Cheboygan	23.3	Manitoulin	14.7
Pine	5.9	Manitoulin	3.7
		total past Manitoulin basin:	*64.7*
Ausable	10.4	Goderich	6.6
Bayfield	6.27	Goderich	4.0
Maitland	40.0	Goderich	25.2
Au Sable	36.8	Goderich	23.2
Thunder Bay	11.9	Goderich	7.5
		total past Goderich basin:	*66.5*
Saginaw	37.9	–	23.9
Au Gres	2.8	–	1.8
Rifle	9.1	–	5.7
Kawkawling	16.9	–	10.6
total present Lake Huron basin:	*274.8*		

*63% of present values.

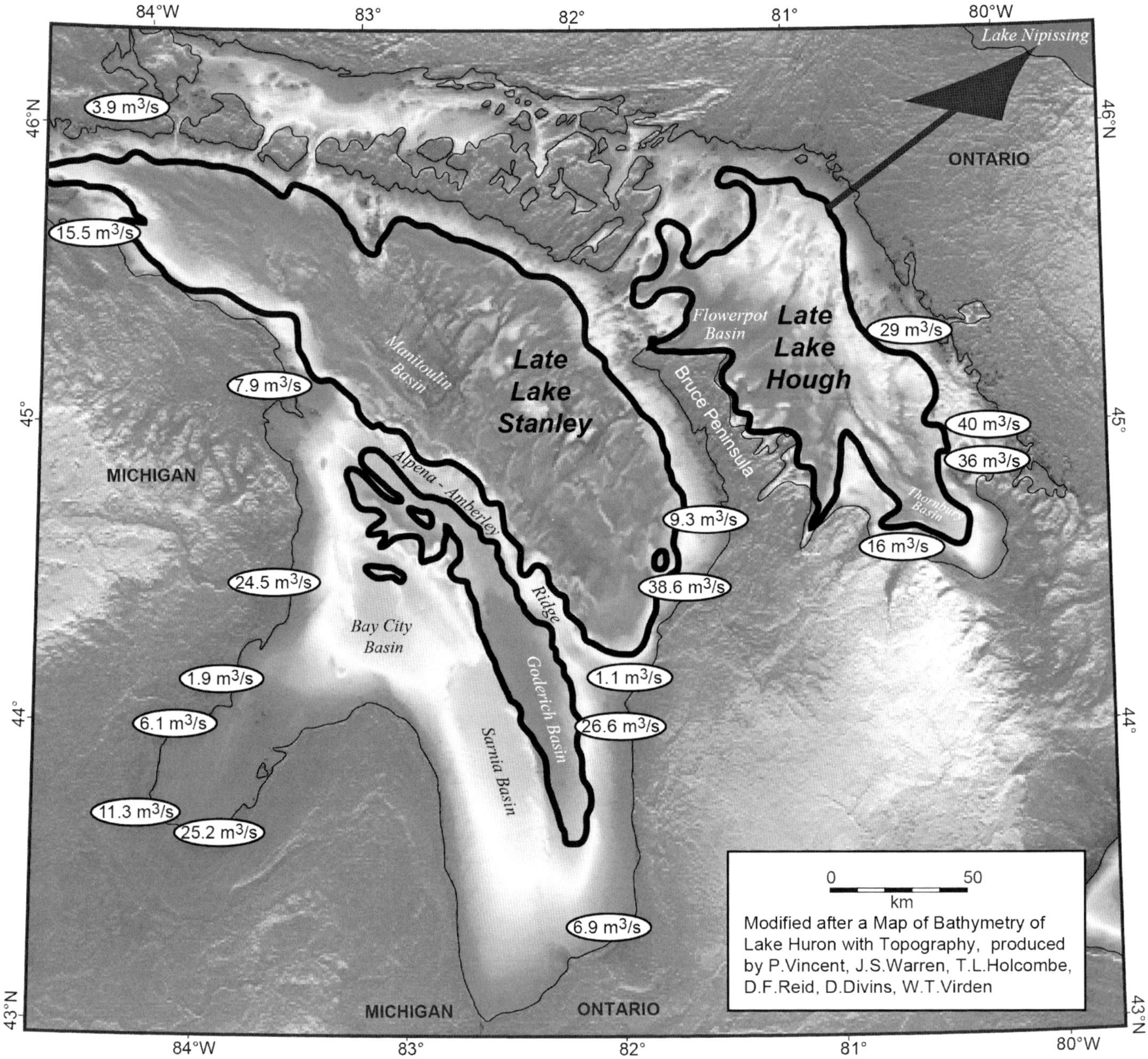

Figure 3.9. Hydrologically closed lakes in the Huron basin during the late Lake Stanley lowstand (ca. 7.9 ± 0.3 ka BP/8464 ± 353 cal BP) received very limited streamflow and no input from the St. Marys River into the North Channel because of hydrologic closure of Lake Superior (McCarthy and McAndrews 2012). The Cheboygan, Pine, Sauble, Penetangore and Saugeen Rivers flowed into the larger Manitoulin basin (a total discharge of 69.6 m^3/s), while the Thunder Bay, Au Sable, Ausable, Bayfield, and Maitland Rivers appear to have flowed into the Goderich basin (a total discharge of 71.7 m^3/s). Based on the bathymetric map of Vincent and colleagues (Bathymetry of Lake Huron. National Geophysical Data Center [NGDC], National Oceanic and Atmospheric Administration. http://www.ngdc.noaa.gov/mgg/greatlakes/huron.html), it does not appear that rivers draining into the modern Saginaw Bay reached either of the large subbasins of late Lake Stanley. Less than 5% of the modern discharge thus entered the Manitoulin or Goderich basins when the Alpena-Amberley Ridge was exposed.

where T is the mean temperature, A is the latitude (degrees), h is elevation, and T_d is the mean dew point temperature. An approximation to the term $(T - T_d)$ can be calculated through the formula:

$$(T - T_d) = 0.0023\,h + 0.37\,T + 0.53\ R + 0.35\,R_{ann} - 10.9$$

where R is the mean daily range of temperature and R_{ann} is the difference between the hottest and coldest months. Present-day values were used to obtain reasonable estimates of R, and the difference between mean January and July temperatures was used to calculate R_{ann}. January and July temperature data obtained from the pollen diagrams (Table 3.1) were averaged and used to calculate January and July evaporation rates. An average h value of 100 m was used for both basins. The latitude values used for the Goderich and Manitoulin basins represented the latitude at the middle of the basin, which approximated to 44°11' N and 45°09' N, respectively. The calculated evaporation rates (mm/day) were then multiplied by the surface area of each subbasin to obtain the total volume of water lost to evaporation (m^3/day). Each basin surface area was calculated using ArcGIS version 10.1 and a detailed contour map of present-day Lake Huron.[4] The surface areas of the Manitoulin and Goderich basins were estimated to be approximately 18,600 and 5300 km^2 respectively, compared to the surface area of modern Lake Huron at 59,000 km^2. The annual mean evaporation rate was taken as the mean of the January and July evaporation rates (Table 3.4).

Approximating each basin to be a rectangular prism, the rate of lake level fall was calculated using the net water budget and surface area of each basin. The rate of lake level fall was 1.0 mm/day and 0.3 mm/day for the Manitoulin and Goderich basins, respectively. At this rate, the lake level would have fallen below the Deane-Tovell Saddle (Echo Sill) between Tobermory and Manitoulin Island within a few centuries, isolating Lake Stanley from Lake Hough. Although rapid, this is consistent with previous illustrations of early Holocene water levels in the Lake Huron basin (see Fig. 3.1).

Direct over-lake precipitation is a major input to the water balance of the Great Lakes (Neff and Killian 2003). Direct rainfall additions were estimated by multiplying mean past precipitation derived from pollen data (Table 3.1) with the surface area of each basin to receive over-lake precipitation inputs of 3.5×10^7 and 1.0×10^7 m^3/day for the Manitoulin and Goderich basins respectively. When comparing various values calculated above, we can achieve a rough estimation of the water budget of each subbasin (Fig. 3.10*A*, *B*). Because the lakes were hydrologically closed, we can assume that loss by evaporation is the only loss in the system. Net water budgets were calculated to be -1.9×10^7 and -1.4×10^6 m^3/day for the Manitoulin and Goderich basins respectively.

4. Bathymetry of Lake Huron. National Geophysical Data Center (NGDC), National Oceanic and Atmospheric Administration. http://www.ngdc.noaa.gov/mgg/greatlakes/huron.html.

Table 3.4. Estimated January, July, and mean annual evaporation rates for the Manitoulin and Goderich basins.

	Manitoulin E_0 (m^3/day)	**Goderich E_0** (m^3/day)
January	-1.96E + 07	-5.47E + 06
July	1.41E + 08	3.95E + 07
annual mean	6.05E + 07	1.70E + 07

Although additions by groundwater are present, no data could be retrieved on these values, although it is known that saline groundwater seeps into the main basin of Lake Huron today (Ruberg et al. 2005). Several studies attempting to model groundwater discharge into the Great Lakes basin indicate that the present direct groundwater discharge to the Great Lakes accounts for only about 5% of the total water budget (Hoaglund, Huffman, and Grannemann 2002; Barton, Mandle, and Baltusis 1996). As such, direct groundwater contribution to the water balance is considered a minor component of the overall budget (Neff and Killian 2003).

Early Holocene Woodland Caribou Habitat and Suitability for Hunting along the Alpena-Amberley Ridge

According to the Ontario Woodland Caribou Recovery Team (2008), woodland caribou (*Rangifer tarandus caribou*) depend on large tracts of mature conifer-dominated forest that produces lichens and other forage. Their historic range extended southward to Lake Nipissing, Manitoulin Island, and the Minnesota border (i.e., near the boundary between the Great Lakes-St. Lawrence forest and the boreal forest; Fig. 3.3). Between AD 1880 and 1990, their range disappeared at a rate of ~34,800 km^2/decade, and their northward range receded at a rate of ~34 km/decade, apparently primarily in response to logging, which promotes early successional vegetation better suited to other wildlife such as moose (Schaefer 2003). Woodland caribou, in contrast, favor late successional to mature taiga (Chowns 2003).

To identify the best modern vegetation and climate analog for the exposed Alpena-Amberley Ridge, the early Holocene pollen rain in the Lake Huron basin was compared with the modern pollen rain in eastern North America (Table 3.5), and the transfer function-derived early Holocene paleoclimate reconstructions were compared with present-day climate normals (Table 3.6). Portage Lake, near Grand Rapids, Minnesota, near the Minnesota-Ontario border (Fig. 3.11), is the most similar, although the comparison is not perfect, particularly with higher abundances of nonarboreal pollen (given the proximity to the prairie) and colder mean January temperature at these higher latitudes (Fig. 3.12).

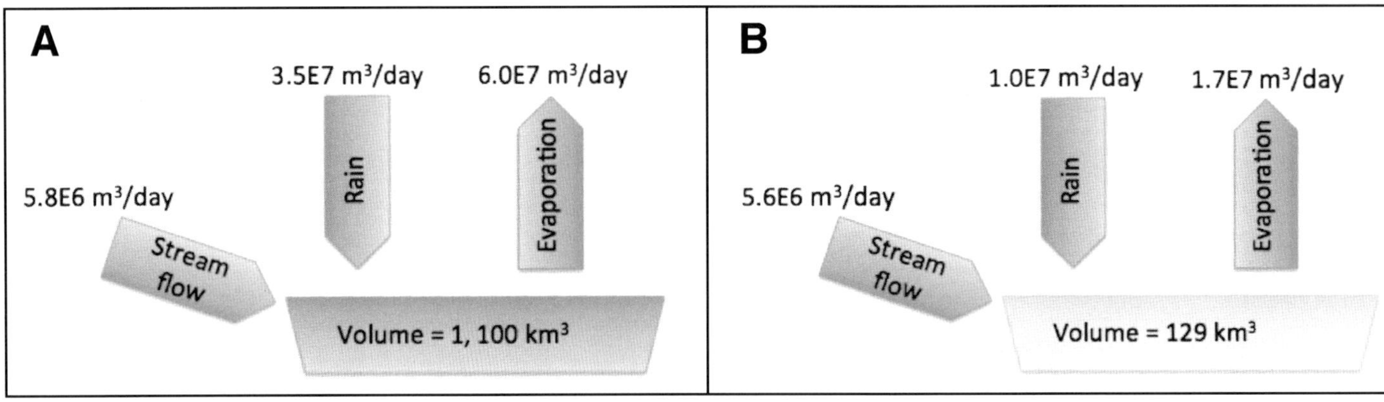

Figure 3.10. Schematic of the paleo water budget for the Manitoulin basin (*A*) and the Goderich basin (*B*) during the most arid part of the Holocene, ~8200 cal BP. The net water budgets of the Manitoulin basin (-1.9E7 m^3/day) and the Goderich basin (-1.4E6 m^3/day) produce estimates of rates of lake level fall ~1.0 mm/day for the Manitoulin basin and 0.3 mm/day for the Goderich basin, accounting for the rapid drawdown of Lake Huron during the early Holocene. The discharge of saline groundwater that seeps into the main basin of Lake Huron (Ruberg et al. 2005) suggests that water on either side of the Alpena-Amberley Ridge was even more saline than the brackish conditions documented for late Lake Hough by McCarthy et al. (2012).

Table 3.5. Relative abundances of key pollen taxa in early Holocene sediments from Shouldice Lake and in modern samples from close modern analogs in northern Ontario (Lake QC) and in northeastern Minnesota (Portage Lake).

Pollen Taxon	**Shouldice Lake** (~8.2 ka)	**Lake QC**	**Portage Lake**
spruce	0.7	6.8	2.2
pine	60.6	55.0	34.8
birch	7.0	18.6	12.5
elm	4.5	1.0	1.6
oak	10.5	2.9	11.8
sugar maple	0.7	0 0	1.3
hemlock	0.7	0.3	0
total herbs	5.6	2.6	22.1

Table 3.6. Precipitation and temperature means at modern analog sites.

Climate Station	**Nearby Lake**	**Modern Precipitation** (cm/yr)	**Modern Temperature** (°C) January	**Modern Temperature** (°C) July
Bemidji	Minnie	63.0	-14.5	19.9
Brainerd	Black Bass	66.0	-14.7	20.3
Cloquet	Kryzewinski	73.9	-13.0	19.0
Grand Rapids	Portage	70.7	-12.8	20.0
Dryden	Hayes	69.0	-17.6	19.2
Sudbury	QC	89.9	-13.6	19.0
North Bay	Three Pines	77.5	-13.0	18.6
Huntsville	Porqui Pond	99.0	-10.5	19.3

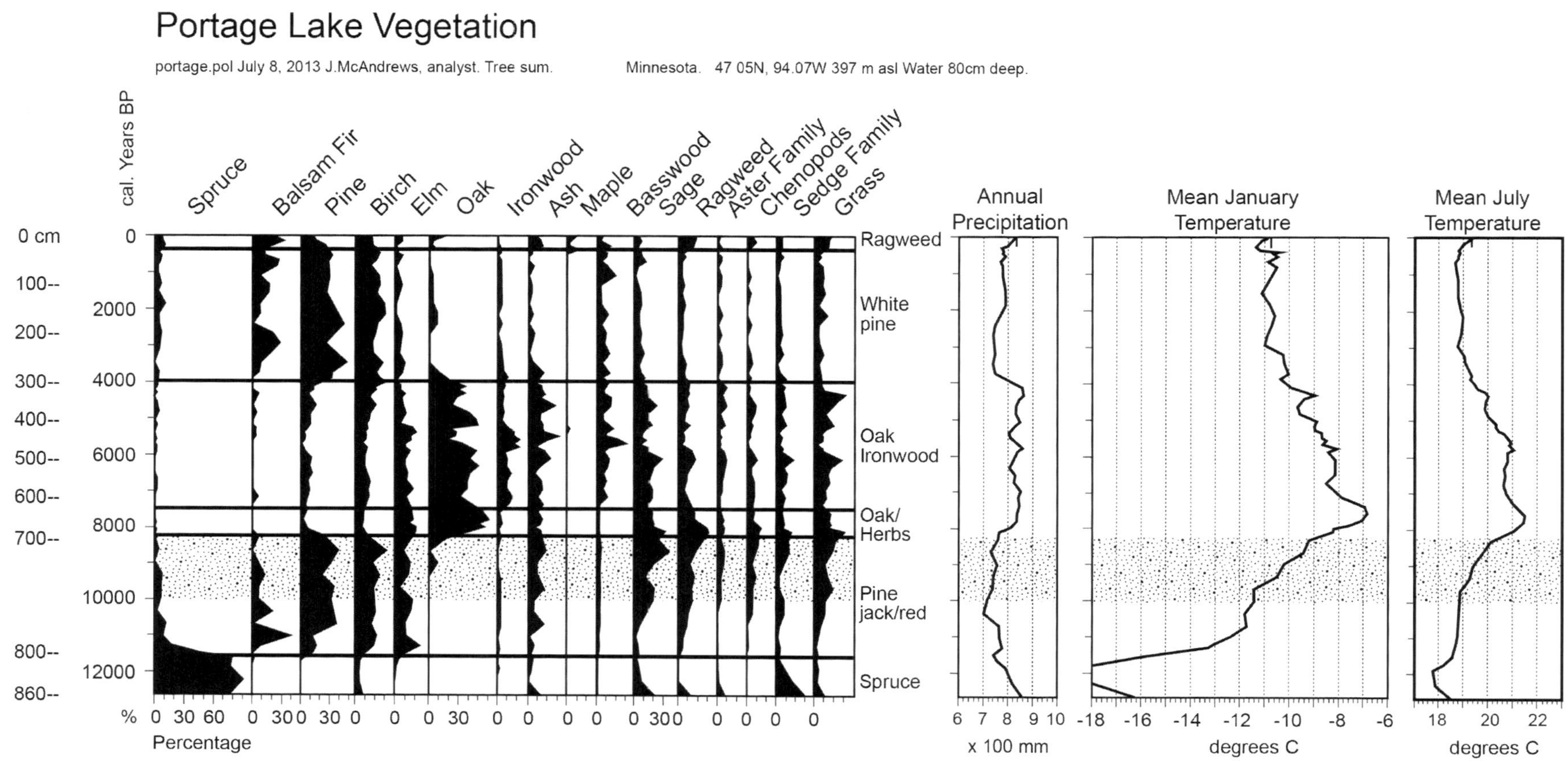

Figure 3.11. The closest modern analog for the region surrounding the main basin of Lake Huron during the early Holocene is Portage Lake, Minnesota. The prairie/mixed forest surrounding the lake in northeastern Minnesota is dominated by pine and birch with balsam fir, spruce, ash, and maple. Climate normals at the nearest climate station, Grand Rapids, Minnesota (Table 3.6), compare well with reconstructed values for mean annual precipitation and July temperature in the Lake Huron basin during the early Holocene (~70 mm/y and 20°C, respectively), but mean January temperatures are about 4°C colder in Minnesota than are reconstructed for the shores of late Lake Stanley.

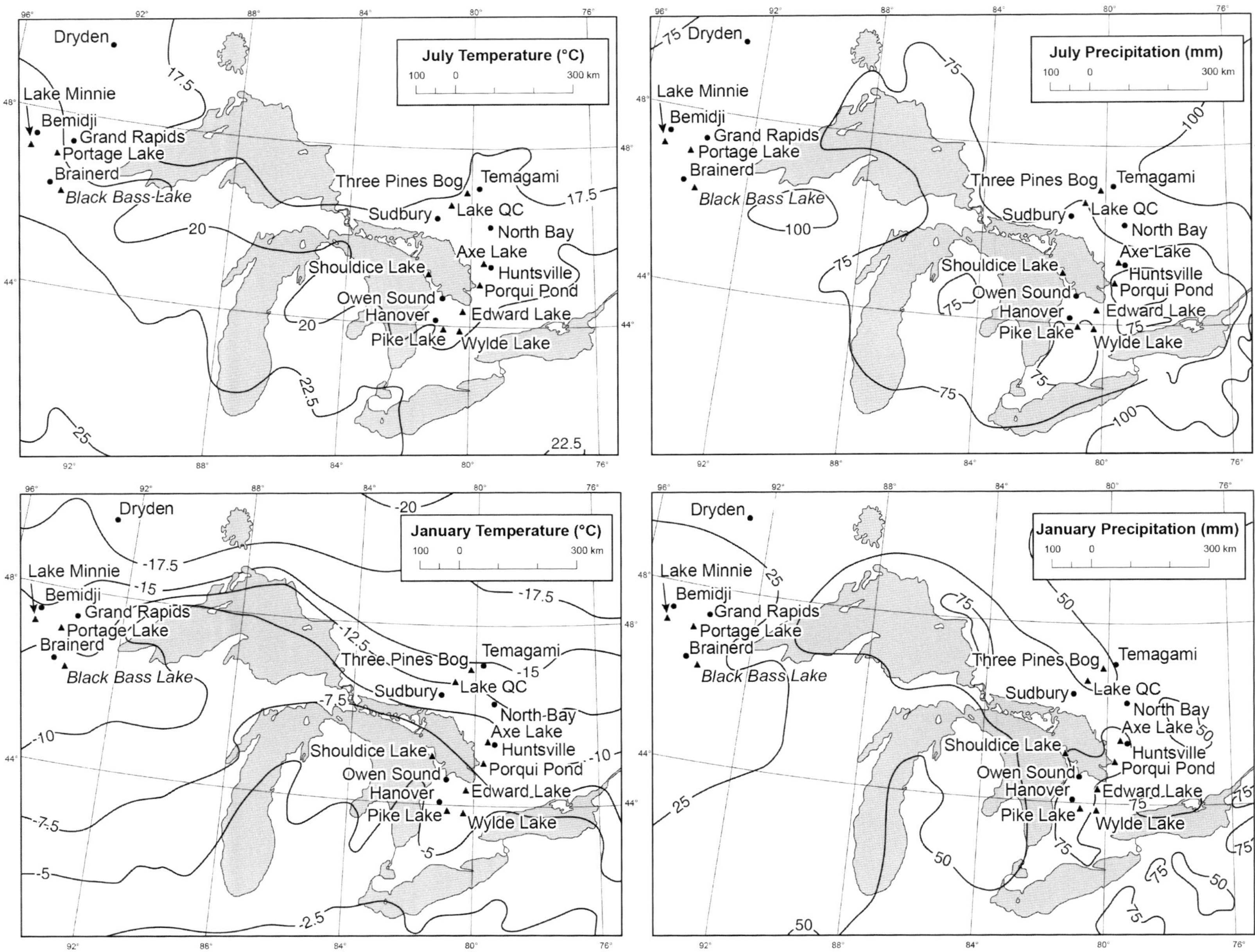

Figure 3.12. Contoured mean modern values of climate parameters from Steinhauser (1979) illustrate the variation from summer-wet in the west to low seasonality with high lake effect snowfall in the east in the Great Lakes region. Small lake core sites (*triangles*) and nearby climate stations (*circles*) from the prairie/mixed forest in northeastern Minnesota (notably Portage Lake near Grand Rapids, Minnesota) are the closest modern analogs to the boreal woodland in the drainage basin of early Holocene late Lake Stanley. Within the Huron drainage basin, Lake QC near Sudbury is the closest modern analog to vegetation around Shouldice Lake, Edward Lake, Pike Lake, and Wylde Lake during subzone 2b, but Sudbury is substantially wetter and the winters are colder (compare Tables 3.1 and 3.6).

The identification of northeastern Minnesota as the closest analog is consistent with the findings of a high degree of similarity between the modern vegetation around Black Bass Lake and Lake Minnie and the early Holocene aspen parkland vegetation in the Georgian Bay basin (e.g., in Porqui Pond; McCarthy and McAndrews 2012). In addition, McCarthy and McAndrews pointed out that climate normals from the climate stations in northeastern Minnesota (e.g., Brainerd and Bemidji) compare well with reconstructions for pollen zone 2b in the Georgian Bay basin.

Within the Lake Huron basin, Lake QC and Three Pines Bog (Fig. 3.12) also currently support vegetation similar to that found around Amberley, Ontario, during the early Holocene. Vegetation subzone L.9 of Rowe (1972) is characterized by white pine with white birch and white spruce and scattered occurrences of the tolerant hardwoods such as sugar maple and yellow birch. The vegetation in this part of the Great Lakes-St. Lawrence forest represents a gradual transition to boreal taxa, and the upland taxa shows a response to past forest fires (Rowe 1972). Winters are colder north of Lake Huron than they are in northeastern Minnesota, however, and modern precipitation values are higher than they were in the Huron basin during the early Holocene.

Thus, even though Portage Lake is in the Superior drainage basin, it appears to be a better analog, particularly given the probable windswept character of the Alpena-Amberley Ridge. Thus, the pine-dominated forest was probably relatively open—more like the boreal woodland that characterized the area east of Georgian Bay at this time (McCarthy and McAndrews 2012)—and would have contained more herbs. The more open vegetation, together with the reduction in flying insects, would have been an advantage to caribou, particularly at parturition, and would also have increased the necessity for hunting blinds, for which there appears to be archeological evidence (O'Shea and Meadows 2009; O'Shea, Lemke, and Reynolds 2013; Chapter 10).

Brackish water in late Lake Stanley is suggested by abundant ostracod valves preserved in sediments from the main basin of Lake Huron (Rea et al. 1994) together with evidence of sustained negative water budgets between the diversions of Laurentide Ice Sheet meltwater ~10,000 cal BP (Lewis et al. 1994). Widespread low lake levels (Newby et al. 2000; Webb, Shuman, and Williams 2004; McCarthy et al. 2012) suggest an increase in solute concentrations in the surface waters. The seepage of brine from aquifers (Ruberg et al. 2005) into relatively small volumes of water in the Goderich and Manitoulin basins would have added high concentrations of Na^+ and Cl^- ions to the waters, probably imparting a salty taste to the waters, as was documented by the Ojibway, who interpreted the saltiness that their ancestors tasted to the tears of Nanabush (Keeshig-Tobias, pers. comm.; Calvert and McCarthy 2010). Perhaps caribou hunters used this salty water, both as a flavoring agent-nutrient and to preserve meat.

Summary and Conclusions

Comparison of reconstructed vegetation during pollen zone 2b (the white pine zone) with modern vegetation, and of estimates of paleoclimatic parameters around 8200 cal BP with those at climate stations in the Great Lakes regions, suggests that the best modern analog for the Alpena-Amberley Ridge during the early Holocene is in northeastern Minnesota. Our water budget suggests a very rapid decline in lake level during this relatively arid interval, consistent with geological evidence for the late Lake Stanley lowstand. The negative water budget, combined with the seepage of briny groundwater into the lake basin, would have produced relatively high salinities that would have been sufficient to flavor meat, and possibly even to help preserve it.

Acknowledgments

We acknowledge the organizers of the workshop at the University of Michigan and the participants for inspiring this study, and Mike Lozon, Brock University, for assistance with drafting.

4 Serious Game Modeling of Caribou Behavior across Lake Huron Using Cultural Algorithms and Influence Maps

by James Fogarty, Robert G. Reynolds, Areej Salaymeh, and Thomas Palazzolo

It has been suggested that in the future, many important archaeological discoveries will take place underwater. This chapter describes a virtual reality-based game that was designed to facilitate the exploration of underwater sites. While the prototype was developed for a particular area—the Lake Huron land bridge—it is felt that the approach can be generalized to other sites as well, given that sufficient data about them are available.

Recent surveys of a stretch of terrain underneath Lake Huron have indicated the presence of a land bridge that would have existed approximately 10,000–8000 years ago, during the recession of ice during the last Ice Age, connecting Canada and the United States. This terrain, the Alpena-Amberley Ridge, was host to a full Subarctic environment, including migratory caribou herds. It is hypothesized that by modeling the behavior of caribou herds in that environment, one might be able to identify hot spots where hunting-related campsites might be located.

The application was designed around these concepts using Microsoft's .Net platform and XNA Framework to visually model this behavior and to allow the entities in the application to learn the behavior through successive generations. By utilizing influence maps to manage tactical information, and cultural algorithms to learn from the maps to produce path planning and flocking behavior, optimal paths were discovered and areas of local concentration based upon these paths were isolated. In particular, paths emerged that supported two different sets of goal priorities for herd movement. One set of evolved paths focused on efficient migratory behavior at the expense of food consumption, which caused some deaths. On the other hand, paths emerged that focused on food consumption with only gradual migration process. There were also paths that emerged that blended both goals together—paths that make effective progress toward the goal without excessive losses to starvation.

Overview

Both computer modeling of group behavior and ecological modeling have seen considerable development, as shown with Walters and Bergman (Walters, Hilborn, and Peterman 1975; Bergman, Schaefer, and Luttich 2000), but what remains to be done is to integrate the two perspectives in a quantitative fashion. Previous research has focused on discovering the ecological basis for behavior by modeling (1) both the terrain and flora (Bliss et al. 1973); (2) the herbivore movements in relative isolation to environments (Bergman, Schaefer, and Luttich 2000); or (3) the individual aspects of herbivore movements without analyzing group behavior as a whole (Walters, Hilborn, and Peterman 1975).

We chose to construct a virtual world model of an ancient environment, the Alpena-Amberley Ridge (AAR), to integrate all these perspectives into one model (O'Shea 2008; Lewis et al. 2007). This project, initiated by O'Shea, a University of Michigan anthropologist, was undertaken to better understand how prehistoric Paleoindians hunted and lived 10,000–8000 years ago. At that time, the level of what is now modern Lake Huron was low enough to expose a 6-mile-wide land bridge that connected what is today Alpena in Michigan to the Amberley area in Canada. O'Shea speculated that the land bridge, now submerged beneath 200 feet of water, might contain evidence of prehistoric occupation, and a preliminary sonar survey of selected areas on the AAR (supported by an NSF High Risk research grant) provided evidence to support this conjecture. The data collection activities were performed using sonar, autonomous underwater vehicles, and scuba divers (Chapter 9). The preliminary results offered tempting insight into what could have existed 10,000–8000 years ago, which resulted in the project being named as one of the top 100 scientific discoveries of 2009 by *Discover* magazine (Barth 2009).

Next, Reynolds and a group of students in the Artificial Intelligence Laboratory at Wayne State University began investigating the possibility of recreating a virtual world model of the region, a model that can be used by the archaeologists to predict where to do further surveys and investigations since the overall area is very large, and surveys, both above and under the water, are costly.

The initial simulations of the region by both Reynolds and Vitale (Reynolds et al. 2013; Vitale 2009) were small in scale, involving small numbers of animals and hunters over a limited region, but returned promising results. Here, we expand on this earlier work to create a large-scale serious game that utilizes a detailed three-dimensional world in which group behavioral concepts are implemented, and where the best and most likely scenarios of life in this Subarctic world can emerge. (A serious game is one designed for a purpose other than entertainment; its main aim is for training and investigation.) Since cultural algorithms, developed by Reynolds, are particularly adept to the process of modeling societies (Reynolds, Peng, and Whallon 2005), we use them to design human and animal group behavior in these extended virtual game models. Cultural algorithms, a branch of evolutionary computation, model the cultural evolution process, where "culture is the fabric of meaning in terms of which human beings interpret their experience and guide their actions" (Geertz 1973).

A cultural algorithm (CA) consists of a belief space and a population model that communicate through an interaction protocol whereby the belief space influences the population and the best individuals can in turn influence the belief space (see Fig. 4.1). This feedback process is based on acceptance and influence functions, and thus the population evolves according to the promotion of the best individuals' beliefs (Liu 2011).

Figure 4.1 displays the cultural algorithm process at an abstract level. The population is initialized in the first step labeled, "population." Each individual is scored, based upon objective criteria, and a predetermined number of elite—those with the best performances—are selected to update the "belief space," which is the foundation for the genetic makeup of the offspring for succeeding generations. Other knowledge sources that describe relationships between objects in the world can be supported and updated through this process as well.

For example, our stated goal is to simulate the emergence of likely caribou behavior, positioning, and survival across the Alpena-Amberley Ridge during various scenarios that are supported by and designed with real-world flora and fauna constraints. These data can be stored and updated in the belief space, and are generalized to provide decision support for the project. One source of evolved knowledge in the belief space are influence maps, which are used to indicate those regions of the terrain most influenced by simulated caribou behavior and corresponding hunter responses. The use of both real-world terrain data acquired during O'Shea's investigations as well as simulated human behavior (that cultural algorithms and influence maps will help to develop) will generate a list of "hotspots" or areas most likely to be occupied by hunters based upon caribou behavior.

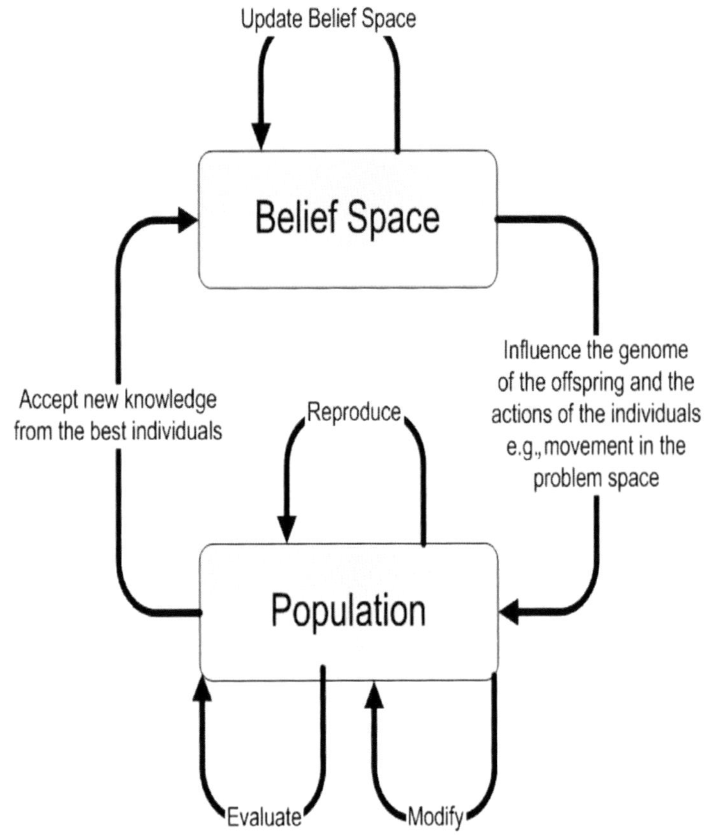

Figure 4.1. Design of cultural algorithms.

Terrain Creation and Modeling

Using underwater depth and latitudinal and longitudinal positioning information provided by O'Shea (O'Shea 2008), the geopositional data were used to construct a grayscale image called a heightmap. This heightmap is the basis for all our results. Using Microsoft's XNA Framework, we generated a 3D model mesh using methods from Lobao (Pereira Evangelista et al. 2009) that allow access to height and normal data throughout the simulation.

The AAR itself extended from Alpena, Michigan, USA, to Amberley, Ontario, Canada, during the last ice age, and is pictured in Figure 4.2 (see also Plate 1; Jin 2011). It was a strip of land that crossed under what is currently Lake Huron. The research has already provided some insight into possible hunting

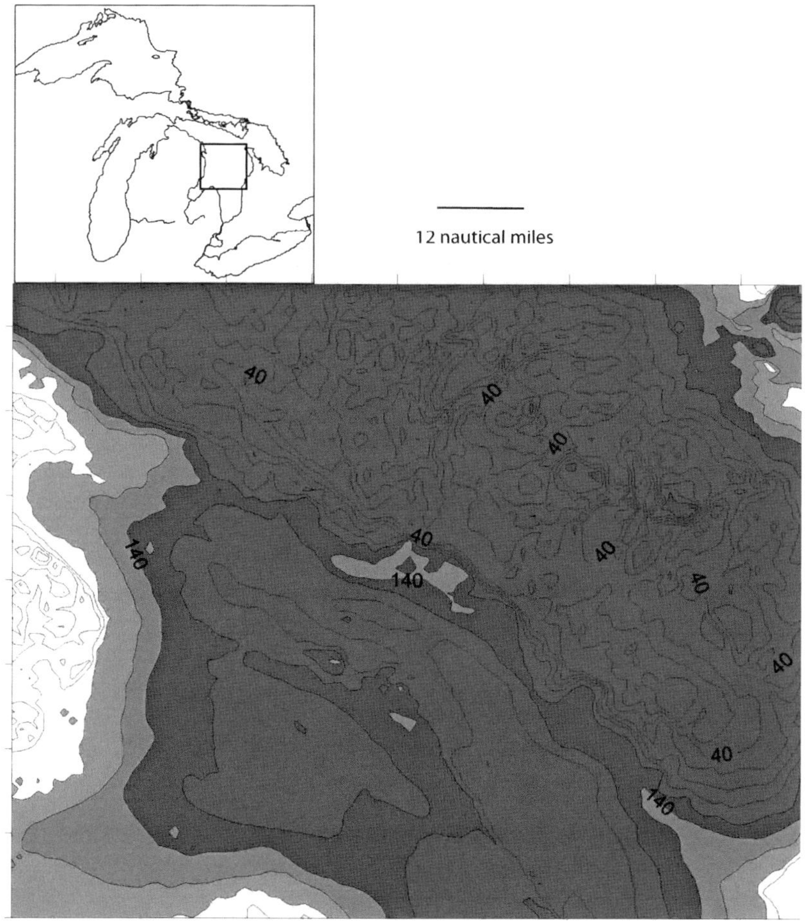

(*left*) Figure 4.2.
Alpena-Amberley Ridge across Lake Huron. (See also Plate 1.)

(*below*) Figure 4.3.
Rigid path-finding nodes or waypoints are shown as dark nodes whereas the lighter regions represent the area that herds can traverse when they reach a given node.

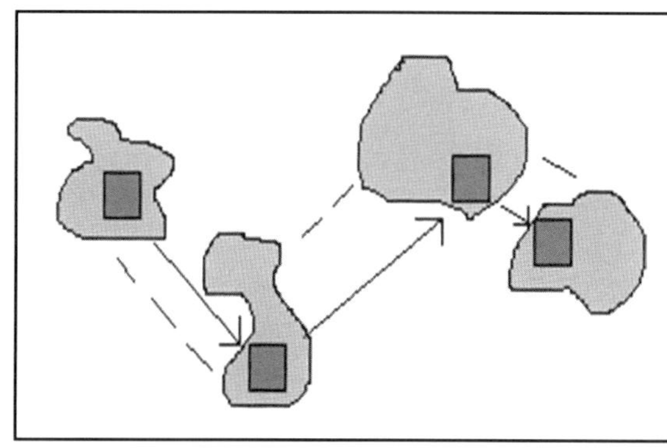

and camping sites (O'Shea et al. 2013, 2014; Chapters 10, 11). The process of using sonar to map the lake bottom has given us the ability to construct a 3D interactive and expandable environment for behavioral and cultural analysis using constructs that will help reveal the possible survival processes of the societies that relied on this terrain. The simulation has been developed to incorporate changes in configurations of terrain and vegetation coverage as well as variables such as water level. The latter becomes important in the future when modeling the impact of rising water levels on land bridge utilization.

Group Behavior

There are a large number of available path planning methods for individuals (McInnes 2003). On the other hand, if we abstract the population into discrete sets of individuals or groups and then plan paths according to the abstract group entity instead of the individual, we can achieve both accurate, low-overhead path planning as well as visibly fluid movement. To prevent the overhead and to tightly integrate behavior to simulate real-world flocking behavior, we look at the flocking behavior models introduced by Reynolds (1987).

Figure 4.3 gives an example of the execution of our path-finding technique. The dark squares are path-finding nodes, which are determined by a path-planning heuristic where each square is an in-order node that the group will navigate toward. However, once the sequence of nodes visited by the group is determined, the individuals in the group can move within the vicinity of the nodes, as indicated by the lighter regions. Their individual actions are determined by the parameters, such as desired proximity to neighbors. This behavior allows groups to have macro-goal decision-making ability while also allowing individuals to make choices within that context.

According to Reynolds' model, entities create a dynamic flocking movement using three primary principles: cohesion, separation, and alignment. That is, as they perform their individual movements, they need to remain close enough to others in the group to show a *cohesive* structure. Still, they need to be far enough from each other to indicate an individual movement activity. That is called *separation*. Thirdly, they need to move in a generally similar direction so that they keep their movements in *alignment* with the rest of the group. Using these three forces, a flow is established that takes into account the individuals in each group. Splitting the total population into groups of dynamic sizes with capacities and orientation centers, as well as establishing individual goal locations and weights for each group, allows multiple interactions with the environment in each generation. These goals and weights are created and tracked through our learning mechanisms, influence maps. These maps then provide information on the general path-planning tendencies of the caribou herds over the virtual landscape. The update of each influence map is done at the end of each generational pass using the cultural algorithm.

Learning Mechanisms

The learning mechanism employed here involves a two-step learning method. The first step is to generate influence maps. Influence maps in games and simulations have a long history (DeLoura 2001), and were found to be of great use in maintaining a statistical tracking of the interactive world in computer games. Influence maps are cellular divisions of 2D or 3D worlds with tactical values assigned to the spaces that they occupy. These values are determined by a problem-specific function and can be accessed during the application execution both for value input into the program or to receive output values for later reference by learning and decision-making algorithms. The map as a function of the game world represents the desirability of a particular cell for traversal by caribou. The factors affecting desirability include positive influences such as availability of food, and negative influences such as terrain accessibility, predation, insects, and water barriers. An influence map is generated by subdividing the world space into smaller segments or cells. These segments can be directly accessed by a number of methods that allow an entity in the world to retrieve informational values concerning the area they require information about.

In our program, the influence maps are generated in real time during the run of the serious game. By using influence maps, we can track valuable components of tactical knowledge that would influence caribou behavior: location of food, rough terrain, or any other positive or negative influence to a segment of 3D space. The influence maps are input into the simulation in terms of grayscale bitmaps.

The second, and most refined, step in the learning process involves the use of cultural algorithms. The CA has proven itself as an adaptable source for both real-time and turn-based game applications (Ochoa et al. 2008; Loiacono et al. 2008), and since the real-time components as well as those that occur at the end of each belief cycle or time step are used, one should consider whether to focus on the real-time or turn-based advantages of cultural algorithms. The Open Racing Car Simulator (TORCS; Loiacono et al. 2008) is closest to what we are developing—a real-time 3D virtual simulation with reward and punishment concepts (win/loss), which we can extrapolate to our own world. The CA in TORCS had access to state variables for a vehicle (such as gear, track position, wheel spin, and fuel), so it would use that information to optimize the output needed to control the vehicle. The TORCS system interface allowed that refined information to generate a set of output parameters to interact with the vehicle (such as acceleration and braking) and move the car within the race pack. Likewise, research by Vitale (2009) used a CA to evaluate a simple wandering kinematic or movement activity in the same situation we now attempt to model.

A key parameter in the kinematic was the jittering parameters that would control the direction and rate of change of movement for a group of individuals. The cultural algorithm in that game simulation was used to learn to adjust the kinematic jittering parameters in order to optimize group movement. Figure 4.4 shows a number of individuals (denoted as triangles) as they attempt to cross a land bridge in a simulation using the wandering kinematic. Each candidate set of parameters in the cultural algorithm population was evaluated in terms of its ability to effectively control group behavior. The overall group performance was assessed in terms of distance traveled and percentage of living entities at the end of a generation, allowing the CA to learn parameters for effectively crossing a portion of the land bridge over a sequence of generations.

Here, the 3D virtual world is developed with the ability to extend the algorithm to multiple animals with a variety of inputs, simply by changing the value files that the program reads. However, the implementation itself sets out to discover valid and hopefully verifiable results on caribou migration over the AAR.

The 3D Virtual World

The terrain and 3D world components of the game are broken into two parts. The first part discusses the detailed terrain generation of a 2D grayscale heightmap for input into the simulation, as well as summarizes the simple way in which foliage is generated and placed into 2D grayscale input files. The second part covers the display of the terrain and vegetation, and caribou movement components (see Tactical Knowledge and Group Movement, below).

Detailed Terrain Generation

Terrain generation can be decomposed into two basic components: (1) generation of the heightmap or topography; and (2) generation of the vegetation content.

Heightmap Generation

Data, provided from O'Shea's study (2008), consisted of actual values read by sonar from the bottom of Lake Huron over a portion of the Alpena-Amberley Ridge. The data were in a tab-delimited format with thousands of records in the format shown in Table 4.1.

These data were mapped to the actual Alpena-Amberley Ridge for the game. Here, a small regional component is selected for demonstration purposes. Figure 4.5 refers to the location of the selected region in terms of the bathymetric data. Michigan is the gray mass to the left, and Canada is to the right. We are focused

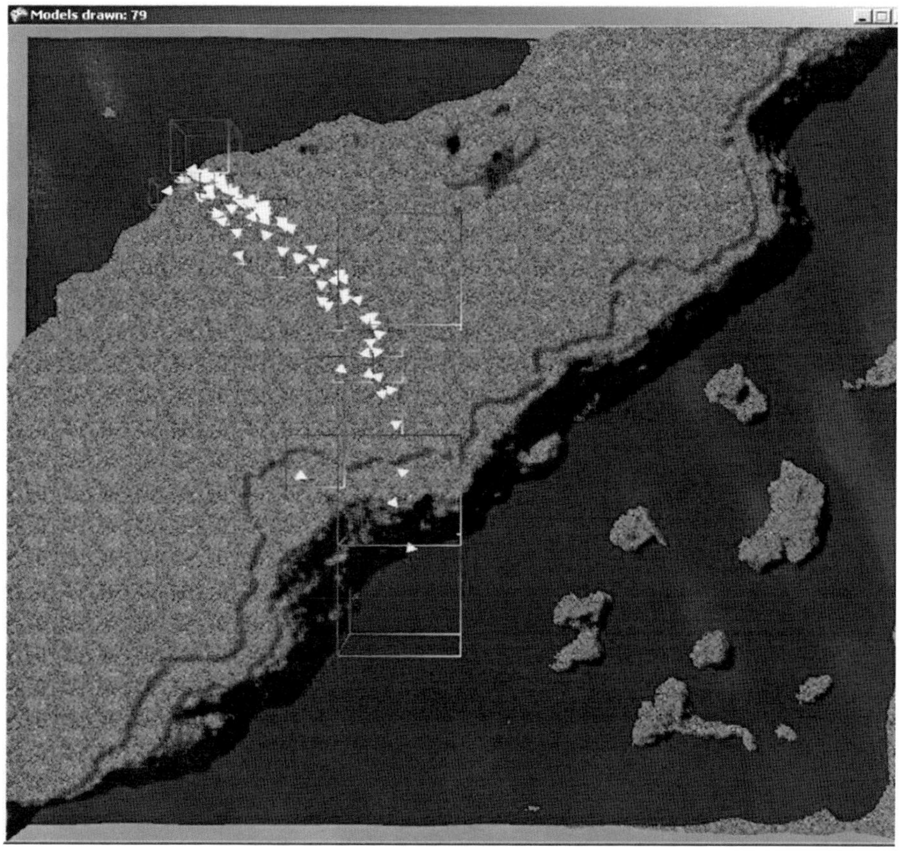

Table 4.1. Initialization values.

Easting	Northing	Elevation (m below sea level)
381571.523	4972936.151	28.5
381637.29	4972934.936	27.6
...	...	...

(*left*) Figure 4.4.
Improved caribou movement over the land bridge (*triangles*, individual caribou).

(*below*) Figure 4.5.
Alpena-Amberley Ridge (Michigan is to the left and Canada to the right). The regional component used for demonstration purposes is outlined.

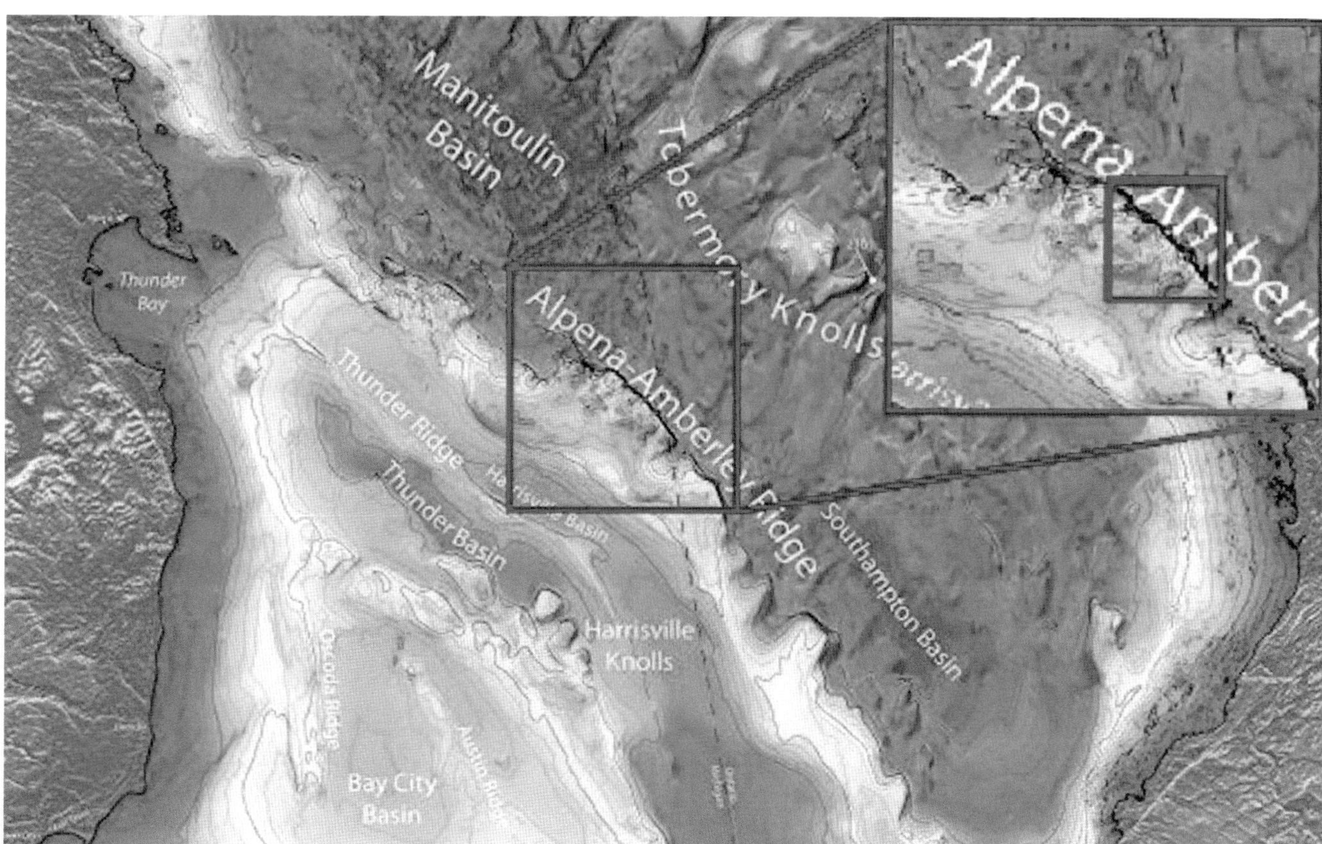

on the small image in the top right corner, or more specifically, to the boxed location within it.

Heightmap generation was begun by dictating a minimum length (in this case, *x*) for the final 2D image, which would be the length or height of the image in pixels; the data that covered the minimum distance were set for the minimum resolution in the display. Using that length as a basis, the minimum easting or northing distance was determined from the data, and that distance was broken up into *x* equal-length "buckets" of a certain range, which will be used later. With that information, the relative length of the other side (*y*) can be determined; it will always be greater than or equal to *x*. That side is broken into equal-length buckets as well.

The maximum and minimum elevations are now determined and normalized, the minimum being assigned the value of 1 with a linear interpolation, bringing the maximum to 255. Assigning the values within this numerical range aligns them with the numerical structure used to form colors in XNA. Next, the easting/northing values are expressed in terms of the proper *xy* coordinates (the correct "bucket") with the correct relative grayscale value. When all values are completed, the image is output. The process is visualized in Figure 4.6.

Some gaps may appear in our resultant 2D image due either to the drifting of the barge that carried the sonar or to the bucket range being too small (i.e., a 128-length side has fewer errors than does a 256-length side due to an acceptable range of *x* and *y* coordinates in each bucket). A gap corresponds to a grayscale value of 0, which can occur only when the data do not fall into that *xy* bucket range. This can be resolved with a number of smoothing algorithms, as discussed in Jain (1986) and Griffin (2000).

One approach to gap removal is by mean filtering, which smooths a small (one pixel) gap with a single pass by replacing it with the average of its neighboring pixels. This approach was selected to smooth the final image with a customized implementation; the resultant smoothed heightmap is shown in Figure 4.7. The images on the left-hand side are based on the raw data, and those on the right-hand side are after smoothing.

Vegetation Generation

Subarctic systems that support a full trophic life cycle consist of living producers and consumers and decomposers of material (Bliss et al. 1973). Caribou consume both living and dead plants, so modeling both current as well as historical plant growth is important in determining food density and caribou survival rate during migration. It is also important to model the tree species variability and location in order to model density of travel paths and to predict the presence of lichen as a food source, as mentioned in Cowling, Sykes, and Bradshaw (2001). Saranhoa (1985) suggested that since consumables also rotate on a multiyearly basis, it was important to pick a particular food level in order to get results in a static environment. The assumption of a certain level of food in the environment was also made here.

Price and Sirois describe the process of vegetative growth in boreal environments (Price et al. 1999; Sirois, Bonan, and Shugart 1994). There are two basic components that are used to compute biomass here: soil water content and available light. In terms of soil water content, the FORSKA 2 model developed and detailed by Price et al. (1999) gives an in-depth model of annual vegetation coverage cover for a particular combination of soil and environment quality. Price et al., in particular, detail the effect of soil water content and biomass on vegetative growth. For example, a decrease in water content decreases the viability of the area for hosting a tundra forest. Since his model's detailed predictions are acknowledged as highly susceptible to small errors in model data, and because an in-depth analysis of boreal environments similar to the FORSKA 2 model is outside the scope of this current project, a simple model by which lower terrain receives a higher proportion of soil water content due to runoff is employed here.

Next, Sirois modeled the relative impact of available light on tree growth. Here, sun angle was calculated from the slope of the topographic data that were collected for each cell by the project. Thus, available light and soil water content were used to produce biomass value relative to available water and light based upon their models. The value was then expressed as a grayscale value and inserted into the virtual world, resulting in a grayscale image depicting the density of vegetation across the selected region.

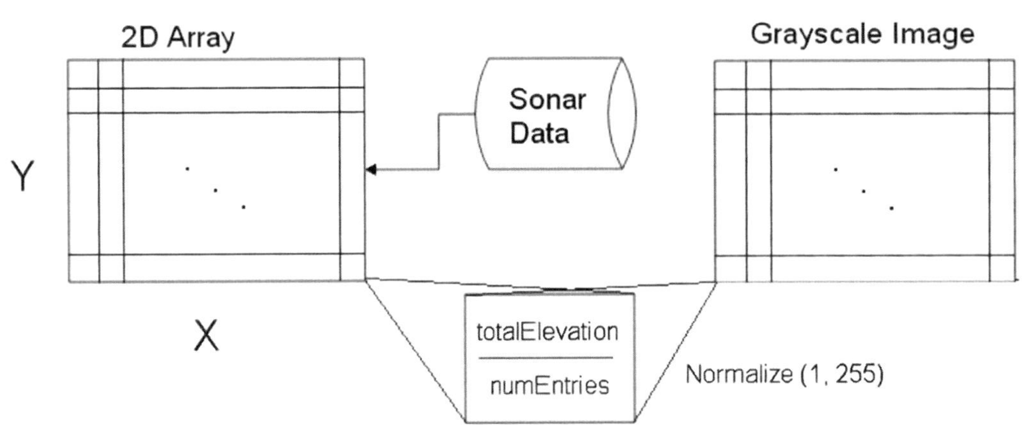

Figure 4.6.
Heightmap generation process.

Terrain Display

Terrain and Caribou Display

After the terrain is generated using the sonar data, techniques described by Pereira Evangelista et al. (2009) allow us to read the white value intensity of individual points in the bitmap and to assign them as a vertex in a 3D model to be displayed in XNA. The terrain uses the angle and height of the terrain to define the features—terrain underwater is rendered with sand textures, peaks with rock, and above water with grass. The water is a reflective and refractive surface, utilizing complex techniques such as the Fresnel term and color modification, as in Figure 4.8. All of the drawing is offloaded to the graphics processing unit (GPU) for speed. The water reflection is achieved through a secondary camera located under the water level, rendering the reflected image into a semitransparent plane displayed on the water's surface.

Vegetation Display

All visible vegetation features—such as trees and scrub—are drawn using billboarding techniques as described by Pettit et al. (2009). In billboarding, a 2D image is rendered as a 3D point with surface area. In this scenario, the images always rotate along the y axis to maintain a perpendicular plane with respect to the camera, while maintaining the y up vector and their x and z positions, to simulate forests and scrub brush, as illustrated in Figure 4.9. The density of the billboards is determined by the relative white intensity of the input files—the higher the white value of the cell, the more likely a cluster is to be dense when it is randomly generated. Further constraints check the slope of the local terrain, and if the terrain is too steep, vegetation will not be generated there.

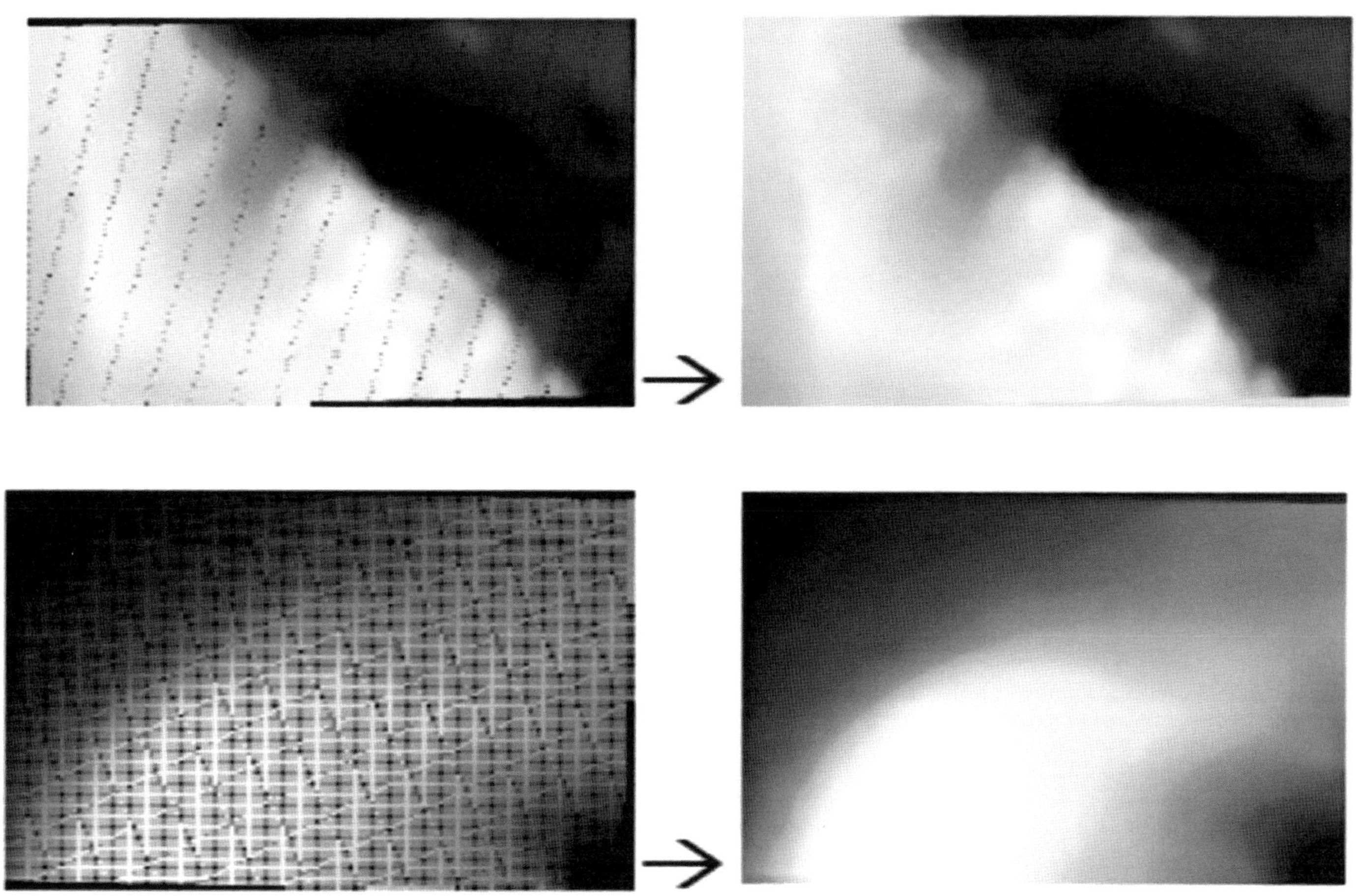

Figure 4.7. Data driven (*left*) and smoothed (*right*) heightmaps for simulation.

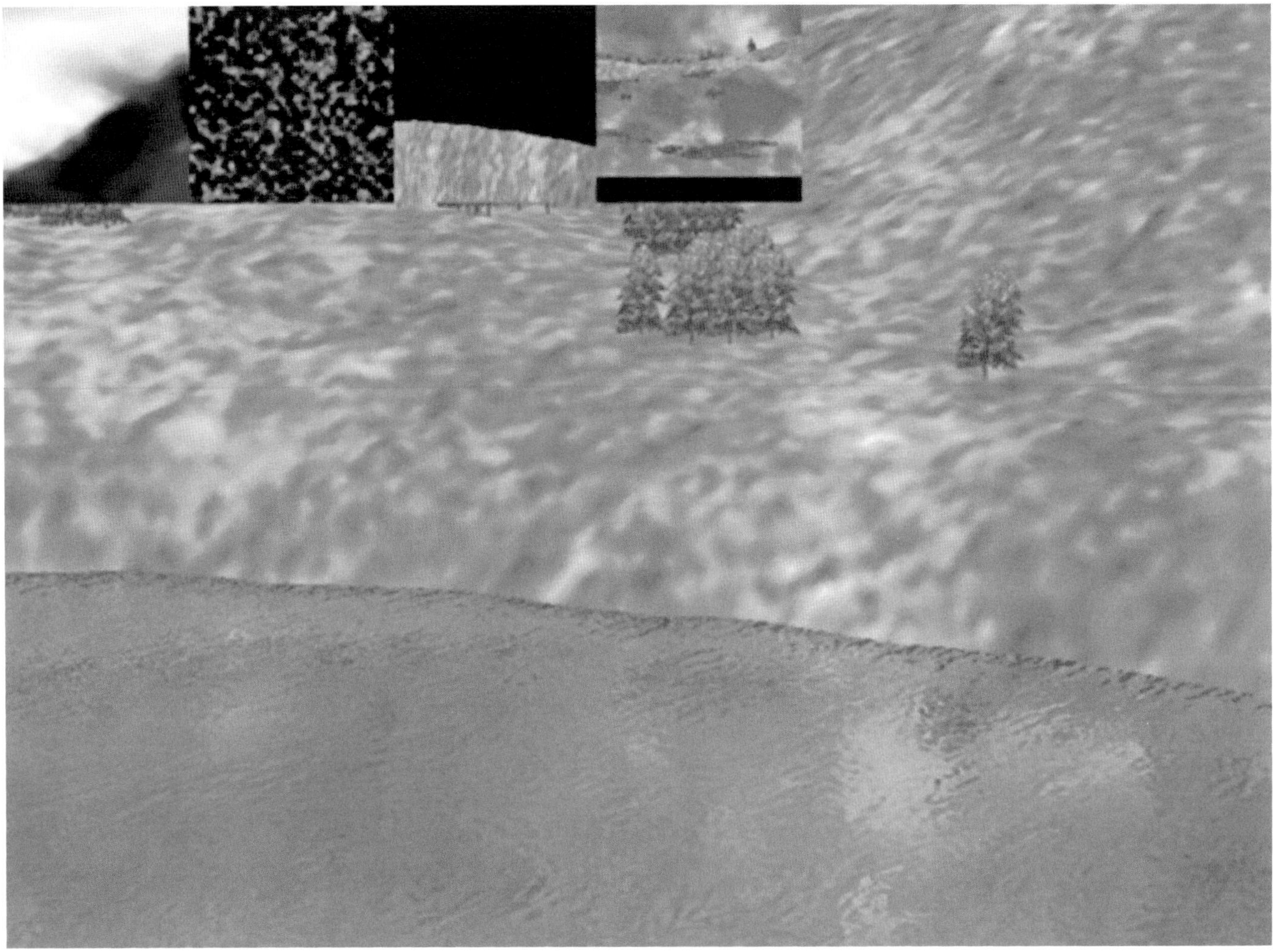

Figure 4.8. Image showing technical details such as billboarding, reflection, and refraction.

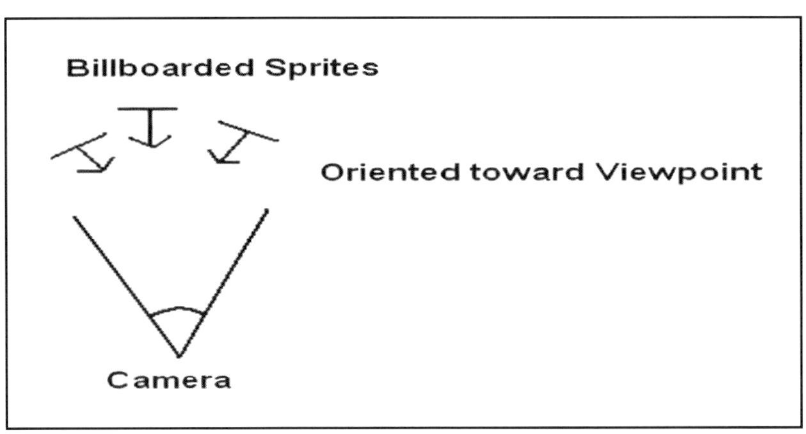

Figure 4.9. Showing xz orientation of billboarding.

The Tactical Knowledge and Group Movement Procedure Used in the Game: Influence Map, Path-Finding, and Flock Behavior

In this section we describe the basic tactical knowledge that is used by the cultural algorithms to make path-finding decisions. The nature of the path-finding algorithms used and the flocking behavior that they must support are also discussed.

The Influence Map Component

Influence maps are commonly used in games since they are easy to calculate and they can be combined in intuitive ways to perform complex spatial reasoning, as described by Zobrist (1969). This design allows the maps to be influenced by external forces as well as to influence the entities in the simulation by providing values for modification or consumption.

The code architecture in this simulation consists of a 3D-centric design with 2D functionality; all influence maps are created in 3D with height parameters, but in this case, there is only one vertical cell that contains the entire height of the land bridge—this emulates a 2D influence map. In other words, although the world is visualized in 3D, the actual height data are expressed in only 2D, with each cell in the 2D array containing its respective height data. The width and length of the map are determined at runtime. There are two possibilities for the creation of an influence map. One approach instantiates the fields to empty values for a fresh learning process while the other takes a grayscale map and generates cells and values from the grayscale cells. In our simulation, this allows us to input and output influence map values at any time in order to branch out simulations with separate values.

During runtime, a number of variables can be used to update the influence map—these consist of negative or positive changes to a cell's value that can affect its total value. Example iterations are given in Figure 4.10, which shows the discovery of new positive points and their influence growing from nearby cells to a distance threshold of three neighbors in all directions from the cell.

Path-Finding

Path-finding is the method of plotting the best route between two points—the best route may be expressed in terms of the shortest distance, the least costly in terms of defined effort variables, or in terms of a number of other parameters as described by Stout (1996). A large number of methods are available, but due to the cellular nature of our influence map and the method in which we use it, we consider only graph-based algorithms.

The major criteria for the selection of a path-planning method from the many available methods, such as breadth-first search or Djikstra's algorithm, was efficiency. This was necessary to make the path-planning process feasible for a large-scale real-time application. As a result, a readily available and efficient path-finding algorithm that suited our cellular design of the influence map was A*, a well-established method that uses heuristics to rank each node in the graph by an estimated value that evaluates routes through the node, using the actual cost so far and the heuristically estimated cost to finish. Since our values are tracked historically, this method allows us to backtrack when we find that our actual values exceed our estimations. The function for the value is as equation (1):

$$f(n) = g(n) + h(n) \tag{1}$$

where our total cost (f) is the sum of actual cost so far (g) and the estimated cost (h) based upon a heuristic (Lester 2005).

Flocking

The concept of flocking as mentioned previously is derived from Reynolds (1987). This synchronized behavior does not directly cause variations in the goals or path-finding of the caribou, but rather, causes indirect variation. The main behaviors in flocking are: cohesion, separation, and alignment, utilized on the basis of individual caribou and averaged over the location and influence of the caribou around them. A number of other weights can be considered when moving the herds as a single entity while flocking. The weights and their behaviors are applied individually to each caribou entity with respect to overall group behavior. For example, detection distance determines how far away an entity can see and react to other members of the same herd. A multiple of this is also used to detect world events such as available food or threats. Separation distance determines how much distance a caribou wants to keep between itself and other members of the same flock.

The fluid motion of a flock allows for not only more realistic visual identification of the herds, but also causes the interesting

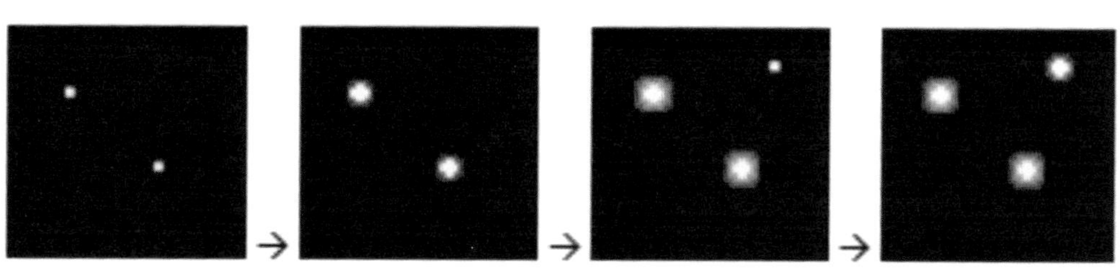

Figure 4.10. The growth of an influence map, showing values growing into nearby cells.

effects of momentum and overflow, which were discovered to influence the final results. Physical momentum helped to control the movement process by restricting not only the turn radius of the individual entities, but also by causing the entities in the front to be driven forward, or those in the back to be pulled up. This meant that in many cases, cells from the influence map that were not meant to be entered were occupied as a result of the group effect on the individual caribou. This also occurred as the result of another effect: overflow or spillover. The herd would sometimes spill laterally into an adjoining cell and influence it, due to the desire of the individuals to maintain a minimum distance from others in the herd.

```
Begin
      t = 0
      InitPop(t)          // init population
      InitBelief(t)       // init belief space
      Repeat
            EvaluatePop(t)
            Vote(Belief(t), Accept(Pop(t)))
            Adjust(Belief(t))
            Evolve(Pop(t), Influence(Belief(t)))
            t++
            Select Pop(t) from Pop(t - 1)
      Until (termination condition)
End
```

Figure 4.11. Cultural algorithm pseudocode.

The Cultural Algorithms Representation

Cultural algorithms are a class of evolutionary models, developed and described by Reynolds (1994; Saleem and Reynolds 2000), that are derived from the cultural evolution process, where culture is described as "that complex whole, which includes knowledge, beliefs, art, law, morals, custom, and any other capabilities and habits by man as a member of society" (Taylor 1920). Using a population of individuals, each with their own set of behavioral traits, the behaviors and shared beliefs guide the population through the cultural adaptation process.

Cultural algorithms are a method for individuals to communicate through a shared belief space (Reynolds, Peng, and Whallon 2005). The experience of individuals in the population space can be collected (accepted) into the belief space. As new knowledge is collected, it can be used to update and generalize on the knowledge that is currently there. These knowledge sources can be interconnected via a network, and the update of one knowledge source can impact the contents of another as a result. The belief space is then used to direct the decision-making of the individuals in the population. These individuals can be networked as well. This network is called the "social fabric" since the relationship needs to satisfy certain constraints in order to be maintained. The basic process for CA in pseudocode is represented as in Figure 4.11.

In this implementation of the CA, the genetic algorithm terminology is used to model our population component as described by Chung (1996). Each member of our population is a herd that is composed of individuals. Each herd is defined in terms of a number of different components or genes, such as herd size, herd goals, and flocking behavior parameters. Each gene of our chromosome is a different component of herd behavior that is represented in a numerical format. Thus, the chromosome is really a structured list of components that is used to construct a herd for the next generation. Each chromosome can be of different length in terms of the number of attributes that it uses.

For this application, the population space is the collection of all the individual herds or chromosomes. The belief space is defined as the source of the cultural knowledge shared by all herd chromosomes. It is broken into five distinct categories: normative, domain, situational, temporal, and spatial knowledge. Each chromosome contains its own specific value for each knowledge source along with the other parameters mentioned earlier, such as herd size.

Normative knowledge is the range of desirable values for individual herd chromosomes in the population space (Saleem and Reynolds 2000)—in other words, it is the acceptable behavior of an individual herd in the population. The normative knowledge is highly useful in this application, as it determines the path-finding mechanism's most acceptable values and nudges individual herds in the population to shift their values incrementally upward or downward in order to meet this cultural norm.

Domain knowledge is information that pertains to patterns of objects within an environment. For example, gradients for various resources can be calculated and used to predict resources over time and space (Saleem and Reynolds 2000). Our domain knowledge for an individual herd chromosome in this application would be to look at influence maps of the terrain and floral and faunal information drawn from our research into the tundra environment in order to identify trends and gradients. This represents the cognitive knowledge that a caribou herd would have about its environment.

Situational knowledge is similar to the "elite" selection mechanisms present in genetic algorithms, as shown in Haupt and Haupt (1998), and involves taking the most effective individual herds as examples and the least effective as warnings. This allows high performance to be present and rewarded for future generations. In this process, we will take the chromosome of the top 10% of individual herds involved in successful land bridge crossings.

Temporal knowledge is the history of the search process in terms of game events that have taken place there, and was first described by Reynolds and Peng (2005). It is closely related to the spatial knowledge in that temporal knowledge can provide guidance in herd movement. Our temporal knowledge is a second set of influence maps representing caribou memories, which are modified permanently during runtime as they track the history and

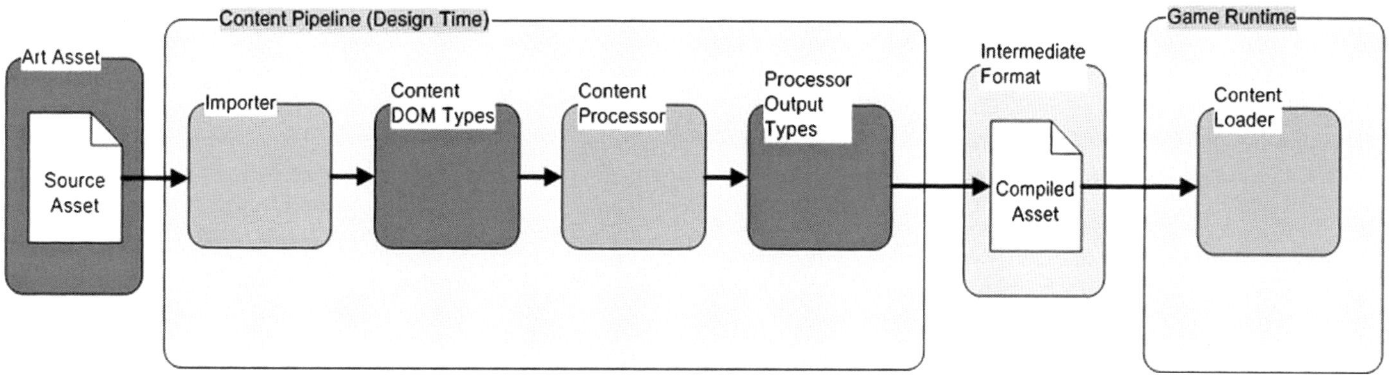

Figure 4.12. Microsoft's XNA content pipeline.

number of caribou deaths in a particular cell. The more caribou that die within a given cell during a time step, the less attractive the cell becomes to caribou herds. Here, that is expressed in terms of a larger negative value. That value can offset other positive aspects of a cell such as its productivity.

Spatial knowledge, described by Jin and Reynolds (1999), provides the ability to reason about the topography of the search space, allowing the distribution of the population over the entire search space. In this case, the population can be placed across the landscape. Originally motivated by constraint optimization, it is used here to identify attractive regions within which to search in more detail. Our spatial knowledge is an influence map of current path-finding node preferences based on unsuccessful and successful herd movement strategies. Herd movements produced by a herd chromosome are tracked and made available as influence maps for future generations to reference in conjunction with the other listed sources of knowledge.

Implementation

Development of the application was executed in Microsoft's C# language on top of the .Net platform. The supporting structure of the graphical components was built around Microsoft's XNA 3.1 framework. .Net is a series of classes and routines that allow for the rapid development of graphical software for display and interaction on multiple .Net compatible machines. The graphics are rendered on the GPU and the game logic and artificial intelligence (AI) procedures are executed on the central processing unit (CPU). The application was designed with both scalability and extensibility in mind.

The basic goal is to evolve an optimal herd path using a path-planning algorithm, A*, for a set of goal weight parameters that leads to the highest survival rate for a herd given when the herd executes the optimal A* plan based upon the herd kinematics and individual flocking behaviors.

The process starts with a collection of herd plans in the cultural algorithm. Each plan is then used by A* to generate an optimal route using the basic plan weights through the modeled terrain (described below). Next, the terrain is broken into cells for the navigation process (the contents of these cells are described in the influence maps below).

Once a path is generated for a plan, it is executed via a herd simulation mechanism (the flocking mechanism is described below). The simulation will model the movement of the herd along the given path. Based upon the herd kinematics, herd individuals will be distributed around the optimal path and move in a relatively common direction.

The performance of the plan is determined by how many individuals survive as the herd moves from its start to finish locations following the plan. The individual herd plans are then reproduced and modified based upon the survivability. Finally, there is a performance assessment that compares the behavior of all herds.

Terrain and Entity Display and Interaction

The terrain display process begins with the conversion of a 2D grayscale heightmap into a 3D mesh model for display on the GPU through the XNA framework, as shown in Figure 4.12. A custom content processor is used instead of the normal content processing in XNA.

There are two important variables that must be specified in order to coerce the pixels to a vector in 3D space: height and spacing. First, the height dictates the maximum range in display units between black and white input pixels. By having a maximum and minimum value for the possible heights and aligning one color to the maximum and the other color to the minimum, a cell's gradation between them can be used to determine its numerical placement between the maximum and minimum values. Second, the spacing dictates the xz (horizontal) spacing between adjacent pixels in the input file.

With that information, each pixel is converted to a point in 3D space given an origin at [0, 0, 0] and growing in positive directions—each point becomes a vertex in a final 3D mesh for display. Textures are mapped onto this model mesh based on local vertex heights and the normals of the faces from three adjacent vertices. The terrain during game time has a useful class called HeightMapInfo, which allows the height and normal of the terrain at any point in space of the simulation to be read and used by the game logic.

Vegetation is read from two grayscale maps: one generated for trees and the other for scrub brush. The input image locations are scaled in the same *xz* manner as the terrain and the height for the billboarded images is determined by the terrain height selected with their *x* and *z* location. Multiple billboards can be placed in close proximity if the intensity of the 2D input image is higher—this random clustering creates a realistic looking environment. The vegetation is constructed as a single mesh for more efficient drawing. There are also two 3D meshes behind the scenes, which duplicate the display of the terrain. They are used to determine the maximum density of vegetation at any 3D point, in the same way that height data are read from the terrain data.

Water bodies are displayed using a highly realistic method using a technique from Pereira Evangelista et al. (2009) that incorporates reflections, refractions, and other high-fidelity options to give a tactile feel to the game world.

All game entities are displayed on the GPU using built-in classes provided by XNA, which allowed for rapid development. The entities also inherit from the XNA class called DrawableGameComponent, which is a class that has overrideable functions for updating and drawing each entity. At each time step, before being drawn, an entity goes through an update phase. During this period, items such as caloric count and living status are updated. This information is used by other processes, especially flocking and CA components.

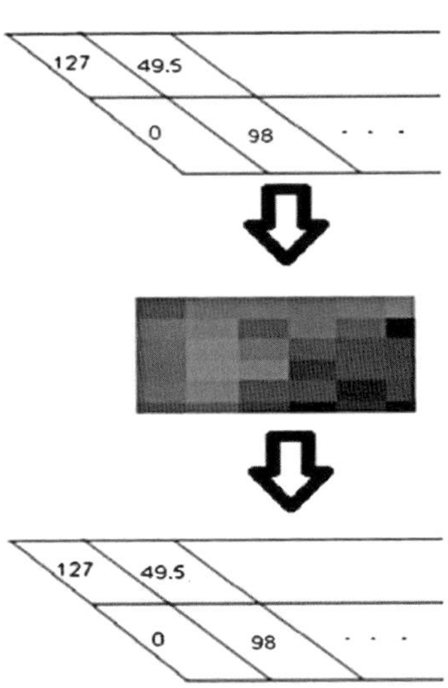

Figure 4.13. Converting an influence map from values to image and back.

Influence Map

The single program class influence map supports all the behavior for the creation and update of the influence maps used throughout the system. When created, a map has a specified number of cells and each of the cells has system-determined dimensions. This means that the dimensions of all cells are equal and that the *xyz* sizes are proportional to both the terrain dimensions and the number of cells specified. The map can be instantiated in one of two different ways.

First, an influence map can be instantiated with the terrain dimensions and the number of cells desired in each of the *xyz* directions. The map is constructed by taking the terrain dimensions and dividing them by the number of cells for height, width, and length. The cells all have an initial value of zero.

A second approach is to provide a 2D grayscale image. The size of the image in pixels determines the number of cells in the *x* and *z* directions and a single *y* level is assigned. The values for the cells are determined by the grayscale values of the pixels, from 0 to 255.

The influence map class supports a number of functions, such as the update of a cell's contents based upon its position on the grid. It can also find the lowest or highest value for cells on the map in terms of a specific content variable. In addition, it has the ability to save the resultant influence map as a bitmap image. This process is shown in Figure 4.13.

The desirability of traversing a given cell when planning a path is a function of the cell's score. That score is computed based upon several factors.

1. Availability of food. To compute this, the vegetation maps are used. In this example, the two underlying vegetation maps are employed to determine the cell's density values, with scaled scores between 0 and 255. Scrub vegetation has a higher relative positive weight than do the tree values, due to more accessible food and less of an impediment to traversal (acts in tandem with aspect 3 below). Therefore, the influence map for vegetation values is based on the formula $(t + (1.5 * s))$, where t is the value of tree coverage from [0, 255] in that cell and s is the value of scrub coverage in that cell from [0, 255].

2. Cell mortality values. The mortality score for each cell takes a value in the range between 0 and 255. At the start of a run, the value for each cell is set to 255. At the end of each time step, .5 is deducted from the current score for each death that occurred there when a plan was executed. No additional deductions are taken once a score of 0 has been reached.

3. Traversal effort. The traversal difficulty is affected by two factors in the model: ground cover and terrain. Ground cover was addressed in factor 1 above, since movement through dense tree stands will reduce accessible food value for a cell. This factor addresses the impact that terrain has on mobility. The focus here is not on rapidly changing values such as jagged locations, but only the maximum undulation. By making higher resolution cells, we can emulate the tracking of jagged materials. The height variation between the center of a cell and its neighbor reduces that cell value by $1/h$, where h is the maximum height of the terrain. In other words, a step of 100 units in terrain with maximum elevation of 1000 is 0.1 reduction in that cell's value. This allows herds to take note of the difference in height between two points, which would yield increased effort in movement.

4. Proximity of the cell to the final goal. The influence map will be seeded with a final "arrival" location that will signal the completion of the path. Upon arrival within that cell, the herd is considered done for that generation. The desirability of a cell is then expressed in terms of the Euclidean distance between that cell and the closest goal cell.

These values computed above represent the initial construction of the influence map. As food is eaten, each cell that contains caribou is reduced by 1.0 for each caribou present in each cell. When selecting nodes for traversal, nodes that are already supporting large numbers of caribou will not be selected. This map is reset at the end of each generation. A second persistent map (retain over the generations) is used to track caribou deaths over each generation.

Flocking

The flocking behavior of a herd borrows heavily from Reynold's research (1987) and Microsoft's Game Development Library (2010), with a few key differences. The flock behavior is defined as not only the interaction between animals, but also in terms of a list of weighted herd goals. Basic flocking implementation is based on the three movement constraints: cohesion, separation, and alignment. Each caribou is assigned to a herd at the start of the simulation and all the herds start at their maximum size. Caribou reassignment during runtime is important to the final evaluation of success of a plan and is calculated as follows:

```
If(Dist(herd[i].center, entity[x]) > Dist(herd[j].center, entity[x]
    && herd[j].count < herd[j].capacity)
        herd[i].remove(caribou[x])
        herd[j].add(caribou[x]).
```

In other words, if an animal is closer to the center of another herd than to their currently assigned herd, and that other herd has not yet reached its capacity, then the individual is allowed to switch herds.

Goals are managed by using a simple list. At the end of every herd behavior update cycle, the goal list is checked. If the list is not empty, the goal with the highest weight for this particular herd is applied to determine the heading in the next time step and each caribou adjusts its direction according to that herd goal direction. The weight varies within certain bounds to prevent unnatural behavior, as excessively heavy weighting will cause erratic movement.

The weighting also has a specific modification that encourages the herd to actually cross the land bridge, as opposed to allowing it to engage in pure foraging or effort reducing behaviors. This weight is calculated and used at two different points in the program. First, it can be used to shift the path direction location further toward the opposing side of the land bridge. Second, it can be used as a variable in the cultural algorithm chromosome for the herd, which is carried and modified through generations as a deciding factor in determining how much emphasis should be placed on path completion. If the value is too low, caribou will not be able to cross the bridge in time. If it is too high, they will pass through areas with more risk and are more likely to lose herd members.

Path-Finding

The path-finding approach employed here uses the A* algorithm to determine the optimal herd path based on the cell weights and distances derived from the influence maps relative to herd goals as described and is associated with a herd plan or chromosome from the population of herd plans. The path computed by the A* algorithm is the optimal path considering the current weight for the cell and the goals of the herds given that the guiding heuristic is admissible. This means that the heuristic is a conservative estimate of distance to the goal. Euclidean distance is an example of an admissible measure. If an A* algorithm uses an admissible heuristic, it can produce an optimal path given the current scenario.

The A* implementation creates a graph by connecting the center of each cell in the influence map to that of each of its neighbors. From this point, the weight of the connecting edges between two cells is determined by the change in cell value between the two. Since A* uses a non-negative directed graph, any negative change is simply set to 0. An example route is shown in Figure 4.14.

7	6	5	6	7	8	9	10	11		19	20	21	22
6	5	4	5	6	7	8	9	10		18	19	20	21
5	4	3	4	5	6	7	8	9		17	18	**19**	20
4	3	2	3	4	5	6	7	8		16	17	**18**	19
3	2	1	2	3	4	5	6	7		15	16	**17**	18
2	1	**0**	**1**	**2**	**3**	**4**	5	6		14	15	**16**	17
3	2	1	2	3	4	5	**6**	7		13	**14**	15	16
4	3	2	3	4	5	6	7	**8**		**12**	13	14	15
5	4	3	4	5	6	7	8	9	**10**	11	12	13	14
6	5	4	5	6	7	8	9	10	11	12	13	14	15

Figure 4.14. Sample A* path-finding route: parallel lines indicate obstacles, zero is start, nineteen is finish, and the numbers inside each cell are the distance so far plus the weight of the heuristic (in this case, distance).

The principal means to assess path distance in A* here is based on the current distance traveled plus the estimated distance left to reach the goal. The estimated distance is heuristically driven. The path with the estimated shortest distance is tried until it is proven that it is longer than the next shortest estimated distance or the goal is reached. Thus, the value for a predicted path is:

$$\text{Path}(i) = g\ (\text{partial path}\ (i)) + h\ (\text{partial path}\ (i))$$

The score for a partially constructed path is the effort expended so far, plus the estimated effort left to achieve the goal. The pseudocode for the A* algorithm is given below:

```
currentPath = 0               // empty list of path
g (S) = 0.0                   // length of optimal path
h (S) = hEstimate(S, goal)    // Estimate the value from between nodes
f (S) = h (S)                 // function is g + h

CreateOpenList(S)             // Create node list containing only start node
CreateClosedList()            // Create empty closed list
while OpenList.Length > 0
        node = lowest(O)      // lowest estimated goal distance on open list
        if (node == goal)
                construct path
                return
        open.remove(node)
        closed.add(node)
        foreach n_node in neighbors (node)
                if closed.contains(n_node)
                        continue
                g_temp = g(node) + dist(node, n_node)

                if (!open.contains(n_node))
                        open.add(n_node)
                        currentBetter = true
                else if g_temp < g (n_node)
                        currentBetter = true
                else
                        currentBetter = false

                if (currentBetter)
                        if (currentPath(n_node))
                                if (f(node) < f(n_node))

                                        currentPath(n_node) = x
                        else
                                currentPath(n_node) = x

                        g(n_node) = g_temp;
                        h(n_node)=hEstimate(n_node, goal)
                        f(n_node) = g(n_node) + h(n_node)
```

The heuristic used to estimate the h value of a cell is as follows:

Normalize the distance from the current node to the goal between [0, 255]. 255 is the start location, 0 is the goal.
Multiply this distance by the finalGoalWeight gene value.
Now find any influence map cell within the individual's detection distance that has a higher value than the current cell.
Multiply that value by (1 – finalGoalWeight).
Select highest node as the best estimate.

Performance Evaluation

The path-planning goal is to maximize the number of arriving caribou across the terrain with each passing cycle until a stop condition is reached. With this in mind, the goal is to produce a chromosome or herd plan whose goal weight parameters produce the optimal path for a herd. A listing of the herd parameters associated with each herd plan in the population and their default initial values is given in Table 4.2. The list from top to bottom can be viewed as a chromosome and each value a gene. At each generation, each herd plan and its weights are used to drive the A* algorithm to produce an optimal path for those parameters. The survival statistics for each plan is then calculated. The goal is to evolve a set of goal weights and an associated optimal plan that maximizes survivability for a herd.

In the first generation, each herd chromosome is initialized by parameter values generated from within a given range, as shown in Table 4.2. These values represent an initial bound on the normative knowledge in the cultural algorithm, as they represent the maximum allowable range for each parameter in this population.

Next, a common herd size and capacity for all herds are selected to prevent certain arriving herds from being unfairly favored or discriminated against due to a poor initial size. For similar reasons, the locations are all initialized for all chromosomes (herd plans) to be within a smaller starting area. This allows the intermingling of herds at the very beginning. This has the added bonus of being a real-world simulation of funneling herds into the land bridge as they move from a larger area to a smaller one. All herds likewise share the same initial goals, since a common influence map is shared between the CA's individuals (herds). An individual herd is considered "arrived" if the calculated center arrives within the box to the right.

We have mentioned that our genome represents the normative knowledge of our belief space. The rest of our cultural algorithm's knowledge is derived from influence maps. The vegetation map—and the intensity to which our individuals seek it—is an important source of individual success. Also, we track caribou deaths via a separate influence map, which is treated as situational and temporal knowledge—caribou that have expired in particular areas at particular times are used as a behavior variable in achieving success of crossing the land bridge.

Once all individuals have arrived, or at least one has arrived after the time allotted has expired, the real-time component ends, and the CA begins to compare the number of surviving individuals across the herds. The individuals are ranked on the following objective function:

$$V = \text{herdCount} * \text{avgHerdCalories} * (1/(\text{herdTransTime}/\text{MaxTime}))$$

where herdCount is the number of surviving members of a herd; the more surviving members, the higher the score. The average calorie count, avgHerdCalories, is normalized between one and the maximum herd capacity to prevent small herds that have been fed extremely well from tilting the results in their favor.

The maximum allowed time for any individual herd to cross the land bridge is maxTime, and herdTransTime is the transition time for the particular herd we are scoring. The last part of the function above scores herds that cross more quickly higher than similar herds that cross more slowly, balanced against survival and nutrition.

This function is useful in many aspects. Herds with the largest number of surviving members are rewarded the most, as are those with high calorie counts. We also consider the inverse of the travel time to be a valuable factor here, as we do not have a fully real-time system capable of changing seasons and we consider this trek to be made during fall and spring migration, where a short transit time is valuable.

The influence maps, representing several sources of knowledge, are updated each time a caribou expires with the negative information associated with the death. The top 10% of surviving herds are elected to update the normative knowledge genome. Based on their scores above, an average successful gene is created and merged with the current best values that already exist in our belief space—this current best value is shifted 50% of the way toward what we have just elected as the best average genome.

This newly updated belief space is now communicated to the individual population to guide changes in herd plans based on the selected topological operator, which in this case is fully connected. That is, every individual receives some knowledge source direction according to the values described in Table 4.3. This has the effect of moving individuals toward those who have already proven themselves to be successful, which is now reflected in the belief space.

Table 4.2. Initialization values.

Parameter	Type	Value
herdSize	int	capacity/2
detectionDist	float	40.0f–100.0f
separationDist	float	30.0f–70.0f
oldDirInfluence	float	0.5f–1.5f
flockDirInfluence	float	0.5f–1.5f
randomDirInfluence	float	0.01f–0.1f
perMemberWeight	float	0.5f–1.5f
finalGoalWeight	float	0.0f–1.0f

Table 4.3. Transition values based on success.

Parameter	Type	Value
herdSize	int	capacity/2
detectionDist	float	± 0.5f
separationDist	float	± 0.5f
oldDirInfluence	float	± 0.01f
flockDirInfluence	float	± 0.01f
randomDirInfluence	float	± 0.002f
perMemberWeight	float	± 0.01f
finalGoalWeight	float	± 0.01f

Results

All the experiments were executed on a single generated terrain heightmap, tree map, and scrub map. The maps were all grayscale images generated and imported by the methods defined in the previous section. The images used for these test runs are shown in Figures 4.15–4.17. These topographical images are the 2D representations of the 3D land bridge across which the caribou will be migrating.

With the terrain information above, 10 separate runs of 100 generations each were made with the starting parameters described in Table 4.4. Runs 1 through 5 were migrations from north to south and runs 6 through 10 were from south to north to simulate fall and spring migration directions respectively. All the weights are randomly initiated within specific ranges. A population space of five herd plans was used for each run. Table 4.4 shows the initial values for each of the ten runs. The best herd from each run is given in Table 4.5. Figures 4.15 through 4.17 provide the gray cell image of the terrain map used for the test region along with the tree and scrub maps respectively. The darker the region, the denser the vegetation component.

Table 4.5, which gives the results of the most successful herd of the final generation, also shows the pertinent weights that were evolved to direct group behavior, as well as the sizes of the finishing herds. In the table, the average nutrition is based on a range from 0 to 100, and the distance traveled is the most accurate distance between waypoints based on estimates of terrain and data synchronicity.

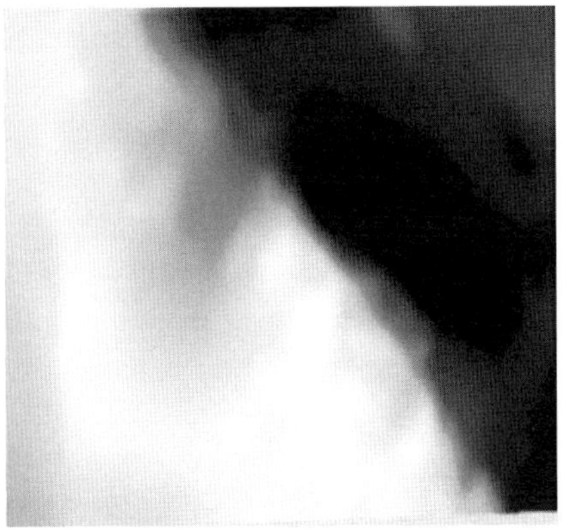

Figure 4.15. Terrain generated for testing.

Figure 4.16. Tree map.

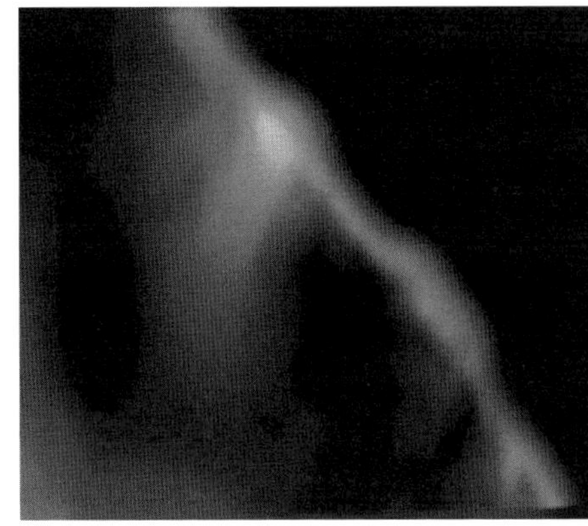

Figure 4.17. Scrub map.

Table 4.4. Starting values for test runs.

Parameter	Run									
	north to south					south to north				
	1	2	3	4	5	6	7	8	9	10
herdSize	50	50	50	50	50	50	50	50	50	50
detectionDist	47.3	65.1	92.5	56.8	80.2	51.4	93.7	76.2	85.6	95.8
separationDist	69.0	45.8	62.2	43.0	64.8	50.1	62.1	52.3	68.9	51.9
oldDir	0.7	0.6	1.1	0.8	1.1	0.9	1.1	1.1	1.2	1.2
flockDir	1.4	0.7	1.3	0.9	1.4	1.3	0.5	1.1	1.1	0.8
randomDir	0.06	0.04	0.05	0.09	0.09	0.01	0.04	0.08	0.03	0.02
perMemberWeight	1.0	1.4	1.1	0.6	1.2	0.6	1.0	0.7	0.8	1.3
finalGoalWeight	0.8	0.0	0.96	0.85	0.61	0.71	0.89	0.01	0.67	0.89

Table 4.5. Results of best herd for final generation for each run.

Parameter	Run									
	north to south					south to north				
	1	2	3	4	5	6	7	8	9	10
starting size	50	50	50	50	50	50	50	50	50	50
finishing size	44	36	41	39	41	42	50	34	47	48
starvation count	6	14	9	11	9	8	0	16	3	2
avg nutrition	73	89	65	21	72	16	25	71	89	21
dist traveled	11710	6581	8423	16715	12451	8189	8634	7731	11314	13459
detectionDist	54.8	54.3	87.1	63.3	90.7	44.9	100.0	41.7	100.0	96.3
separationDist	61.0	37.5	53.7	51.5	45.3	61.3	65.6	53.3	72.4	50.4
oldDir	0.51	0.5	1.35	0.92	0.85	1.44	1.41	0.61	1.19	1.1
flockDir	1.41	1.5	0.81	1.05	1.35	1.12	1.01	0.95	0.86	1.5
randomDir	0.06	0.048	0.06	0.1	0.18	0.032	0.028	0.1	0.054	0.06
perMemberWeight	0.78	1.0	0.82	0.2	0.90	0.45	0.93	0.46	0.51	0.69
finalGoalWeight	0.762	0.510	0.932	0.81	0.642	0.941	0.812	0.6	0.814	0.932

We now discuss the differences in the 10 runs based upon the evolved parameters. Figure 4.18 shows the direction the caribou are traveling across our digital land bridge as tied to the actual bathymetric data. Figure 4.19 (see also Plate 1) shows how the survival rate changes for the best program in each generation of the cultural algorithm for the 10 runs. Notice the steadily increasing values for all individuals, indicating a continuous improvement based on changing belief space values. The *y* axis is the number of surviving herd members, the *x* axis the generation number.

Runs 7 and 9 were the most successful, with some of the highest survival rates at the end of the 100 requisite generations; the migratory pattern carried the caribou from south to north. By comparing relative values, it can be observed that a middle-to-high finalGoalWeight, which directs the herd toward the destination, did not overwhelm the search for food, allowing a greater number of caribou to consume enough and survive the transit. Also, it is clear that a high detection distance allowed there to be a higher selection range of cells to choose for the path nodes. These paths combined both the grazing and migration goals.

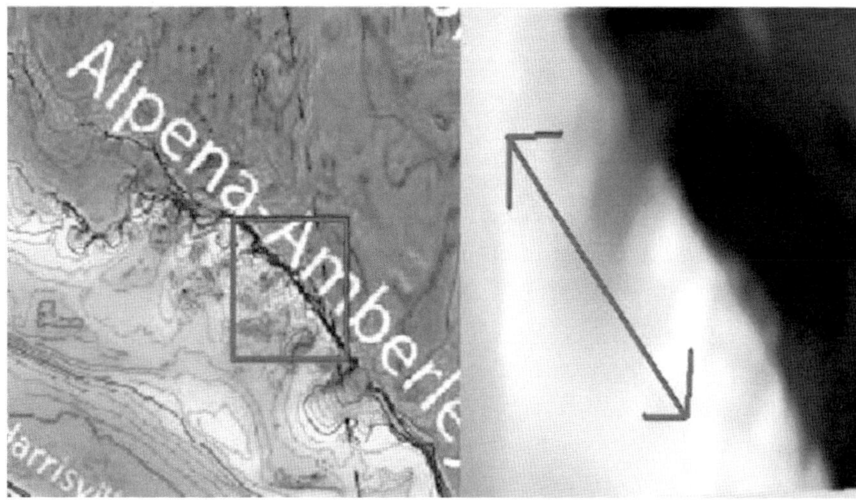

(*right*) Figure 4.18.
The direction and location of our simulation.

(*below*) Figure 4.19.
The comparison between the learning curves for each of the 10 runs. (See Plate 1.)

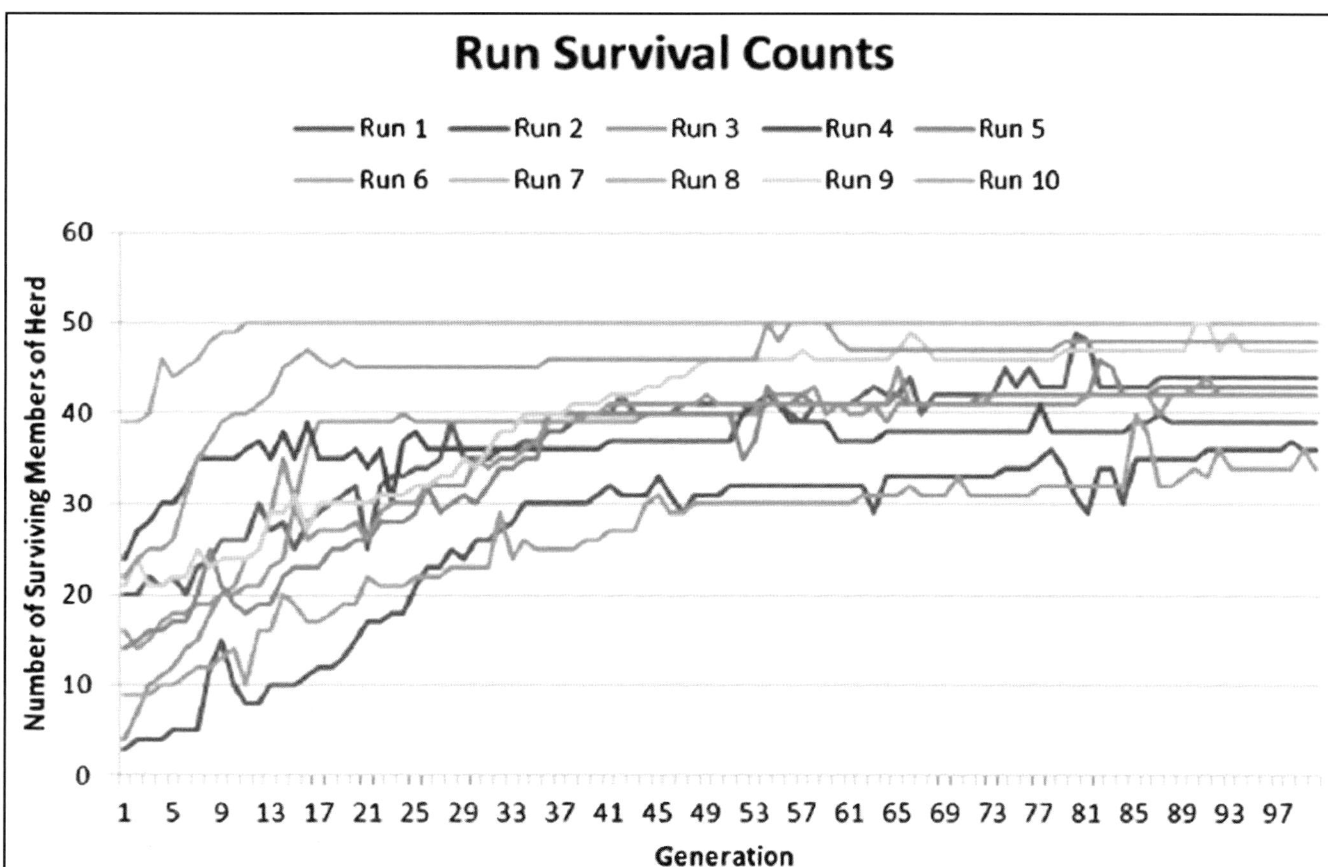

On the low end, runs 2 and 8, with the herds running north to south and south to north respectively, evolved a low goal-seeking weight that resulted in the herds staying in a high yield area and not making progress toward the goal. They did not starve, except they grazed until the allocated time began to run out and they drifted through areas already consumed. Thus, paths 2 and 8 represent more of a grazing approach than a migration pathway. With a higher goal-seeking desire, they would have traversed the bridge faster.

Runs 1 and 3 are both examples of north to south runs that lost few individuals during the traversal. Due to a high finalGoal variable, the caribou were able to guarantee that they would migrate across the land bridge in time. Also, their high detection parameter allowed them to plot a transitory path that would lead them through certain areas of high nutritional value. However, their very high goal weights made them cross with little respect for food, leading to low nutrition, even with a high survival rate.

By comparing the run results, some basic findings about successful configurations of parameters emerge. If the goal-seeking weight is too high, the herd will miss locations that have a higher proportion of food and thus will begin to starve out. Also, the wandering variable cannot be too large since it will produce fruitless wandering over the terrain. Also, a high old direction weight will keep caribou trapped in particular locations or vectors for too long. A high detection distance, which is utilized in both the ability to plan paths and to find other members of the herd to follow, is also useful in locating efficient pathways by giving a broader spectrum of possible choices. Therefore, one needs to blend or balance the two goals to get a migration pathway that does not take too long when browsing, but, on the other hand, does not lose too many individuals. A high success rate, being based on timely completion and well-fed caribou, should have high detection distance, a moderate migration goal, and a moderate random component for food discovery.

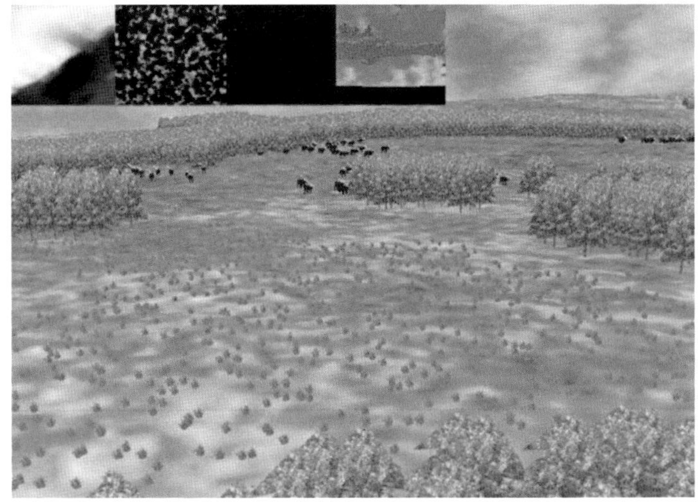

Figure 4.20. Caribou grazing.

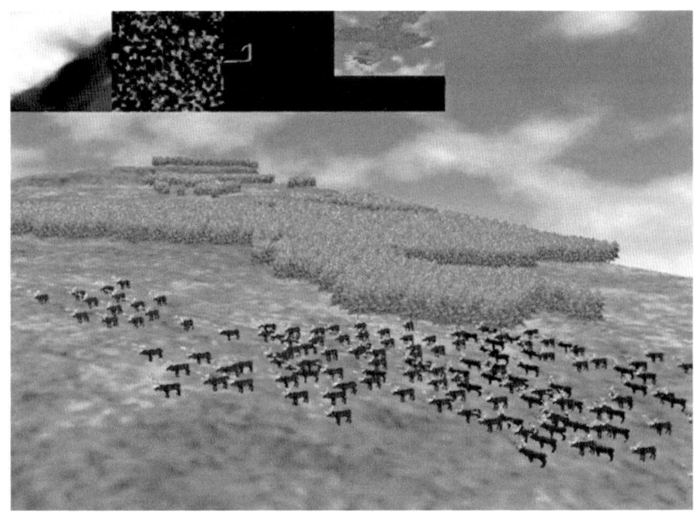

Figure 4.21. Caribou movement. (See also Plate 1.)

In Figures 4.20 and 4.21 (also see Plate 1), screenshots of successful behaviors as the caribou move across the land bridge are provided, showing their grazing and migratory actions. Notice in Figure 4.20 that there are several small herds grazing near the areas of higher vegetation, each spaced a certain distance from the others to avoid crowding. Figure 4.21 shows the variable behavior of herds on the move. Some herds, such as the one in the lead, are avoiding the vegetation areas and are moving directly to the goal, whereas other herds are moving closer to the stands of dense vegetation, browsing as they go.

Figures 4.22 and 4.23 illustrate the path-based learning that has taken place during the runs. In Figure 4.22, segments of early herd paths are given. Notice that the herd paths spread out in a variety of directions but, in general, move through the heart of the dense vegetation. In Figure 4.23, the paths are more tightly clustered and move along a relatively straight trajectory toward the goal but close to the edge of the denser vegetation to facilitate foraging along the way.

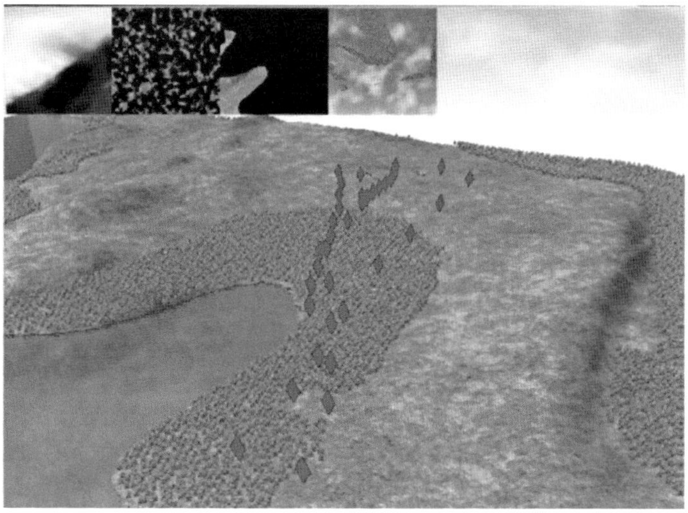

Figure 4.22. Path nodes at the start.

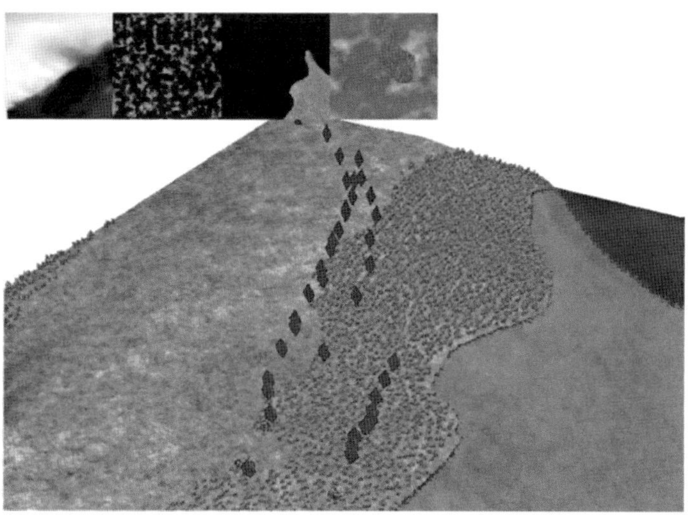

Figure 4.23. Path nodes at the end.

Conclusion

In this chapter, an approach to learning migratory behavior using cultural algorithms was described. The cultural algorithms generate and use influence maps to compute path-planning behavior using the A* algorithm. The resultant runs show the different degrees to which the goals of migration and food procurement can be combined. That is, if a herd moves too quickly, some caribou will not be able to get sufficient amounts of food and will die along the way. On the other hand, if a herd tends to focus on food procurement, then migration behavior can slow down substantially. This might be behavior exhibited by the caribou during the fall migration.

To produce a solid and sustained migration, one needs to balance the food procurement goal and the directional goals together. These behaviors emerged from the system as a result of the cultural learning process. What remains to be done is to integrate in a defensive component in herd migratory behavior relative to human and other predators.

Future Work

The serious game modeling of caribou migration using cultural algorithms and virtual world technology to learn successful migratory behavior has successfully generated plausible herd behaviors. However, there are a number of aspects that are open for further and more refined development. Many of these suggested extensions, such as a more precise terrain generation process, can be integrated within the simulation. Some suggestions are:

(1) Paleolithic hunters constructed drive lanes, cairns, and campsites relative to their knowledge of caribou path planning. While the current model allows the inclusion of an influence map to simulate the existence of such constructions in affecting animal behavior, further work would allow more detailed specifications and implementation of identified material remains according to archaeological records.

(2) The addition of other fauna would complete the ecosphere with the inclusion of food competitors and hunters of the caribou. For example, particular types of herbivores in the tundra environment may compete directly with caribou and should be modeled as such. Also, threats to caribou such as insects, disease vectors, and wolves, along with other predators, can be considered in the future.

(3) The knowledge used here is specific to the AAR environment. In the future, it would be of interest to allow the influence maps to be created automatically for different application areas so that the results could be compared across cultures and environments.

PART II

Cultural Background and Archaeological Context of the Alpena-Amberley Ridge

5 | Archaeology of the Late Paleoindian/Early Archaic in the Lake Huron Region, with New Data from the Sheguiandah Site

by Patrick J. Julig and Gregory Beaton

The archaeological visibility, identification, and preservation of Late Paleoindian/Early Archaic sites and assemblages (ca. 10,000–7000 BP) have been problematic with relatively few excavated sites in the upper Great Lakes region. This has been attributed in part to Great Lakes water level changes during this time, coastal geomorphic factors and isostatic uplift, and poor organic preservation, as well as other factors such as relatively few regional surveys and excavations of known sites. Some Early Archaic sites of this era may also lack clear diagnostic artifacts. Many sites in the boreal forest are associated with proximity to permanent water margins, and the low-waters in the Lake Huron basin during this period mean that numerous Early Holocene sites are now inundated—similar to those on the submerged Alpena-Amberley Ridge—and others along the northern shores are uplifted and are now very remote from modern water margins. Some sites along lake margins and wetlands are buried below Holocene peat deposits and are invisible unless deep testing is conducted. This chapter reviews the archaeological record for Late Paleoindian/Early Archaic sites and assemblages of this period for regions across the upper Great Lakes, on both ends of the Alpena-Amberley Ridge, and for the Manitoulin Island and Killarney region to the north. Early Archaic assemblages are known from certain northern strandline and quarry/workshop habitation sites such as the Sheguiandah site on Manitoulin Island. We present a deeply buried Early Archaic quartzite uniface tool assemblage dating to this time period, from near the base of Swamp 4, a small bog area on the Sheguiandah site. In addition, we consider that the Bruce Peninsula and Manitoulin Island were connected across the Lake Huron basin during the Early Holocene, at the same time as the Alpena-Amberley Ridge, and may be considered an archaeological and environmental model for our understanding and interpretation of the now submerged southern Alpena-Amberley Ridge. Finally, we discuss some of the challenges related to archaeological surveying for sites from this time period from a geoarchaeological perspective.

Introduction

The Alpena-Amberley Ridge is tentatively dated between 10,000 and 7000 BP, fitting within the Late Paleoindian/Early Archaic period in the upper Great Lakes (O'Shea and Meadows 2009), a period that is not too well studied and is perhaps the least understood of the region's prehistory. One of the primary reasons for this data gap is the generally accepted principle that many of these sites either are now inundated by current Great Lakes water levels or are located further back from the shore in isolated and heavily forested areas. This problem is exacerbated by differing isostatic uplift between various Great Lakes regions. Additionally, evidence from several sites suggests that normal archaeological survey strategies may be failing to locate deeply buried artifacts—which are now often located at greater depths and are sometimes under peat bogs (Julig 1994, 2002; Pilon and Dalla Bona 2004).

Compounding the insufficient understanding of this time period, many sites remain only partially tested/excavated, and many lack formalized tools (Bursey 2012). For instance, in the modern world of cultural resource management (CRM) survey procedures, many sites have likely been identified as "lithic scatters"—with minimal interpretation/excavation when those can be avoided by developers. This dominance of industry-led excavation and survey seems to have resulted in government grey literature reports—rather than the published record—serving as a major source of new information to researchers. Thus, what information that actually is available comes in the form of a few "well-known" unpublished reports or older mainstream publications.

Further exacerbating this problem, less CRM and research have been undertaken in the often remote and difficult-to-access northern Great Lakes settings—regions that could provide additional evidence for this period. With a comparatively low population and minimal development, many areas of the upper Great Lakes remain relatively unsurveyed, thus providing little evidence of the Late Paleoindian/Early Archaic periods. Furthermore, the region is fairly devoid of academic institutions focused on regional archaeology. Thus, at least on the Canadian side of the border, sites of the era are clustered around Sudbury and Thunder Bay, Ontario, correlating with the presence of two universities.

Perhaps as a consequence to the aforementioned difficulties, it is unclear what actually is representative of Late Paleoindian and Early Archaic groups. It appears that Eastern Plano groups populated the region during the early portion of this period, circa 9500 BP, and are associated with the northern range of the Great Lakes as a late expression of Paleoindian culture. Most often, sites are found on ancient beach ridges and within the coniferous forest zone, and, in northern Ontario, near locally available raw materials, but radiocarbon dates are rare. Early explanations for the obvious clustering of Plano sites along ancient beach ridges led to the development of the term "Aqua-Plano" (Quimby 1959). Based on the characteristic lanceolate technology, Plano is most often associated with earlier Paleoindian groups and contemporary western counterparts. However, mixed tool assemblages with differing hafting technology appear on many sites.

Perhaps the most important aspect of Late Paleoindian/Early Archaic culture from 10,000 to 7500 BP in the upper Great Lakes and particularly northern Ontario would have been the ability to adapt to changing environmental conditions. This includes fluctuating lake levels with coastal instability, changing vegetative zones (and as a result, changing fauna), and continually changing travel routes affecting the seasonal round and trading networks (Julig 2002:308).

It has been assumed that Plano is associated with the boreal forest while other lithic traditions of this time period, represented by Hi-Lo, Kirk corner notched, side notched, and bifurcate technologies, are focused on the northward expanding deciduous forest (Ellis, Timmins, and Martelle 2009). Some sites, particularly in transition zones of this forest environment from boreal to parkland, have evidence for coeval populations (Mason 1981; Shott 1999). Much like during other periods, the Great Lakes were a dynamic region of social interaction at this time. With the development of new transportation technology, evidenced by woodworking tools and changing hunting technology, the diffusion and spread of ideas within the changing environment of the Great Lakes system between 10,000 and 7000 BP has confounded researchers for half a century.

According to many, the beginning of the Early Archaic period is often heralded by the arrival of notched haft elements in lithic technology (Sassaman 2010). A handful of point types as northern expressions of southeastern counterparts have been identified in the changing forest environment of the central and southern Great Lakes, including Dalton, Big Sandy, Kirk, and bifurcate. All contain notched haft elements with the exception of Dalton. It would appear that while Eastern Plano has been influenced by western populations traveling along glacial lakes, these Early Archaic intrusives are from cultural development occurring further to the south (Ellis, Timmins, and Martelle 2009; Sassasman 2010).

The following is a brief review of current culture historical evidence of the period between circa 10,000 and 7000 BP across the upper Great Lakes, with a focus on Eastern Plano groups that appear to have inhabited the boreal forest region of the upper Great Lakes (see Fig. 5.1 for site names).

Southern Ontario

Southern Ontario was a rapidly changing environment from 9500 to 7000 BP as the forest changed to a more deciduous dominated overstory. This has been outlined recently by Ellis, Timmins, and Martelle (2009), who postulated that the Early Archaic period begins at approximately 10,000 BP with the appearance of notched and markedly stemmed point forms largely replacing Paleoindian. Ellis summarizes the point forms (Dalton, Big Sandy, Kirk, and bifurcate) using the Ontario terminology of Hi-Lo, notched, corner notched, and bifurcate. He acknowledges that Eastern Plano and other forms occur contemporaneously but generally have different geographic distributions based on coniferous and deciduous forested locations. In general, the Eastern Plano forms are considered the earliest, along with Hi-Lo, followed by notched, corner notched, and bifurcate. The only firmly dated sequence on the bifurcate is based on a single radiocarbon date of 8320 ± 60 BP, with the other sequences based on well-established southeastern counterparts (Ellis, Timmins, and Martelle 2009).

The Point Clark region of southern Ontario—the area where the Alpena-Amberley Ridge would connect with mainland historical Ontario—offers little evidence during the period from 10,000 to 7500 BP. With the exception of occasional Archaic lithic scatters, there is a confounding lack of evidence for use of the ridge on the Ontario side, although the presence of Fossil Hill chert among some of the CRM collections is interesting to note (these, however, may be Early Paleoindian). There are undated Middle Archaic sites, possibly Laurentian Archaic (Lee 1952). Further to the east, the Flesherton point of Sheguiandah quartzite and other Sheguiandah quartzite artifacts, sourced by instrumental neutron activation analysis (INAA), have been found near Waterloo (Julig, Pavlish, and Hancock 1987). These quartzite finds may show connections to the Manitoulin region

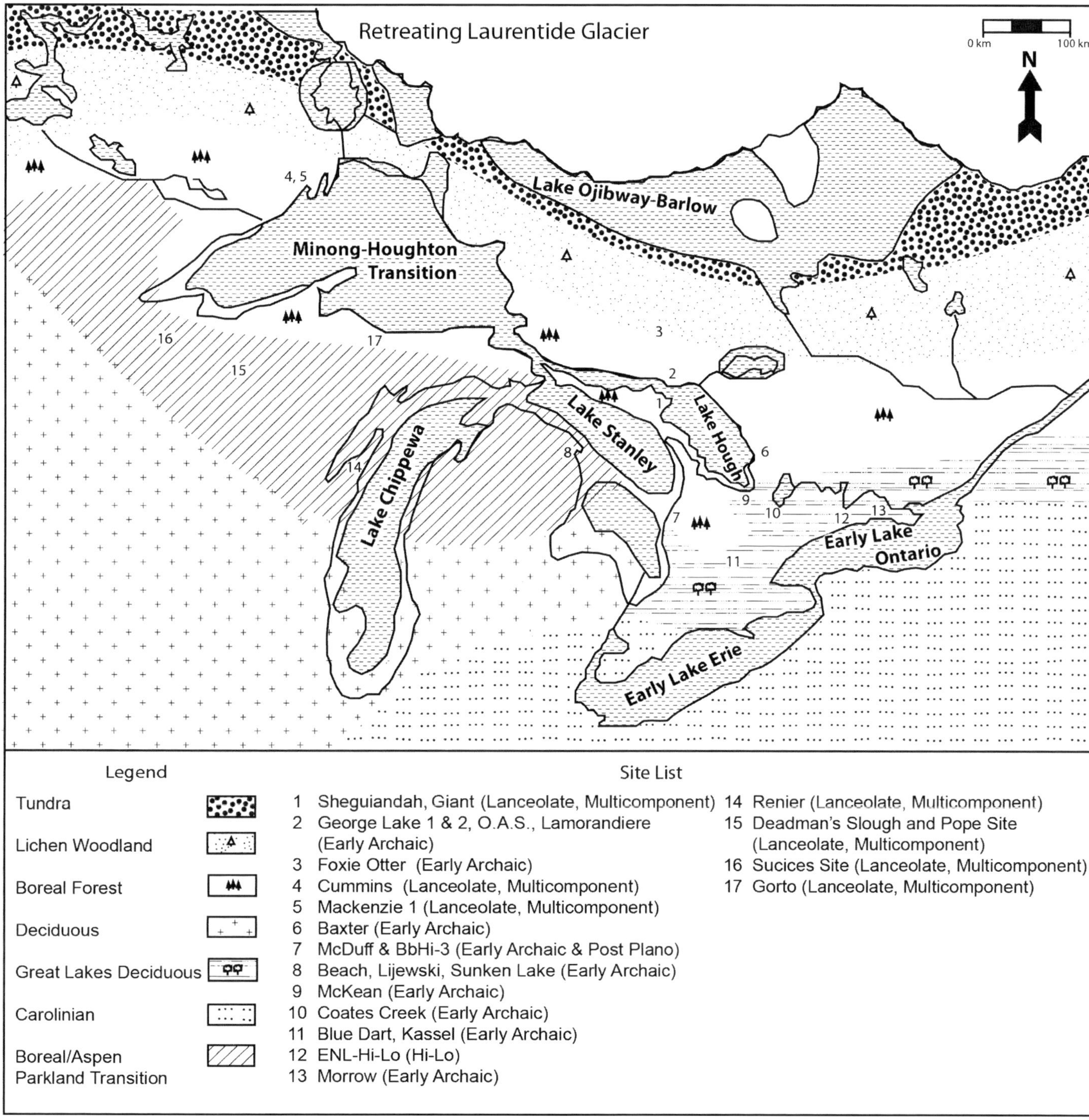

Figure 5.1. Great Lakes water levels circa 9000 BP, vegetation zones, and sites, with site names from text.

during the low-water period of the Early Holocene (Fig. 5.1); however, such Bar River formation and other quartzite from the north may also have been glacially transported to the southern Lake Huron regions. We suspect that the paucity of Early Archaic/Late Paleoindian data is mostly a geoarchaeological problem—with many of the sites in the south and western parts of the basin now underwater, while others in the central and northern parts of the basin have been undetected due to being buried beneath Holocene peat deposits in and adjacent to wetlands. Some sites and assemblages of this era are evident in upland quarry/workshop locations such as the Sheguiandah and Cummins sites, and a few other locations, as discussed in subsequent sections. However, many sites are not located owing to a sampling bias based on traditional methodologies.

Wisconsin and Michigan

As is the case in south central Ontario, the known record from the Early Archaic period of the upper Great Lakes of Wisconsin and Michigan is relatively poorly represented and generally lacks radiometric dating. The forest cover during this period was dominated by boreal forest along the south shore of Lake Superior but transitioning to a mixed boreal forest/aspen parkland in more southerly areas (Chapter 3).

What is interesting from this region is the presence of some Eastern Plano and Kirk lithic traditions from the same sites displaying some degree of contemporaneity (Shott 1999). For instance, the well-known Renier site (an Eden-Scottsbluff cremation site located on the eastern shore of Green Bay) in northeastern Wisconsin contains a Kirk Horizon point associated within a Plano cremation burial (Mason and Irwin 1960; Shott 1999; Pleger and Stoltman 2009). Another site with both Kirk and Plano representations is the Gorto site, located in the Upper Peninsula of Michigan and consisting of an Eden-Scottsbluff cache and possible cremation (Buckmaster and Paquette 1988; Shott 1999). Both Renier and Gorto are associated with elevated, fossil beach ridges similar to those of the Lakehead complex Late Paleoindian/Early Archaic sites located in northwestern Ontario (Fox 1977; Julig 1994). Sassaman (2010) also implies that the burnt biface caches of the Deadman Slough site and Pope site from Wisconsin could be possible cremation burials in the Great Lakes region. These are the earliest sites attributed to burials in the Great Lakes region. The Deadman Slough site consists of a mix of lanceolate and Kirk traditions and also contains a substantial amount of preserved faunal material. Coupled with the Sucices site (also in northeastern Wisconsin, with preserved faunal material), these sites suggest a generalized diet of faunal resources from a wide variety of environmental settings (Kuehn 1998). A generalist strategy would be advantageous during a period of significant Holocene climate change with a dry period and the northward expansion of deciduous forest into the upper Great Lakes. Only slightly postdating Eastern Plano, an early date from the Upper Peninsula of Michigan is available from site 20KE20 on the Keweenaw Peninsula at 7182–6408 cal BP, indicating possible early copper usage (Lovis 2009; Martin 1993).

On the Michigan side of the Alpena-Amberley Ridge, several previous and some recently identified Late Paleo/Early Archaic sites are known mostly from surface collections, including the Lijewski site (Krist and Brown 1994; Frank Krist, pers. comm., 2012; Fig. 5.1). Some of these sites contain Eastern Plano points, including Holcombe type. The lithic assemblages include chert types that are not typical of those generally found in the northeast region of Michigan's Lower Peninsula (Frank Krist, pers. comm., 2012). These sites are on or above the fossil beaches of Main Lake Algonquin, and adjacent to wetland complexes, as has been found elsewhere. Sites are typically in upland locations, which would provide a good view of migrating caribou, and would be good caribou hunting positions in the Early Holocene (Krist and Brown 1994).

Northern Ontario

Much is known about the Late Paleo period in portions of northwestern Ontario, specifically the Lakehead complex (Fox 1977; Julig 1994) and Interlakes composite (Ross 1997), but not too much is known about the Early Archaic. What does seem to be characteristic of this period in northern Ontario is the expression of Eastern Plano lithic technology and point forms, and also certain western Plano point styles, associated with ancient beach ridges and occasionally with wetland/estuary environments. Furthermore, local raw materials from bedrock sources are preferred across the north, from the Thunder Bay region with Gunflint formation taconites and cherts (Julig 1994), and in northeastern Ontario and Georgian Bay, with a focus on Bar River and Lorrain formation quartzite (Julig 2002), especially a glassy recrystallized phase (Julig and Long 2010).

The sites tend to cluster, likely owing to a mixture of geomorphological/lake level factors, suitable bedrock lithic sources, and surveyor geographical bias (based on amount of development and locations of study areas in a large, sparsely populated region). An excellent example would be the Thunder Bay area and the density of sites located on Lake Minong beach ridges. Many Lakehead complex sites were discovered along these ridges (including Brohm and Cummins), associated with usage of locally available taconite to the west of Thunder Bay. The Cummins site contains a cremation burial that is dated to 8480 ± 390 BP (Dawson 1983; Julig, McAndrews, and Mahaney 1990).

Furthermore, residue analysis was undertaken on a sample of lithics from the Cummins site, revealing a mix of blood protein residues including the expected large ungulates such as moose and caribou but also medium-size game such as porcupine and beaver, suggesting a fairly generalized diet (Newman and Julig 1989). The residue study also uncovered human blood. Similar to other large quarry/workshop sites of this era—like Sheguiandah—the archaeological deposits at Cummins are stratified, with side notched points clearly elevated above the lanceolate horizon (Julig 1994) on the main Minong-age beach. In addition, in the adjacent Cummins pond bog excavations, artifacts were located in organic sediments with associated zone 3b pollen, dating circa 7000–8000 BP in the Thunder Bay region (Julig, McAndrews and Mahaney 1990; Julig 1994). Hinshelwood (2004) has found continued use of selected Lakehead complex Paleoindian sites into the Archaic era, as was reported also at the Cummins site. These beach ridge sites would have continued to be used for caribou procurement, where rivers crossed the beach ridges, and also for lithic raw materials, similar to the earlier occupants.

The ridges in this area have a relatively high density of sites circa 9500 BP (MacNeish 1952; Dawson 1983; Fox 1977; Hinshelwood 2004; Julig 1994; Norris 2012). With increased development in the Thunder Bay area, new sites have recently been located, including one of the largest Paleoindian sites in Canada (Markham 2012; Norris 2012). Similar to the Cummins site to the west, Mackenzie 1 contains a range of different Eastern Plano biface forms from the same area, while other adjacent sites have only a single lanceolate point form. Further information about these new sites as it becomes available will likely influence what we know about Late Paleoindian/Early Archaic adaptations and Early Archaic origins throughout the upper Great Lakes region.

New sites to the north of the Great Lakes, in far northwestern Ontario, are also revealing that populations were expanding into northern locales, possibly moving in a northeasterly direction following the receding Laurentide Ice Sheet (Hamilton 2013). However, certain artifact forms such as the ground stone grooved gouge found at (and possibly associated with) the Wapekeka burial is a typical Laurentian Archaic artifact, suggesting a movement of such diagnostic artifact types and possibly populations from the southeast, rather than the southwest. Another Archaic tool form possibly used for woodworking and associated with the Early Archaic in this region is the trihedral adze, and examples have been found associated with the Early Archaic horizon at the Cummins site (Julig 1994), far to the east at the Foxie Otter site on the Spanish River (Hanks 1988), and to the west of Thunder Bay at the Allen site dating to circa 8100 BP (Pilon and Dalla Bona 2004).

Toward the later temporal end of the Alpena-Amberley Ridge, circa 7600 BP, there is evidence of non-cremation human burials associated with red ocher and grave goods in the far north of Ontario toward the Tyrell Sea (Hamilton 2004), and the previously mentioned grooved Laurentian Archaic gouge. Furthermore, a deeply buried site with a dated, occupied paleosol suggests that the northern regions of the province were beginning to be occupied by approximately 8100 BP (Pilon and Dalla Bona 2004).

At this point, there is a paucity of evidence between northwestern and northeastern Ontario. The next nearest scatter of sites from the Late Palaeoindian/Early Archaic time period is evident along the north shore of Lake Huron between eastern Manitoulin Island and Killarney, Ontario. Much like the cluster around Thunder Bay, sites in this area are associated with locally available raw material and the presence of ancient beach ridges. Interestingly as well, they seem focused on glassy recrystallized quartzite outcrops while mostly ignoring locally available chert such as Fossil Hill formation materials available on Manitoulin Island, until the appearance of Early Archaic point forms in post-Plano times (Storck 2002). It seems that trade networks in the northeastern Great Lakes north of Manitoulin Island are somewhat closed off while the western counterparts remain open, as evidenced by some southern and western exotics on Lakehead complex sites. This is likely due to the high water levels in Lake Huron; the land bridges at Alpena-Amberley and Manitoulin to Tobermory were not available until the low-water phases of Lake Stanley. Alternatively, this could simply be the result of sampling bias, with many excavations taking place at or near quarry sites.

Sites including George Lake 1 and 2, the Giant site, and Sheguiandah were the focus of archaeologists during the 1940s and 1950s, and Sheguiandah was later reexamined and more fully documented (Greenman and Stanley 1941; Lee 1953, 1954a, 1954 b, 1955, 1956, 1957; Julig 2002). These sites are focused on lithic resource extraction at Bar River formation quartzite outcrops. There is a large cluster of sites around Sheguiandah on Manitoulin Island (Fig. 5.2), while George Lake 1 and 2 are located across the water on the northeastern Georgian Bay coast, near Killarney. In addition, the Foxie Otter site, located further inland up the Spanish River, also dates to the Early Archaic period but is not associated with glacial lake shorelines or quartzite outcrops (Hanks 1988). Perhaps this is early evidence of a late fall/winter occupation in the interior as part of the presumed seasonal round during the Late Paleoindian/Early Archaic period.

Sheguiandah Site

The Sheguiandah site is located on the eastern shore of Manitoulin Island within the village of Sheguiandah (Fig. 5.2). One of the area's most characteristic features is the quartzite outcrop located on a hill overlooking Lake Huron (Georgian Bay) toward Killarney, Ontario. This "Sheguiandah quartzite" (Bar River Formation) was a focus of prehistoric Late Paleo/Early Archaic groups in the region, extending across the water to Killarney, where it is called "Killarney quartzite." It contains stratified Paleoindian and Archaic artifact assemblages, one of few such sites in northern Ontario. Initially, the site was interpreted as a very early North American "pre-Clovis" site since the artifacts came from "till-like" deposits (Lee 1953, 1954a, 1954b, 1955, 1956, 1957). It was later reinterpreted based on geoarchaeological investigations whereby the archaeological assemblages were found to be younger (Early Holocene) and representative of the Paleoindian and Archaic periods (Julig 2002; Julig and Mahaney 2002; Storck 2002).

Based on limited radiometric dating, the main portion of the site was occupied between 9500 and 7000 BP. This date is supported by the lithic assemblages that have been recovered, revealing Eastern Plano as the dominant tool type with some early Archaic (side notched and corner notched) in more shallow deposits (Julig and Mahaney 2002; Storck 2002). Some of

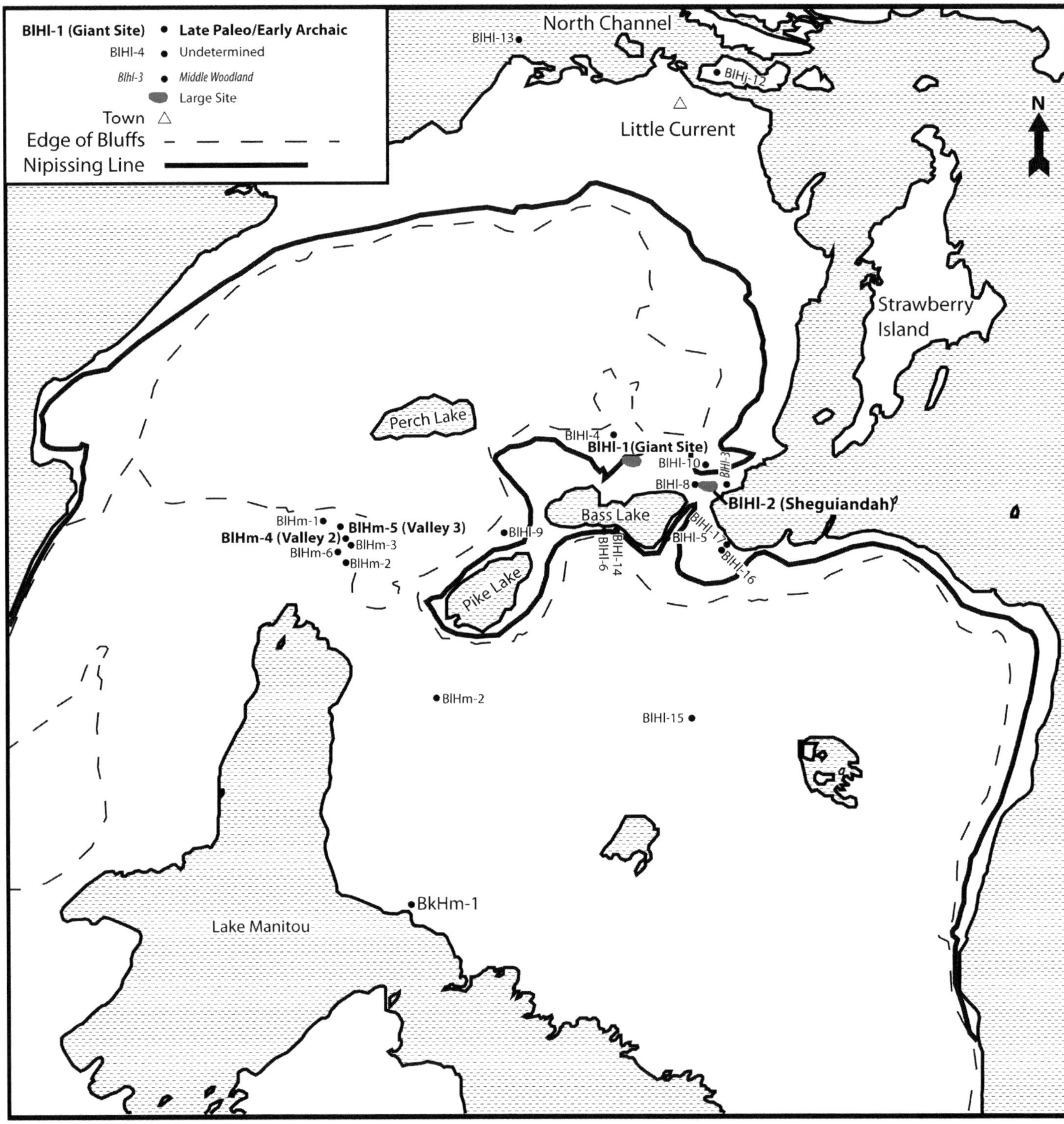

Figure 5.2. The Sheguiandah site area, showing aceramic sites, the Nipissing strandline, and upland bluff areas. These upland bluffs may have been ideal caribou habitat, and the constrictions between the lakes where sites are located may have been interception areas in post-Plano Early Archaic times.

these post-Plano points are on southern chert types, and while not tested, they may include Fossil Hill varieties, Michigan basin, or possibly Onondaga from southern Ontario. Some Middle and later Woodland materials were also recovered from the site, and at the eastern end of the site, a Middle Woodland component has been recorded as a separate site known as Sheguiandah East.

The presence of some water-worn tools suggests an initial site occupation along an active beach around the Korah phase of Lake Algonquin or before the early Mattawa flood event circa 9600 BP (Julig and Mahaney 2002; Barnett 2002). Further investigation is needed to obtain subsistence information, but an Eastern Plano littoral focus is implied, based on the site location with the aid of shoreline reconstruction data (Julig 2002; Von Bitter 2002). The dynamic and changing shorelines, as shown in the Alpena-Amberley Ridge area as well, suggests caribou as a focal resource in Early Holocene times.

During additional geoarchaeological tests at the Sheguiandah site in 1991, a small stratified component that was present between 55 and 65 cm deep was identified within Swamp 4 peat deposits (Julig and Mahaney 2002). Two dates were obtained, placing the component between approximately 7900 and 6900 BP. No diagnostic artifacts were identified but the site was likely occupied while the Alpena-Amberley Ridge was above current water levels, and may be characteristic of similar sites that one would expect along this land bridge. Some of these may also be below peat/organic deposits, which may have protected them from subsequent disturbances.

Manitoulin Island would have been similarly connected to the Bruce Peninsula during this time, likely all the way to the Sault Ste. Marie area. In many ways it would have been similar to the Alpena-Amberley Ridge, a southeast to northwest land bridge connection across the Huron basin, but on a much larger scale. Furthermore, the bluffs located around the Sheguiandah site area may have provided ideal caribou migration habitat with possible valley crossing locations where they could have been intercepted. It is acknowledged that no faunal evidence has been recovered to this point; rather, we only suggest that the area would have provided an ideal hunting locale with a plethora of lithic raw material to utilize. This raw material was likely recovered from ideal habitation locales based on food resources that were close to good quarry facies as there are outcrops throughout the region. Many of the sites recorded are around Sheguiandah, including the Giant site, as shown on Figure 5.2. Most of these are located at or above the circa 5500 BP Nippising strandline, but below the Korah level at circa 9500 BP that marks the habitation area at Sheguiandah (Julig 2002). These sites are mainly quartzite lithic scatters, and some are adjacent to quartzite outcrops of Bar River and/or Lorrain formation quartzite, but the extraction focus was on the glassy facies (Julig and Long 2010). As with the post-Plano point assemblages from Sheguiandah, there are some southern chert artifacts evident (possibly Fossil Hill cherts in small frequencies), suggesting that the Early Archaic populations had connections across the land bridge to the south at this time.

The following is a description of an informal lithic cache of Sheguiandah quartzite unifaces, relatively deeply deposited within a Late Paleoindian/Early Archaic component of the Sheguiandah site. These uniface tools suggest an obvious focus on hide processing.

Swamp 4

All the artifacts from Swamp 4 of the Sheguiandah site came from a 1 × 2 m test trench. This test was mainly for geoarchaeological purposes, to check the stratigraphy, and to obtain ^{14}C dates on the base of the depressions and associated artifacts (Fig. 5.3). The cultural level consisted of an approximately 10–15 cm deep sandy, silty clay overlain by half a meter of peat (Fig. 5.4, Plate 2). No cultural features were noted within the stratigraphy. Two radiocarbon dates were obtained from organic samples in close association with the artifacts, including 6870 ± 70 BP (charcoal) and 7930 ± 80 BP (peat). The basal peat may be the more reliable date for the associated lithic artifacts as the wood charcoal (possible charred root) may be from a later forest fire.

The artifacts from Swamp 4 represent an informal cache of tools dominated by unifaces. The artifacts can primarily be described as large, utilitarian tools, likely used for processing game, and possibly for working bone and antler (burins and burin-like tools). In total, 197 artifacts were recovered from the cultural horizon of the 1 × 2 m trench. Sixty of the 196 artifacts (30%) are unifacially modified, 13 (7%) are polyhedral cores, and 123 are debitage (63%), with only 1 bifacially flaked tool recovered, a spokeshave (Table 5.1). The entire assemblage is made up of Sheguiandah quartzite with varying degrees of staining, which we have attributed to contact with the overlying peat deposit: the artifacts in direct contact with the overlying peat are highly stained (Fig. 5.5, scrapers) while those in contact with the regolith below (Figs. 5.6, 5.7) are relatively fresh and unstained.

The uniface assemblage ($n = 60$) is made up of 36 scrapers, 7 burins, 3 blades, and 14 multifunctional tools (Table 5.1; Figs. 5.5–5.7, Plate 2). These artifacts can easily be described as part of a butchering toolkit and for processing hide and bone. The assemblage is a mix of 6 side scrapers, 9 endscrapers, and 21 informal scrapers. Fourteen multifunctional tools with scraping edges and burin facets were also identified, along with 7 burins. Three blades were identified, contributing a possible butchering element to the toolkit. The tools appear to have been heavily used but no formal use wear studies were undertaken. One biface preform or notch/spokeshave was also identified, although it is at a relatively early stage. It was likely used much in the same way as the rest of the uniface tools. The uniface assemblage overall would appear to be an ideal butchering and hide processing kit, and undoubtedly with further excavation, additional tools would be recovered from the immediate surroundings.

Thirteen cores were also identified within the cache, 4 of which had blade-like scars. The 2 smallest cores with blade scarring were used to generate microblades. Although 1 is identified as a core tool owing to visible macroscopic use, most of the as-

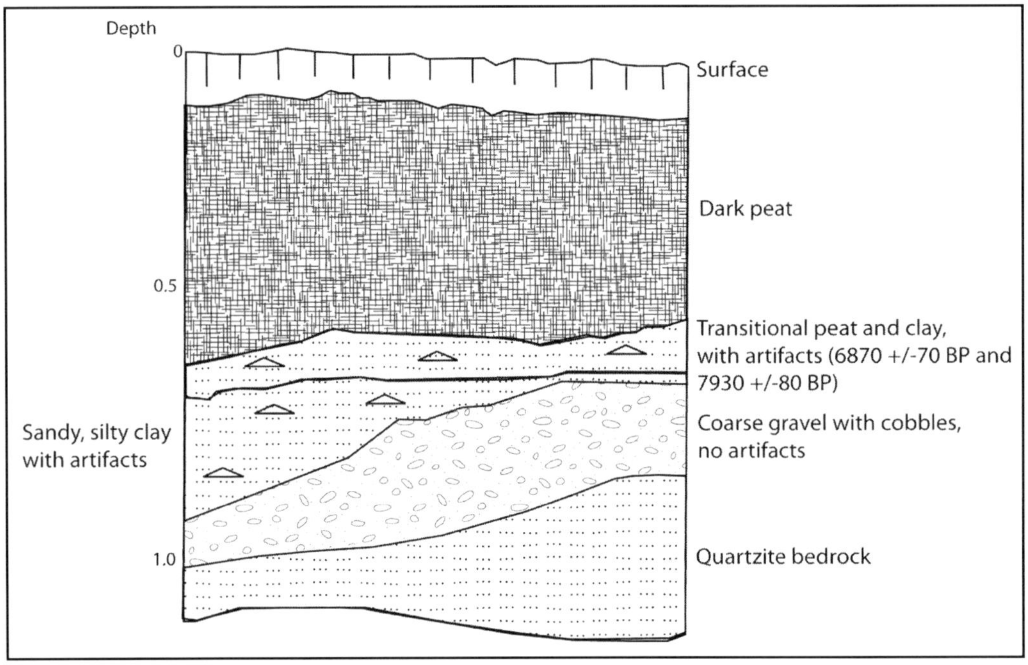

(*above left*) Figure 5.3. Stratigraphy from Swamp 4, Sheguiandah site, showing Holocene peat deposits overlying Early Archaic uniface assemblage (after Julig 2002).

(*left*) Figure 5.4. View of test pit location from Swamp 4 (taken in 2013). Although described as Swamp 4 by Lee (1955), this is actually a small flat shallow depression in the quartzite bedrock ridge of the Sheguiandah site, protected by knobs. (See also Plate 2.)

Table 5.1. Artifact counts.

Artifact Type	Count
Bifaces	
spokeshave	1
Cores	
polyhedral	13
Flakes	
broken flakes	23
complete flakes	16
fractured flakes	23
shatter	61
Unifaces	
blades	3
burins	7
multifunctional	14
scrapers	36
Total	197

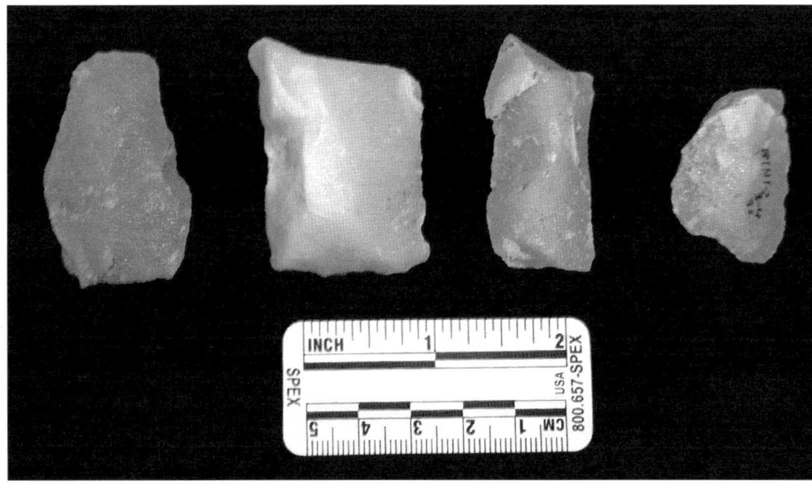

Figure 5.5. Quartzite scrapers showing staining from overlying peat deposits. (See also Plate 2.)

semblage was likely used to generate additional expedient tools and cutting flakes. It is also possible that larger pieces were used as pieces of site furniture to process hides or to bash bones. The cores fit nicely within what would be expected from an expedient butchering/processing toolkit.

Later primary flake debitage from Swamp 4 may also have been used as game processing tools, including 14 retouched flakes and 14 utilized flakes. The remainder was a mix of secondary flakes and shatter. Although some retouched and utilized flakes were noted, the ratio of debitage to the number of tools present is relatively low. This may indicate that the tools were not generated in situ but were instead moved to this location after manufacture and use.

Additional excavation of the area would be required to fully assess the site function; however, several inferences can be made with the collected sample. The unifaces likely represent an informal cache of processing tools that were discarded after use. Although the artifacts were not found within a cultural feature and few formal tools were identified, they appear to have been meaningfully placed or left within a relatively finite area (1 × 2 m). This may represent a small shelter in this protected location. The high ratio of tools to debitage in a quarry workshop site is atypical, as is the relative lack of biface technology. At the Sheguiandah site, the major manufacturing activity appeared to be biface preform production (Julig 2002).

The mostly informal tool types within the assemblage are not surprising, owing to the location of several quarry faces in close proximity to the cache. Many of the informal uniface tools are similar to the uniface assemblage at other quarry workshop sites such as the Cummins site (Julig 1994). The Swamp 4 assemblage would appear to be a toolkit utilized to process animal remains that were brought back to a habitation area close to the quarry. Once the processing was complete, the tools were left or discarded in this particular area. If any faunal material was deposited with the tools, it was not archaeologically visible, possibly owing to the acidity of these quartzite outcrop areas (these are the only places where blueberries will flourish around Shequiandah, as they prefer acid soils).

As mentioned above, the lack of debitage compared to unifaces suggests that they were generated elsewhere and likely transported to this locus. Furthermore, 28 pieces of debitage had retouch or were utilized (macroscopic observation). Much of the discarded assemblage could also be categorized as useful for future use, or relatively lightly utilized, while the debitage

Figure 5.6. Sheguiandah quartzite: *top row (left to right)*, blade, backed blade, and backed side scraper; *bottom row*, backed side scrapers. (See also Plate 2.)

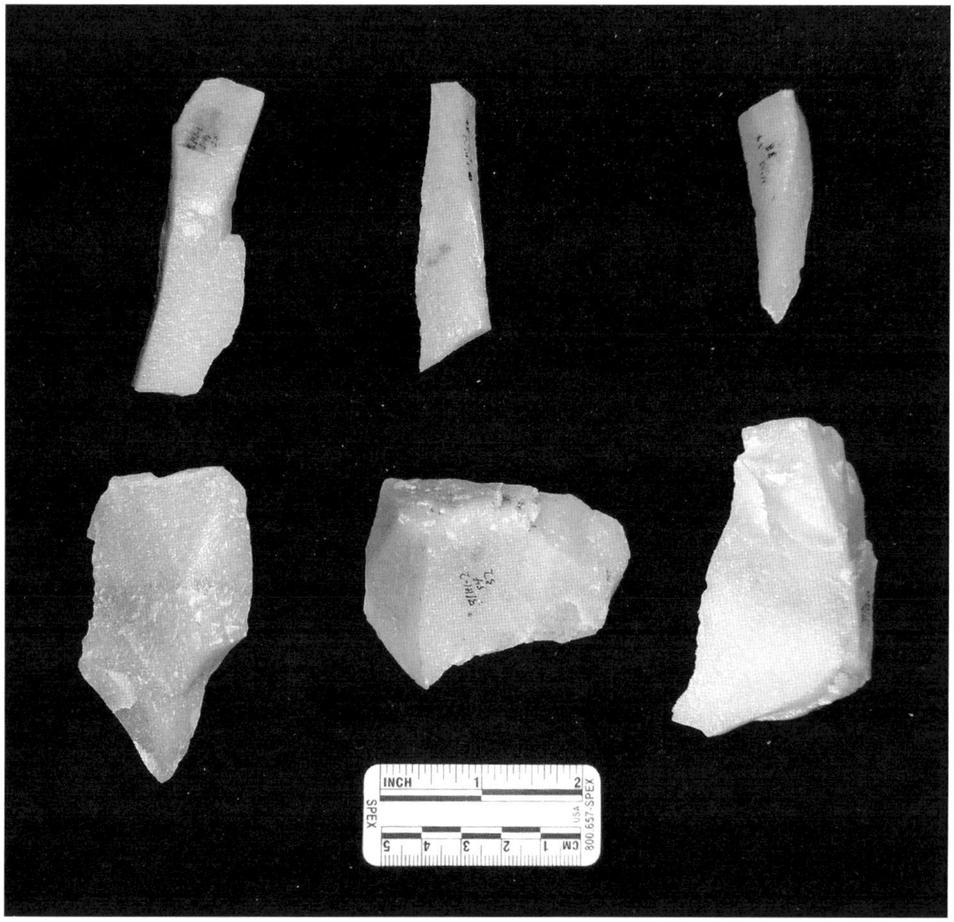

Figure 5.7. Sheguiandah quartzite: *top row*, blades; *bottom row*, large flake cutting tools with burins. (See also Plate 2.)

had either visible retouch or use. Microwear analysis could clarify this issue.

The small Swamp 4 depression may have been a grassy or mossy meadow in Early Holocene times circa 8000 BP, and situated at the side of the bedrock knoll that is the Sheguiandah site, it may have been located near a caribou trail. Caribou often migrate around the sides of ridges following the contour lines, and Sheguiandah may have been a viewshed location (Krist and Brown 1994) and actual hunting/processing site as well as a quarry workshop and habitation site (Julig 2002). If caribou were taken on the edge of this knoll near Swamp 4, it may have been a location suitable for processing and caching the animals or meat, as such boggy areas with sphagnum moss are often used for temporary caches by more recent northern caribou hunters (Taylor and Turner 1969).

Discussion

The Sheguiandah site is a habitation site with multiple occupations, similar in terms of lithic technology to the larger and slightly later Giant site to the west (Fig. 5.2). It is postulated that lithic procurement was likely tied to the seasonal round of its inhabitants. The evidence presented by the Swamp 4 tool types suggests that large game was processed between 7900 and 6900 BP in this part of the Sheguiandah site area. Despite no clearly diagnostic type artifacts, the time period is the Early Archaic and the end of the emergence of the Alpena-Amberley Ridge. It has been hypothesized—based on the identification of many Sheguiandah quartzite lithic scatter sites at key points (Fig. 5.2)—that these beach and rock ridges leading to the northern uplands could indicate procurement along a caribou migration corridor.

There are some intact rock features, possibly hunting blinds or meat caches, recorded on ridges around Manitoulin that may be of considerable antiquity, but these are not yet studied in detail. However, it is very certain that caribou would have been present along the Manitoulin Island corridor during this time period since the native vegetation would have been fairly typical boreal forest, possibly with more conifers than the Alpena-Amberley Ridge, which is considered ideal caribou habitat. There were caribou present on Manitoulin until the start of the twentieth century, and some faunal remains are present in sites such as the Shawana site and nearby Killarney Bay 1.

There is as yet no direct evidence from faunal material at the Sheguiandah site; thus, subsistence activities are implied from tool types and location. The Sheguiandah site is located in close proximity to upland environments that could have been related to caribou migration during the Early Archaic period. Caribou, therefore, could have been obtained right at the Sheguiandah site or in close proximity, such as is implied at Swamp 4. Lithic quarrying is often attributed to snow free conditions, and it would make sense that the Sheguiandah site would be occupied during a fall migration. The tool types certainly suggest processing of large game animals, which was likely a regular occurrence right on the site. Possible residue analysis of the tools in the future could shed light on what exactly was processed, but for now, the specific use of these tools remains speculative.

What the Swamp 4 artifacts do clearly demonstrate is the possibility of finding relatively deeply deposited Early Archaic artifacts under peat bogs. These areas are often avoided by surveyors; this particular area was found while attempting to determine geoarcheological data and coring for palynological analysis. The Cummins site from Thunder Bay contains similarly deeply deposited artifacts in peat deposits, of a similar age, as does the Allen site from Sioux Lookout (Julig 1994; Pilon and Dalla Bona 2004). These combined findings present a unique challenge to researchers trying to combat the geoarchaeological problems associated with documentation of certain types of sites of the Late Paleoindian/Early Archaic. Most sites are either on beach ridges, or quarry/workshops, on bedrock outcrops. Thus, when looking for early sites in the upper Great Lakes, surveyors need to remember that upland sites may be inundated with water in bogs and swamps, and that they possibly are fairly deeply buried under a blanket of Holocene peat. Perhaps such deposits will provide some of the best stratified and preserved assemblages from this time period, keeping in mind the amount of coastal change (isostatic uplift and flooding) that has taken place. They may also provide organic and faunal remains, as was the case for sites to the west, such as the Sucices site and Deadman Slough, as mentioned previously.

Peat bogs and swamps themselves, in general, however, are typically ignored by CRM archaeologists when survey strategies are developed by government ministries, and these areas are thus rarely tested outside pure research archaeology.

In northern Ontario, with the typical absence of datable organic material from this period, these organic sediments provide the additional bonus of yielding radiometric dates and pollen sequences. If additional components are found in association with other early sites, this could provide chronological information that is often sorely lacking, particularly on the unforgiving Canadian Shield's acidic soils. At both the Cummins site (Julig 1994) and the Sheguiandah site (Julig 2002), trenching and excavating into bog deposits yielded Early Holocene artifact assemblages. The dry period in the Early Holocene (ca. 8000–6000 BP) may have made wet areas available for habitation, and with the return of normal climatic conditions in the latter half of the Holocene, these boggy areas became covered with peat.

Swamp 4 as a Cache, or Special Purpose Site?

The lithic assemblage at Swamp 4 was interpreted as a possible uniface cache, but maybe the peat bog was used for other activities. The association of peat bogs and wetlands to Paleoindian and Early Holocene archaeological sites is a well-known association in the southern Great Lakes region (Deller 1979). Bogs contain a plethora of resources and characteristics that are beneficial to human habitation and that are sometimes not located in other environments. The most obvious aspect of bogs and wetland environments that would draw human occupation is the presence of game and other useful resources; they would have likely been ideal hunting areas—for migrating birds to large game such as caribou—during certain times of year, while providing plant food resources and traditional medicines during other times. Ethnographically, at least with the Anishinaabe people of northwestern Ontario, plants that are associated with bogs or muskeg are often given the prefix *mashkiigo-*, highlighting their specific importance to indigenous inhabitants of the region (Davidson-Hunt et al. 2005).

In addition to game and other subsistence resources, the peat could have provided a fuel source for fire, as has been documented in the ethnohistoric record (Taylor and Turner 1969). Occupation of these areas would likely have led to the observation that blueberry bushes and other plants are "reinvigorated by fire," particularly in peat bogs (Eastman 1995). Additionally, peat could be lit for long-burning fires—potentially for long-duration burning as well as for carrying fire to the next location. If the peat bog was used to cache meat and other resources, long-burning fires would perhaps decrease the possibility of scavenging by wolverines, black bears, and wolves, as has been documented as a wolverine deterrence strategy by the Labrador Inuit (Taylor and Turner 1969).

Swamp 4 has definitive evidence of burning with some burnt logs remaining. The peat deposit in Swamp 4 is also shallower than that in adjacent Swamp 3, suggesting that much of the peat was burned off, maybe by natural fires, but maybe by anthropogenic processes by Early Archaic bands camping there and using the adjacent quarry exposures within 50 meters, on the south side of the ridge.

As a result of peat harvesting (for a source of fuel) in northwestern Europe, well-known archaeological discoveries have been discovered. In northern and western Europe, archaeologists associate bogs with their ability to preserve organic remains. There are several instances of major archaeological finds that have been pulled out of these types of environments, but perhaps the best known are bog bodies. Such finds exemplify the ability of bog environments to preserve soft tissue for thousands of years in acidic, cold, and low oxygen environments (Sanders 2009). Humans have noted the preservation phenomena in bogs for millennia and have purposefully utilized this effect as exemplified by bog butter, which to this point has been found only in Ireland and Scotland, and is found both on its own and within containers (Earwood 1997).

Little has been reported on bog preservation in archaeological contexts from North America as relatively few data exist. Experimental methods have shown preservation within ponds and bogs related to research on megafaunal predation by Paleoindians and extinctions (Fisher 1995, 2009). Ethnographically, William Turner mentions this type of caching while living among the Labrador Inuit in a setting where the Inuit are employing traditional caribou hunting methods (Taylor and Turner 1969). During his travels, he observed that ungutted caribou would be thrown in a lake and could be preserved up to a year later, particularly for nose and brain parts that were relatively preserved as well as marrow bones and some flesh (Taylor and Turner 1969). Storing caribou meat "under the moss" has also been noted ethnographically among Chipewayan hunters, possibly for short-term storage (Sharp 1977). To build on the largely negative evidence of caribou hunting in the Great Lakes region during the Late Paleoindian/Early Archaic period, it is possible that the caching of meat in bogs would have provided a semi-reliable method to protect meat from scavengers and to help prevent spoilage from flies. A possible, accidental side effect would be preservation over longer periods, such as caching for entire seasons (like fall to spring) as a strategy to prevent starvation.

Small bog areas and swamps may also be used as ideal game ambushing sites when located in mostly upland environments. In northern Canada and elsewhere, caribou are often driven into water and then taken by small watercraft and spearing (Taylor and Turner 1969).

If caribou hunting had been taking place at Sheguiandah, or nearby, the herds would likely have followed trails along the sides of the ridges in the area. Caribou could also have been driven into these areas, or the hunters could have utilized such areas as natural hunting pits and ambushed animals from the herd relatively undetected. Hunting pit complexes are noted in several areas of Scandinavia that might draw a parallel to this type of strategy, and hunts in the Arctic were often conducted along ridges in a similar manner (Manker 1960; Julig 1993). While hunting pits are not recorded as commonly in North American circumpolar regions, such strategies may have been used in the past.

Alpena-Amberley Ridge Implications

The relative paucity of information from the Late Paleoindian/Early Archaic period in this region is attributed to a range of possibilities, including depopulation after full boreal (closed forest) reforestation, poor site visibility, and lack of post-Plano and Early Archaic diagnostics. A depopulation in the Early Holocene may have occurred in the upper Great Lakes region owing to an unstable local environment with constantly changing coastlines. We also observe a reliance mostly on locally available raw materials during this time, similar to the generalized Archaic pattern in the south. Travel may have been more difficult due to the lack of open terrain and less stable beach areas, and trade routes and social interaction may have declined. However, there are some indications of southern cherts in some of the post-Plano assemblages, possibly attributable to new connections and movements enabled by the Manitoulin to Bruce Peninsula land bridge during the low-water phase.

Poor site visibility is generally due to site inundation and hidden ancient beaches being located further back from the water. There are also a variety of coastal processes that affect visibility, including eolian erosion, wave action, and downcutting of rivers during falling water levels. Once water levels returned to near modern levels, deltas—which would provide ideal camping locations—would be inundated, with sites obliterated during this process. Gradual rising water may have preserved some sites while others would still be susceptible to complete destruction. Herein lies the problem with survey along the portions of the Amberley Ridge. Perhaps coring peat bogs and trying to locate areas similar to Swamp 4 is the solution to find intact stratified deposits under the water.

Also, as in the case with Swamp 4, there may be a lack of clearly diagnostic material, which we suggest has led to poor site visibility for the Late Paleoindian/Early Archaic period. In southern Ontario, some Early Archaic assemblages contain diagnostic biface artifacts; however, some sites appear to lack biface technology, and are attributed to the Early Archaic mainly by the type of chert raw material used. The same situation may be present in the more northern regions, such as Amberley/Alpena and Manitoulin, as we find at Swamp 4. However, some of the post-Plano points from Sheguiandah, including the corner notched, some stemmed lanceolate, and side notched "Big Sandy," may be found in good dateable contexts. But in some sites and assemblages, we may possibly be left with expedient technologies on specific raw material types as the predominant hallmarks of this little-understood period. Although the use of certain raw materials such as Fossil Hill chert offers archaeologists clues, as does the presence of so-called "big expedient technologies," there is little in the way of concrete evidence to link artifacts to particular time periods, unless they are found in datable contexts, such as in peat deposits. Another suggestion may be from other tool forms; for example, the many burins and burin-like tools may indicate that a bone point technology may also be used for caribou and other game procurement, as is fairly common in other northern and Arctic contexts.

Ultimately, it may be the lack of focused research that has hampered efforts to clearly understand this time period in the upper Great Lakes. New research is needed, incorporating geoarchaeological techniques to locate sites that are either inundated or preserved on landforms and strata from the Late Paleoindian/Early Archaic time periods. This is where the current research that is taking place under Lake Huron on the Alpena-Amberley Ridge will assist archaeologists. Site survey and feature mapping taking place underwater with the use of submersibles may ultimately provide key information that is sorely lacking, and perhaps encourage researchers who are studying areas above current water levels to survey not only in areas that may have been dry shorelines in the Early Holocene but are now peat bogs and wetlands, but to dig a few centimeters deeper and to look a bit harder. We also need to study rock features, pits, and other traces of possible early caribou hunting on likely game trails in areas that have never been cleared, near the known quarry workshop sites of this era.

Acknowledgments

We thank the organizers of the Caribou Hunting Symposium and editors of this volume, including John O'Shea, Elizabeth Sonnenberg, and Ashley Lemke. We also thank the symposium participants, including Bill Fox and Andrew Stewart. We also benefited from discussions we have had with Frank Krist, Brian Deller, Chris Ellis, Jeff Bursey, Peter Storck, Peter Barnett, Bill Ross, Brian Gordon, and Scott Hamilton. The Swamp 4 collections were excavated by Julig during the Sheguiandah site reinvestigations done in 1991, under the direction of Archaeological Services Inc., and we thank Ron Williamson and all members of the project study team for access to these data.

6 | Chert Sources and Utilization in the Southern Huron Basin during the Early Holocene

by William A. Fox, D. Brian Deller, and Christopher J. Ellis

While considerable research has focused on fluted point chert utilization in the lower Great Lakes region (Deller 1989; Ellis 1989; Storck and von Bitter 1989), less attention has been paid to subsequent industries spanning the Late Paleoindian through Early Archaic periods. Chert and other toolstone sourcing around the Huron basin is now well established (Fox 2009; Janusas 1984; Luedtke 1978, 1979; Long, Julig, and Hancock 2002). The authors review biface collections derived from the circum-Lake Huron region in an attempt to correlate diagnostic form with raw material preference. The resultant database is understood to reflect seasonal population movements and intergroup exchange of toolkits during the low-water stages of the Lake Huron basin.

Introduction

Lower Great Lakes chert acquisition patterns during the eleventh millennium BCE have been interpreted to reflect initial colonization of the emergent post-glacial landscape by southern fluted point bands occupying present-day Ohio in the west and upstate New York in the east. Gainey phase assemblages often include bifaces of central Ohio Mercer formation chert (Simons, Shott, and Wright 1984:267), and some specimens of Onondaga formation chert may derive from quarries such as Diver's Lake in western New York, as opposed to the Ontario deposits to the west. While Collingwood chert from the more northerly von Bitter quarry in the Beaver valley (Storck and von Bitter 1989) is present in these earliest assemblages, it comes to dominate toolkits characteristic of the later Parkhill phase (Deller and Ellis 1992:11; Storck 1997:17, table 2.4). At this time, Bayport chert from the Saginaw Bay vicinity is a popular raw material to the west (Ellis 1989:143, table 6.1). The Crowfield assemblages begin to display some acquisition of Kettle Point chert from the southern Huron basin, as this source was exposed by retreating lake levels following the main Algonquin stage (Deller 1989: 211), while the type site is dominated by Onondaga chert (Deller and Ellis 1984:43, 2011:15–19, 25). Subsequent Holcombe preferences are similar, including a heavy dependence on Bayport chert at the type site in southeastern Michigan (Fitting, DeVisscher, and Wahla 1966:18–20, 126), and long-distance embedded chert procurement systems appear to continue into Early Archaic times (Ellis, Wortner, and Fox 1991:5–7, 26; Ellis et al. 1998:162).

Toolstone Sources in the Lake Huron Region

Geologically, Lake Huron is situated in the northeastern perimeter of the Michigan basin, bounded to the north by the Precambrian formations of the Canadian Shield and underlain by a series of Paleozoic sedimentary formations of the Ordovician to Mississippian periods. Cherts are abundant in certain of the latter formations, as well as the Huronian Supergroup of late Precambrian formations along the north shore (Fig. 6.1, Plate 3). Quartzites also outcrop in the Lorrain and Bar River formations of this northern region, and these were extensively quarried and utilized for biface and uniface production by Late Paleoindian and Archaic groups, as evidenced on the Sheguiandah site (Lee 1953, 1954b; Julig 2002) and Killarney Provincial Park sites

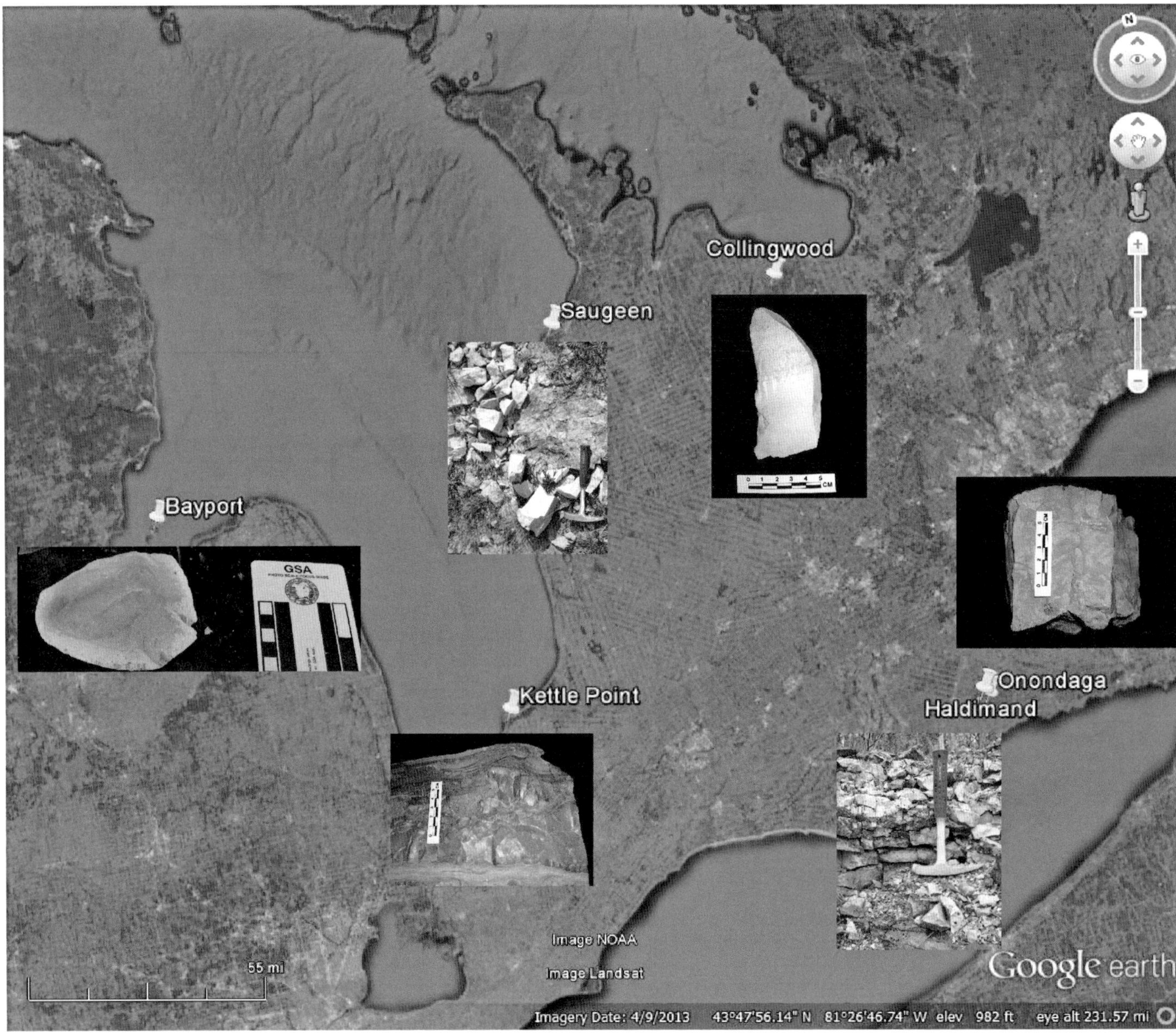

Figure 6.1. Southern Huron basin chert sources. (See also Plate 3.)

(Greenman 1943; Storck 1974). Substantial chert deposits also occur in the Gordon Lake formation (Fox 2009:358, 2014:5).

To the south, nodular cherts have been documented in the Silurian Fossil Hill formation, the Devonian Bois Blanc and Ipperwash formations (Eley and von Bitter 1989; Fox 2009), and the Mississippian Bayport formation (Dustin 1935; Luedtke 1978:416). Cream-colored cherts occur sporadically within the Fossil Hill formation, as it is exposed from the Beaver valley to the east (Collingwood variant), up the Bruce Peninsula (Bruce variant) to Manitoulin Island (Wike and Providence Bay variants), and on westward into upper peninsula Michigan (Detour and Campbell quarry variants; Fox 2009:360, fig. 3). The latter three display a transition to blue and brown colors in the analogous Cordell formation of the Manistique group (Luedtke 1979:745). Cherts in the lower Devonian Bois Blanc formation are also cream to beige in color, while Kettle Point chert at the top of the middle Devonian Ipperwash formation ranges from blue-gray to maroon in color and occurs in, at times, massive beds (Fox 2009:363, fig. 5). Similarly, the gray to brown cherts in the middle Mississippian Bayport formation occur in beds, but also, as large nodules in exposures on islands in Saginaw Bay (Dustin 1935:467).

Beyond the aforementioned primary or bedrock exposures of toolstone, Native groups also acquired stone for working from secondary or glacially transported deposits of cobbles. A range of Precambrian metamorphic rock toolstone was available from glacial deposits as far south as central Ohio. This included not only siliceous material for flaked stone tools, but also siltstones and argillites used by later Native groups to produce polished stone artifacts such as atlatl weights, pendants, and pipes. Igneous gabbro and diorite cobbles were also fashioned into axes, and metasediments were used to produce expedient spall tools during the Archaic period (Fox 2013:136, fig. 9.3; Kenyon 1959:37, plate III, 41, plate V-7).

Paleozoic bedrock exposures containing cherts to the east, south, and west were quarried and provided toolstone throughout most of the Native occupation of the region. Specific nonlocal sources appear to have been preferred over others during certain time periods, such as the Mercer formation cherts from central Ohio that were popular with some Paleoindian and Early Archaic groups that occupied the southern Lake Huron basin.

Archaeological Evidence for Specific Toolstone Use in the Southern Huron Basin

The period of interest includes the low-water stages between 10,000 and 8000 years ago, when the Alpena to Amberley ridge corridor existed across the Lake Huron basin. Current shoreline chert exposures in Saginaw Bay and at Kettle Point and McGregor Point along the east coast of Lake Huron would have been more extensively exposed for chert acquisition by contemporary Native communities and would have been many kilometers from the then-active shorelines. Obviously, east-west pedestrian transport across the Huron basin would have facilitated the movement of cherts between the present areas of Michigan and Ontario. The exposed landmass on the ridge and points south would have provided an opportunity to acquire glacially transported toolstone pebbles and cobbles derived from the Canadian Shield, as well as Silurian and Devonian formations to the north. This also means that such materials can be expected to be scattered across the subsequently inundated bottomlands of the southern Lake Huron basin. On the contrary, cherts outcropping to the south and west of the study area, such as Mercer and Bayport formation cherts, respectively, cannot have been deposited naturally along the ridge. Their discovery, along with other popular exotic cherts such as western Onondaga formation material, must signal human intervention in the deposition of such materials within the study area.

Over the summer of 2013, the senior author revisited a number of museums and private collections in southern Ontario in an effort to document the raw materials utilized to produce diagnostic Late Paleoindian and Early Archaic bifaces roughly contemporary with the Lake Huron basin low-water stages (Ellis et al. 1998:161–62). This was done to develop some sense of which materials would most likely be represented on Native sites of various functions within the study area. As no cherts are known to outcrop along the Alpena-Amberley Ridge, it is expected that all final stage bifaces would have been carried onto the ridge, presumably by highly mobile hunting parties. There is a possibility that expedient flake tools may have been produced using glacially deposited cobbles of toolstone from northern outcrop sources in the study area; however, it is extremely unlikely that biface tools or debitage relating to biface edge maintenance from such sources would be included in assemblages from contemporary sites.

A number of factors mitigated against a quantitative approach to this study, including the limited provenance available for many donated specimens held by institutions and, sadly, the disappearance of specimens from these collections since the author's previous visits three decades ago. Luckily, a photographic record remains concerning some of the latter specimens (Fig. 6.2, Plate 3). Larger and better provenanced site assemblages are reported from Ontario, Michigan, and Ohio, and these are referenced in the following overview.

Given current age estimates, the Huron basin low-water stage contemporary diagnostic forms are considered to range from Late Paleoindian Deavitt (Dibb 2004) and Hi-Lo lanceolate to Early Archaic notched forms including Thebes and St. Charles (Justice 1995:54–60), Kirk corner notched/Nettling (Ellis, Wortner, and Fox 1991; Justice 1995:71–80), and early bifurcate base forms (Bowen 1994; Justice 1995:86–96; Lennox 1993). Late Paleoindian lanceolates from Ontario include a 14 cm long quartzite biface from the town of Kincardine in Bruce County (Storck 1976:3, table 1.5). This specimen appears to have been thermally fractured, and may have accompanied a cremation, similar to those recorded west of Lake Michigan (Buckmaster and Paquette 1988:121; Kuehn and Clark 2012:133). Further south in Middlesex County, the Heaman site (Deller 1976) produced specimens manufactured of Mercer, Onondaga, and Bayport formation cherts (Fig. 6.3, Plate 3).

Hi-Lo bifaces from the southern Huron basin are manufactured of Onondaga, Haldimand (Bois Blanc Fm. variant; Parker 1986a, 1986b; Fox 2009:361, fig. 4; Fig. 6.4), and Kettle Point cherts (Deller 1979:15, figs. 8, 9). The former two materials can be acquired from outcrops a short distance from each other, 150 km to the east of the present Lake Huron shoreline (Moerschfelder 1985). The Stelco 1 site, situated just southwest of these Onondaga and Haldimand chert outcrops, produced a Hi-Lo assemblage totally dominated by the latter chert type (Timmins 1995:4), as is the Koeppe II Hi-Lo component located 45 km north of these bedrock sources (Woodley 1997:160). Throughout the history of Ontario's Native occupation, Haldimand chert was not favored as a raw material, as compared to Onondaga chert, so its popularity at this point in time has been interpreted as indicating a particular significance to Hi-Lo knappers, perhaps relating to its whitish

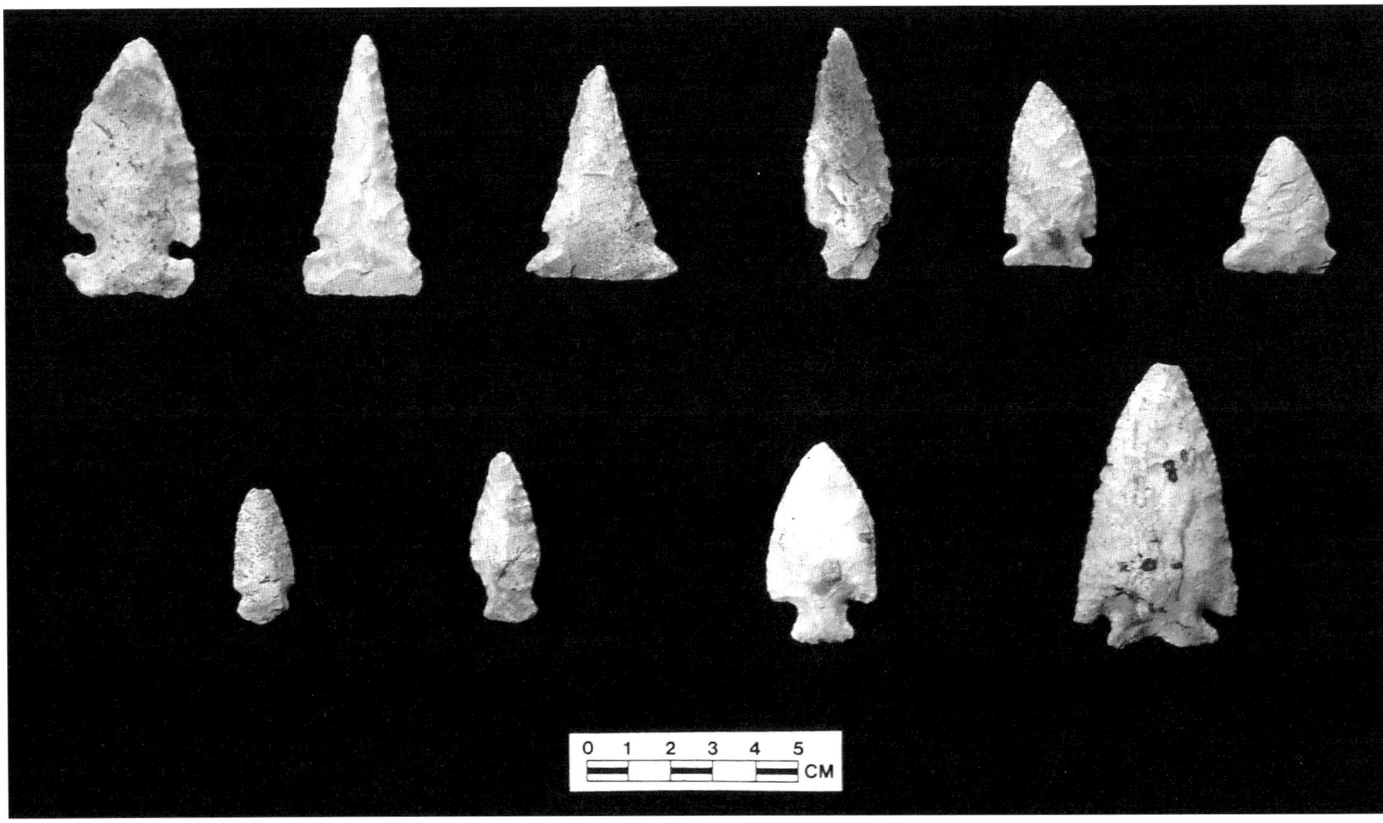

Figure 6.2. Collingwood chert Archaic period bifaces from southwestern Ontario. (See also Plate 3.)

color. Located to the west toward Kettle Point, the Southwinds Hi-Lo component produced equal numbers of Kettle Point and Haldimand chert artifacts (Timmermans 1999:11), which is typical of sites to the west of London (Ellis and Deller 2013: table 3).

Around this time, there is an east-west and apparently somewhat permeable interface between southern Early Archaic notched biface-using populations and northern Late Paleoindian "Plano" populations. Limited evidence for an occupation of southern Ontario by groups utilizing Thebes and St. Charles-style bifaces exists in southwestern Ontario, and, interestingly, a St. Charles specimen from the vicinity of Hanover in Bruce County appears to be manufactured of Mercer formation chert (Fig. 6.5). To the east, a notched Collingwood chert biface associated with lanceolate Late Paleoindian forms on the Coates Creek site displays all the attributes of a St. Charles-style biface (Storck 1978:31, fig. 5). And just to the north, Lennox reports a Thebes component at the McKean site, including a lightly ground Collingwood chert biface base with angled notches (Lennox 2000:44, fig. 19*e*). Other than local Collingwood chert, this Early Archaic assemblage is manufactured of Onondaga chert, leading Lennox to suggest that, similar to local Early Paleoindian seasonal movements, the site occupants "had recently returned to the site from the Niagara Peninsula area with tools of Onondaga chert" (Lennox 2000:54). Further north yet, the Sheguiandah site produced two quartzite bifaces of "enigmatic" cultural affiliation (Storck 2002:149), displaying angled corner notches and convex ground bases (Storck 2002:150, fig. 5.7 *4*, *5*), among a Late Paleoindian assemblage dominated by lanceolate forms.

Mark Seeman (pers. comm., 2014) has observed that in Ohio, "there are proportionately many more St. Charles points in and around the Coshocton quarries in relation to Thebes than anyplace else in the state we have sampled." Elsewhere, Thebes-style bifaces dominate, manufactured from a range of Ohio cherts (many Upper Mercer) and including the occasional Indiana and Michigan (Bayport) chert examples (Amanda Mullett, pers. comm., 2013). The Nobles Pond site Thebes component

Figure 6.3. Deavitt lanceolates from the Heaman site and vicinity. (See also Plate 3.)

Figure 6.4. Hi-Lo bifaces from southwestern Ontario.

Figure 6.5. Mercer chert biface from the Hanover vicinity in Bruce County, Ontario.

includes bifaces manufactured from Kettle point chert (Seeman, pers. comm., 2013). Don Simons (pers. comm., 2013) has noted Bayport chert Thebes bifaces in collections from the region south of Saginaw Bay in Michigan, and Abel (1990:16) reports that 25 percent of Thebes bifaces in northwestern Ohio are manufactured from Bayport chert (see also Bechtel 1988).

The eighth-millennium BP Nettling site to the southeast in Ontario produced an extensive biface assemblage. The biface blanks are primarily of local Onondaga chert, while the majority of the serrated, corner-notched refined bifaces are Ohio cherts (Pipe Creek and Mercer variants), suggesting a north-south seasonal pattern of movement across what would have been a low-water configuration of the Lake Erie western basin, between present-day Sandusky Bay and Point Pelee. Contemporary Early Archaic assemblages to the north and east are dominated by Onondaga chert, although the Culloden Acres site did include some Kettle Point chert (Ellis and Deller 1991). The latter material appears to be rarely utilized for serrated biface production (see Fig. 6.6).

No excavations have occurred on bifurcate base sites southeast of the Huron basin; however, bifurcate base projectile points have been documented in surface collections. Similar to assemblages in northern Ohio (Bowen 1994), points manufactured on Mercer formation chert are not uncommon. Two sites in the Grand River drainage further to the east are dominated by Onondaga chert, but do include limited amounts of Kettle Point chert (Lennox 1993:5, 20–21), and a third produced slightly more Haldimand than Onondaga chert by weight (Woodley 1996:41–42). No Ohio chert is present on these sites. While Early Archaic sites are known southwest of the Huron basin, unfortunately, there has been an "absence of systematic work on Early and Middle Archaic adaptations in the Thumb [of Michigan]" (Shott and Welch 1984:43; W. Lovis, pers. comm., 2014).

Figure 6.6. Kettle Point chert serrated biface from Grey County, Ontario.

Final Thoughts

Similar to the hypothesized Saginaw region Archaic population's expanded range of interaction to "encompass portions of the southern Lake Huron and western Lake Erie basins" during the post-Nipissing period of lower-elevation lake levels (Cook and Lovis 2014:69), it may be that the dramatic post-Algonquin drop in lake levels and the creation of a nascent landscape in the southern Huron basin not only allowed, but encouraged, wider ranging mobility and stronger intergroup relations. Certainly, the low-water stages exposed, for the first time since the colonization of the region, primary chert sources of future importance to Archaic period groups. The somewhat surprising abundance of Bayport chert Thebes bifaces in northwestern Ohio (Bechtel 1988:122, table 1) appears to support this model of enhanced long-distance interaction, as does the Bruce County (infra) Mercer chert St. Charles biface. While Bayport chert had been available to Early Paleoindian groups in the Saginaw region, the post-Algonquin lake levels exposed abundant and massive deposits of this desirable toolstone, some on striking topographic features such as the Charity Island hills in the Saginaw valley. This raw material would be expected to dominate Late Paleoindian-Early Archaic toolkits in use on the Alpena-Amberley Ridge and throughout the southern Huron basin. Indeed, it is represented in Late Paleoindian and Hi-Lo assemblages to the southeast (see Fig. 6.3, Plate 3). Contemporary Alpena-Amberley Ridge components may well have included tools, particularly bifaces, manufactured from exotic central (i.e., Mercer) and northern Ohio (i.e., Delaware or Pipe Creek) cherts, while Onondaga or Collingwood chert bifaces would also be an expected component of contemporary toolkits, albeit in limited quantities. Evidence for post-Hi-Lo Early Archaic utilization of local Kettle Point chert in Ontario is so far limited, despite its presence to the south on the Nobles Pond Thebes component (infra), possibly due to a realignment of macro-band territories and movement, combined with the abundant Bayport sources to the northwest. Finally, there is a possibility of locating Precambrian quartzite tools and/or debitage on Huron basin low-water stage sites; however, evidence for Saugeen chert use at this time is extremely limited and equivocal.

Acknowledgments

The authors wish to thank staff of the following institutions for study access to their collections—Joan Hyslop of Grey Roots, Barbara Ribey and Laura Leonard of the Bruce County Museum, and April Hawkins of the Royal Ontario Museum. Larry Zimmer and Brian Deller kindly shared their personal collections, while valuable supplementary observations were provided by Mark Seeman and Amanda Mullett (Kent State University), Jeb Bowen, and Don Simons.

7 Comparing Global Ungulate Hunting Strategies and Structures

General Patterns and Archaeological Expectations

by Ashley K. Lemke

While drive lanes and other caribou hunting structures are best preserved and best known from the Arctic, hunting structures targeting diverse species of ungulates represent a global phenomenon. This chapter presents a brief summary of ungulate hunting structures across the globe, followed by a more targeted discussion of caribou hunting strategies in North America and Europe. The comparison of these structures from disparate contexts reveals a similar pattern of exploitation strategies that tap into innate characteristics of ungulates and demonstrate a detailed knowledge and use of regional landscapes and local topography. These detailed comparisons provide general archaeological expectations for further research into these unique archaeological sites and have the potential to provide significant details concerning the diversity of ungulate hunting adaptations in the distant past.

Introduction

Hunting strategies and structures for capturing ungulates are found across the globe—commonly in the North American Arctic and interior, but also in southwest Asia and South America. These built stone, wood, and dirt structures target a diverse range of hoofed and herd animals yet they share several general characteristics. And while the specifics of ungulate hunting vary according to local landscapes, the targeted species, and the cultural group, common trends are apparent when the process of ungulate hunting is considered on a worldwide scale (Brink 2013:26). These shared attributes include the targeted exploitation of specific characteristics of ungulate behavior and the placement of hunting structures on the landscape in strategic positions.

Within the category of ungulates, caribou are an important resource not just for ethnographically known Arctic hunters and herders, but as a prey species for many disparate prehistoric groups in Subarctic environments as well. Reindeer were important for food, clothing, and artifacts since the Upper Paleolithic was first referred to as "l'Age du Renne" (Lartet and Christy 1875), and recent research documents reindeer as an important resource earlier in prehistory (e.g., Britton et al. 2011; Niven et al. 2012). Additionally, long-speculated ideas of caribou exploitation in northeast and midwest North America are gaining traction (Simons 1997; O'Shea, Lemke, and Reynolds 2013); these animals were likely an important resource for Paleoindian and Archaic hunter-gatherers in these regions during the Terminal Pleistocene and Early Holocene.

This chapter begins by globally comparing ungulate hunting features; it then examines caribou hunting structures specifically, discusses the characteristics shared across these different strategies, and concludes with the general archaeological expectations that can be drawn from these comparisons. This overview of global ungulate hunting provides archaeological expectations at both the regional and site level, including the relationship between hunting structures and campsites and spatial distribution of artifacts within these structures.

Global Ungulate Hunting

Southwest Asia

In southwest Asia, large, stone built game traps named kites first appear in the Neolithic between Yemen and Armenia (Zeder et al. 2013). These low stone walled structures have a semi-enclosed round or oblong shape with funnel or V-shaped openings, and are used to hunt a range of wild ungulate species, most commonly gazelles (*Gazella* spp.), but also onager (*Equus hemionus*) and oryx (*Oryx leucoryx*) (e.g., Bar-Oz et al. 2011; Betts and Yagodin 2000; Helms and Betts 1987; Kennedy 2011, 2012; Legge and Rowley-Conwy 1987; Nadel et al. 2010; Van Berg et al. 2004; Zeder et al. 2013).

These hunting structures vary in terms of their placement in relation to each other (i.e., one or many kites), their placement on the local topography, and the size and density of their walls. For example, groups of kites or chain kites are interpreted to channel migrating herds of Persian gazelle, and single or pair kites from the Sinai and Negev highlands were most likely used to target smaller numbers of nonmigratory prey, such as other gazelle species, onager, and oryx (Nadel et al. 2013). Moreover, substantial kites with massive walls in hilly areas were most likely targeting larger-bodied ungulates such as onager, in contrast to thinner-walled kites on the flat plains, which most likely targeted gazelles (Nadel et al. 2013).

In accordance with the variable habits of these different ungulates, specifically if they migrate in large herds or not, kites were placed in strategic spots on the landscape, either intersecting migration routes, near common game trails, or adjacent to grazing areas where browsing animals could be taken by surprise and driven into enclosures (Bar-Oz and Nadel 2013; Zeder et al. 2013:115). Desert kites targeting an array of ungulate species demonstrate the adaptability of these methods of capture across ungulate size classes and range of behaviors.

South-Central Andes

In the south-central Andes, elaborate hunting blinds and structures were used to exploit camelids such as vicuñas (*V. vicugna*). Intensive, systematic survey of the Antofalla Valley in Argentina identified five different types of stone structures used in camelid hunting from 9000 BP to modern hunting with rifles. These structures include stone wall trenches, butchering tables, landmarks, shelters, and water hidings (Moreno 2012).

The stone wall trenches are arrow or half-moon-shaped, and are placed on high points on the landscape, usually on the steep slopes overlooking the valley where animals would be drinking and grazing. These structures appear to function as blinds to conceal hunters for observing and hunting the animals, and to protect hunters from the wind and sun. They are often found in clusters or groups, presumably so many hunters could hunt together, since most structures are large enough to conceal only a single hunter. Tables (the local name given to large piles of rocks with flat rocks across the top) were presumably used for butchering camelids after a successful hunt, and provided a place to butcher the animal while protecting and keeping the hide intact. Landmarks are standing upright stones or stacks of stones that may serve to mark hunting territories, or were part of the hunting structures themselves. The nature of these landmarks is very similar in form to *inuksuit* from the North American Arctic, which served a range of functions: to mark the beginning of drive lanes, to form part of a drive lane themselves, and/or to otherwise mark significant spots of the landscape (e.g., meat cache, burial, directions; e.g., Brink 2005). Shelters are small circular or semicircular structures that would usually fit one person, and served as hunting blinds and additional shielded areas on the landscape to protect and hide people from sun, wind, and animals. Lastly, small stone constructions, which are designed to give constant shade, most likely acted as hiding spots for water. Ceramic sherds were often found in these structures and were probably the remains of water vessels (Moreno 2012).

These structures demonstrate a detailed knowledge of animal behavior and the local topography. Many structures acting as hunting blinds were located on the highest points on the landscape in order to offer the best viewshed of the valley and of grazing prey animals. Additionally, these structures seem to be placed near common game trails used by camelids as they moved from higher to lower elevations and back throughout the day (Moreno 2012:113).

Camelids in general and vicuñas in particular are adapted for high altitude and rocky steep slopes, and therefore can quickly escape or outrun hunters that are actively pursuing them. The highly modified hunting landscape developed in the central Andes with a focus on ambush hunting of large groups of animals by small numbers of hunters demonstrates that prehistoric hunters had a detailed knowledge of animal behavior (Moreno 2012).

North America

Central Plains

In the North American central plains, bison (*Bison bison*) hunting that used constructed jump and drive lane structures has a long history; the earliest bison trap, Jake Bluff, dates to 10,838 ± 17 BP and is a late Clovis bison kill (Bement and Carter 2010). Behavioral traits of bison—such as herding in large groups at certain times of the year, and tending to stay together and flee as a herd when threatened—made them a prime target for human hunting using traps and structures. Diverse forms of bison traps include arroyos, corrals, and jumps (Carlson and Bement 2013).

Arroyo walls often functioned similar to drive lanes as bison were driven into dry river channels with steep walls and dead ends. Once the lead bison reached the dead end and tried to turn around, they were blocked by the rest of the stampeding herd (Carlson and Bement 2013). Arroyo traps such as Jake Bluff are the earliest forms of bison hunting structures while elaborate jumps over cliff faces seem to have been developed later.

Bison jumps may be the best known and most illustrative example of people taking advantage of the local topography to complete large-scale hunts. For bison jumps, the herd of animals is actively moved from a grazing area and stampeded over a predetermined cliff or precipice, to fall to their death or to be killed by hunters waiting at the bottom. Only certain points on the landscape can function successfully as jumps so hunters had to take many factors (such as hiding spots for the hunters, milling areas, and the cliff itself) into account to find the perfect spot. Once the location was decided, drive lanes consisting of cairn-marked lines were added to lead the way to the jump. These bison drives can be very prominent on the landscape; one such bison jump, Head-Smashed-In in Alberta, Canada, has over 500 stone cairns (Reeves 1978:154).

These bison hunting features have been the subject of archaeological study for decades (e.g., Agenbroad 1978; Brink 2008; Carlson and Bement 2013; Frison 1970, 2004; Reeves 1978; Reher and Frison 1980). Numerous archaeological investigations and detailed geographic information system (GIS) analysis of drive lanes in the American plains have concluded that prehistoric hunters had a sophisticated knowledge of animal behavior and natural topography, as drive lanes often followed least-cost paths across the landscape, and certain aspects of bison behavior were actively exploited (Carlson 2011).

Great Basin

Over 100 large-scale hunting structures are known in the North American Great Basin, dating from the Early Archaic (approximately 5000–6000 years ago) to the historic era (700–800 years ago). These structures target ungulate species common in the region: most often pronghorn antelope (*Antilocapra americana*), but also bighorn sheep (*Ovis aanadensis*), mule deer (*Odocoileus hemionus*), and elk (*Cervus canadensis*) (Burnett et al. 2008; Hockett et al. 2013).

Most pronghorn traps are elaborate hunting sites with many different kinds of structures functioning together. An example of this is the Whiskey Flat trap complex, which includes a drive lane or drift fence, corrals, and hunting blinds (Wilke 2013). These hunting stations or blinds are small V-shaped, U-shaped, or semicircular single person stone constructions (Wilke 2013).

While bison were driven in the Central Plains, in the Great Basin pronghorn were lured (Brink 2013). Pronghorn have an innate curiosity and tend to run uphill when startled, and the layout of drive lanes such as the Barnett site in Alberta display an exploitation of these behaviors, as these particular drive lanes are settled on an elevated ridge (Brink 2013). Pronghorn were attracted to the drive lanes by many methods that are ethnographically documented, including lying down and raising a hand, kicking feet in the air, or raising and lowering a sort of flag. These methods rely on pronghorns' innate sense of curiosity and lure them slowly into traps. Unlike bison, pronghorn are more skittish and tend to scatter, double back, or even run in circles to escape predators. Great Basin hunters clearly knew these attributes of pronghorn behavior and rather than attempting to stampede them over a cliff or into drive lanes, the animals were tricked and lured close to trap sites. As Steward highlights, these luring methods "would have been less effective with other species" (1941:219).

Caribou Hunting

The record of caribou (*Rangifer* spp.) hunting in the North American Arctic is well known and is covered in detail in this monograph (Chapters 8, 10). Although disparate methods of hunting caribou exist, drive lanes and their associated hunting structures are by far the most common method (Spiess 1979). Caribou hunting features include drive lanes, hunting blinds, *inuksuit*, and caches.

Prehistorically, caribou are thought to be one of the primary prey species of Paleoindian and Early Archaic hunters in the Great Lakes and Northeast (Gramly 1982; Simons 1997). Although caribou remains (as all faunal remains in this region of acidic soils) are found only rarely—at the Holcombe Beach site in Michigan (Cleland 1965), Bull Brook in Massachusetts, Whipple in New Hampshire, and Udora in Ontario (Jackson 1990; Spiess, Wilson, and Bradley 1998; Storck and Spiess 1994)—other lines of evidence including site locations (Gramly 1982, 1988; Jackson 1990, 1997; Robinson et al. 2009; Roosa 1977; Simons 1997), distributions of lithic material (Ellis 2011; Chapter 5), and technological variation (Johnson 1996; Newby et al. 2005; Chapter 6) have been used to support caribou exploitation. Research on the Alpena-Amberley Ridge, a now inundated feature that was dry land around 9000 RCYBP ago, is providing a record of caribou hunting in the Subarctic Great Lakes. To date, numerous caribou hunting structures—ranging from simple, one-person hunting blinds to complex drive and blind features—have been identified (Lemke, O'Shea, and Sonnenburg 2013; O'Shea, Lemke, and Reynolds 2013; Chapter 10).

While hunting structures have not yet been identified in the Paleolithic (but for a possible Mousterian hunting blind at Molodova 1, see Binford 1983; Chernysh 1989; Hoffecker 2002; Klein 1999; Kolen 1999; Stringer and Gamble 1993; Svoboda, Péan, and Wojtal 2005), the archaeological record demonstrates similar exploitation patterns in targeting and intercepting migrating caribou. In Upper Paleolithic sites, hunters appear to have targeted caribou during their migrations and positioned themselves to intercept the animals from strategic positions (Burch 1991; White 1989). Some eastern Gravettian/Pavlovian sites in central Europe, particularly in Hungary, that are located on hilltops and ridges may represent specialized interception sites for migrating reindeer (Dobosi 1991:199; Thacker 1997:92). Moreover, zooarchaeological assemblages in central and western Europe demonstrate that reindeer exploitation during migrations was important for both modern humans and Neanderthals. Reindeer remains in Magdalenian sites in the Paris basin consistently represent autumn hunting (Enloe and David 1997; Enloe 2003). The Mousterian occupation at Chez-Pinaud Jonzac has the remains of reindeer butchered by Neanderthals; these reindeer have isotopic signatures of migrating (Britton et al. 2011; Niven et al. 2012).

Discussion

General Patterns

This brief global summary of ungulate hunting structures illustrates that the placement and nature of hunting features demonstrate both a detailed understanding of animal behavior and an intimate familiarity with the environment.

The form and nature of hunting structures reveal a detailed knowledge of ecology and behavior of targeted species and exploitation of predictable movements and certain aspects of animal behavior (Brink 2008; Nadel et al. 2013; Smith 2013; O'Shea et al. 2013). Ungulates share several characteristics in both anatomy and behavior that make their exploitation similar across the globe. For example, in terms of eyesight, pronghorn, like bison and caribou (Brink and Rollans 1989; Brink 2005), are particularly sensitive to moving objects (O'Gara 2004:111). Thus, drive lanes are usually elaborated with flags, brush, or other objects that will move in the wind—both to attract animals and to make them sufficiently nervous so that they stay within drive lane boundaries. Many ungulates, including caribou, bison, horse, and pronghorn, will often run alongside barriers, go around them, or try to go under them rather than cross or jump over them (McCabe et al. 2004:14). Therefore, drive lanes did not need to be substantial, and simple rock lines just 20–50 cm high were substantial enough to channel ungulate movements (Brink 2013). Additionally, these animals are relatively social, and their herding together in groups during certain times of the year makes them susceptible to large-scale hunting by humans. This herding behavior also generally corresponds to seasonal variation in animal condition; it is during autumn that most of these prey species—such as caribou, bison, and pronghorn—are at their peak condition (in terms of body weight, fat context, skin and sinew condition, etc.), and many zooarchaeological assemblages of these species are indicative of autumn hunting (e.g., Blehr 1990:320; Dobosi 1991:199; Enloe 2003:24; Enloe and David 1997; Frison 2004:125; McCabe et al. 2004:15; Reimers and Ringberg 1983; Stefansson 1951:337).

To exploit these behavioral attributes, ungulate hunting structures from across the globe share many common elements, including standing or stacked stones such as *inuksuit*, cairns (Wilke 2013), or landmarks (Moreno 2012); long linear structures collectively referred to as drive lanes; and hunting blinds. On a broader scale, the placement of structures on the landscape is not random, but demonstrates an intimate familiarity with the local environment, often taking advantage of the natural and existing topography either to channel animals to kill zones or to intercept animals, as structures are often situated at natural bottlenecks, along migration routes or common game trails, near grazing areas, or on elevated ridges (Bar-Oz and Nadel 2013; Nadel et al. 2013; Moreno 2012; Smith 2013; Chapters 4, 10). These constructions tap into the innate curiosity of ungulates, their tendency to follow lines, and their herding behavior—to both attract and trap groups of animals at strategic points on the landscape for a successful hunt, often when animals are in their peak condition.

Archaeological Expectations

From comparing ungulate hunting structures across the globe, some general archaeological expectations can be developed at both the regional and site level.

Regional Expectations

It is often the case that while blinds and other features may occur individually, they are often found in groups; for example, desert kites often have four or more hunting blinds associated with them (Kempe and Al-Malabeh 2013), and the Rollins Pass game drive complex in Colorado has numerous drive lanes and blinds (LaBelle and Pelton 2013). Considering a larger region, one can therefore expect to find many different types, but also different configurations, of hunting features—including individual blinds, several hunting blinds together, groups of hunting blinds and other structures such as drive lanes, standing stones, and/or elaborate complexes incorporating several of these different types. When surveys have been done (e.g., Moreno 2012) or in areas where there is a long history of research concerning hunting structures, such as the North American plains (e.g., Agenbroad 1978; Brink 2008; Carlson and Bement 2013; Frison 1968, 1970, 1971, 2004; Frison, Wilson, and Wilson 1976; Reeves 1978; Reher and Frison 1980; Todd et al. 2001), the larger regional picture is one of a complex, modified hunting landscape with a diverse set of features, usually grouped and functioning together, which were most likely reused, refurbished, elaborated, and modified over vast stretches of time (Smith 2013).

In addition to large-scale configurations of hunting structures, other regional expectations include other site types and their spatial distribution in relation to hunting features. When known, camps and habitation sites are usually some distance away from the hunting structures and kill sites since camp activities, smells, and noises would likely disturb the animals and thwart any efforts to hunt them (Bar-Oz and Nadel 2013; Brink 2005:15; Smith 2013; Stewart et al. 2000; Stewart, Keith, and Scottie 2004; Zeder et al. 2013:119). Additionally, in some regions, including southeast Asia and the Great Basin, rock art is found near or within hunting structures, and often depicts hunting of specific ungulates (Eisenberg-Degen 2010; Harding 1953; Hershkovitz et al. 1987; Hockett et al. 2013; Lemaître and Van Berg 2008). These brief examples demonstrate that expanding research at a more regional level is appropriate to gain the best understanding of hunting structures and the overall modified landscape in any given area.

Site-Level Expectations

In cases where artifacts have been recovered, lithic assemblages tend to be limited to projectile points and fragments, bifacial knives and other tools, and resharpening flakes (e.g., Carlson and Bement 2013). The spatial distribution of lithic artifacts, particularly weaponry, is clustered around hunting blinds. For bow and arrow hunting, the ethnographically documented range is 11–20 meters (Blehr 1990; Dalton 2011), and at the Olsen game drive in Colorado, most projectile points and fragments were found at the intersection of numerous drive lanes, within the shooting range of several hunting blinds (LaBelle and Pelton 2013: fig. 15). While the ranges for different weapons would be variable (with use of atlatls, for example), this model of spatial distribution around hunting blinds is nonetheless a critical first step to understanding spatial patterning.

Faunal assemblages vary considerably: from the large bone beds known from bison kills in the North American plains to a complete absence of faunal remains such as some kites in southwest Asia. In general, larger bodied animals, which are killed in large numbers, tend to be butchered at the site—resulting in the large bone beds. Many bison jump and kill sites, such as Head-Smashed-In, Gull Lake, and Calderwood, have distinct layers of burned bones. These burned bone beds are inferred to be the result of cleaning out the drive lanes and removing the stench of butchered bison so that the drives could be reused (Brink 2008:166). Contrary to this pattern of butchering large-bodied animals at or near the hunting structures, smaller ungulates such as gazelles and pronghorn are usually removed whole from the kill sites and butchered at other locations. It is ethnographically documented that in many communal pronghorn kills, the animals were killed with clubs and were taken whole from the kill site to the campsite (Lubinski 1999). This pattern of removing whole carcasses from the hunting structures is also demonstrated archaeologically, as some habitation sites in southwest Asia have large faunal assemblages of gazelle, which seem to have been moved from desert kites to be butchered and distributed in the camp (Zeder et al. 2013). The lack of faunal remains from many caribou drives is interpreted as the carcasses having been moved to and butchered at nearby camps (Brink 2005:14), in addition to having been stored in frozen caches (Binford 1978b; Chapter 8).

While burning episodes of large bison bone beds leave a clear archaeological signature, both the intense cleaning of hunting structures and the potential for removing smaller animals whole from the hunting features would leave little in the way of cultural materials. Even in cases of large complex hunting structures, only five out of twelve excavated blinds yielded artifacts (LaBelle and Pelton 2013:50), and it is not uncommon for caribou drives to be devoid of artifacts entirely (Brink 2005:15). Furthermore, detailed ethnoarchaeological studies of hunting blinds, such as those by Binford, reveal that food and weaponry residues may not always become part of the archaeological record (Binford 1978a:347). Thus, overall artifact densities can be expected to be low. It is important to remember that artifact densities are a function of faunal preservation and site formation processes, as well as being highly contingent on a number of factors of the kill itself, including the number of people available to butcher, transport, and eat the meat; the number of animals killed; the size of the animals; the availability of storage; transport options; and distance to camp (Binford 1978b). Due to this range of factors, faunal expectations are best made for particular environments where each of these factors can be taken into account.

Despite the lack of cultural materials that may characterize hunting features, the formal attributes of the structures themselves can be used to infer a range of other variables. Because the nature of the features and their placement on the landscape are so contingent on certain aspects of ungulate behavior, their formal attributes can be used to infer other information when direct evidence is lacking. For example, even in the absence of faunal remains or other archaeological materials, formal attributes such as the size, shape, and orientation of hunting structures have been used to surmise the targeted prey species (Brink 2013; Nadel et al. 2013), the types of weaponry (Freisen 2013), the season of use of hunting structures (Morrison 1981:182), and the number of animals hunted.

Comparisons of the formal attributes of hunting structures with faunal remains to those without have also been informative. For instance, the Barnett site in Alberta had no surface faunal or lithic artifacts and no excavations have been done; however, the structures are very similar in form to the drive lanes at the Laidlaw site, a site also on the Canadian plains that had pronghorn faunal remains. Due to the similarity in the drive lanes and their placement on the landscape, Barnett is inferred to be a pronghorn hunting locality (Brink 2013). Similarly, in southwest Asia, although many kites are lacking faunal material, archaeologists have been able to hypothesize the different types of ungulates targeted by these hunting structures by combining what is known about kites with faunal remains, the formal attributes of the structures themselves, and animal behavior. It is hypothesized that different types of structures were targeting different species of ungulates available in the region and that large, more substantial drives on the sloped areas were targeting larger game such as onager, while less substantial drives on the plains were targeting gazelle (Nadel et al. 2013).

Also, examining the formal attributes of hunting structures from the Canadian Arctic, Friesen argues that wide gaps, shallow hunting blinds, and diffuse discontinuous drive lanes were indicative of bow and arrow hunting, where the shooting range is longer and animals need only be channeled, not actively panicked (2013). This is contrasted with other types of hunting structures with robust and continuous drive lanes with narrow gaps between them, and substantial and continuously walled hunting blinds necessary for lance hunting, which requires the animals to be panicked in order for the lance-armed hunters to be in close enough proximity (Friesen 2013).

In addition to inferring prey species and the types of weapons used, the formal attributes of hunting structures have been used to deduce seasonality. Since the general orientation of migrations is often known, the orientation of drive lanes can be used to determine the season of use with great accuracy (Morrison 1981:182).

Besides the formal attributes, the grouping and diversity of different structures can be used to infer the number of animals hunted. The complexity of the hunting structures (measured by the number of different types of structures, and by how elaborate or substantial individual elements are) may also be related by the number of animals being targeted. For example, it has been hypothesized that the elaborate game drive complex at Rollins Pass, Colorado, targeted smaller groups of alpine game such as bighorn sheep since these animals likely did not aggregate in very large numbers, and the gaps in the drive lanes could allow only for small numbers of animals to pass through at any given time (LaBelle and Pelton 2013:59). Narrow gaps may equate to a panicked state of animals so they passed closer to hunters (Friesen 2013). And, similar to Spiess' (1979:118) suggestion that bigger and more complex drives are needed when caribou are few or dispersed, the complexity and narrow gaps of the Rollins Pass region are most likely intended to ensure a successful hunt of these inherently smaller groups of animals in an alpine environment. Conversely, simpler structures or individual blinds may be sufficient when larger groups of animals are being hunted, such as during caribou migrations. These examples illustrate that while no simple correlation (such as: complex hunting features equal large groups of animals) exists, the formal attributes of the structures themselves can be used to infer the number of animals able to move through and be targeted by the hunting features.

These archaeological expectations are only general, and more specific expectations should be generated for particular regions or where the particular prey species is known since although these hunting strategies share many similarities, there are species and cultural specific differences. All these expectations could improve by a systematic survey of the ethnographic and ethnohistoric literature where accounts of hunting structures and their operation are given in great detail.

Conclusion

From this survey of ungulate hunting strategies and structures a few points are made clear, specifically concerning the diversity, complexity, and deep time depth in patterns of ungulate hunting using structures.

While the geographic and temporal distribution of these sites and their shared characteristics underscore a common solution to ungulate capture and hunting and serve as an example of convergent evolution (Smith 2013), diversity in these methods is also apparent. While clear differences exist in the local environments and species, each case demonstrates the sophisticated knowledge and use of local landscapes and a detailed understanding of animal behavior. However, the diversity that is perhaps most interesting concerns the assumptions we make as archaeologists about the numbers of people and animals involved in these hunting structures.

Certainly, the creation, use, and maintenance of many hunting complexes often involved sizable groups of people for large-scale hunting of ungulates. Prehistorically, the structures may have served as the locus for family and band aggregations during cyclical nucleation (Carlson and Bement 2013; Smith 2013; Wilke 2013), and a substantial amount of labor was needed to build large constructions and carry out complex chores during the drive (Brink 2008; Frison 2004; Kornfeld, Frison, and Larson 2010; Nadel et al. 2013). It is also ethnographically documented that trapping ungulates such as pronghorn was as much a ceremonial activity as it was a subsistence venture (Sundstrom 2000); for Great Basin peoples, it was often the largest social gathering of the year (Liljeblad 1986:645).

However, while these aggregations of people and surpluses of animals are important social and economic phenomena that should not be ignored, we cannot make the assumption that all game drives, corrals, or other hunting structures mean that large groups of people are taking large numbers of animals. Targeting these animals with the aid of built drive lanes or other hunting structures is not always a large-scale event. Given the geographic spread of these structures, not all environments at all times supported large populations of ungulates. The low-density population of bighorn sheep in alpine environments is just one example. Also, hunting structures can be constructed, maintained, and operated by small numbers of people. Some drive features or corrals can be quickly constructed and can result in limited numbers of animals (Spiess 1979:119). The diversity that is apparent here—from small groups of hunter-gatherers in the Rocky Mountains targeting small groups of bighorn sheep to the large-scale process of pastoralists targeting huge numbers of gazelle—is important for future investigations of ungulate hunting strategies.

Along with the diversity apparent in hunting structures in terms of the number of people or animals involved, the complexity of hunting features, alignments, and concentrations is clear from this global overview. When considered at a regional level, the large number of hunting structures and elaborate complexes reveal multipurpose and multiseasonal hunting landscapes. While individual blinds or drive lanes may have been used by small numbers of hunters during one season, the same groups of hunters and their families may have returned to those structures or to others close by at another time of year. Hunting landscapes need to be examined with an eye for diversity, complexity, and use over time at different scales—from seasonal, annual, and generational use to much longer term maintenance and reuse of hunting structures and their change over time.

Indeed, there is a deep time depth in patterns of ungulate hunting using structures. Hunting features and modified hunting landscapes serve as examples of ecological inheritance, as they are modified and elaborated over time by subsequent generations, and knowledge about their use and manufacture is passed down (Smith 2013). Specific regions, such as the long record of bison hunting in the Central Plains, show great diachronic change as different methods and structures came into, and perhaps fell out of, use (Carlson and Bement 2013). It is the animal behavior that remains constant in these scenarios and reveals why humans have such a long history of predating on ungulates. The aid of hunting structures is just a more archaeologically visible method of exploiting these unique animals that group together in peak times of the year, a trait that can be exploited successfully and fairly regularly with the correct understanding of this behavior. Hints of these patterns even early in prehistory are becoming apparent. Although complex drives or other built hunting structures have not yet been systematically identified in the Paleolithic, faunal assemblages indicate that both humans and Neanderthals were targeting ungulates, specifically caribou, during migrations and at peak times of the year (e.g., Britton et al. 2011; Enloe and David 1997; Niven et al. 2012). Further research may reveal consistency in these patterns over vast areas of time and space.

Understanding the entire range of variability and complexity in ungulate hunting strategies—specifically those that involve aspects of a built environment such as drive lanes, corrals, and blinds—will help to fill in the gaps of these types of adaptations in the distant past and help to document the vast range of variability among prehistoric economies.

8 | Searching for Archaeological Evidence on the Alpena-Amberley Ridge—Is the Arctic Record Informative?

by Andrew M. Stewart

The surface record of cultural boulder features constructed by Inland Inuit caribou hunting families who lived year-round on the Arctic tundra west of Hudson Bay for much of the nineteenth and twentieth centuries provides guidance in the search for archaeological features on the now-submerged Alpena-Amberley Ridge, where caribou likely contributed to the subsistence of hunting societies that occupied this region during the early Holocene. The form, scale and prominence of these features in the archaeological record of this part of the Canadian tundra—where the most common rock forms are standing stones, stone rings, boulder clusters/clearings, cobble/boulder field depressions, and continuous stone rings or arcs—suggest patterns that might be useful in focusing attention away from natural and onto cultural distributions of rocks on the ridge, on the bed of Lake Huron.

Introduction

What might we look for in the way of cultural remains in an open or sparsely vegetated landscape that was occupied by hunter-gatherers for two to three millennia, then abandoned as rising water levels forced people to move to higher ground? What might remain for us to see on the now inundated ground that is not buried in lake sediment? Recent identification of stone constructions—specifically a game drive and associated hunting blinds—on the Alpena-Amberley Ridge (AAR; O'Shea and Meadows 2009; O'Shea, Lemke, and Reynolds 2013; O'Shea et al. 2014) suggests that a range of cultural features constructed with cobbles and boulders may occur there. These features may be associated with caribou hunting as well as with land use and settlement generally along the ridge.

Although specific ethnographic analogies with recent hunter-gatherers are usually thought limiting rather than helpful (Levine 1997; Wobst 2011), it might still be worth considering the range of stone constructions occurring in an "analogous" circumstance—one in which mobile hunter-gatherers are living in an open landscape (e.g., prairie or tundra) where rocks must substitute for wood in an environment where trees are small, infrequent or remote, and costly to access (Fig. 8.1). One such circumstance where I am familiar with the archaeological record is found on tundra west of Hudson Bay, in the area occupied by the Caribou or Inland Inuit since about 1800 (Burch 1986; Burch and Csonka 1999; Mannik 1998). Here, stone constructions relating to year-round land use (e.g., residence, caribou hunting, trapping, fishing, commemoration) are both widespread and prominent in this treeless landscape. They occur in greater density at locations such as caribou water crossings that were frequently used.

A review of these forms might be helpful in broadening the search for archaeological features on the Huron lakebed and being able to recognize a diverse array of forms there. Comparison with known forms from the Inland Inuit landscape might help in the discrimination between cultural constructions and natural rock distributions—the result of sediment transport by water or ice. In other words, they might be useful in defining templates for search and quick identification of at least some cultural features.

Figure 8.1. Forest-tundra transition environment along the Clarke River in Canada's Northwest Territories (late June, 2003).

This does not rule out the existence of, and need to identify, other features of unique construction and purpose that may be associated with this time and place (Wobst 2011).

The logistics of working underwater make it desirable, at least in the early stages, to tune the search, perhaps, to coarse patterns in the distribution of rocks that are easily recognized as cultural, rather than to the more fine-scale evidence of portable artifacts (which are more easily overlooked because of their small size or because they are buried by lake sediment). The material cultural landscape of recent northern hunter-gatherers is a rich "comparative collection" that might aid in this coarse-grained search.

Basis for Interregional Comparison

Comparison of the archaeological landscape of the AAR and the Inland Inuit rests on two points of similarity: a relatively open landscape (Fig. 8.1), and the possibility that caribou may have migrated along the AAR and were intercepted en route.

Vegetation succession on the mainland on either side of Lake Huron during the early Holocene, including the period when Lake Stanley and the AAR existed (Fig. 8.2*A*), occurred at a time of persistent dry conditions in the Great Lakes region (McCarthy and McAndrews 2012; Shuman, Webb, et al. 2002). Boreal forest in Michigan (to the west) and mixed forest in southwestern Ontario (to the east) at about 8000 BP may have been somewhat open under these dry conditions, when boreal parkland dominated an area to the northeast of the Huron basin (McCarthy and McAndrews 2012). Conditions on the AAR itself, with mostly bedrock and boulder substrate (limestone and dolomite), thinly mantled with till, would have been more open still.

Faunal remains, site distributions, and lithic technology have been used to characterize Early Paleoindian lifeways in the Northeast and Great Lakes region as caribou-reliant, like those of some recent northern North American hunter-gatherers of the Arctic and Subarctic: the Caribou Inuit of interior Nunavut west of Hudson Bay; the Northern Athabascan Dene along the treeline west of Hudson Bay to the Mackenzie delta; and the Innu of Labrador and northern Quebec (Fig. 8.3). Faunal evidence from Paleoindian sites, as well as a consideration of local topographic site contexts, supports an argument for major reliance on caribou (Cleland 1965; Jackson 1997; Simons 1997; Storck 2004; Storck

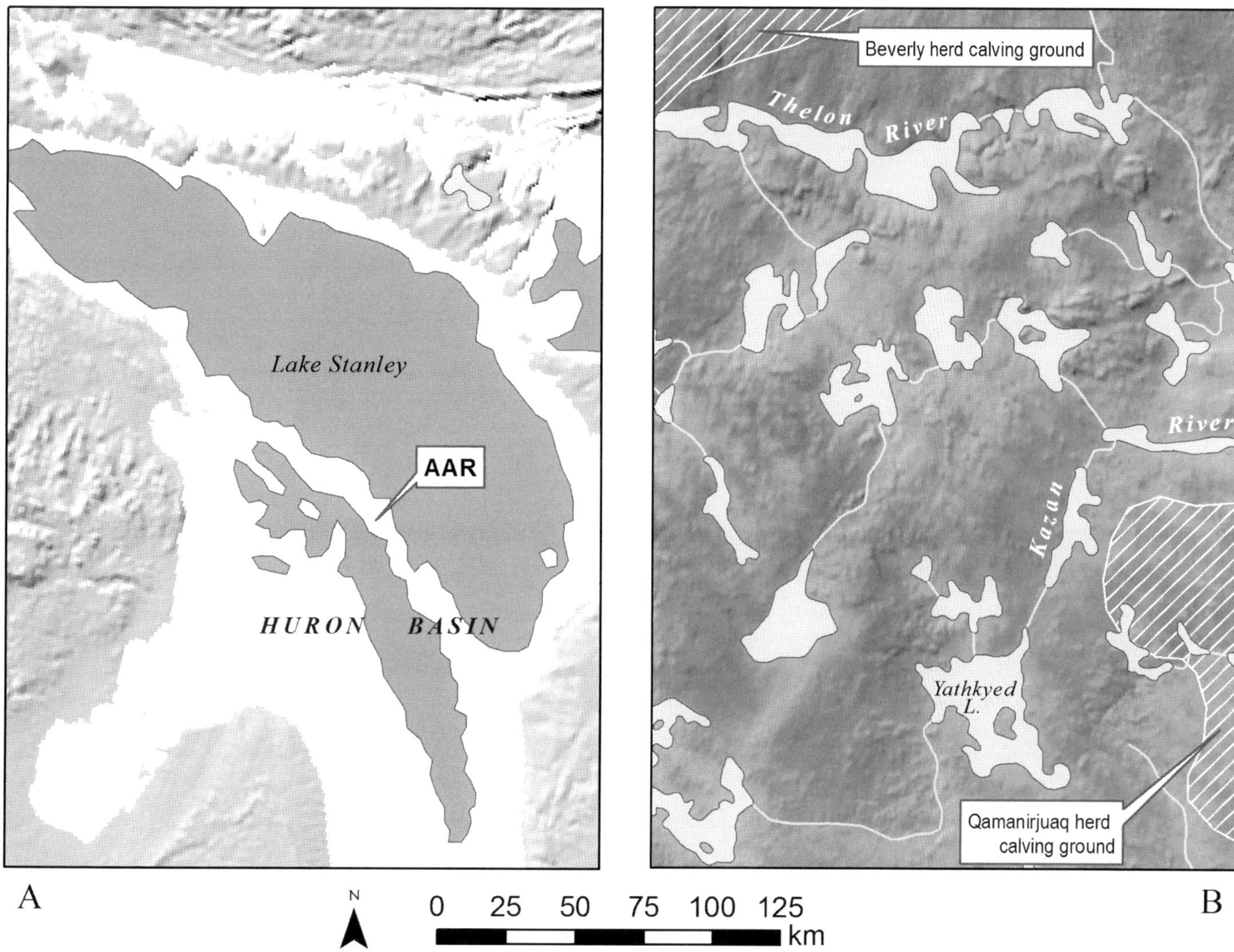

Figure 8.2. The Alpena-Amberley Ridge in the Huron basin and part of the barrenground caribou range west of Hudson Bay shown at the same scale. *A*, the AAR at the time of late Lake Stanley about 7900 rcyrs BP (after Lewis, King, et al. 2008); *B*, part of the spring and summer range of the Beverly and Qamanirjuaq herds, with hatched areas indicating calving grounds. See Figure 8.4 for location of this map within the larger annual caribou range. (Sources: Lewis, King, et al. 2008; Beverly and Qamanirjuaq Caribou Management Board n.d.)

and Spiess 1994), but not necessarily a near-exclusive, specialized exploitation of this species. Its use within a more generalized, broad spectrum of resources is more likely, particularly for the Late Paleoindian period (Kuehn 2007).

The persistence of Hi-Lo and Agate Basin projectile points in this region after the Younger Dryas suggests that Paleoindian subsistence practices continued into the earliest Holocene (Ellis, Carr, and Loebel 2011). These practices may have included hunting migratory or woodland caribou as part of a broad spectrum of resources (Kuehn 2007; Lovis 2009:749). The evidence from the Holcombe site suggests the persistence of caribou, at least as one element of the subsistence base of Late Pleistocene/early Holocene peoples in the Great Lakes (Cleland 1965). During the Early Archaic in the western Great Lakes region, there is some support for extensive, long-distance mobility and the continuation of a Late Paleoindian pattern of extensive movement across large areas (Ellis et al. 1998:162; Lovis 2009). Some sites are thought to have been exploited for resources during only a limited period and then abandoned—for example, lithic resources at the Bass site in northern Wisconsin (Pleger and Stoltman 2009:702).

The use of the AAR may be considered in the context of the possibility of episodic or repeated long-distance mobility by both

Figure 8.3. Peter Avalak from Cambridge Bay butchering a caribou at Bathurst Lake, August 2004.

animals and people along its length between land masses to the northwest (Michigan) and southeast (Ontario), respectively, at either end. Locations along the AAR may have acquired significance as large game were intercepted, killed, and stored, similar to "fixed points" associated with meat caches along northern coastlines (Stopp 2002).

The scale of mobility implied by the length of the ridge is consistent with the scale of chert exploitation in the Late Paleo/Early Archaic periods (Ellis, Carr, and Loebel 2011). It is also consistent with the scale of mobility of Chipewyan hunting families that traveled, at least occasionally, far out onto the barrenlands to hunt caribou during the period of their post-calving, summer aggregation from the main settlement area along the forest-tundra ecotone during the early contact period (Heard 1997; Smith 1978; Smith and Burch 1979; Figs. 8.2, 8.4). The width of the AAR (averaging 16 km) would have permitted occasional or seasonal camps (and not just isolated hunting facilities, such as blinds, or caches) to be located far out on this connecting landform, serving as base or logistic camps for families or individual hunters. Although the landform persisted for roughly two millennia, perhaps favoring consistent, patterned use, Mattawa flood events during this period (Lewis and Anderson 1989, 2012) might have destabilized any long-term subsistence and settlement patterns.

The Inland Inuit

The area west of Hudson Bay, north of the treeline, preserves a material and historical record of settlement and land use by the Inland (Caribou) Inuit. This is one of many areas in the Arctic and Subarctic for which archaeology has been documented in tandem with oral history supplemented, in places, by a detailed historic record (e.g., Andrews and Zoe 1997; Friesen 2002; Keith and Friesen n.d.; Janes 1983; Lyons et al. 2010; Stopp 1994, 2002). Consequently, we have some idea not only about facilities built of rock that are found in the landscape but also about the circumstances of their construction and use.

Several Inland Inuit societies inhabited the tundra landscape between Hudson Bay and approximately the Dubawnt River to the west, and between the northern edge of the boreal forest and the Thelon River and Chesterfield Inlet to the north (Fig. 8.4) during the nineteenth and early twentieth centuries (Burch 1986). This region was occupied year-round. Individuals and families moved often—by foot, by sled aided by dogs (in winter and early spring), and by *qajaq* (kayak) along rivers and lakes (in summer)—among various hunting-fishing camps. This settlement pattern was part of a subsistence hunting, trapping, and trading way of life that gave way, during the 1960s and 1970s,

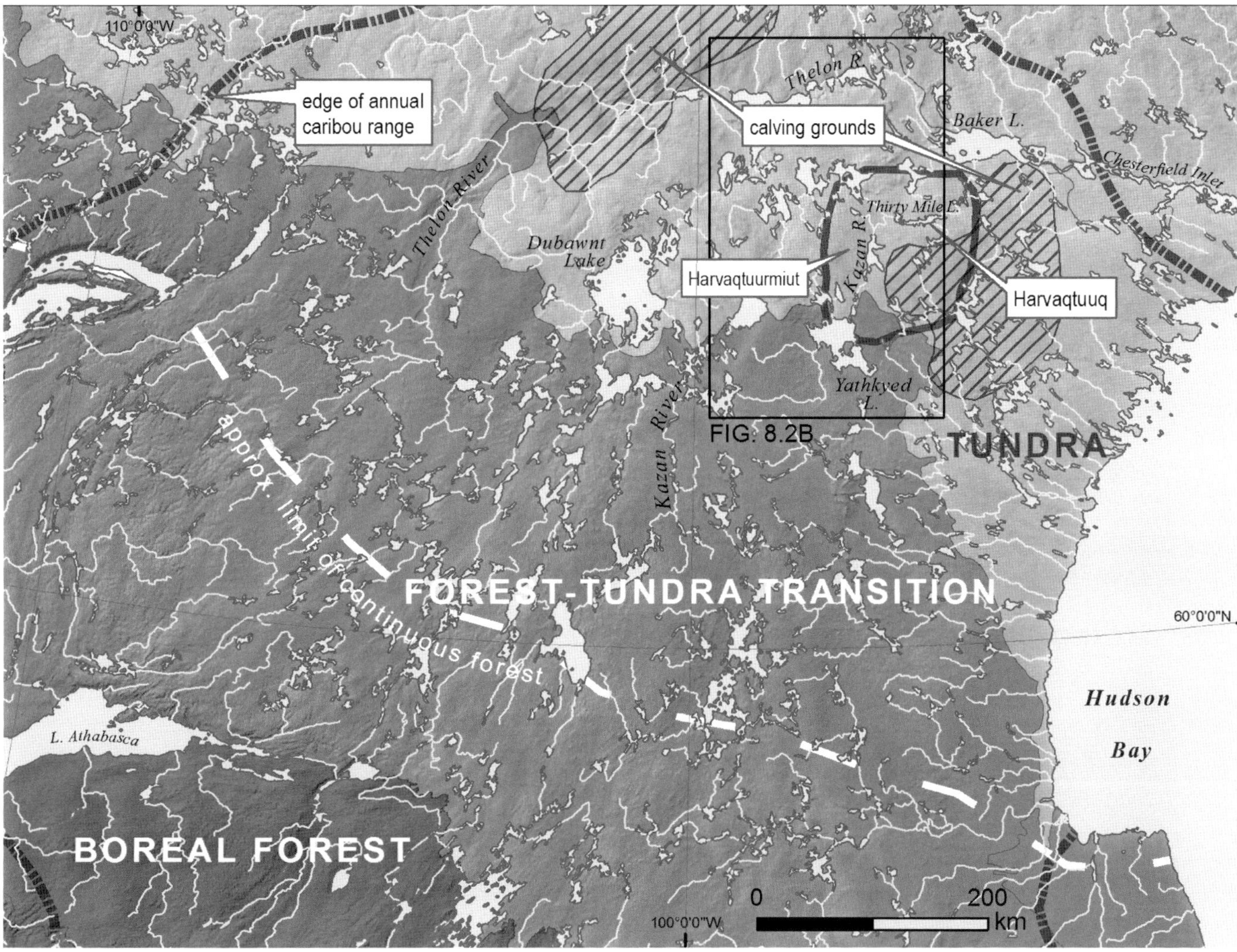

Figure 8.4. Area of most of the range of the combined Beverly and Qamanirjuaq caribou herds (based on government surveys, 1940–1995) and land use by Inland Inuit and Caribou Eater Chipewyan, in context of generalized vegetation zones and treeline. Approximate area of land use by Harvaqtuurmiut, circa 1890, is shown in the vicinity of the lower Kazan River. (Sources: Beverly and Qamanirjuaq Caribou Management Board n.d.; National Atlas of Canada; Burch 1986.)

to settlement in government-built hamlets and a wage economy supplemented by hunting and fishing (Arima 1984; Burch 1986; Damas 1988; Mannik 1998; Rasmussen 1930; Tulurialik and Pelly 1986; Vallee, Smith, and Cooper 1984).

Before the 1960s, the Harvaqtuurmiut, one of the Inland Inuit societies, lived mainly along the lower Kazan River (Fig. 8.4) where caribou hunting was pursued, almost exclusively, supplemented by fishing and trapping. Hunting was particularly focused, spatially, during spring, summer, and fall, when a series of camps were occupied along the Kazan River with the purpose of intercepting caribou during migratory and post-calving (summer) herd movement (Gates 1989). The summer and fall camps were located at or near river water crossings. Thus, camps came to be reoccupied, if not annually, then regularly, for generations (Mannik 1998). Stone facilities such as tent rings, caches, caribou waiting places, and hunting blinds were built and often reused, maintained, or robbed for rebuilding nearby.

Much of the archaeological evidence of camps is visible today on the surface. The landscape, which was deglaciated only between 7000 and 8000 years ago (Dyke and Prest 1987), is bedrock covered with only a thin veneer of till (Aylsworth, Cunningham, and Shilts 1989). Vegetation consists of Low Arctic plant communities dominated by dwarf shrubs, grasses, mosses, and lichen (Scott 1995:45–51).

Some of this archaeological record on the lower Kazan River—known as the Harvaqtuuq—was recorded in the 1990s (Stewart et al. 2000; Friesen and Stewart 2004, 2013; Stewart, Keith, and Scottie 2004). Understanding of the record was furthered by oral history with Harvaqtuurmiut elders, also recorded during the 1990s in Baker Lake and at some of the former camps, now archaeological sites, on the Harvaqtuuq (Harvaqtuurmiut Elders et al. 1994; Keith 2004; Mannik 1998).

Cultural features recorded on the ground surface during the Harvaqtuuq surveys included rock structures as well as concentrations of artifacts and faunal material (usually caribou bone exhibiting signs of cultural processing). Rock structures included tent rings, boulder caches, and the distinctive standing stones (*inuksuit*; sing. *inuksuk*) that are so visible in this open tundra landscape, as well as many other kinds of features (Stewart et al. 2000).

Archaeological work in the Harvaqtuuq was directed primarily toward recording the locations of features as well as naming and interpreting their use-history with the help of elders. For this discussion, however, I step back from interpretation in order to describe and generalize about the outward forms—the physical appearance of features and what distinguishes them from their setting in the tundra landscape. What is the range of forms and what are the most common forms encountered? How are they associated with the specific background setting?

Lower Kazan River Boulder Features

The most common forms encountered during the Harvaqtuuq surveys, in order of frequency (with percentages; $n = 1554$), are described below. (Scatters and isolated artifacts and bones, which account for nearly 9 percent of the total number of features, are excluded here.)

Standing Stone (20 percent; Fig. 8.5A, B)

Most common of all cultural features recorded in the Harvaqtuuq were standing stones ($n = 316$). These were markers put up across the Arctic for many reasons (Bennett and Rowley 2004:255–61), some related to caribou hunting in the context of drift or drive systems (Arima 1987:59; Rasmussen 1930:39; Friesen 2013). Other standing stones served to mark the location of caches, fishing locations, and other resources (Jenness 1922:148; Tataniq in Mannik 1998:220, 231), while still others were more idiosyncratic and of unknown significance. They range in size from single cobbles (less than 25 cm in diameter) to upright boulders measuring more than 2 m in length. They also include structures of two or more boulders, but single rocks are most common. They are usually distinguished by color or context. White quartzite rocks can be placed on darker bedrock, for example, and/or on top of and at the leading edge of a large, naturally emplaced boulder (an erratic or bedrock block). Stones that are part of a larger drive system may be quite small and unobtrusive, visible as silhouettes only from lower elevations by caribou ascending slopes (e.g., Friesen 2013:16).

Discontinuous Rock Ring (20 percent; Fig. 8.6A, B)

A circular alignment of rocks (boulders or cobbles) on the ground surface in which rocks are discontinuous (spaced apart). These are mostly tent rings. Smaller rings sometimes represent features for drying caribou hides (rocks are used for securing hides to the ground), and for equipment caches (rocks are used for securing hides or canvas coverings over sleds and other large items that are used only seasonally). Caches made for equipment or dried meat that was being stored during the warm season when it was subject to mold or rot were often made on gravel substrate, which provided drainage (Bennett and Rowley 2004:252).

Boulder Cluster/Clearing (16 percent; Fig. 8.7A, B)

A concentration of boulders or cobbles (or both) on the ground, sometimes heaped, rising into a low cairn, sometimes next to, or partly surrounding, an area on the ground cleared of rocks, which is usually less than 1 m across. Many of these features represent field caches for caribou—whole carcasses or parts thereof in a relatively unprocessed state (Friesen and Stewart 2013). Where clearings are observed, these features may represent caches that have been opened for removal of caribou. They are usually found near the site of a kill (Peryouar in Mannik 1998:167). Some represent graves or animal bone repositories, relating to cultural proscriptions for bone disposal (Aasivaaryuk in Harvaqtuurmiut Elders et al. 1994:132; Rasmussen 1930:50; Stewart and Friesen 1998). Other clusters or piles of rock represent collapsed fox traps. Where clearings are observed, adjacent concentrations of boulders tend to be distributed haphazardly.

Hearth (9 percent; Fig. 8.8A, B)

This form is culturally specific to Inuit. The *kiklu* (Inuktitut for "hearth") is a small (20 to 40 cm^2) enclosure of three long boulders placed on the ground. They include two boulders that are parallel (placed 20 to 40 cm apart) and the third one placed across one end. The hearth end of the fireplace is open.

Walled Ring or Arc (5 percent; Fig. 8.9A, B)

A continuous boulder ring, at least part of which is coursed, that forms a low wall, or an arc of coursed rocks. In both cases, some of the boulders around the base of the wall may be set on narrow edge. This type of feature may make use of (or incorporate) a large, naturally emplaced boulder (e.g., an erratic, or the vertical face of a bedrock outcrop). A section of the wall is usually more built up. Large, complete rings likely represent locations for heavy tents or *qarmat* (walled dwelling with hide or canvas roof) occupied during the early spring or late fall season (Rasmussen 1930:30). Some may be

Figure 8.5. Standing stones (*inuksuit*). *A*, white quartzite cobble placed on dark lichen-encrusted bedrock contrasts strongly against its background (length of scale is 15 cm); *B*, rock slab (*foreground left*) placed on edge on bedrock overlooking a swale (*right, receding into background*), probably to influence caribou movement along this lower ground.

Figure 8.6. Discontinuous rock rings. *A*, Roy Avaala of Baker Lake crouched on the far side of a light tent ring, which is positioned on an outcropping of bedrock and a shallow gravel substrate, with other tent rings in background; *B*, insubstantial ring of small cobbles where caribou hides were probably dried (scale length in this and following figures is 2.5 m).

Figure 8.7. Boulder cluster/clearings. *A*, opened cache on a gravel substrate, for meat or equipment; *B*, grave or cache (*foreground*) with standing stone *inuksuit* in background.

Figure 8.8. Inuit hearths—variations on a three-sided enclosure. *A*, two upright slabs extending out from a bedrock scarp; *B*, boulders arranged to form a square with three sides (length of scale section is 50 cm).

Figure 8.9. Walled ring or arc features. *A*, Roy Avaala sitting behind a hunting blind that faces onto caribou trails (*background*); *B*, walled dwelling (*qarmaq*), with walls of coursed boulders, consisting of two joined "rooms," one of which may be a cache (*left foreground*). Total length is 3 m. Behind the *qarmat* (*middle background*) is a single-coursed, continuous boulder ring.

caches or waiting places (game lookouts). Arcs may represent short-term shelters, sleeping places (Bennett and Rowley 2004:227), or waiting places (game lookouts) where convex faces are oriented toward game trails.

Boulder Field Depression (5 percent; Fig. 8.10A, B)

An excavated area (usually circular) in a natural cobble or boulder field substrate, sometimes surrounded by a ring of the boulders that were excavated from the center. They may represent caches that have been opened (see boulder cluster/clearing). Sometimes these features are more substantial and obvious when the pit sides are formed from, and defined by, upright slabs set on edge. These more substantial forms may represent caches, particularly for dried meat, graves, or *qajaq* storage areas (Tunnuq in Mannik 1998:224–25).

Continuous Rock Ring (4 percent; Fig. 8.11A, B, Plate 4)

A continuous ring of a single course of rock or partial rings (arcs). Larger examples are likely to be heavy tent rings (for early spring and late fall use). Smaller examples tend to represent graves, equipment caches, sleeping shelters, hunting blinds, and places to wait for game. They may be circular, oval, or rectangular in outline.

Twinned Boulder Lines (4 percent; Fig. 8.12A, B, Plate 4)

Closely set parallel lines or linear arrangements of rocks are sometimes associated with *qajaq* storage and construction (Arima 1987:33). A set of four individual long boulders set upright on the ground in two pairs, the pairs being about 2 m apart, are *qajaq* stands. Boulders of each pair lean away from each other, forming a cradle for the ends of a *qajaq*. These may be culturally specific structures, but stands and storage places for wood-framed, hide- or bark-covered boats might also be present around shorelines of the Great Lakes. In the boreal forest, cached canoes have been found resting upside down on logs (Government of Yukon 2013).

Rectangular Structure or Enclosure (2 percent; Fig. 8.13A, B)

A rectangular or square enclosure, or structure, of boulders. Along the coastlines of Hudson Bay and the Arctic Ocean, square enclosures, 1 m or less, can represent fish oil caches. Here, in the interior, they may represent a number of things, including children's play structures. A square structure of upright slabs of rock may be a *pullat*-type fox trap (Bennett and Rowley 2004:67)—sometimes with a rock slab positioned across the top. Rectangular enclosures (single course of adjacent rocks placed on the ground) between 1 and 2 m long may represent graves. Often, the enclosing rocks are set on narrow edge.

Tower Enclosure (2 percent; Fig. 8.14A, B)

Tower-like boulder-ring structure of coursed rock, massive near its base, enclosing an interior storage chamber, measuring about 2 m in diameter at base and standing between 1 and 2 m high, approximately. The interior is sometimes semi-subterranean (e.g., when it is excavated into a boulder field). The tower usually has an opening at the top constricted by inward-leaning boulder walls. The top may also be closed with a rock slab. Specific examples were identified as caches for storing dried meat, bones, skins, and so on. Others were identified as *ullisauti*-type fox traps (Bennett and Rowley 2004:67).

Cobble or Pebble Cluster (2 percent; Fig. 8.15A, B, Plate 4)

Concentration of cobbles (i.e., rocks between about 7 and 25 cm in diameter) and/or pebbles (less than 7 cm). They may represent disturbed features such as the edge of a sleeping platform where the rest of the tent ring has not survived. This feature type also includes toolstone caches (rounded pebbles and cobbles of siliceous stone). It may also represent places where remains of meals (caribou bone) were covered with rocks to prevent them from being exposed to carnivores.

Boulder Field Platform (1 percent; Fig. 8.16A, B)

A circular area on a naturally occurring boulder field that has been cleared and leveled (e.g., for a tent or cache). A ring of boulders may surround this area, but more generally this is a negative-relief feature, where the platform is excavated into a boulder field. Platforms that represent the floors of dwellings were probably early spring occupations, adapted to the conditions of the spring thaw: the choice of location (rocky substrate) facilitated drainage for melting snow (Birket-Smith 1929:73).

Small Rock Structure or Outline (1 percent; Fig. 8.17A, B)

Construction, alignment, or concentration of pebbles or cobbles by children representing toys or games and areas for play.

Summary of Feature Data

The categories just described for the lower Kazan River reflect only broad contrasts in outward appearance of features, rather than function or use (though some indication of use or range of uses has also been given). Formal contrasts emphasize differences in size and construction. In some cases, these formal categories coincide with a single function—the distinctive Inuit hearth (*kiklu*) and the *qajaq* stand being two examples. Assuming that these culturally distinctive designs do not appear outside the Inuit cultural context, the specific forms may be disregarded for

Figure 8.10. Boulder field depression features. *A*, cache excavated into a boulder field and ringed with boulders; *B*, semi-subterranean cache in a shoreline boulder ridge.

Figure 8.11. Continuous rock ring or arc features. *A*, heavy tent ring of large boulders; *B*, hunting blind facing the river. (See also Plate 4.)

Figure 8.12. Twinned boulder lines. *A*, Brian Ookowt at far end of a double line of rocks; *B*, four upright, leaning boulders form a *qajaq* stand among other boulders. (See also Plate 4.)

Figure 8.13. Rectangular structures or enclosures. *A*, two fox traps; *B*, possible grave.

Figure 8.14. Tower enclosures. *A*, long-term cache (*right foreground*), measuring between 2 and 3 m across at base, mainly for dried meat (*qimatulivvik*); *B*, probable cache on the Thelon River.

Figure 8.15. Cobble clusters. *A*, white quartzite toolstone caches (*right foreground* and where Roy Avaala is pointing); *B*, quartzite toolstone cache next to tent ring. (See also Plate 4.)

Figure 8.16. Boulder field platforms. *A*, area cleared in boulder field for double or elongated tent; *B*, clearing for small tent on pebble substrate; partial ring of boulders is visible on far side of clearing.

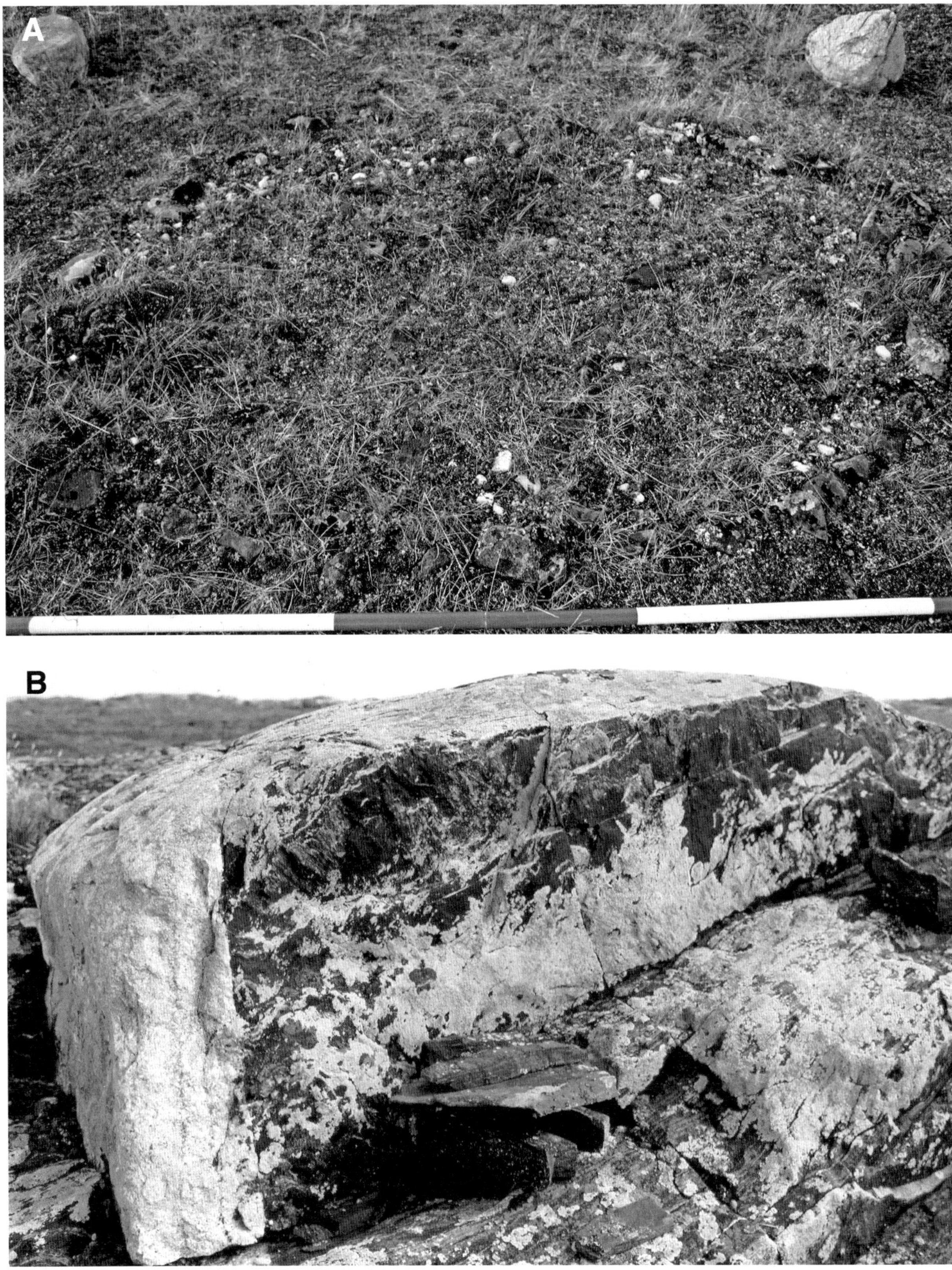

Figure 8.17. Small structures, alignments. *A*, a play tent ring of pebbles, complete with sleeping platform outline (lines of pebbles through center of ring); *B*, probable play structure (20 cm square) on bedrock shelf.

purposes of further comparison in the effort to identify possible shapes of cultural features on the bed of Lake Huron. *Inuksuit* are a distinctive element of Inuit material culture (Bennett and Rowley 2004; Hallendy 2001), but marker stones for many different purposes might easily be used in open landscapes further south. Examples of other large-scale constructions of stone from the ethnohistoric and archaeological record of recent northern foragers include: large tents used for social gatherings and exchange (e.g., Friesen 2004a:227; Friesen and Stewart 1994; Walls 2009); long tents with linear arrangements of hearths for formal occasions (Stopp 2002:13); corrals for molting geese (Bennett and Rowley 2004:72; Jackson and Nasby 1987:49); and fish weirs (Rasmussen 1931:63; Bennett and Rowley 2004:75).

The most common categories in the lower Kazan River data that account for more than 60 percent of structures and that might be useful for comparative purposes are: standing stones (*inuksuit*); rings of stone (mostly tent rings); boulder clusters/clearings; cobble/boulder field depressions; and continuous rings or arcs of stone, both coursed and uncoursed.

Standing stones often relate to drift fences, funneling caribou to blinds (e.g., Friesen 2013). These stones may be small and subtle, forming a pattern only when considered from a distant perspective (and often from the perspective of someone, or an animal, moving upslope, where they are silhouetted against the sky). Some standing rocks relate to the marking of caches and fishing locations. To the extent that people returned to these areas in the winter, marker stones could be expected, particularly near former shorelines.

Tent rings, too, might be expected where families moved onto the AAR in the warm season. But what if logistic parties exploited its resources for shorter periods during the year? In this case, smaller but continuous arcs of rock might be more common than tent rings, marking shelters, sleeping places for individual hunters, and hunting blinds.

A common substrate for cultural features throughout the Arctic and in coastal and river shoreline settings is the cobble beach (Stopp 1994). These features are thought to include food caches among hunter-gatherers with relatively predictable patterns of seasonal procurement and movement. Cobble pits that have been identified as cultural rather than natural features, though most contain no artifacts, are found along the eastern shore of Lake Superior and northern relict beaches and elsewhere on the gravel and cobble beds of some river and lake shorelines on the Precambrian Shield of Ontario (e.g., Noble 1968, and as reviewed by Stopp 1994). Boulder field depressions and platforms along the Kazan River are part of this widespread practice of using cobble and boulder natural formations as well-drained places for storage and spring habitation. Whether cobble and boulder beaches existed along the shoreline of Lake Stanley, which would provide a suitable substrate for such features, remains an open question.

The AAR might have served to channel human movement seasonally between what is now Ontario and Michigan, providing an incentive for caching along this used route, untethered to camps (Stopp 2002:319). If wood was scarce, stone caches might appear as clusters of rock. Alternatively, the use of this area as a hunting ground in summer or especially in fall might have employed caches as a hedge against winter and spring scarcity.

Discussion

Drawing on a previous analysis of settlement patterns on the tundra west of Hudson Bay (Friesen 2004b), some consideration can be given to the overall settlement pattern on the AAR as it might be manifested by the distribution of boulder features there. Assuming that a migratory population of caribou used the AAR in the course of its annual range, we should not necessarily expect to find a complex Inland Inuit-type range and distribution of features.

Two contrasting settlement and mobility patterns, each focused on caribou as the key resource, have been linked to distinct culture groups and their histories on the barrenlands: Inuit and Dene (Irving 1968; Friesen 2004b; Smith and Burch 1979). Inuit settlement includes large base camps and outlying locations with diverse facilities. Residential camps are established near major river crossings, where people expected to intercept migrating caribou, procuring them in large numbers as they crossed the river. Archaeological sites representing base camps are large and complex, reflecting both social aggregation and annually repeated occupation of these sites during the spring, summer, and fall (Stewart et al. 2000). This pattern conforms to a collector type of subsistence-settlement organization, described originally for the Nunamiut (Binford 1978b, 1980).

Dene settlement, by contrast, consists of smaller camps with fewer facilities distributed much more widely between forest and tundra. Conforming somewhat more closely to the subsistence-settlement organization of foragers (Binford 1980), the Dene followed the caribou north onto the tundra in spring, hunting them mostly on land in small herds, falling back to the treeline in late summer to pursue larger herds as they migrated to their wintering ground in the forest. Dene archaeological sites generally consist of a small number of tent rings at places that are not limited mainly to river crossings, as well as concentrations of lithic material at lookout locations (Gordon 1996). These sites do not appear to contain the structured set of facilities seen in the boulder feature data along the Kazan River. The difference in settlement patterns between Inuit and Dene cannot be explained entirely by differences in available raw materials for building facilities—perishable wood along the treeline versus durable stone on the tundra. In other words, these contrasting patterns show how dramatically different archaeological signatures can emerge from the use of the same resource (barrenground caribou) in essentially the same environment and landscape (Friesen 2004b).

In the same way, the landscape of the AAR might have been used in contrasting ways by different people at the same time. On the one hand, people focused on a seasonal and concentrated migration of animals might have developed a range of facilities reflecting their residential occupation of this area, as well as procurement and processing of animals at locations away from base camps. Favorable sites for large, complex base camps might occur particularly at narrowings of the AAR where movement was constricted by the shoreline, or at gaps through areas of topographic relief. On the other hand, if the AAR were used for hunting individual or small groups of animals browsing or grazing there in the warm season as part of a larger annual range, we might expect a less prominent archaeological signature in isolated or small numbers of grouped tent rings. This does not preclude the use of more favorable locations (e.g., narrowings and gaps; areas of steep relief next to fishing holes)—annually or on a less frequent schedule—where game drives might have been constructed and where archaeological evidence for occupation might have accumulated over time (Friesen 2004b:306–8; Wilson and Rasic 2008).

Conclusion

The purpose of this discussion has been to consider the archaeological potential of the early Holocene landscape of the AAR, using the perspective of another—the Low Arctic Inland Inuit landscape—to guide the search for the most visible remains. Cultural features constructed from boulders are both visible and enduring in the Inland Inuit landscape. Smaller features and quartzite artifacts are also highly visible but are more culturally or geologically specific to that region. For many uses (e.g., caches, game drives, hunting blinds, graves), boulder features replace equivalent wooden features that can be seen in the forest-tundra zone to the south and west (Andrews and Zoe 1997; Clark 1987). As on the tundra west of Hudson Bay, and elsewhere across the Arctic, the archaeological record in this exposed early Holocene landscape should contain boulder features in the absence of available wood.

In the Lake Stanley early Holocene, caribou herds might still have been a prime target of coordinated procurement involving drives operated by family or large social groups. Finds on the lakebed seem to confirm the existence of at least one drive with associated lithic material (O'Shea, Lemke, and Reynolds 2013; O'Shea et al. 2014). Coordinated procurement at a small number of seasonally occupied sites with favorable topographic conditions might imply the existence of large residential base camps with a potentially large inventory of features, especially if caching was practiced here. Even if resources were abundant, however, it is not clear that people would concentrate and coordinate their efforts from a residential base on the AAR. Instead, the ridge could have been used at the extreme end of a settlement range that was centered on the mainland at either end of the AAR. If so, scattered tent rings might dominate the visible record on the AAR.

Finally, one type of feature prominent in the archaeological record of both the Arctic/Subarctic region and the upper Great Lakes is the boulder field depression and boulder field platform. Cobble and boulder fields clearly were important settings for a range of activities that may include caching, hunting, residence, and perhaps spiritual activity. It's not clear that storm-impacted cobble beaches can be found along the AAR but, if so, they would represent a key landform for archaeological search.

Acknowledgments

Documentation of features discussed here was carried out for Parks Canada and the Harvaqtuuq Historic Site Committee of Baker Lake between 1993 and 1997. Photos were taken by Andrew Stewart. Figures 8.5–8.18, except where noted, were taken on the lower Kazan River. Thanks to Lisa Sonnenburg, Ashley Lemke, and John O'Shea for inviting me to contribute to their ongoing research on hunting structures in Lake Huron.

PART III

Hunting Ancient Caribou Hunters—Archaeological Finds on the Alpena-Amberley Ridge

9 | Strategies and Techniques for the Discovery of Submerged Sites on the Alpena-Amberley Ridge

by John O'Shea

This chapter describes the methods and theoretical underpinnings that have shaped the research efforts on the Alpena-Amberley Ridge (AAR). The chapter first describes the impetus for the research, and the assumptions that guided the initial field investigations. It then considers the full set of techniques and approaches that have been employed to discover and understand the early human occupation of the AAR.

While it has long been recognized that many of the critical locations for Late Paleoindian and earlier Archaic occupation in the Great Lakes region lay beneath the waters of the Great Lakes (cf. Karrow and Warner 1990; Shott 1999), most researchers have considered that recognition the end of the story. It seemed unlikely that archaeological sites would survive the subsequent inundations of the Nipissing transgression intact, and any that might survive would surely be deeply buried beneath later sediments, making them effectively undiscoverable. Renewed research on the Lake Stanley low-water stage in Lake Huron, particularly the new bathymetry that for the first time showed the Alpena-Amberley Ridge (AAR) as a continuous feature across the basin, and the discovery of preserved forest remains beneath southern Lake Huron (Hunter et al. 2006), reopened the question of whether early archaeological sites might be preserved beneath the lake.

Of course there is a big gap between entertaining the possibility that sites might be preserved and actually going out and finding them. Even on land, where time and access are relatively unlimited, it is difficult to find Paleoindian sites, and even with increasingly elaborate predictive modeling and systematic survey, most finds continue to be accidental discoveries or based on information from local collectors. While "accidental" finds from submerged sites do sometimes occur, particularly in coastal areas where drag line fishing is practiced, none of these discovery techniques would be applicable to central Lake Huron. Clearly, if there was any hope of finding submerged sites on the AAR, it would be necessary to develop a way to predict where sites ought to be located, and to determine what the sites would actually look like.

To address these questions, the University of Michigan Museum of Anthropological Archaeology (UMMAA) work in Lake Huron began with a series of assumptions. First, we posited that there would be little in the way of post-Lake Stanley sediment on the AAR. We based this assumption on anecdotal reports from lake geologists involved in the collection of lake cores, and on the mid-lake location of the AAR, which is presently 50 km or more from the nearest sediment sources. As such, we began work believing that if there were preserved archaeological sites, they would not be obscured by thick layers of lake sediment.

The second assumption was that the AAR corridor would have figured in the semiannual migration of caribou, and that caribou would have been the principal attraction for ancient hunters. This assumption was based on paleoclimatic reconstructions of the Lake Stanley environment, which was characterized as cold and tundra-like (see Chapters 3, 12), and on the belief among many terrestrial archaeologists working on Late Paleoindian in the Great Lakes region and the Northeast that caribou were an important game species of the period (Jackson 1997; Simons 1997; Robinson et al. 2009), even though the preservation of actual faunal remains is woefully limited due to the poor preservation of animal bone in the acidic soils of the northern forests.

The final assumption, following from the second, was that ancient hunters on the AAR would use techniques similar to those known historically and ethnographically by Arctic and Subarctic caribou hunters (cf. Stewart et al. 2000; Friesen 2013), and specifically that they would use the readily available stone on the AAR to construct hunting structures, such as drive lanes (Brink 2005). Such features would be large enough to discover using remote acoustic techniques, and they would likely have survived any but the most catastrophic kind of final inundation event.

The first assumption, if correct, meant we could hope to discover ancient sites, while the second and third assumptions allowed us to make predictions concerning where sites, or at least one category of site, should be located and what the sites should look like. These predictions in turn enabled us to select the initial search areas and the search techniques that would have the greatest chance for success. Of course, as with all archaeological predictions, the proof would be in the pudding.

The starting point for all that followed was selecting the initial target areas in which to work. For this we looked at the bathymetry of the AAR and experimented with varying potential lake levels to gain an understanding of the terrain that would have been present when the feature was dry land. This was accomplished by creating digital elevation models (DEM) from the National Oceanic and Atmospheric Administration (NOAA) bathymetry and then creating three-dimensional land surface images using ArcGIS 10. This landscape was evaluated against the extensive literature on caribou behavior and how they are hunted. From these macro-scaled considerations, three target research zones were selected that represented different kinds of topographic settings for caribou. These three zones are shown in Figures 9.1 and 9.2 (see also Plate 5), and their spatial characteristics are described below.

Area 1 is the largest area and the most varied, topographically. It is dominated by a long linear bedrock outcrop, which we hoped might contain chert quarry sites, and considerable variation in elevation, including the shallowest point of Six Fathom Scarp. Search Area 1 represents the zone of highest elevation (i.e., shallowest water) and has the potential of containing intact remains attributable to the final Lake Stanley lowstand (7900–7500 BP). The area is roughly 56 km^2 (21 mi^2), and contains upland areas and a portion of the high northeast-facing cliffs (Table 9.1). Our expectation was that this would have provided an area for a larger base and rearmament. It seemed likely that the area might provide a highland pass along the caribou migration route. There is also a possibility that the cliff area might contain cave or rockshelter sites.

Area 2 is the nearest to shore, yet presents some of the deepest areas on the ridge, which we hoped might capture evidence from the earliest stages of Lake Stanley. Topographically, Area 2 contained a potential water crossing, where caribou would have had to swim across a narrow strait. Ethnographically, many groups prefer to hunt caribou either from boats while they are swimming or from shore as they emerge from the water. This locality would provide a setting where either strategy could be employed. Area 2 is approximately 49 km^2 (19 mi^2) in extent and would have been a narrow and low-lying area, possibly a ford (Table 9.1). It would have represented a choke point through which migrating caribou would have had to pass and as such would have been an excellent setting for creating ambush points. In this area we expected kill sites, along with locations used for the primary and secondary processing of the kills. The natural shape of the landform probably precluded the necessity of creating artificial structures to channel caribou movement, but higher elevations might contain ephemeral lookout sites and other evidence of human activity. This low-lying area would have been rapidly submerged by rising lake levels, and probably was exposed only during the Early Lake Stanley phase. As such, it offered the best candidate for intact archaeological traces representing the earliest human use of this ancient landscape. To date, only limited survey has been conducted in Area 2.

Area 3 presented a region where the AAR narrowed with a pronounced slope. This would thus be a location that would provide hunters with a valuable overlook position when the herds were moving toward the south, and at the same time produce a natural funneling effect on the movement of the animals. Area 3 is an area of roughly 17 km^2 (12 mi^2) and presents an upland setting overlooking a narrow shoreline (Table 9.1). This is another ideal area for base camps. It also presents a setting similar to those in which built structures, such as cairns and long barricades, are constructed to channel the movement of caribou into kill areas. Given its intermediate elevation, it may have presented a significantly different kind of landform, depending on the changing elevation of the lake.

For the initial examination of the three test areas, side scan sonar (SSS) survey was employed. SSS was well suited to the job since it emphasizes details of bottom topography and, when operated in extensive mode, can be used to cover wide areas. SSS survey was conducted using a digital side scan sonar unit (Imagenex), at a frequency of 330 kHz at depths between 20 and 30 m, in overlapping swaths of roughly 200 m (cf. Fish and Carr 1990:62–63). The linear arrangements of stone we expected to encounter, along with concentrations of angular reflectors as might be produced by quarry rubble, would produce strong acoustic signals that should be recognizable even at moderate ranges. The SSS results also produced a finer-grained image of the submerged landscape than that derived from the DEM, and provided important information on the composition of the lake

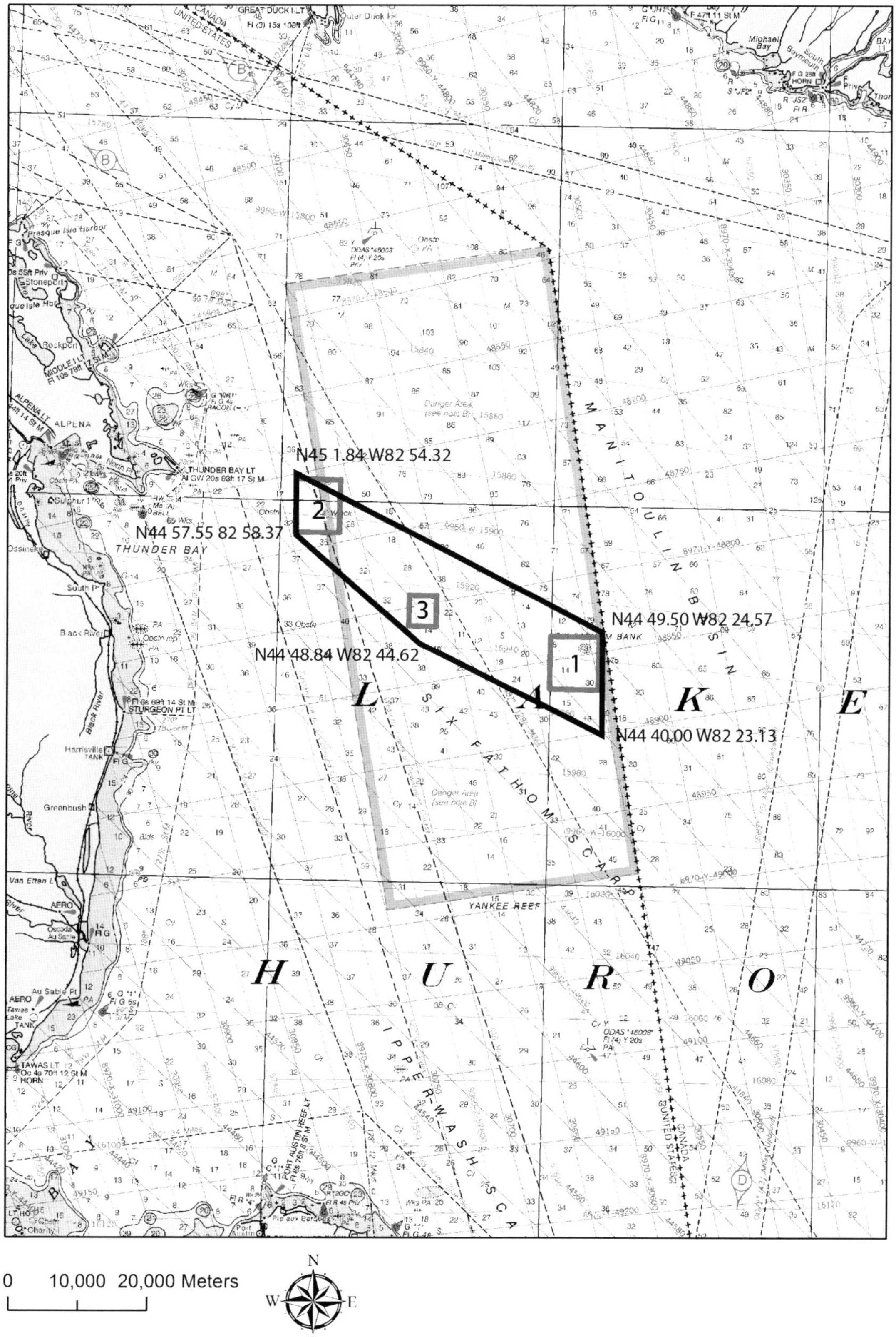

Figure 9.1. Location of principal research areas overlain on the nautical chart for central Lake Huron.

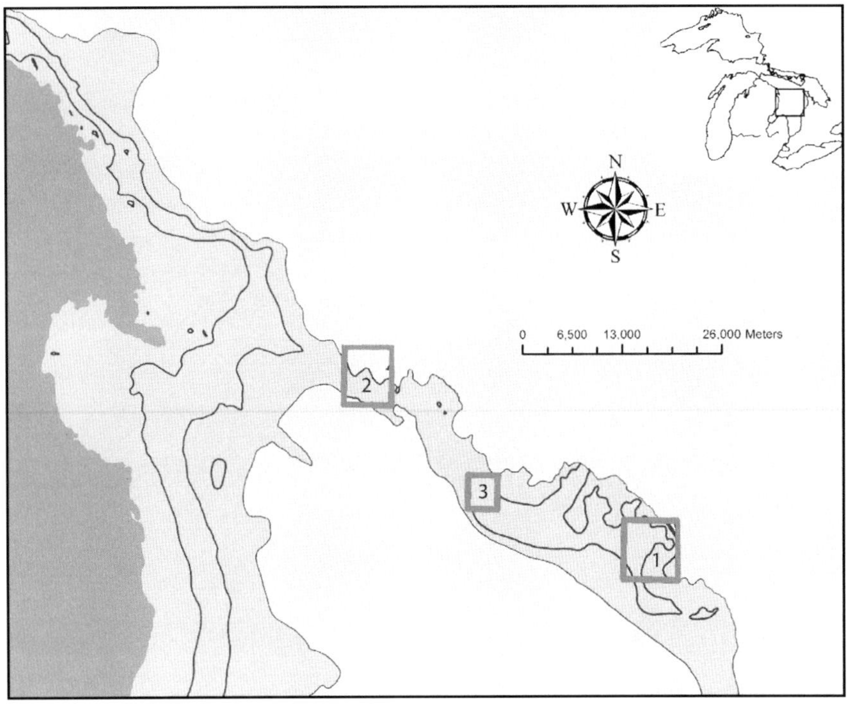

Figure 9.2. Location of principal research areas overlain on the exposed landform of the Alpena-Amberley Ridge. The darkest area is the modern land surface, while the lightest areas were underwater during the Lake Stanley stage (less than 140 m amsl). Contour interval is 10 meters. (See Plate 5.)

Table 9.1. Research areas.

Zone	Size (km^2)	Distinguishing Character	Depth (m)
Area 1	56	outcrops	15–80 (155)*
Area 2	49	water crossing	30–80
Area 3	17	overlook	30–50

*Deepest actual part of area.

floor, distinguishing softer sediments, such as sands, from rock based on the acoustic reflectivity. These differences in bottom characteristics were subsequently confirmed via video and direct examination, and provided important clues to the presence of ancient swamps, waterways, and bogs. The acoustic maps produced via SSS were post-processed and mosaicked (Figs. 9.3, 9.4), and draped over the DEMs to provide a realistic portrayal of the once dry landscape.

Subsequent to the completion of the SSS survey, a portion of the central AAR—an area of 115 km^2, which partially overlapped Area 1—was mapped using multibeam sonar (MB; Figs. 9.5, 9.6, Plate 5). MB survey produces an extremely fine-grained map of depths, and can be used either in a small area to image a three-dimensional bottom feature, such as a shipwreck, or in a more extensive mode to map small changes in bottom elevation. MB survey was conducted using an R2 Sonic 2024 multibeam echosounder with an F180 vessel attitude and position system. Like SSS, acoustic backscatter from MB provides important information on the character of the lake bottom sediments based on their acoustic reflective properties.

The SSS and MB coverages presented a detailed view of the submerged landscape, which formed the basis for subsequent environmental and cultural modeling. They also highlighted a series of specific targets of interest, relating both to landforms and to potential cultural features, which were subsequently investigated via video and SCUBA.

From this basis, the research efforts went in two distinct directions. The first, involving a hand deployed remotely operated vehicle (ROV) and SCUBA-trained archaeologists, began a more directed examination of the AAR and specific targets and locations identified from the SSS and MB surveys. The second strand of the investigation involved computer simulation, first to model the AAR environment as dry land given differing lake levels, and second to model the movement of caribou across this reconstructed landscape so as to provide predictions for the likely locations of ancient hunting sites. Chapter 4 describes the simulation work in more detail, while Figure 9.7 illustrates how the simulations are integrated with the program of field research. The goal of the simulation modeling is to narrow search efforts by identifying locations with a high likelihood of containing hunting sites. In the initial stages of the research (reported here), the majority of targets were selected manually, based either on suggestive features visible in the acoustic imagery or by investigating specific landscape features that intuitively seemed suitable for use, based on known historical and ethnographic data. As the artificial intelligence (AI) models become more complete and realistic, they will gradually assume more of the burden for selecting locations for investigation.

Perhaps the most important relationships illustrated in Figure 9.7 are the dashed lines that return to the AI model. These represent data flows back to the AI model, which may be specific pieces of environmental data, the discovered presence of new structures, or indeed, the absence of structures in a given location. In light of new information, the AI model is iterative updated and refined. In one critical sense, the AI model is in fact the ultimate database for the research, reflecting all that

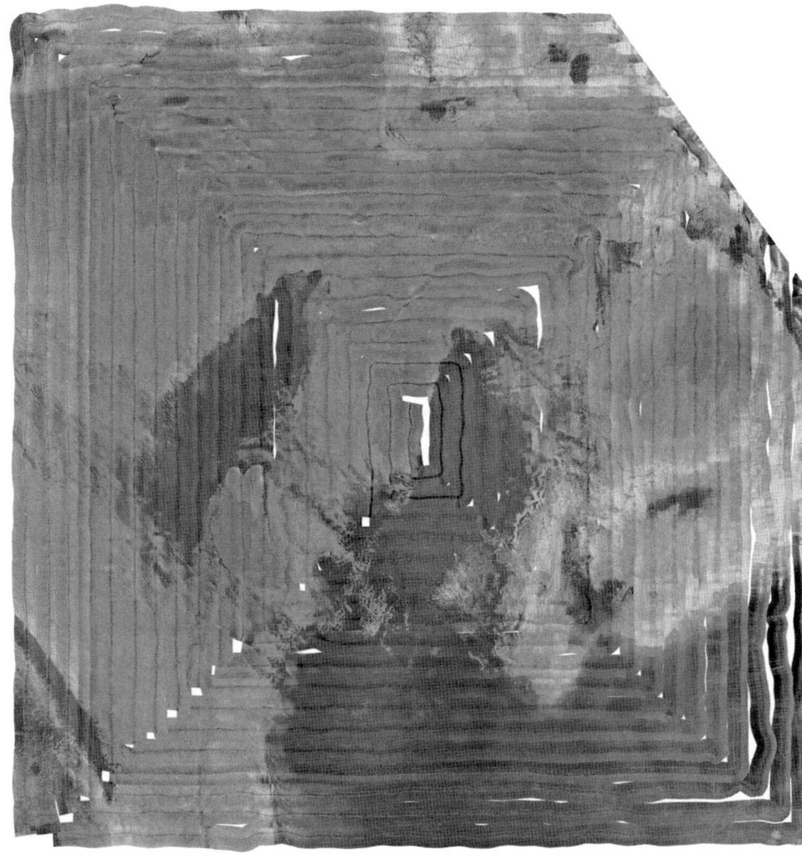

Figure 9.3.
Side scan mosaic of Area 1. Each swath is 200 m wide. Dark areas on the mosaic indicate areas of sand.

Figure 9.4.
Side scan mosaic of Area 3. Each swath is 200 m wide. Dark areas indicate areas of sand or clay.

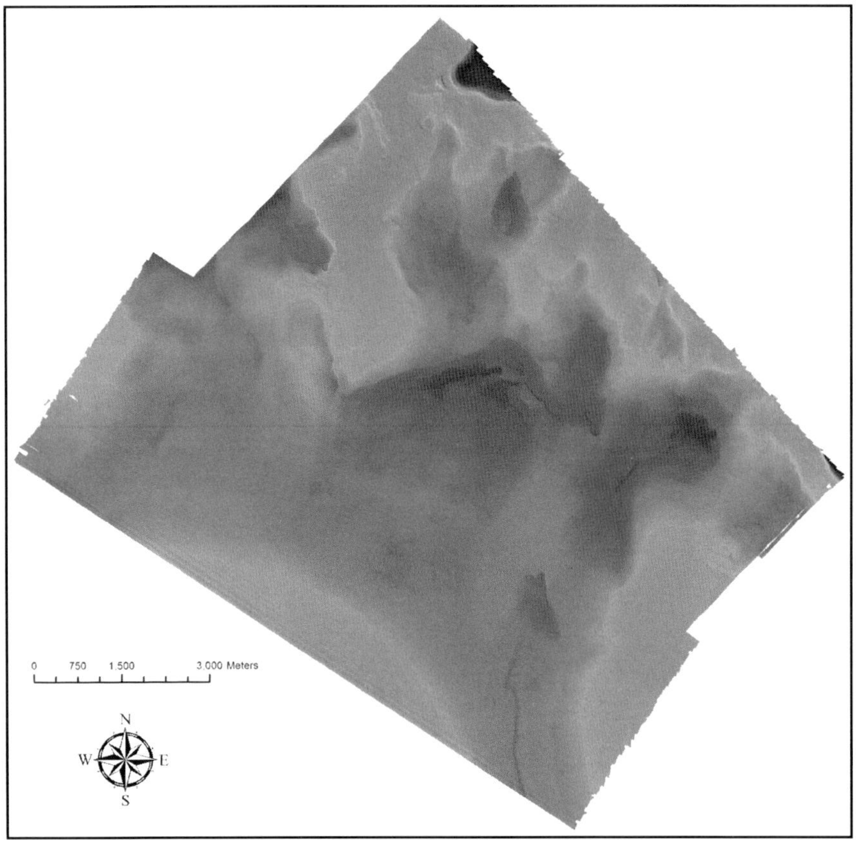

Figure 9.5. Multibeam sonar image of Area 1 and adjacent bottom areas. Redder colors (see Plate 5) denote shallower depths. The central limestone ridge creating Six Fathom Shoal is prominent in the center of the image.

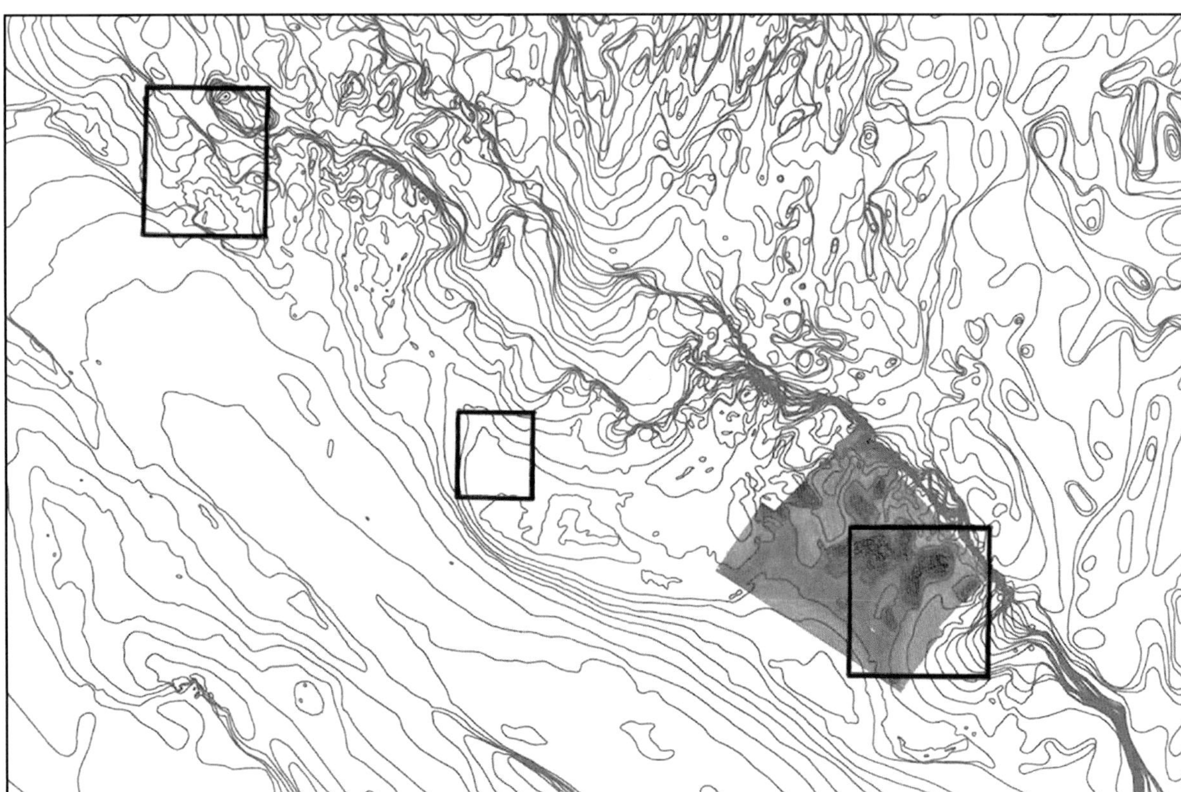

Figure 9.6. Multibeam sonar coverage and principal research areas overlain on the contour bathymetry of the lake bottom and Alpena-Amberley Ridge. Contour interval is 5 meters.

is known about the research area at any given time.

Figure 9.7 also summarizes the more detailed levels of site investigation on the AAR. As presented in the figure, the activities progress from extensive to more intensive. In our initial planning, extensive search efforts would be followed by more detailed coverage generated via autonomous underwater vehicles (AUV). Hand deployable AUVs are now available that can carry side scan sonar, video, and rapid fire frame photography, and offer a number of advantages over surface deployed assets. They can be programmed to follow precisely defined search patterns and are much less affected by surface wind and waves, which often limit the effectiveness of surface deployed SSS. They also can operate much closer to the bottom, which reduces the inherent "blind spot" immediately beneath the SSS unit, and results in much more efficient coverage of the search area. The idea was to use AUVs to create coverage of small localities that might contain complex hunting structures or multiple hunting sites. To date, however, this scale of coverage has not been realized.

The workhorse of the research, to date, has been the use of a surface deployed ROV that provides direct high definition (HD) video access to locations of interest and has a limited capability to collect specimens. The UMMAA project has utilized an Outland 1000, equipped with UWL-500 LED lights, UWC-360D dual HD video cameras (color, and black and white), and a manipulator (Fig. 9.8). Two mission-specific modifications to the ROV have been made. The first was the addition of a Tritech MicroNav100 tracking sonar to allow the ROV location to be viewed and recorded in real time. The transponder allowed the ROV to record the location of specific features on the lake bottom. The ROV's current location and track are also displayed in real time on an acoustic map of the lake bottom and are stored permanently in the shipboard geographic information system (GIS). This tracking feature has proven particularly useful when subsequent review of video imagery reveals interesting features that were not noted during operations. The second addition to the ROV is a pair of fixed forward-facing lasers. These two small lasers become visible in the video

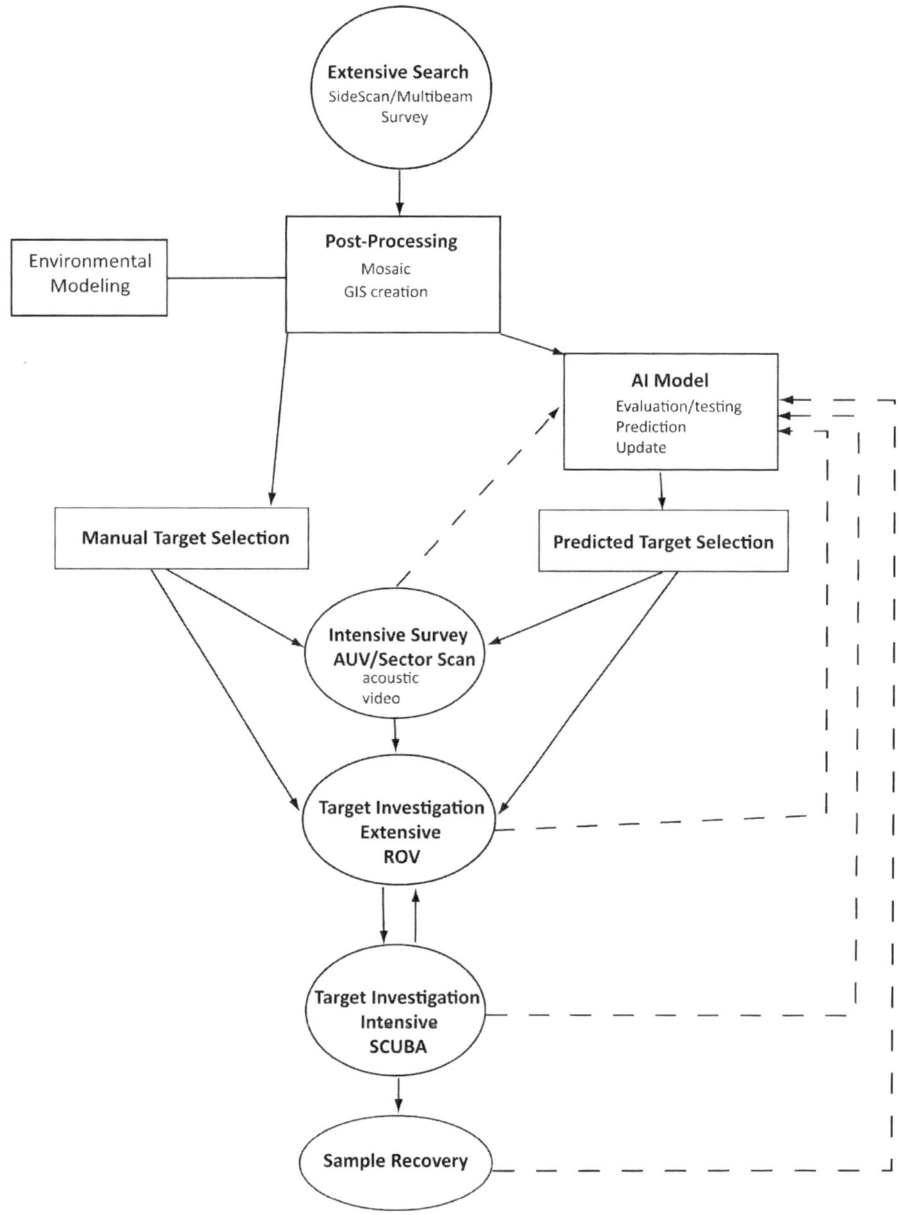

Figure 9.7. Schematic representation of AAR research design. Dashed lines represent the flow of research findings back to the AI simulation.

imagery whenever the ROV is close to an object, and provide a means of remotely measuring the object.

In addition to its solo role in site investigation and documentation, the ROV operates as an important adjunct for the follow-up analysis of sites by divers. Lacking the limits on bottom time that constrain divers, the ROV is deployed first to ascertain that the vessel is accurately positioned and that all supporting dive gear is properly in place. During the actual dive, the ROV follows the progress of the dive, providing real-world coordinate locations for the samples collected and providing video documentation of locations and sample collection, which lessens the task burden on divers. The ROV also creates an important link between deployed divers and the surface. Not only does this provide an added layer of diver safety, it enables the ROV to "lead" divers to sampling points.

Figure 9.8. Outland 1000 remotely operated vehicle (ROV), aka Jake.

Figure 9.9. MS 1000 scanning sonar unit mounted on a tripod prior to deployment. Scanning head is located at the base of the cylindrical unit.

A second intermediate range mapping technique that has been utilized with great success recently is scanning sonar (Fig. 9.9). In essence, the sonar head is held in place by a tripod on the lake bottom, and the sonar head then rotates through 360 degrees to produce a scaled acoustic map of the immediate area. The digital images are viewable in real time, and by varying the sonar frequency, it is possible to increase the range or the resolution of the recovered image. The real advantage of the scanning sonar is that it can produce a highly detailed map of an archaeological structure in a fraction of the time it would take divers to even complete the measurements. The resulting map is much more accurate than that produced by divers and is immediately available as a digital image. The maps of both complex hunting structures discovered—the Funnel Drive and Drop 45—are based on scanning sonar images (see Chapter 10). It might also be noted that the Drop 45 structure was actually discovered via the scanning sonar.

The most intensive work conducted on the lake bottom is performed by SCUBA-trained archaeologists. Divers collect cores and environmental samples (Fig. 9.10), including wood specimens, for analysis (see Chapter 12); they measure and sketch submerged features for the later construction of plan maps; they collect opportunistic or systematic sediment samples in the search for cultural debris; and they have been employed to systematically collect samples in geological outcrops in the search for local chert sources. Most diving to date has been in the range of 20 to 35 m (60–120 feet).

The collection of bottom samples is a topic in itself (see Chapter 12 for a discussion of the collection of cores and environmental samples). Sample collection for potential cultural materials has presented a series of problems, some common to all underwater research, and some unique to the contemporary conditions of Lake Huron and the Great Lakes. Following from the initial assumption that archaeological deposits should not be deeply buried, there was the hope that cultural materials might be exposed on the bottom and might be observed via the ROV. While the assumption concerning sediment has been borne out, what was not anticipated was the complete covering of all hard surfaces by invasive mussel species. This factor immediately heightened the importance of direct observation by divers, who could move or scrape off the dense masses of mussels to view the underlying material.

As investigations progressed, a more nuanced appreciation of that first assumption emerged. It was correct that little in the way of recent overburden covered the lake bottom on the AAR. When sediment has been encountered, it is typically sand, which appears to have been deposited during the time that the ARR was above water. In shallower areas, particularly on top of the Six Fathom Scarp in Area 1, the rock surface exhibits considerable subaerial erosion and scouring, with virtually no sediment cover. In somewhat deeper water, the relatively thin sand deposits represent one-time lakes, streams, and shorelines, and sit immediately on top of bedrock. In these areas, topographic variation is primarily due either to intact outcrops of limestone and dolomite, or to linear piles of rocks and cobbles, which are remnant glacial features. When the AAR was above water, these features would presumably have been covered with thin layers of soil and vegetation, all of which were washed away as the AAR was flooded. Cultural materials on these landforms at that time would presumably have dropped into the gaps between the cobbles. By contrast, as lake levels rose, prime waterside occupation areas would have been inundated and covered over with a thin layer of sand. Since these sand deposits sit directly on bedrock, any cultural materials that were displaced or came to rest in lag deposits should be present on the bedrock immediately beneath the sand. This is, in fact, precisely the circumstances in which cultural debris has been recovered in the Drop 45 structure (see Chapter 10).

Figure 9.10. Diver manually collecting a sediment core.

This more nuanced appreciation of the formation processes has directed the sampling efforts for cultural materials. While all potential structures are sampled for cultural materials, a particular focus for testing and systematic sampling are stream, lake, and bog margin areas that are covered with ancient sand. In such sampling, the focus is not so much the sand deposit, but rather, the contact between the sand and the underlying bedrock.

While standard vial and core samples that were collected for environmental data occasionally contained cultural materials such as charcoal and microdebitage, the target sampling for cultural materials bears a strong resemblance to shovel test sampling in terrestrial archaeology. A metal scoop is used to remove a roughly 30 × 30 cm area of overburden (sand) and to scrape along the surface of the bedrock to recover potential cultural materials. In the initial stages, the entire sample of sand and rock was collected and taken to the surface for sorting and analysis. Current practice is for divers to carry #3 one-quarter-inch (6.3 mm) scientific sieves and to screen the material in situ, returning only the screen residue to the surface. This technique was first used in a fully systematic manner at the Drop 45 Drive Lane and produced excellent results—recovering a number of small flakes, and clearly demarcating those areas that did, and did not, produce cultural debris (O'Shea et al. 2014).

As with hunter-gatherer sites in terrestrial archaeology, the low density of cultural debris can hinder site discovery, and it may be that more intensive sediment screening (as with airlifts or water dredges) may be necessary. Such an approach would be most suitable once a demonstrable site has been located, as with Drop 45, and would require a different configuration of surface support. The current sampling system is best suited for exploratory and site discovery efforts.

Techniques for the discovery and documentation of archaeological sites on the AAR continue to evolve, as do the approaches for integrating the results of simulation with real-time examination of the lake bottom. A particular emphasis on these developments has been the focus on equipment and methods that can be deployed by hand from a small vessel. Fortunately, advances in electronic miniaturization and computing have made it possible, as everything from side scan sonar to multibeam can now be accommodated. The emphasis on small vessel-based research is not simply a question of aesthetics. The reality of underwater research is that it is expensive, and can rapidly exceed the kinds of budgets that are available for normal archaeological research. This also reflects the fundamental difference between the focal character of shipwreck archaeology, and the more extensive and sustained research effort required for the archaeology of a submerged landscape (O'Shea et al. 2013). The ability to integrate the diverse types of equipment and examination methods on a small vessel makes the conduct of prehistoric research on the sea floor possible.

Of course, investigations can reach a point where small vessel operations become ineffective or impossible. For example, once a substantial site is located and the research moves into large-scale data recovery, it will be necessary to shift technique and include water dredges or lifts to process quantities of sediment. Likewise, and particularly in the case of the AAR, the ability to maintain position on the site for multiple days to allow for ongoing dive operations without the daily necessity of transiting back and forth to port would be a major advantage. Nevertheless, for survey and exploratory work of the kind currently underway on the AAR, the system employing modular hand deployable assets has proved its ability to produce significant scientific results on what continue to be relatively modest means. Or as our colleague Guy Meadows of Michigan Technological University termed, "big ocean science on a bathtub budget."

10 Constructed Features on the Alpena-Amberley Ridge

by John O'Shea

This chapter provides descriptions of the principal types of stone constructions identified to date on the Alpena-Amberley Ridge, and provides preliminary data on their relative frequency and distribution. These features include simple and more complex constructions thought to have been used for the hunting of caribou, along with other ancillary features, such as rectangular caches. The chapter contrasts the occurrence of constructed features within the two research areas investigated on the Alpena-Amberley Ridge, and provides information on the topographic settings in which the stone constructions are located.

Introduction

Since the initiation of research in 2008, a number of stone arrangements or constructed features have been identified and investigated. The first of these, the Dragon Drive Line and Blind, was identified in the original side scan sonar (SSS) mapping of Area 1, due to its fortuitous alignment with the survey transects. For the most part, however, hunting features do not resolve in the extensive acoustic searches using either SSS or multibeam sonar (MB; see Chapter 9 for a description of these techniques and their roles in the search effort). What these extensive search techniques did accomplish was to provide an accurate and detailed view of the ancient land surface. This resulting surface topography has been used to identify likely locations for hunting sites using both intuitive methods (initially) and the results of simulation modeling of caribou behavior as described in Chapter 4. The discovery of potential sites then involved visual examination of the localities and potential features, initially via the video of the remotely operated vehicle (ROV), followed by direct investigations by archaeologists in the water.

This chapter describes the basic kinds of stone constructions that have been identified on the Alpena-Amberley Ridge (AAR) and provides a preliminary sense of their frequency and distribution. A more synthetic treatment of the stone constructions as elements in the prehistoric occupation is presented in Chapter 14. The survey localities used in the descriptions are illustrated for Area 1 (Fig. 10.1) and for Area 3 (Fig. 10.2).

Description of the Alpena-Amberley Ridge Structures

Ethnographic (Stewart et al. 2000; Chapter 8) and archaeological (Brink 2005) descriptions of caribou hunting structures are consistent in their representation as relatively simple constructions that take full advantage of local landforms and materials. Indeed, some could easily be missed altogether if not actively sought out or pointed out by an informant. The same features characterize the structures identified on the AAR. There is a clear economy of effort in the selection and arrangement of materials, and in most cases, the structures are used to enhance existing

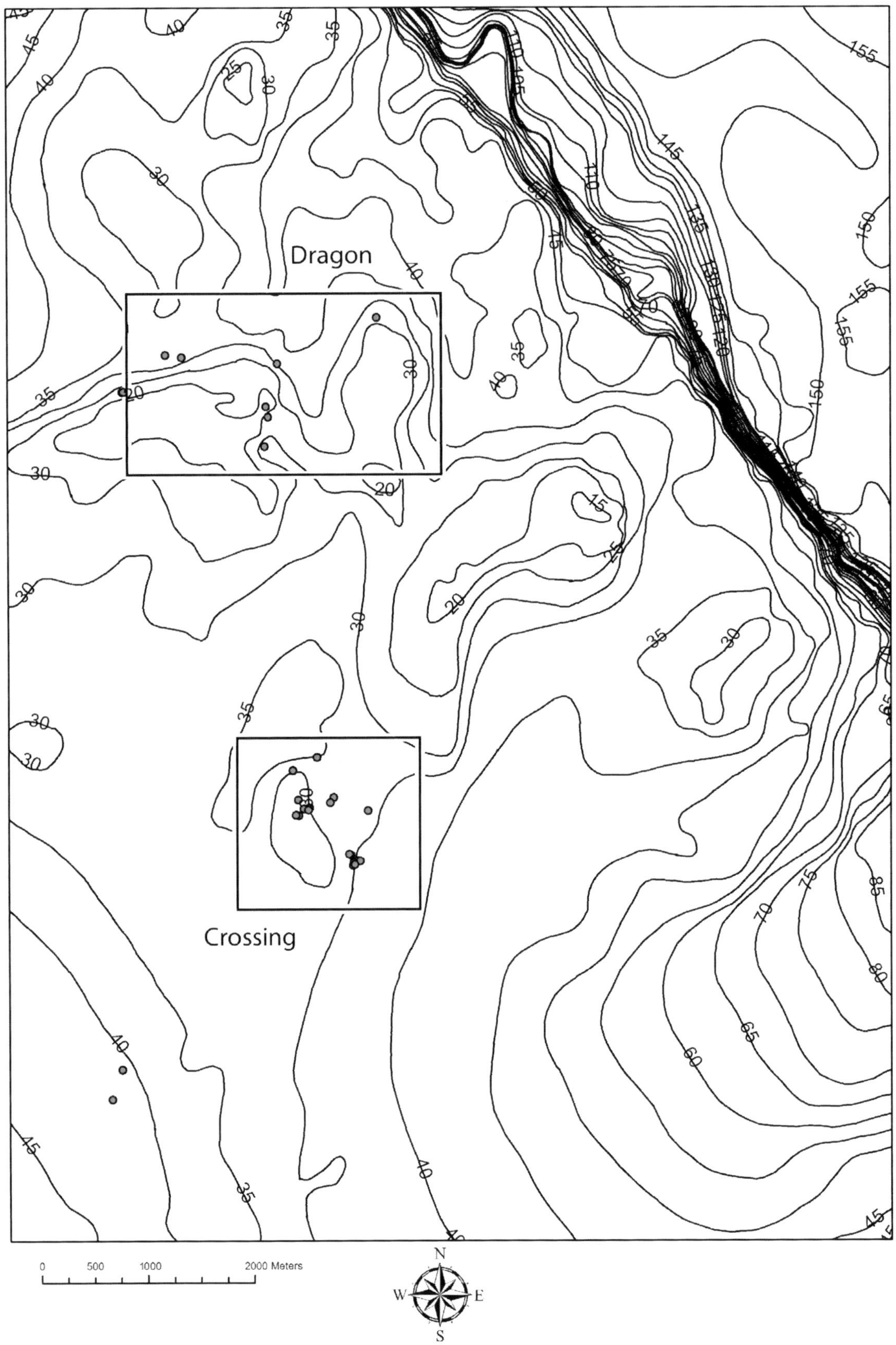

Figure 10.1. A contour map of potential stone structures in Area 1. The two localities mentioned in the text are indicated by boxes. The contour interval is 5 m and reflects depth below surface. Modern datum for Lake Huron is 176 m.

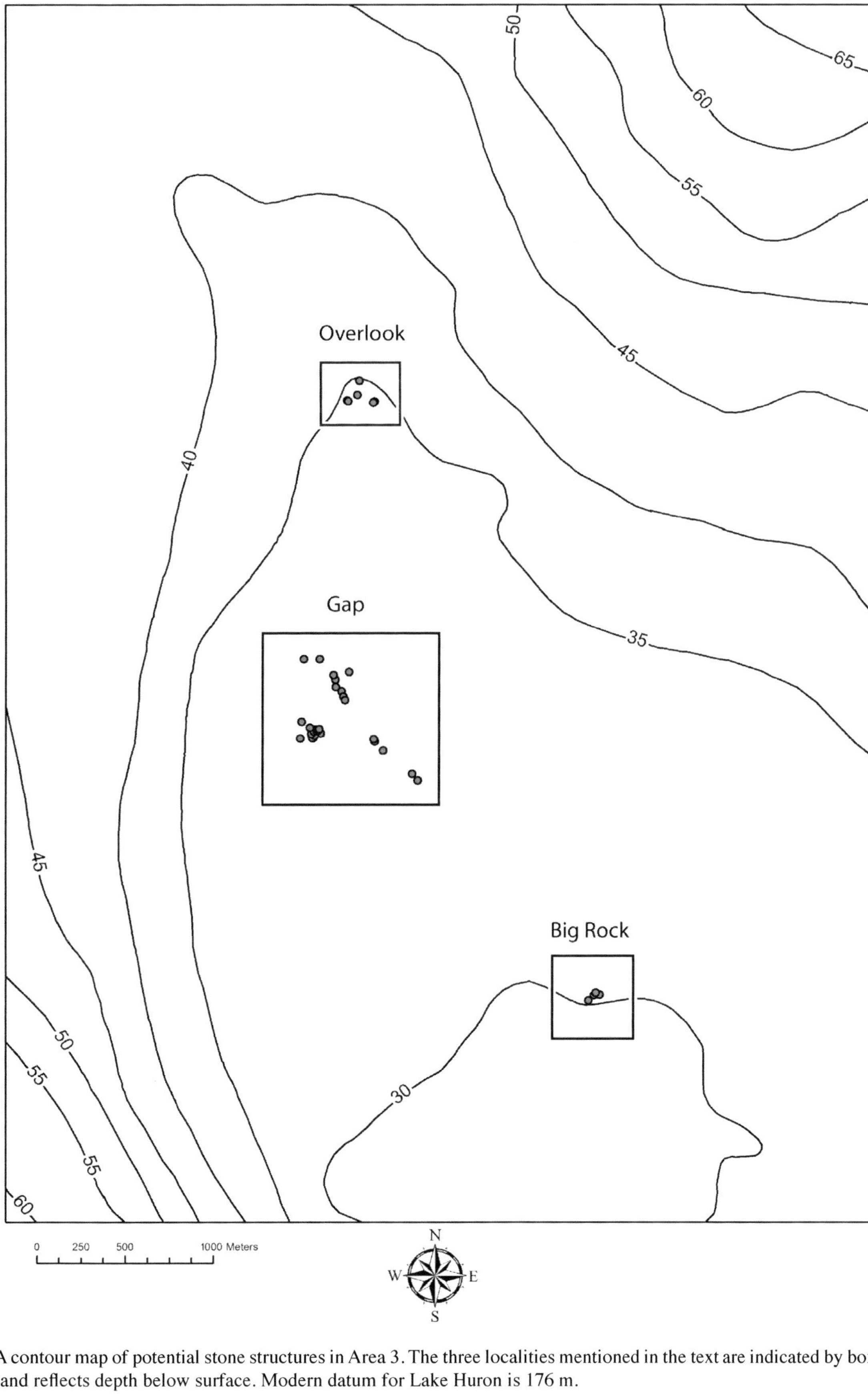

Figure 10.2. A contour map of potential stone structures in Area 3. The three localities mentioned in the text are indicated by boxes. The contour interval is 5 m and reflects depth below surface. Modern datum for Lake Huron is 176 m.

features in the landscape. Given the expected simplicity of form and modification, it is likely that substantial numbers of these structures have gone unidentified due to limited conditions of visibility underwater and the all-pervasive covering of hard surfaces by invasive mussels. Nevertheless, those that have been identified provide a first glimpse of how ancient peoples used the AAR.

The basic shapes and forms observed are relatively simple and rudimentary. They are also modular in the sense that they can be used alone or they can be combined to create more elaborate and complex features (see also Chapter 7). In the description below, the simple structures are described first, and then the discussion moves to a consideration of more complex combinations of structures.

Simple Structures

Simple structures come in various shapes and sizes and can tentatively be linked to differing functions. Fundamentally they can be divided into enclosures of various shapes that presumably operated to enclose or conceal, and lines that directed movement. Among those structures that could have operated to conceal, it is possible to distinguish open and closed varieties.

Open or V Structures

Open or V-shaped structures are the simplest form of modification that can still be reliably identified. They are believed to have served primarily to conceal hunters and, given their open form, their orientation provides a clear indicator of the direction in which the animals would approach. Given the open form, it is unlikely that these structures served other functions (such as caches), although it is possible they might have been used for shelter or windbreak.

V structures are typically based on a single large stone, which forms the apex of the "V," and two lines of other, typically smaller, stones that extend back from this apex to create a wedge shape. The core "V" on these structures may be supplemented by further extensions of lines composed of smaller stones. These extensions usually begin after a distinct gap, and often turn outward at a sharper angle than the core "V." The stones and boulders used in the construction of the "V" are variable in size, although the apex stone is typically a meter across and 60–110 cm high. The total width of the main "V" is in the range of 3 to 4 m.

The first V blind identified (Fig. 10.3*A*, *B*, Plate 5) is located in the Gap locality of Area 3. It is composed of five boulders with some smaller cobbles used to fill in gaps. The apex of the structure is oriented to the north, and the arms form an angle of about 50 degrees. Each arm is 3 m long. In this particular structure, there is a second line of stones, not shown on the figure, which begins about 1.5 m south of the westerly arm, and extends outward toward the southwest at a 40-degree angle. This extended line is 4 m long.

A second example of a simple open structure is the AshGap V, located in the AshGap portion of the Gap locality (Fig. 10.4) at a depth of 32 m. This is a more rudimentary blind composed of two large central boulders and a series of smaller rocks that approximate a "V"; additional placed rocks form an interior line. The total length of the structure is 4 m, and it measures 3.5 m at its widest extent. The functional importance of the interior stone line is not immediately apparent. It is possible that this was a later add-on to the main "V" and might represent part of an internal shelter. A second V structure in the immediate vicinity had a rectangular structure immediately behind it, which may suggest that additions were a common feature in this locality.

An alternative variety of simple open structures is represented by the Overlook Blind (Fig. 10.5), a feature located in the Overlook locality of Area 3, in 33 m of water. This variety of structure is focused on a single very large boulder, with lines of much smaller rocks projecting back from it. Here, the focal boulder is 2.2 m long and stands 0.8 m high. The rocks making up the two arms of the "V" are uniformly in the range of 24 cm high.

The structure is situated on level bedrock, but it is backed onto the foot of an uphill slope, which effectively provides a back for the structure. While it meets the basic definition of a V structure, both the construction and orientation of the feature (it is facing east) are anomalous, which may suggest that it served some function other than that of a hunting blind, such as a temporary shelter. On the other hand, it is located in the immediate vicinity of other V structures in an intensively utilized kill area.

Enclosed Structures

The initial category of enclosed structures recognized in the AAR survey was termed a three stone blind, even though subsequent investigation has revealed that, in some cases, more than three stones were used to create the structure. The first three stone blind identified on the AAR is the Dragon Blind (Fig. 10.6*A*, *B*, Plate 6), located in 31 m of water in Area 1. The structure received this name due to the long sinuous line of rocks revealed in the SSS image of the locality; this drive line is discussed further below.

The structure is composed of three large, flat topped boulders that are visually striking due to the bright white layer of dead algae that covers their upper surfaces. Each of these central boulders stands roughly 90 cm high. The main structure is triangular and measures approximately 2.5 × 2 m, although the area is larger if adjacent stones are included. A fourth large rock is immediately adjacent to the core three and is triangular in cross section, with the flat face down. It is less apparent in the photos because it is covered with mussels and adhering algae.

Inspection of the structure via ROV and SCUBA has shown that two of the three large boulders are red sandstone. It has also revealed that a number of smaller rocks and cobbles have been wedged beneath the three core stones, lifting the central portions of each stone upward and outward, to effectively increase the interior of the structure. While not represented in Figure 10.6*A*, Figure 10.6*B* (see also Plate 6) clearly shows the presence of a series of additional rocks, particularly to the immediate west of the structure. The function, if any, of these additional rocks is not known, but a similar pattern is seen at the T-V Blind (below).

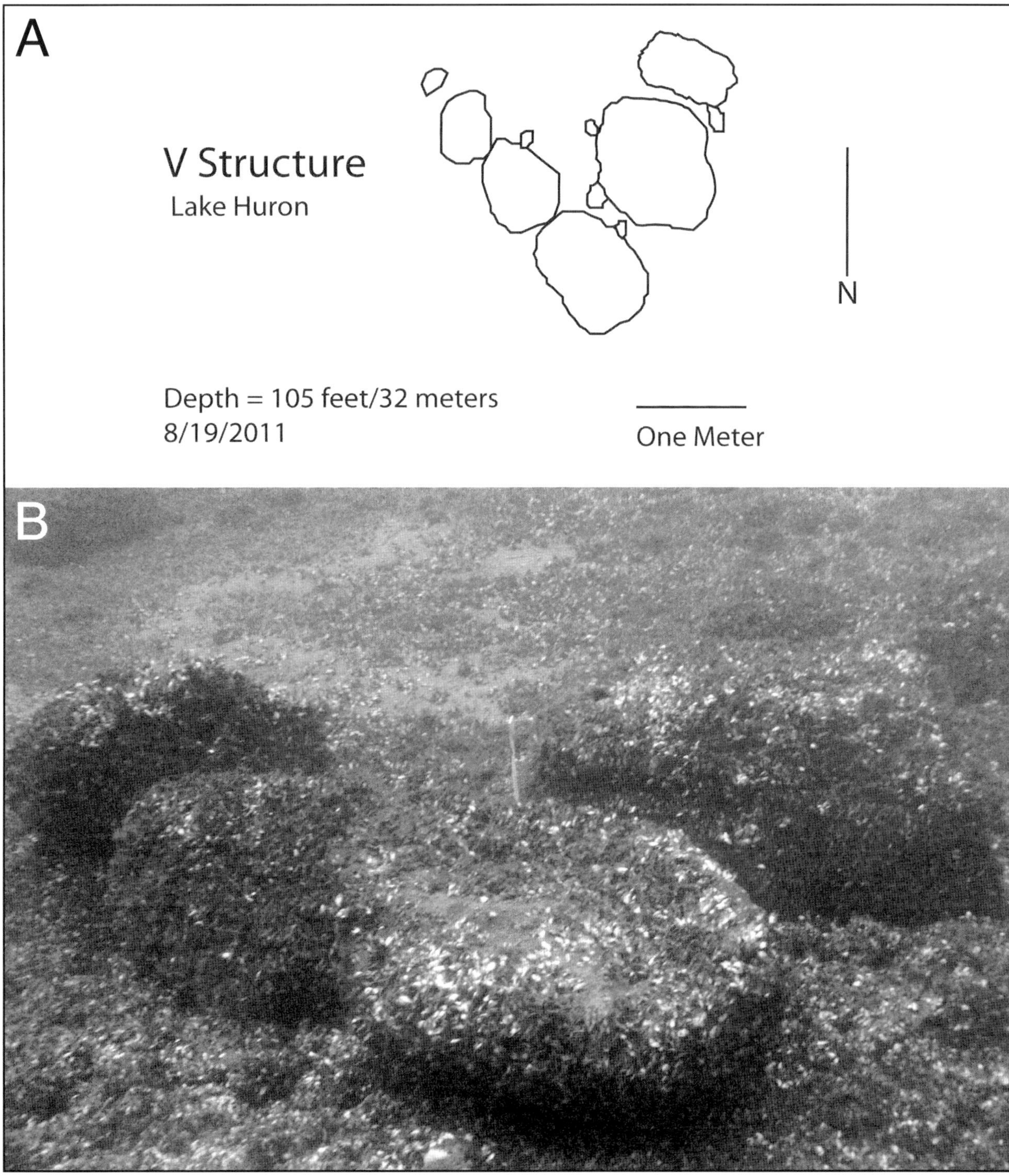

Figure 10.3. A V structure from the Gap locality in Area 3. The "V" is oriented to the north and is located at a depth of 32 m. *A*, scale drawing of the main stones in the construction; *B*, photograph of the feature with the same orientation. The object in the center of the "V" marks the location of a bottom sample. (See also Plate 5.)

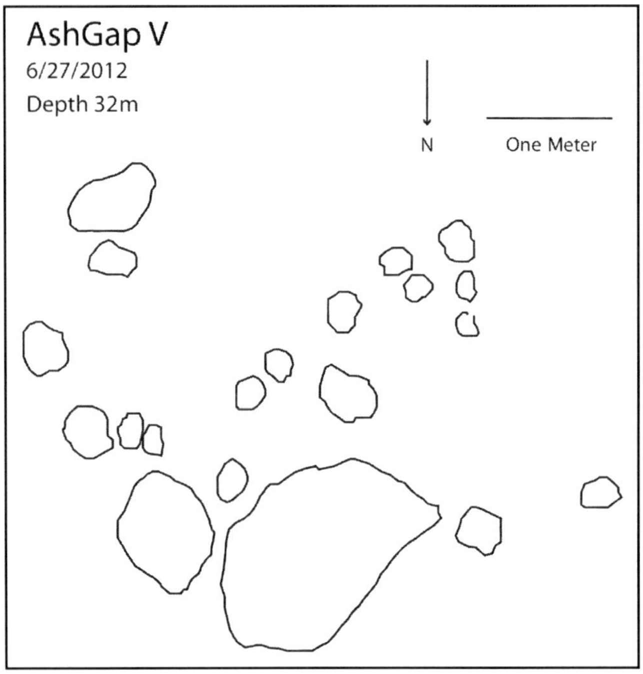

Figure 10.4. A V structure from the AshGap portion of the Gap locality in Area 3. The structure has an anomalous interior line of stones that may have been associated with a small internal shelter.

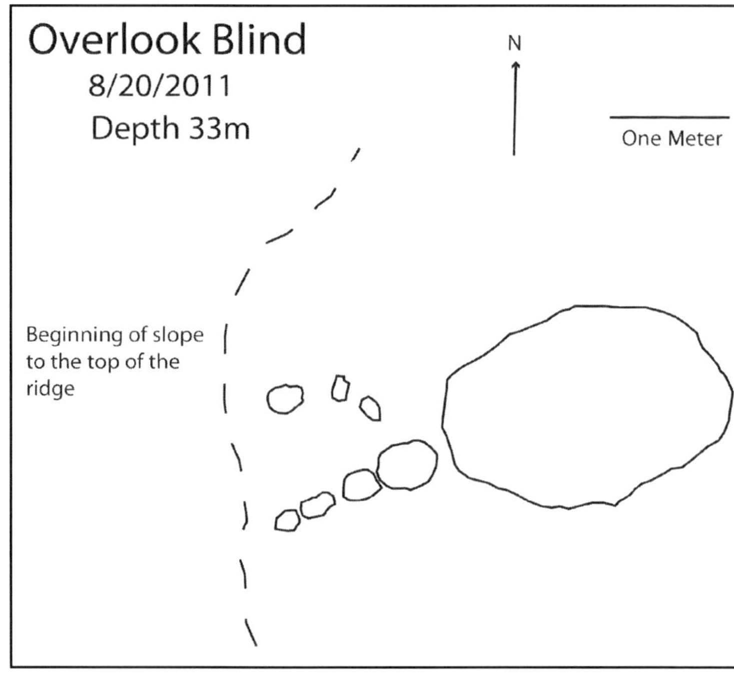

Figure 10.5. The Overlook Blind is located in the Overlook locality of Area 3 in 33 m of water. This feature is focused on a very large boulder, with lines of smaller rocks extending away from it, and abutting an uphill slope.

An important property of the three stone blinds is that they allow for rapid, multidirectional egress from the blind's interior. In contrast to the V structures, three stone blinds are not inherently directionally dependent, and could conceivably be used regardless of the direction in which the animals were moving.

A second example of a simple three stone enclosure is the T-V Blind, located in Area 3, in 32 m of water. Like the Dragon Blind, the T-V structure is composed of three large boulders that create a triangular enclosure (Fig. 10.7). Overall, the structure is 2.5 m × 2 m. The structure sits in an area of limestone bedrock with very few other stones. Figure 10.7 illustrates the distribution of stones in the vicinity of the T-V structure (note that these locations are not drawn to scale, although the headings are accurate). Again, it is not clear whether this haloing of cobbles had any specific function, although the placement of pairs of stones together may suggest they had been intentionally situated.

As the name suggests, this feature was assumed to be a V structure when originally encountered, and indeed, it is possible that it was used in only one orientation (in this case it would be facing the south, which suggests a spring season of use). On balance, however, it is probably most reasonably thought of as an enclosed structure.

A second variety of enclosed structures have a rectangular shape. A representative example of a rectangular structure is the West Blind in the Overlook locality of Area 3, in 35 m of water (Fig. 10.8). The West Blind is 3.5 × 3 m and is composed of a total of four boulders and three additional large stones. While a structure such as this could certainly provide concealment for a hunter, the relative close packing of the stones would have made rapid egress more difficult than for the three stone enclosures. There is also ethnographic precedent (cf. Stewart 2014: fig. 13) for the use of rectangular structures as caches rather than as hunting blinds.

Rectangular structures are not common on the AAR. Three have been recorded in survey to date, and in two of the three cases, the rectangular structures occur in the immediate vicinity of V structures. In the case of the West Blind, it sits to the side of a line of V structures in the Overlook locality. In the case of the one V structure in the AshGap locality, the rectangle is situated immediately behind the V structure (i.e., on the opposite side from the expected arrival of animals).

Linear Structures

Linear alignments of stones are one of the principal ways in which caribou drive lanes are created (Brink 2005; Stewart et al. 2000; Friesen 2013). Of course, it is rare that such lines would exist in isolation, but rather, would be an element in a kill locality

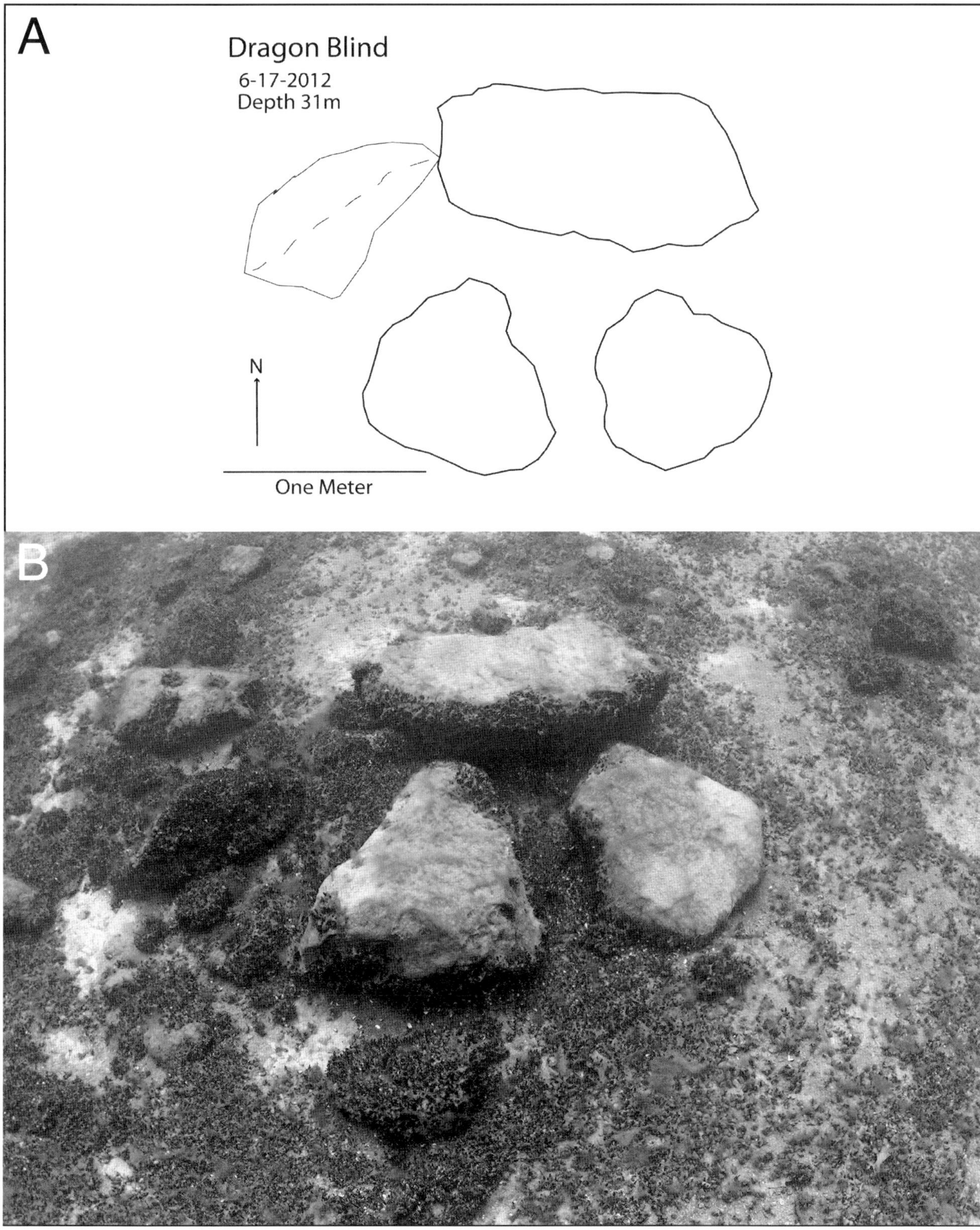

Figure 10.6. The Dragon Blind in Area 1 is associated with a long drive lane (see below). *A*, plan drawing showing the four main rocks comprising the blind; *B*, photograph that shows these stones, along with a series of small rocks around the perimeter. The upward tilt of the main stones is visible in this photo. (See also Plate 6.)

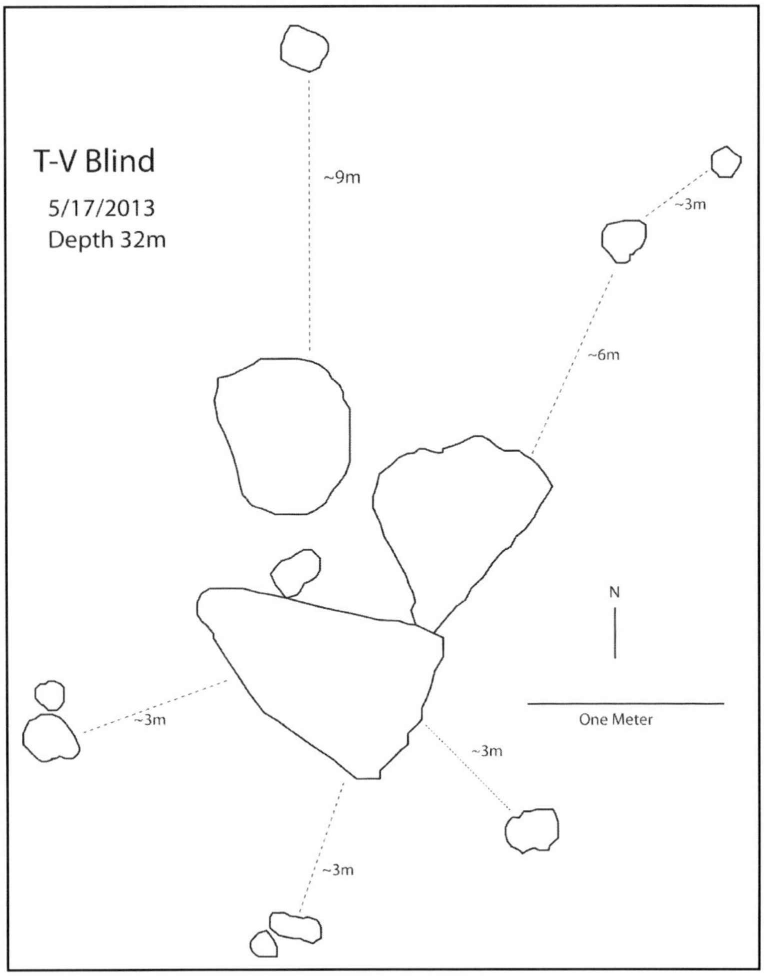

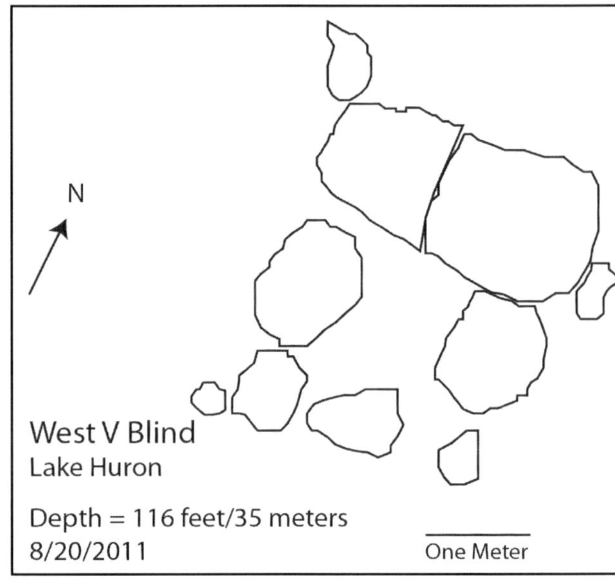

(*left*) Figure 10.7. The T-V Blind. This is a three rock-type closed blind in the Gap locality of Area 3. The blind has pairs of stones placed around its perimeter.

(*above*) Figure 10.8. The West V Blind is actually an enclosed rectangular structure located in the Overlook locality of Area 3. The rectangle is located behind a normal V structure and, following ethnographic accounts, may have functioned as a cache rather than a hunting structure.

that typically would include multiple lines, hunting blinds, and stone piles or cairns (*inuksuit*). From a practical perspective, a constructed line on the AAR that lacked other hunting features would be difficult to distinguish from linear features produced by any number of natural processes. As such, it is likely that the number of constructed features identified to date on the AAR is an underestimate of the total that exists. On the other hand, linear features can produce very obvious acoustic signatures that can be identified even during the extensive phase of SSS sonar. While the present discussion focuses on constructed linear features, both exemplars are associated with other constructed features, blurring the neat distinction between simple and complex hunting structures. Further, as discussed in Chapter 14, linear stone alignments are integral to both of the known complex hunting features.

The first linear structure that was identified in the AAR survey is the Dragon Drive Lane and Blind (see above). It was first recognized on the initial SSS survey of Area 1, in large part because of its fortuitous orientation relative to the sonar track. It was later confirmed by ROV observations at the central blind (Fig. 10.9*A*, *B*, Plate 6). The Dragon Drive Lane is located in the northern portion of Area 1 and is a southwest to northeast trending line of small rocks and boulders that form a line 365 m long along a basically level limestone bedrock floor. The line has a distinct bulge near the northeast end and it is in this bulge that the Dragon Blind is located. Several large boulders or rock piles are also associated with the beginning and end of the lane, as well as one at the midpoint. This central pile may actually be a second blind but it has not yet been directly examined. A view of the rock line as seen from the Dragon Blind is presented in Figure 10.10 (Plate 7).

As in Arctic examples, the drive lane is not so much a trapping structure as it is a feature designed to channel movement toward a predictable kill zone. The stones used in the Dragon Drive Lane seem larger than those used in the examples illustrated by Brink (2005) and Steward et al. (2000), but they would still not have created a solid barrier to the movement of animals. Depending on the location of the kill zone, linear features may, or may not, show directional dependency. In the case of the Dragon Lane, it would appear to be associated with the autumn movement of animals.

A second variety of linear construction is a line with built-in enclosures. An example of this kind of feature is represented by the New Gap Lane in the Gap locality of Area 3 (Fig. 10.11). The line is roughly 12 m long running north-south, and is made up of a spaced line of larger rocks with smaller rocks and cobbles filling the gaps between the larger stones. In four locations along

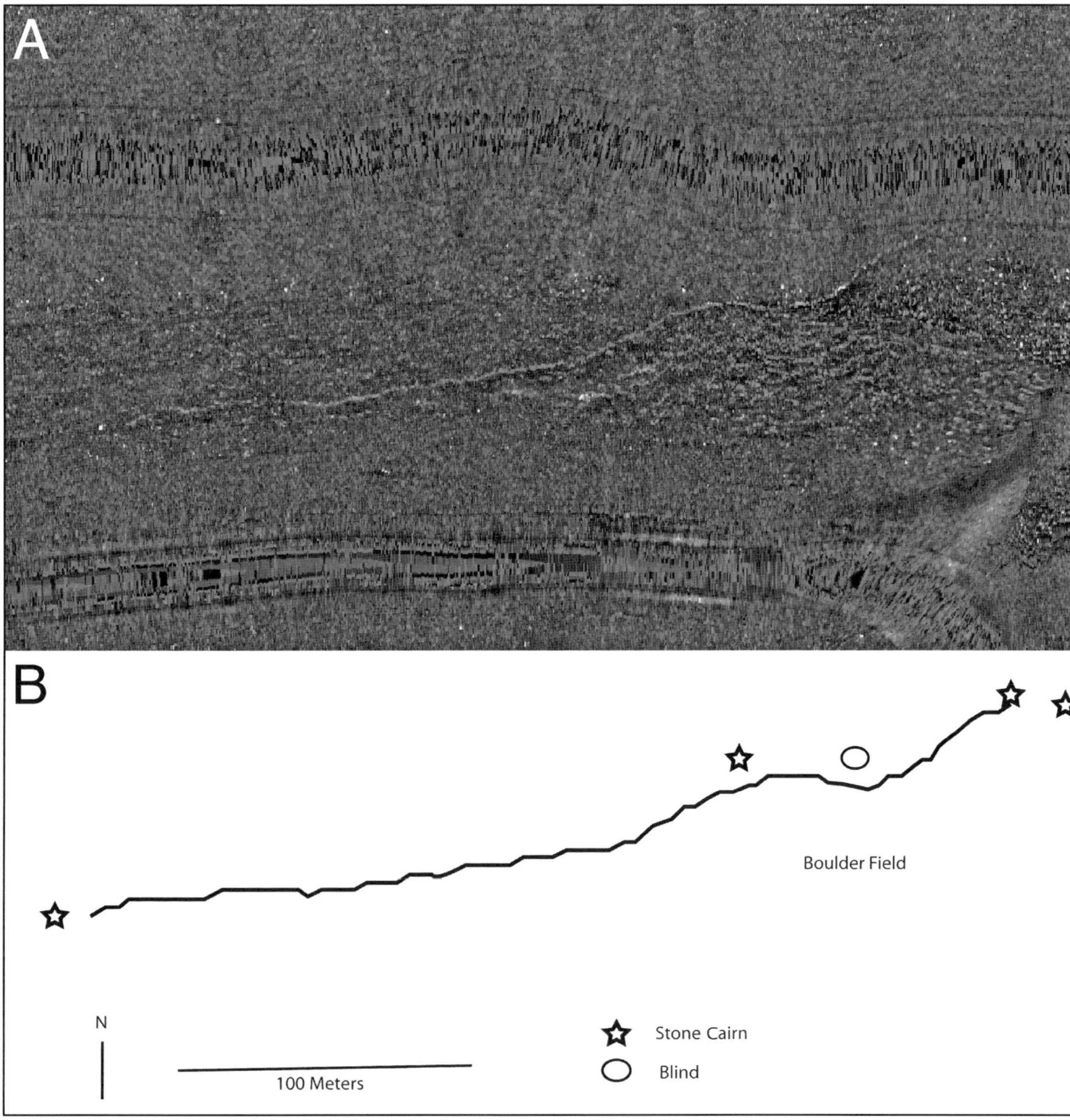

Figure 10.9. The Dragon Drive Lane. This feature in Area 1 consists of a long linear stone feature, with several associated stone cairns, and at least one hunting blind (the Dragon Blind, see Fig. 10.6). *A*, a sonar mosaic of the feature; *B*, plan drawing that highlights the principal constructions making up the drive lane. (See also Plate 6.)

Figure 10.10. A view of the linear rock line of the Dragon Drive Lane as viewed from the Dragon Blind. It should be noted that the compass rose on the image is inverted and the actual view is to the south. (See also Plate 7.)

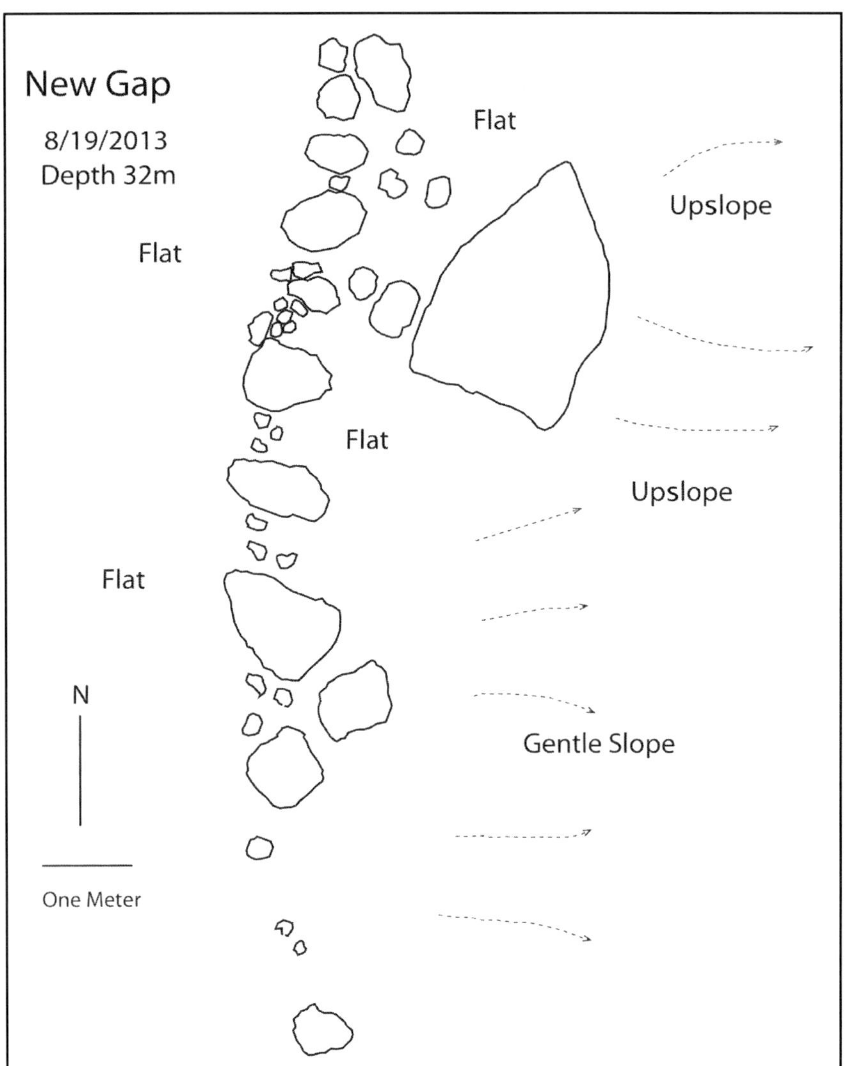

Figure 10.11. The New Gap Lane in the Gap locality of Area 3. This linear feature is roughly 12 m long and consists of a line of larger boulders with the gaps being filled by smaller stones. It appears that the structure was used primarily to provide concealment for hunters, but may also have served as a temporary shelter or cache.

this line are blindlike enclosures that are created by adding stones behind and perpendicular to the main line. Two of these perpendicular stone alignments are closed off in the rear (east) by a very large boulder, and the entire line is situated at the base of an upsloping landform to the east.

In looking at the placement of this feature, it appears that the line was located both to enhance the channeling effect of the existing slope and to provide concealment for hunters. The alignment of stones near the large boulder creates a normal-sized rectangular structure that might represent a caching feature, as previously discussed, or some manner of temporary shelter for hunters. There is nothing inherent in the orientation of this structure to limit the seasonal use of this feature, and given its siting within a north-south trending pass, it presumably could have been used for both spring and autumn hunts.

Other Constructed Features

Beyond lines and enclosures, a series of other constructed features have been identified by the AAR survey, including small rings, circular structures, stone piles, stacked stones, and upright stones. The archaeological recognition of these less regular constructions is made difficult by both the pervasive covering of all hard surfaces with mussels and attached algae, and the uncertainty in distinguishing true cultural modification from natural occurrences. This latter factor is exacerbated by the tendency of hunters, both modern and ancient, to make maximum use of what is naturally present in the environment and to make only the least modifications necessary to achieve their desired goals (Chapter 8).

Small rings and circular structures are the simplest categories to describe. The small rings encountered so far are composed of round and angular cobbles that form a hollow ring with a diameter of roughly 1 m. In both shape and size these small features resemble fire rings. In the one example that was directly examined via SCUBA, the surrounding stones did not appear to be fire cracked, but the core taken in the center of the ring revealed a layer of oxidized sediment and charcoal (see Chapter 12) that would seem to confirm the initial identification as a fireplace. No other cultural debris was encountered in the core. At least one of the other rings is made up of strongly angular rocks but they have not yet been examined to determine whether they have been thermally fractured.

Only one larger structure has been identified that is circular in shape. Unless additional obviously circular structures are observed, the present find is probably best thought of as an awkwardly shaped enclosed structure. Given the absence of clear egress pathways, they may also represent an alternative shape for caching.

Rock piles and standing and stacked stones are all categories of constructed features that are documented by Stewart et al. (2000) in their ethnographic work in the Falls River locality. All three can perform the guiding and marking functions attributed to *inuksuit*. Yet each has its own peculiar problems as archaeological phenomenon on the AAR.

In several instances, large glacial erratics have formed the anchor for stone constructions, such as stone lines, and in these cases it seems likely that they were opportunistically used in place without additional modification. Yet it would be clearly wrong to assert that any large erratic found on the landscape would necessarily have been utilized by early hunters.

A good example of the difficulties and potentials of these large unmodified features is the Big Rock in the southern portion of Area 3. This boulder stood out on the initial SSS survey as a very large rock that occurred in the middle of a very flat undifferentiated plateau. As such, it did not seem to warrant investigation, but was, by chance, selected as the target for a student practicing with the ROV. After the boulder was dutifully imaged and measured, the ROV began looking at its surroundings, which revealed the presence of an associated linear feature and a rock pile that might be a blind. Neither was visible in the initial SSS coverage. In this instance, the boulder as the most prominent feature on the landscape appears to have been used to anchor a small hunting feature. Overall, it seems that individual large boulders either can serve as a central component of a hunting feature, or can act like a large cairn or *inuksuit* to guide and channel movement.

Rock piles are another feature that are sometimes directly visible in the SSS imagery, but which, at other times, resolve only when viewed directly. Some of the larger piles may originally have been enclosures of one kind or another that have collapsed or been modified by post-use processes. Smaller piles, such as those already described for the Dragon Drive Lane, probably functioned more like cairns. Clearly, great caution must be exercised before declaring a rock pile to be a cultural feature since they are also produced by a variety of natural processes.

Stacked and upright stones present a different kind of archaeological difficulty since they are the types most vulnerable to disturbance during the inundation of the AAR. Upright stones—those standing with their long axis in a vertical plane—while common ethnographically, are less so on the AAR. Only one example can be argued with reasonably certainty, and that is the upright stone in the Funnel Drive complex. This stone is roughly cylindrical in shape and sits now in a tilted position near the outer opening of the funnel (see discussion below). In this case, the upright stone appears to have been an integral part of the hunting complex, serving to channel animals into the kill zone.

Stacked stones, particularly if they are of modest size, are probably the least likely type of construction to be preserved on the AAR although their recognition, if present, is unambiguous. Ethnographically, stacked stones appear to be used either to construct cairnlike structures in the manner of *inuksuit*, or, when spaced linearly, to create lines to channel movement (and in lieu of a continuous line of rocks).

The small stacked stone feature pictured in Figure 10.12*A* was one in a linear series of similarly constructed stacks found in Area 1, and bears an uncanny resemblance to similar constructions documented in the Falls River area (Fig. 10.12*B*; see Stewart et al. 2000). Small stacked features of this kind are extremely vulnerable to disturbance and it must be assumed that their preservation and discovery should be a rare occurrence. The fact that a sequence of them did survive for discovery may suggest that they were a common feature at one time.

Complex Structures

As has already been noted, the simple structures described here are modular, in the sense that they can be combined to create larger and more complicated hunting features. They can be thought of as providing a grammar for these more elaborate constructions. Several features already discussed, such as the Dragon Drive Lane or the New Gap Lane, combine elements of linear and enclosed structures, as well as rock piles and large boulders. The two features considered in this section are seen as being an order of magnitude more complex than any of the constructions described so far. They are complex in that they have more associated parts that are tightly integrated in a relatively small area, and complex because they would have required a great number of people to successfully operate them. While sharing these properties, the two complex hunting features so far documented on the AAR—the Funnel Drive and the Drop 45 Drive Lane—are distinct in their construction and operation.

Funnel Drive

The Funnel Drive was the first complex hunting feature identified on the AAR and was also the first feature to be mapped using scanning sonar technology (Fig. 10.13*A*, *B*, Plate 7). The feature is located near the high limestone ridge that gave Six Fathom Shoal its name, in Area 1, in 25 m of water. The immediate kill area is roughly 150 m^2, while its total area of extent is roughly 900 m^2 (.09 ha).

The central portion of the funnel is formed by a tightly set line of six boulders on one side and an equally solid—but more complex—line opposite, which appears to have functioned both as a block and as an extended blind (Fig. 10.14, Plate 8). These two lines converge in the northwest, producing a gap of 5 m, although a large stone placed in the middle of the gap divides the opening into two openings of 2.5 m (Fig. 10.15, Plate 8). The complex also incorporates a pair of three rock blinds: one at the east end of the back line and the other opposite the gap in the central portion of the feature. Immediately behind this second blind is a large stone that appears to have originally stood upright.

The Funnel Drive is situated to take advantage of two natural features—an irregular boulder field to the southwest and an approximately 1 m drop-off to the northeast, produced by the naturally outcropping limestone bedrock. These two features would have tended to channel the movement of animals along the level bedrock surface that the funnel effectively blocks. To enhance this blocking effect, a discontinuous line of large stones runs from the end of the interior wall out to the edge of the boulder field (Fig. 10.16, Plate 9). This line would not have been able to actually block the movement of animals, but would have been sufficient to channel their movement in toward the funnel structures.

The orientation of the Funnel Drive would favor the movement of animals moving toward the north and west—that is, the spring migration—with the large Six Fathom Shoal outcrop itself tending to dictate distinct routes for movement. It should be noted, however, that the feature is situated between this high ridge and a marsh, and it is alternatively possible that the locality was used to actively drive browsing animals into the feature. Regardless of the seasonal scenario, the operation of this complex hunting structure would have necessitated a large group of cooperating hunters. Whereas many of the simple structures could be operated by a small group of hunters waiting for the animals to pass by, the Funnel structure would have acted to compress animals into a small and volatile area (see Friesen 2013). This implies not only a sufficiency of hunters in the component blinds to make an effective (and safe) kill, but probably also implies other participants on the peripheries to move the animals forward into the kill zone. In this the Funnel Drive bears a closer resemblance to classic bison jumps than to the more passive drive lanes.

Drop 45 Drive Lane

The Drop 45 Drive Lane is the most complex hunting feature yet identified on the AAR. It is located in 37 m of water in the Overlook locality of Area 3. The feature is constructed on level limestone bedrock, and is composed of two parallel lines of stone leading to a naturally formed cul-de-sac created by a raised cobble pavement (Fig. 10.17*A*, *B*, Plate 9).

The stone lane proper is 8 m wide and 30 m long. It is bounded to the west by a naturally occurring raised cobble surface, and to the east by an area of bog. The two lines of stone that create the lane incorporate three enclosed blinds, two at the entry, and a third near the cul-de-sac. In addition to the main lane, the complex includes a series of linear alignments. Two are west of the lane on the cobble surface and extend perpendicularly from the lane, and a third is found immediately beyond the end of the lane on the raised surface. Further to the northwest are a boggy swale and a second crest that is also populated by a perpendicular arrangement of boulders. Taking all these elements together, the total area in which caribou would have been ambushed is roughly 100 m long and 28 m wide (.34 ha).

The interior of the drive lane is covered with clean sand to a depth of about 6 cm overlaying the limestone bedrock. Systematic sampling along the length of the lane yielded a total of 13 chert flakes. These and other lithic artifacts from the AAR are presented in Chapter 11.

The Overlook locality, the site of Drop 45, is a narrow (less than 2 km) southeast to northwest sloping isthmus, which contains a substantial concentration of structures. Near the crest of the slope (to the southeast) are at least five simple enclosures, including V structures and one rectangular structure. Downslope from the hunting area, acoustic imagery indicates the present of two long converging stone lines that narrow to a gap of about 400 m just below the Overlook area (Fig. 10.18).

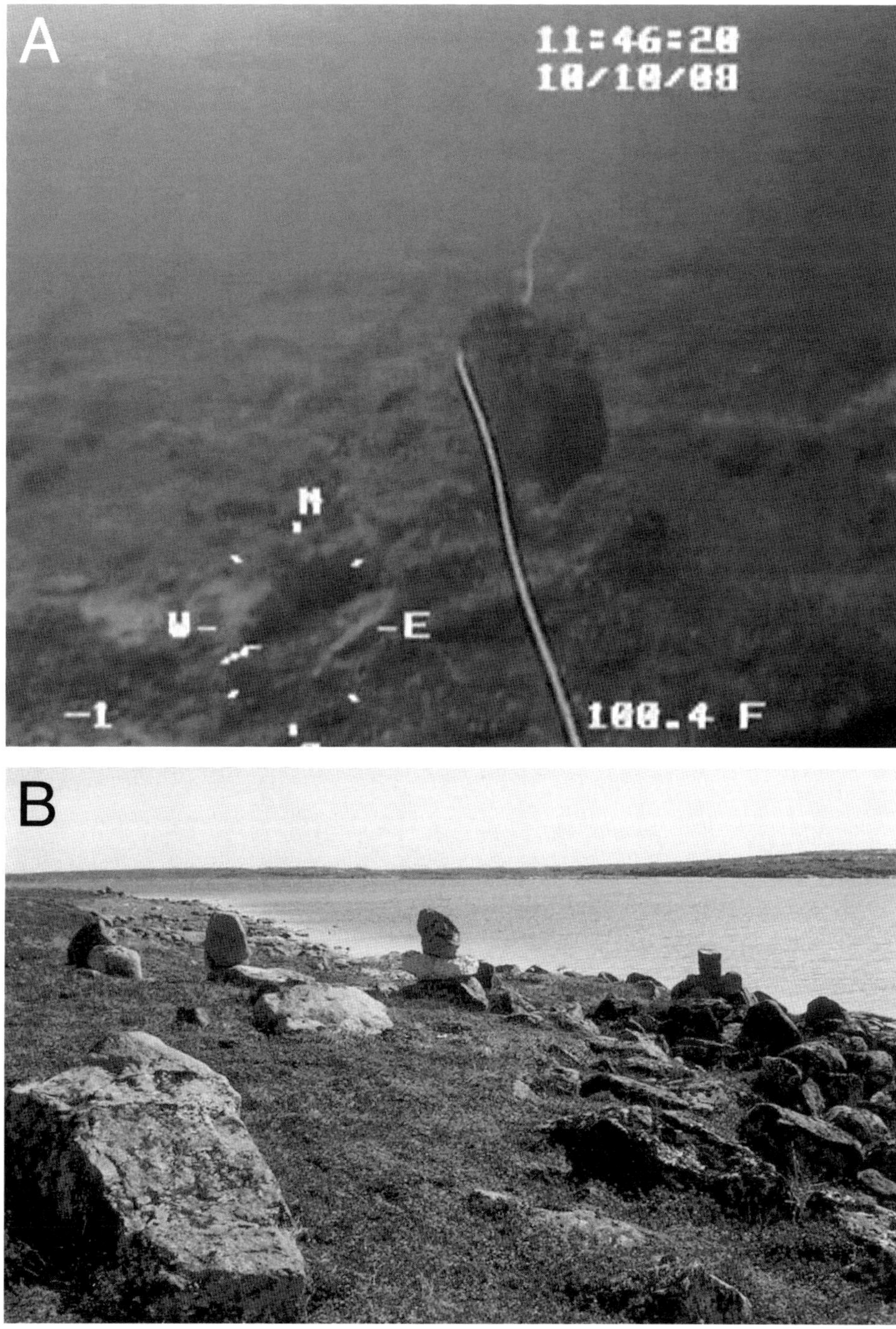

Figure 10.12. This figure compares an upright stone feature from Lake Huron with similar features of the Falls River area in Ontario. *A*, one of a series of stacked rocks identified in Area 1 of Lake Huron. The cable stretching across the features is the umbilical for the ROV; *B*, an illustration from Stewart et al. 2004:189.

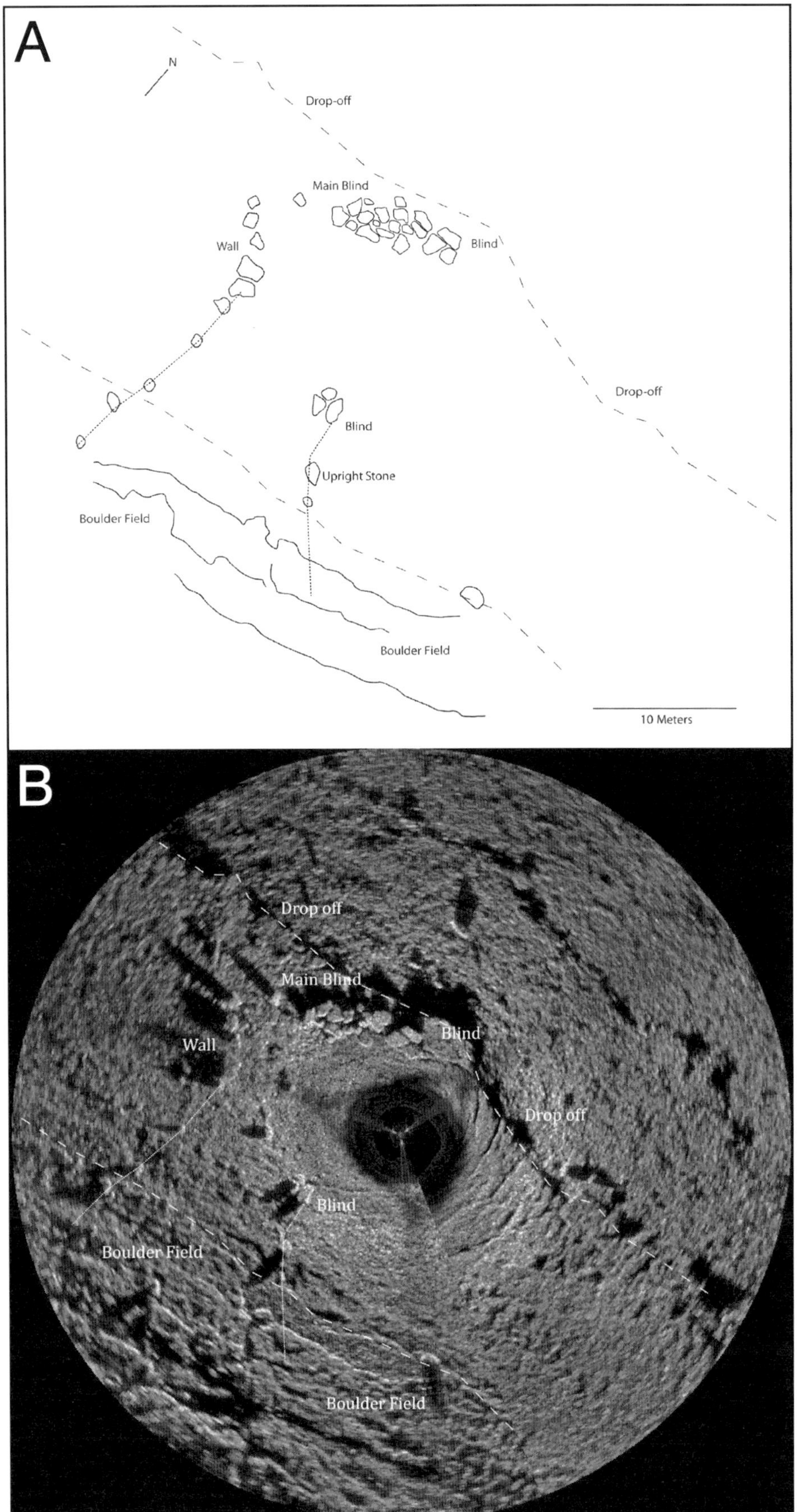

Figure 10.13. The Funnel Drive in Area 1. *A*, plan drawing of the feature highlighting its component parts; *B*, scanning sonar image of the drive. The dark circular area in the center of the image is the location of the tripod suspending the scanning sonar head. (See also Plate 7.)

Figure 10.14. The main blind of the Funnel Drive looking north. (See also Plate 8.)

Figure 10.15. The gap produced by the convergence of the main blind and stone line at the Funnel Drive. Note that a large stone has been placed in the center of the opening. Divers in the center of the photo are collecting bottom samples. Photo courtesy of Tane Casserley of the Thunder Bay National Marine Sanctuary. (See also Plate 8.)

Figure 10.16. Photograph of line of spaced boulders extending out from main wall of Funnel Drive. (See also Plate 9.)

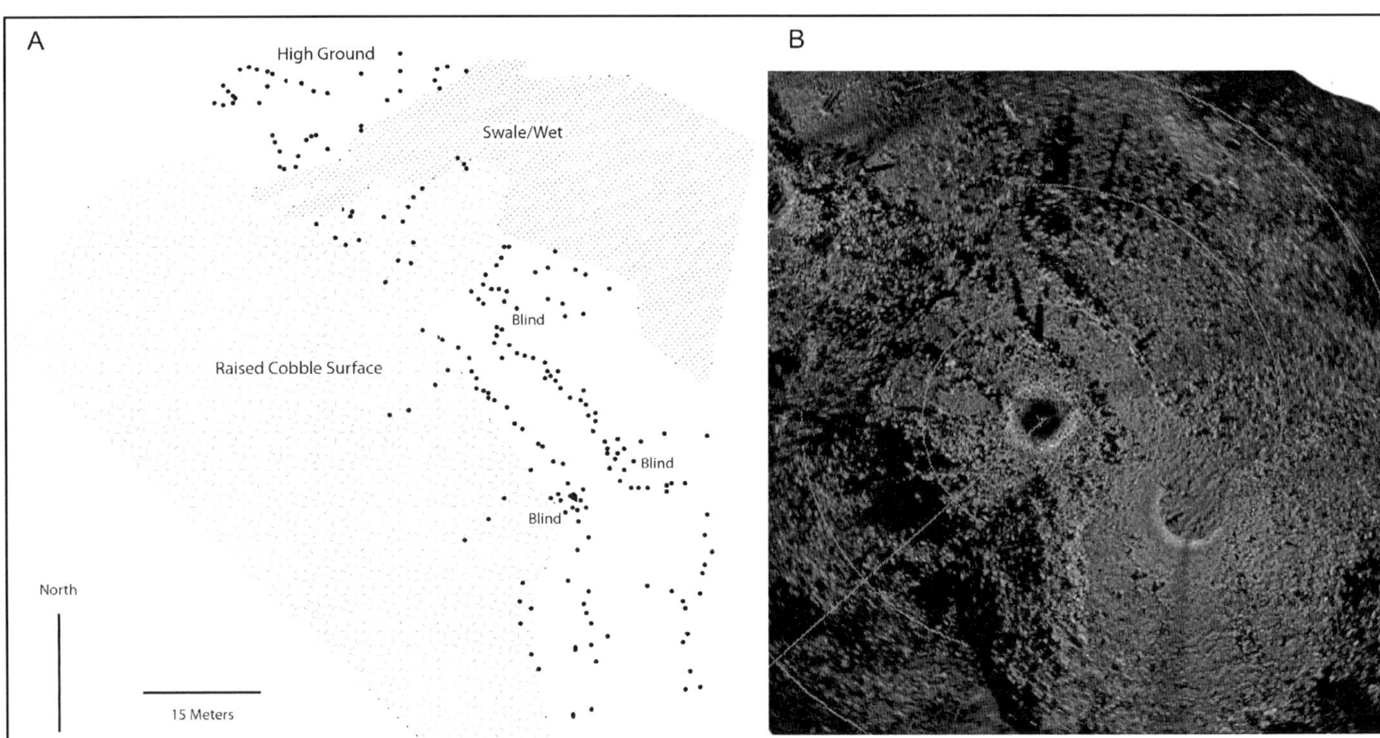

Figure 10.17. Drop 45 Drive Lane in Overlook locality of Area 3. *A*, plan view of the feature, highlighting the component elements; *B*, a mosaic of two scanning sonar images. The arcs in the scan image are spaced at 15 m intervals out from the central scan location. (See also Plate 9.)

Drop 45 is located near the top of the slope but below the crest, and is oriented with its broad opening to the southeast. This orientation would associate it with the spring migration of caribou, and would envision the animals transiting over the crest of the hill and immediately entering into Drop 45. As with the siting of many of the structures, a line of sight analysis demonstrates that they are located so as to be invisible to the approaching animals until they are effectively within the structure. Considering the likely season of use, it is interesting to note that the V structures that are located at the top of the slope in the Overlook locality are oriented to the northwest, suggesting a use in the autumn. As suggested by O'Shea et al. (2014), the explanation for the concentration of structures in this area, and their association with both spring and autumn movement, may reflect the locality's status as a "choke point" in the annual migrations, in which the predictability of the animal's passage (and thus the hunter's ability to intercept) is maximized.

As with the Funnel Drive, Drop 45 incorporates a number of stone lines and enclosures to create its final form. And as with Funnel Drive, the layout of the feature suggests the participation of numerous hunters to guide, drive, and kill the animals entering the feature. The stone alignments on the high ground beyond the main kill zone were presumably also populated by hunters who would have attacked those animals that escaped the main kill area. This need to populate a number of locations within the complex to make the hunt work is in contrast to the simple structures on the hilltop above, in which any combination of one or many of the structures could have been occupied passively, until the migrating animals were within range to strike.

The Frequency and Distribution of Structures on the Alpena-Amberley Ridge

Since 2008, research on the AAR has identified a number of potential and confirmed structures in both Area 1 and Area 3. In some cases, the structures were recognized during survey, which permitted limited mapping and measurement to be conducted remotely. In other cases, subsequent review of the video records revealed features that were not noted during the survey. From all these contacts, a master listing of potential targets has been constructed that will guide future investigations.

Taking only those features that were recognized during the actual survey, it is possible to form a preliminary sense of the frequency and distribution of the differing kinds of bottom features. Table 10.1 follows the preliminary classification of structures used in the description above. The terms "circle," "cluster," "line," "pile," "rectangle," and "V" describe the nonrandom shape or configuration of stones that may have constituted either a hunting structure or a component in a larger structure. The same is true of "upright stones," which are unusually (for the locality) large rocks that appear to be in an upright position. "Rings" are circular arrangements of stones that are too small to have been a hunting structure, but may have been a different kind of cultural feature, such as a fireplace. The final category, "complex," includes those features that contain a series of structure elements that are tightly integrated to create a single structure. As noted in the descriptions, elements occasionally do occur together in what seem to be an intentional grouping, and as such the division between complex and simple structures is somewhat artificial. The justification for the division is that the elements within a construction termed "complex" are integral, in the sense that they are all dependent elements, whereas other near placements of elements seem potentially to have grown through addition, in the sense that the individual elements could have functioned and been used as self-standing hunting features. This distinction is considered in more detail below.

The numbers in Table 10.1 must be viewed as first approximation since many of the structures have only been examined remotely. It, likewise, is not possible to estimate the overall density of constructions on the submerged landscape because search efforts have been directed at examining likely hunting locations, without an equivalent examination of less likely localities. Such searches are planned for the future. While we cannot speak directly to area density, it is possible to offer a first approximation of the local density of construction in areas that contain structures, and to consider the environmental context in which the encountered structures occur (the siting of hunting structures is considered in more detail in Chapter 14).

Based on surveys conducted to date, potential hunting sites do appear to be clustered on the landscape within plausibly predictable locations relating to the intercept of migrating animals. The location where we have the best evidence of this is in Area 3 (Fig. 10.18). In this region, there are numerous stone constructions, which have been directly examined, as have the areas adjacent to and in between the clusters of structures.

Looking at the Gap locality (Fig. 10.19, Plate 10), there are two distinct clusters of features, both of which are anchored on landscape features that would have constrained or guided the movement of caribou. The more southerly cluster represents an area of 1.2 ha and contains 14 identified structures, for a density of 11.7 per hectare. The more northerly cluster has an area of 2.5 ha and 10 identified structures, yielding a density of 4.0 per hectare. If the Gap locality is taken as a whole, it represents an area of 29 ha containing at least 31 structures, or a density of 1.1 per hectare. By comparison, the Overlook locality in the northern portion of Area 3 (Fig. 10.20, Plate 11) included at least 6 structures, including 1 complex construction, within an area of 6.2 ha, yielding a density of just under 1 per hectare.

Considering Area 1, the locality that is most similar to the Gap locality in terms of the amount of survey and the number of structures is the Crossing locality (Fig. 10.21, Plate 12). This large area comprises 98.7 ha and contains at least 21 constructions, yielding a density of 0.2 per hectare. Similarly low densities are observed in the Dragon locality (Fig. 10.22, Plate 13), which is 30.3 ha and contains at least 5 constructions, including 1 complex structure, yielding a density of 0.2 per hectare.

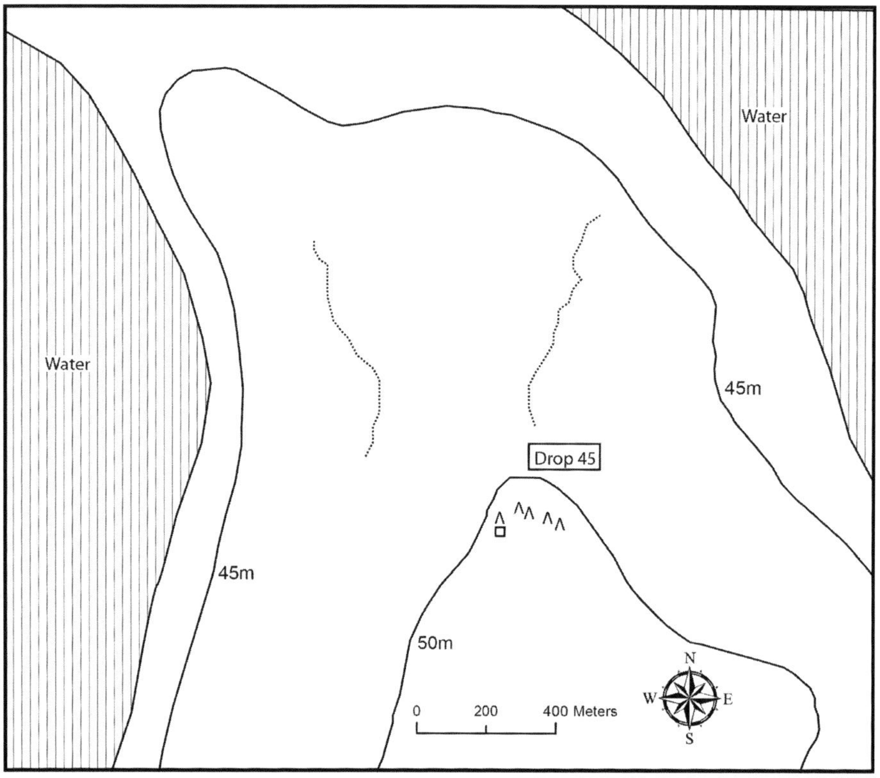

Figure 10.18. The Overlook locality in Area 3, showing the topographic setting of the V blinds and the Drop 45 Drive Lane and associated features. Contour interval is 5 m and is reported in meters above mean sea level (modern Lake Huron datum is 176 m amsl). Hatching reflects areas believed to be underwater at time the locality was in use.

Table 10.1. Frequency of different stone structure types by search area.

Category	Area 1	Area 3	Total
circle	0	1	1
cluster	15	10	25
line	9	8	17
pile	1	3	4
rectangle	1	3	4
ring	3	0	3
upright stone	0	1	1
V	3	14	17
complex constructions	1	1	2
total	33	41	74

As stated previously, these density figures must be taken with several grains of salt since the bottom survey to date does not approximate a systematic or complete coverage survey, and the definition of relevant localities is entirely arbitrary. Yet they are sufficient to show that in favorable locations, the density of structures can be quite high, and that the structures are not evenly distributed across the landscape.

One potentially interesting contrast in the distribution of the differing constructions is the contrastive emphasis on closed vs open blinds between the two research areas. While the occurrence of differing types of structures cannot be shown to be significantly different between the individual localities or areas, there is the suggestion that V-type structures are more common in Area 3 and that closed structures, such as three stone blinds, are more common in Area 1 (Table 10.2).

The explanation for this regional distinction is not obvious. One possibility is that the V structures in Area 3 are situated to exploit specific migration events, whereas the enclosed structures of Area 1 were more generalized in their use, and would have been situated to exploit a specific seasonal movement of animals. This possibility fits with the simulation of caribou movement across the AAR (see Chapter 4), which predicts that the animals would have been effectively channeled in their movement over the portions of Area 3 examined, while their movement would have been more diffused in Area 1.

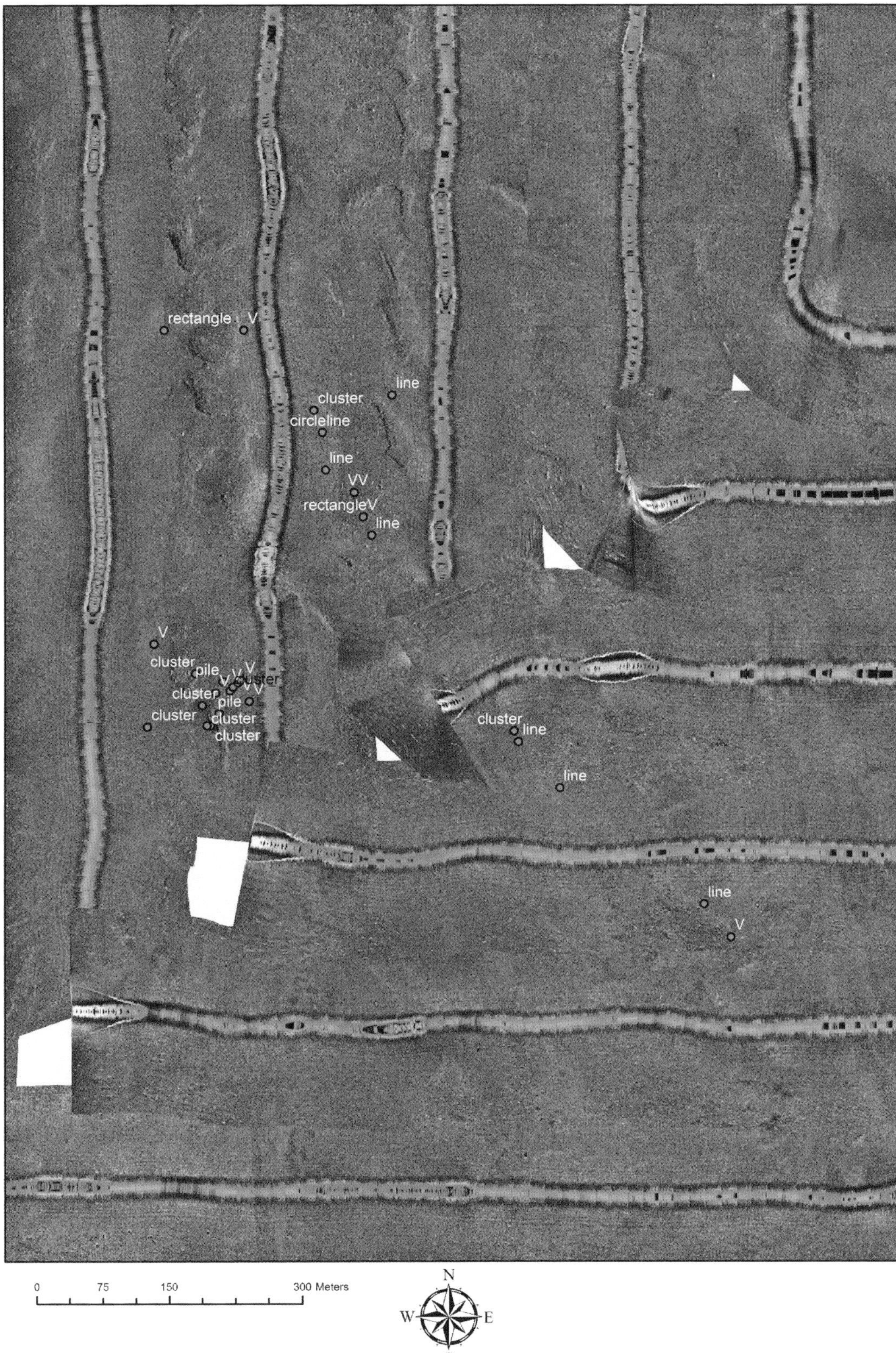

Figure 10.19. The Gap locality in Area 3, showing the main concentrations of features identified. Distribution is overlain on a side scan sonar mosaic of the locality. Channeling glacial deposits are in clear evidence in the areas of main feature concentration. (See also Plate 10.)

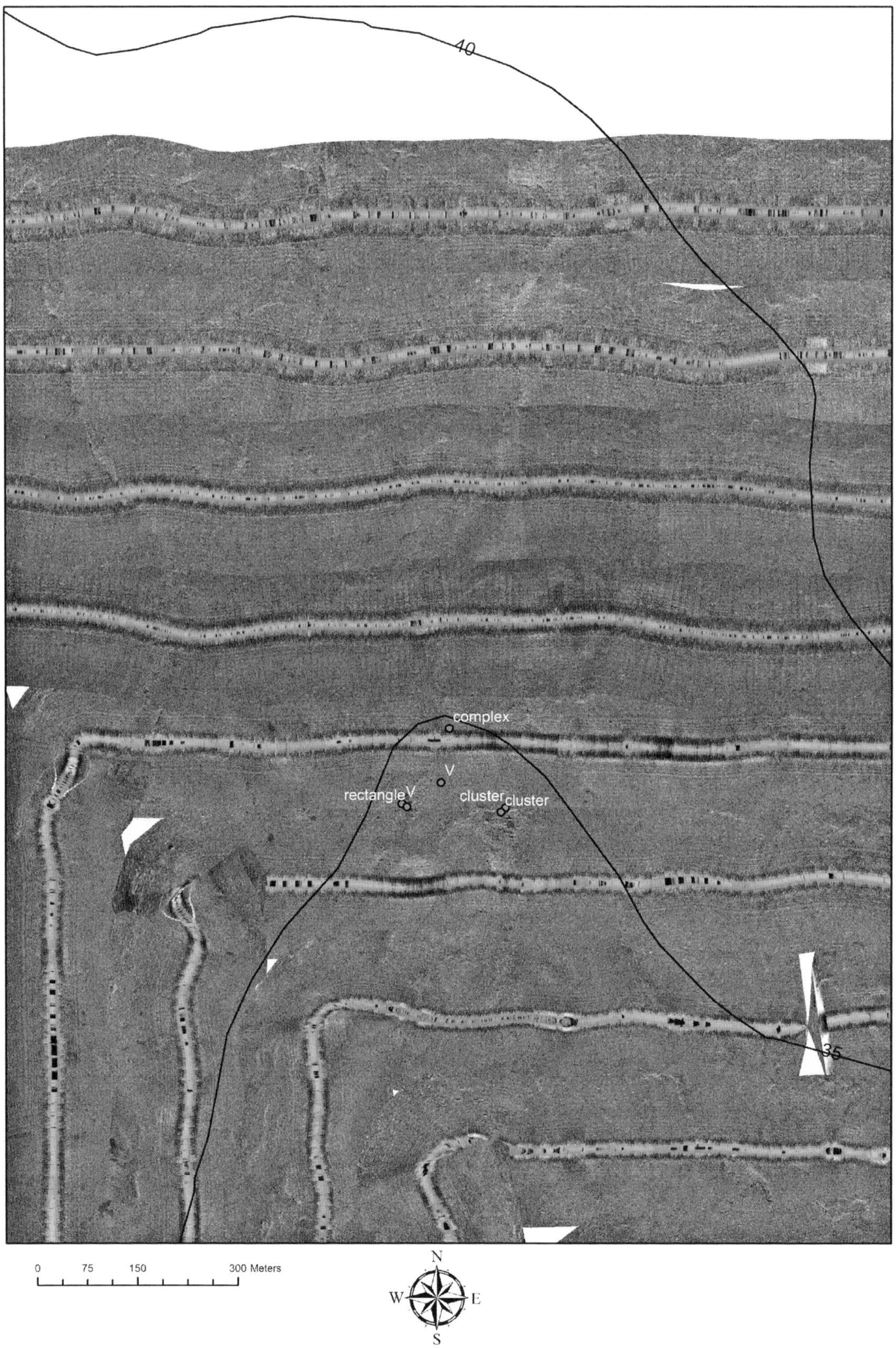

Figure 10.20. The Overlook locality in Area 3 showing the locations of structures near the top of the ridge. The distribution is overlain on a side scan sonar mosaic of the locality. Contour interval is 5 m reported in depth below surface. (See also Plate 11.)

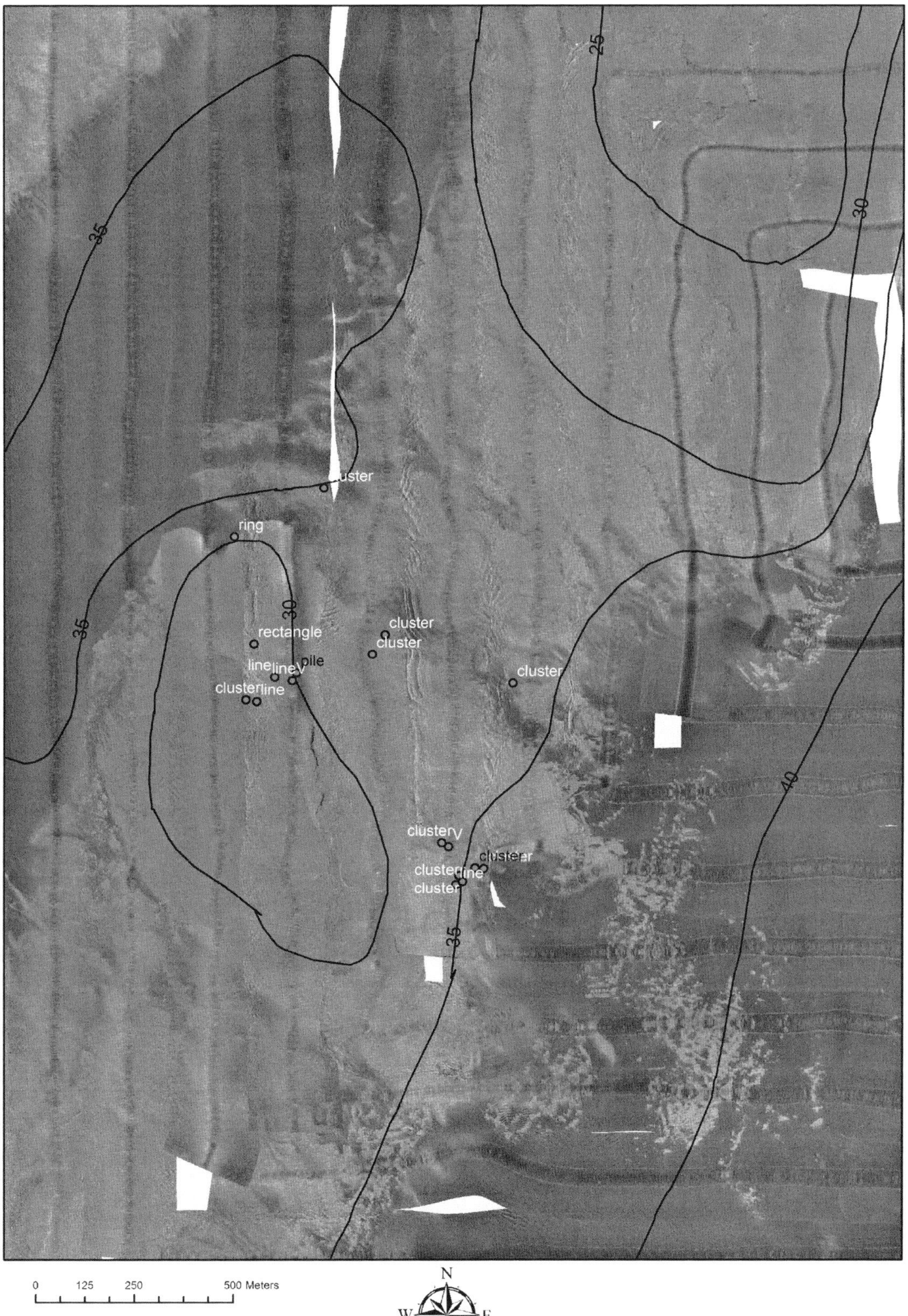

Figure 10.21. The Crossing locality in Area 1 showing the location of identified features. The distribution is overlain on a side scan sonar mosaic of the locality. Dark areas in the side scan image are areas of sand that would have been underwater during the occupation of the AAR. Contour interval is 5 m reported in depth below surface. (See also Plate 12.)

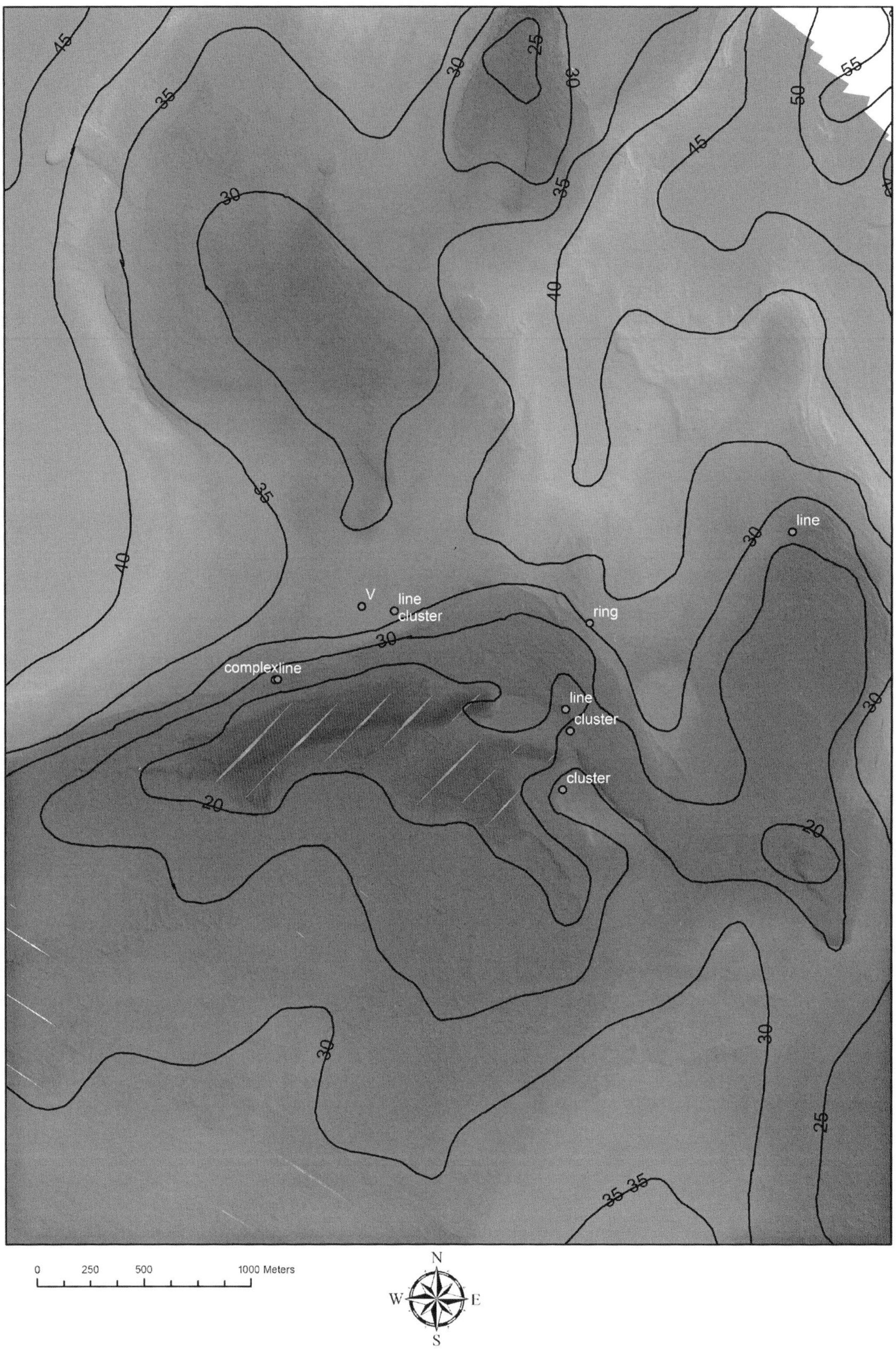

Figure 10.22. The Dragon locality in Area 1 showing the location of identified features. The distribution is overlain on a multibeam sonar mosaic of depth. The contour interval is 5 m reported in depth below surface. The location labeled "complex line" is the Funnel Drive. (See also Plate 13.)

Table 10.2. Distribution of major structure types by research area.

Structure Type	Area 1	Area 3	Total
cluster	15	11	26
line	9	8	17
pile	1	4	5
rectangle	1	3	4
V	3	14	17
total	29	40	68

Pearson chi-square = 9.069, $df = 4$, $p = 0.059$

Discussion

The purpose of this chapter has been to describe the salient characteristics of the stone constructions that have been identified to date on the AAR and to briefly note how they might have functioned during their time of use. A fuller consideration of function and seasonality is presented in Chapter 14. What is left to be considered here is how the structures came to be constructed on the landscape and what significance should be attached to the differing forms that are observed.

It is clear, first and foremost, that the occupants of the AAR were not interested in creating a lot of extra work for themselves. They took advantage of the natural alignments and barriers that this post-glacial landscape offered, which were many, and they used the readily available stone to create whatever additional features were needed to turn the natural settings into effective hunting sites. In some cases, this may have been as simple as moving cobbles out of the way to create open lanes; in others, it meant shifting a couple of boulders into a more desirable location. While these boulders are substantial, spruce poles of the type that have been recovered from the AAR would have provided sufficient leverage to move them (see Chapter 12). While it is probably safe to assume that hunters attempted to minimize the effort involved in creating these structures, there are at least two pieces of evidence to suggest that substantial amounts of effort and labor were expended in their construction.

One example is the observation that two of the three main boulders forming the Dragon Blind were of old red sandstone. Large specimens of this sandstone are not rare, but they are not particularly common either, which raises the possibility that they were specifically selected and used, perhaps because of their red color (see Chapter 8). It is also noteworthy that at this same feature, several of the large boulders appear to have been partially lifted so that small stones could be wedged beneath them to increase the interior area of the blind.

A second instance is found at the Funnel Drive. While the Funnel complex is entirely composed of larger boulders, it probably was initiated at the site of a fortuitous natural concentration of rock (such concentrations often result from the breaking up of layers of limestone bedrock). This cannot be said, however, of the extended line of boulders that stretches out from the main structure. As is evidenced in Figure 10.16, these boulders have been placed in a spaced line on a level bedrock surface that is otherwise entirely devoid of rocks. In this instance, it was not simply moving a couple of existing rocks into place—the boulders had to have been moved a significant distance to the location, and then placed with some precision to form this discontinuous line.

The fact that ancient hunters were able and willing to undertake this kind of construction when necessary should not be surprising, as historical and ethnographic cases aptly illustrate this capability. The more interesting question is how was the process realized and to what extent were the final features planned?

The modular character of the structures suggests that the constructions could grow by aggregation without any specific initial plan in mind. A key feature of the simple structures is that they are usable on their own, when placed in suitable natural settings. If a particular location proves productive, additional features can be added either to increase the effectiveness of the location or to accommodate a greater number of hunters. The continued improvement of a desirable location may also have served to denote a particular individual's or group's claim to the use of the location. Both processes—a growth by progressive addition or accretion, and the elaboration of a permanent facility to assert a claim to use—are supported by ethnographic cases.

Yet, it is not clear how the more complex features, such as the Funnel Drive or Drop 45, could have been built up in such a progressive and unplanned manner. Even the Dragon Drive Lane contains a series of interlinked components that are needed for the structure to operate. In each of these cases, it is possible to envision a simpler, prior version of the complex form that occupied the same location, but that simpler construction would have had to be entirely reworked to create the complex hunting structures that were ultimately created.

In light of these considerations, it is probably not a coincidence that the features that were the most complex to construct were also the hunting sites that implied the participation of a great number of people. It will be left to Chapter 14 to synthesize these and the other observations regarding the organization of hunters on the AAR.

11 Lithic Artifacts from Submerged Archaeological Sites on the Alpena-Amberley Ridge

by Ashley K. Lemke

Seventeen flakes and 1 unifacial scraper have been recovered from submerged archaeological sites on the Alpena-Amberley Ridge, a landform across the Lake Huron basin that was dry land 7500–9500 years ago. These lithic artifacts—recovered during systematic sampling and excavation by SCUBA divers—were in close association with stone constructed caribou hunting features. They most likely indicate tool maintenance and scraping activities during hunting, butchering, and hide processing behaviors. The majority of lithic artifacts (13 flakes and the scraper) come from an elaborate caribou hunting site with drive lanes and hunting blinds: Drop 45. The remaining 4 flakes come from two localities with additional hunting structures. This chapter describes all the lithic artifacts recovered to date, including metrics, raw material types, and context, and discusses what these artifacts demonstrate about hunters and hunting on the Alpena-Amberley Ridge.

Introduction

The Alpena-Amberley Ridge (AAR) is a rocky limestone and dolomite outcrop that runs across the central Lake Huron basin in the Great Lakes. Historically known as Six Fathom Shoal, this ridge would have been dry land during the Lake Stanley lowstand phase of Great Lakes prehistory (7500–9500 cal BP), where water levels were as much as 120 m below modern levels. These low-water levels exposed the AAR, a post-glacial environment that would have been inhabited by plants, animals, and humans during the early Holocene. Paleoenvironmental reconstruction indicates that the AAR was a Subarctic environment with marshes, shallow lakes, rivers, and wetlands. The preserved spruce and tamarack trees that have been recovered from the AAR indicate that it was a prairie parkland between 8000 and 9000 BP. In addition, recovered microfossils reveal an ideal habitat and forage for ranging caribou (Chapters 3, 12).

It has long been acknowledged that Late Paleoindian and Early Archaic sites dating to this time period would now be underwater due to rising Holocene water levels (Ellis, Kenyon, and Spence 1990; Karrow 2005; Karrow and Warner 1990; Shott 1999). To date, more than 60 stone constructions have been discovered on the AAR that appear to have been created and used by Late Paleoindian/Early Archaic caribou hunting peoples. Archaeological research has focused on surveying this preserved ancient hunting landscape and excavating stone constructed features (see Chapters 9, 10). During systematic sampling and excavation, lithic artifacts have been recovered from three different areas. This chapter describes and discusses these artifacts and their contexts, and considers what they can tell us about human activity on the AAR.

Lithic Artifacts

Lithic artifacts, including 17 flakes and 1 unifacial scraper, were recovered during systematic sampling and excavation operations performed by SCUBA divers on the AAR (Table 11.1). The flakes are small, with average length, width, thickness, and weight of 9.39 mm, 5.62 mm, 2.26 mm, and 0.21 g respectively.

Table 11.1. Lithic artifacts from submerged archaeological sites on the Alpena-Amberley Ridge.

Spec. No.	Research Area	Site or Locality	UTM Easting	UTM Northing	Material	Type	Length (mm)	Width (mm)	Thickness (mm)	Weight (g)
DE-1a	1	Crossing	383383	4960599	chert	debitage	6.08	1.16	3.20	0.08
Vial 1a	1	Crossing	383371	4962702	chert	flake	7.88	5.55	1.92	0.13
DA-1a	3	Gap	362075	4968223	chert	flake	7.31	6.50	1.64	0.07
DA-1b	3	Gap	362075	4968223	chert	debitage	2.30	2.93	0.42	0.01
DP-1-1a	3	Drop 45	362314	4970264	chert	debitage	15	8	2.61	0.27
DP-1-1b	3	Drop 45	362314	4970264	chert	debitage	6	5.50	3.05	0.12
FE-1-2a	3	Drop 45	362319	4970292	chert	flake	11	10	2.11	0.26
FE-1-2b	3	Drop 45	362319	4970292	chert	debitage	6	5	2.61	0.08
EG-1-2a	3	Drop 45	362314	4970258	chert	debitage	14	6	1.17	0.13
EG-1-2b	3	Drop 45	362314	4970258	chert	debitage	15	7	4.05	0.44
FA-1-2a	3	Drop 45	362314	4970268	chert	flake	10	6	1.80	0.10
EZ-1a	3	Drop 45	362322	4970266	chert	flake	6.50	5	1.32	0.05
EO-1-2a	3	Drop 45	362317	4970282	chert	debitage	17	7	2.26	0.16
EO-1-2b	3	Drop 45	362317	4970282	chert	flake	6	5	1.79	0.87
FB-1-1a	3	Drop 45	362322	4970262	chert	cortical flake	11	4	4.14	0.21
Unit 1a	3	Drop 45	362362	4970280	chert	flake	8.43	3.26	1.60	0.06
Unit 3a	3	Drop 45	362323	4970290	Bayport	thumbnail scraper	9.15	7.97	3.48	0.20
Unit 8a	3	Drop 45	362322	4970279	chert	cortical flake	10.15	7.64	2.75	0.50

The thumbnail scraper is larger, with a maximum length, width, thickness, and weight of 9.15 mm, 7.97 mm, 3.48 mm, and 0.20 g. In Table 11.1, a type is listed for each lithic artifact. Flakes are defined as thin, angular specimens that had one or more diagnostic features of lithic manufacture—that is, bulb of percussion, intact platform, and/or feathering/ripples from impact pressure ($n = 9$). Debitage is defined as specimens that are thin, angular, and easily distinguished from background sediments (i.e., rounded, thick, natural sediments and pebbles; $n = 8$). This debitage category is similar to specimens from terrestrial archaeological sites where bulbs and/or platforms may be sheared off or to specimens that are diagnostic of bipolar shatter. All the artifacts are made on chert, with four main raw materials represented: gray-brown cherts, which are common in the local Devonian Age Traverse formation (Hough 1958; $n = 11$); a black and orange glacial chert ($n = 3$); a high-quality black semitranslucent chert ($n = 2$); and Bayport chert, located in the Saginaw Bay region of Michigan, which was used to make the scraper. The use of Bayport chert by Late Paleoindian and Early Archaic hunter-gatherers on the AAR is expected since lower water levels during this time period would have led to greater exposures of this raw material source (Chapter 6).

Context

There are two primary research areas on the AAR: Areas 1 and 3 (Fig. 11.1). Area 1 is the largest (56 km^2) and most varied topographically, and has the highest elevation on the AAR. Area 1 was selected for research for two primary reasons: (1) these high elevations have the potential for containing intact archaeological remains dating to the Lake Stanley lowstand (7500–9500 cal

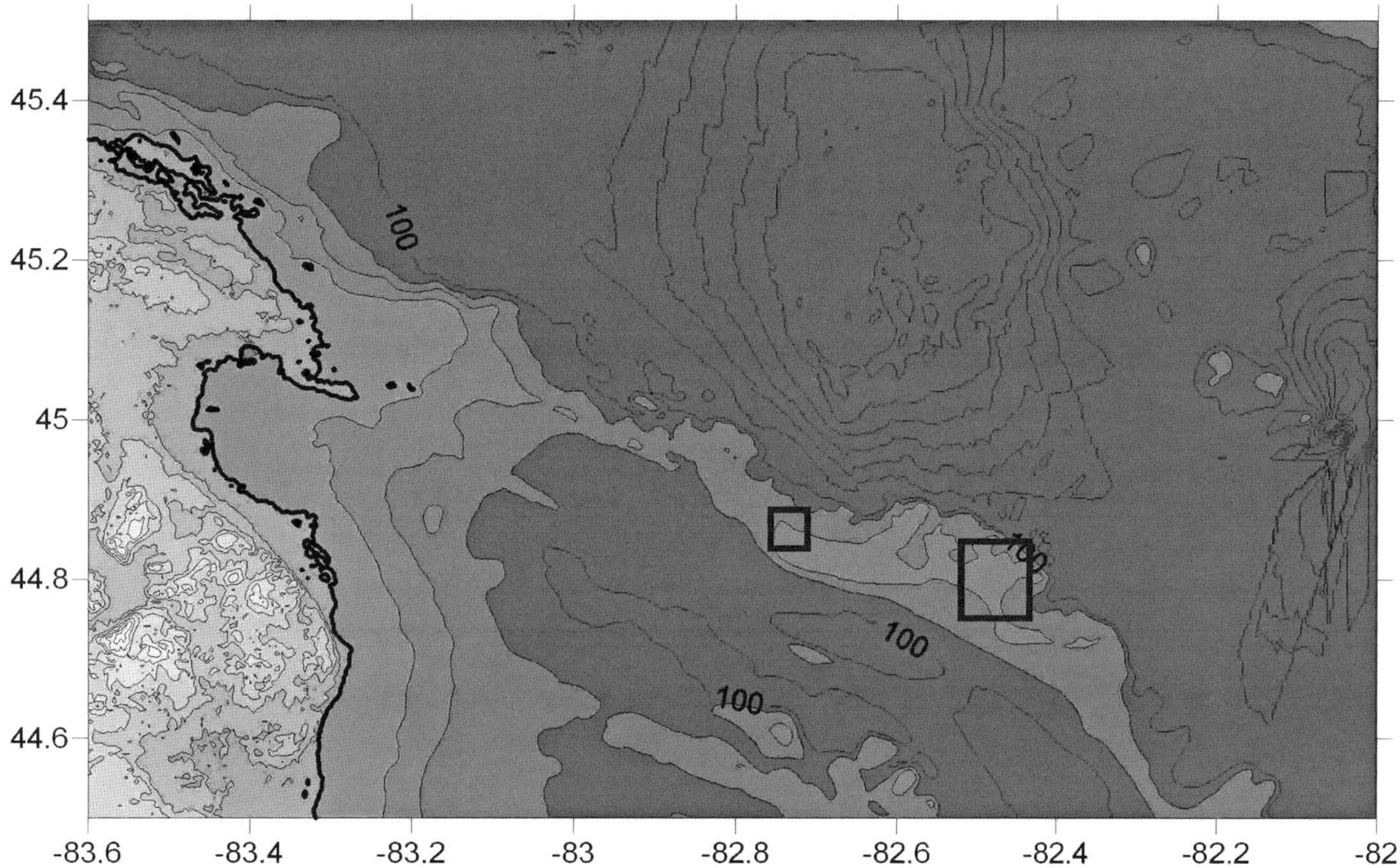

Figure 11.1. Primary research areas on the United States portion of Alpena-Amberley Ridge. Area 1 is the larger rectangle on the central AAR and Area 3 is the smaller rectangle.

BP), and (2) it is dominated by a long linear bedrock outcrop that may contain bands of chert. Area 3, in contrast, is smaller (17 km^2), and is a location where the AAR landform narrows with a pronounced ridge. This area is hypothesized to be an overlook location for hunters awaiting migrating herds passing through the narrow valley. Each area has been the focus of systematic mapping using sidescan sonar, and Area 1 has additional multi-beam sonar coverage. Targets on the sonar mosaics were selected for ground truthing using a remotely operated vehicle (ROV), and confirmed archaeological structures were selected for finer scale mapping using scanning sonar and systematic sampling by SCUBA divers (see Chapter 9 for further discussion of methods). Stone constructed hunting features in the form of hunting blinds, rock clusters, and rectangular structures have been located in both areas, and complex hunting structures with drive lanes and associated hunting blinds have also been located and tested in both research areas (see Chapters 10, 14). Lithic artifacts come from both Areas 1 and 3.

Crossing Locality, Area 1

In Area 1, the Crossing locality has two paleolakes; the smaller one, to the northwest, is connected by a stream or water channel to the larger lake to the southeast. The Crossing locality comprises 98.7 ha and has 21 stone constructions (Chapter 10). Two lithic artifacts were recovered from this locality within bulk sediment samples collected by SCUBA divers: DE-1a and Vial 1a. DE-1a was recovered from a sample taken south of the smaller paleolake and the water channel, at a depth of 94 feet. The area sampled was just outside a stone rectangle that is situated near other hunting features including lines and a V-shaped hunting blind. DE-1a is a small brown flake on high-quality chert (Fig. 11.2, Plate 14).

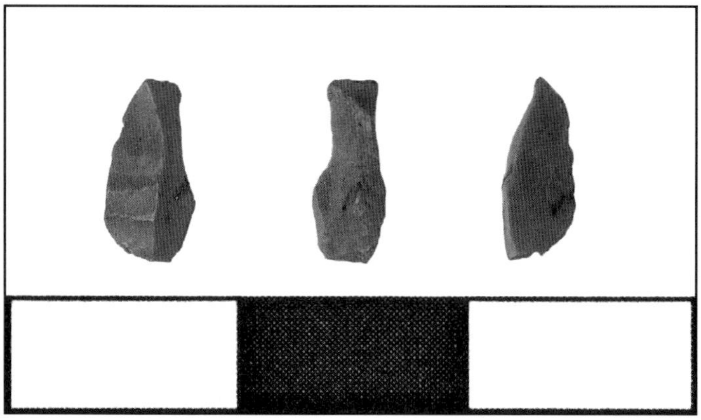

Figure 11.2. DE-1a flake from the Crossing locality, Area 1. Scale bar is in centimeters. (See also Plate 14.)

Figure 11.3. Vial 1a flake from the Crossing locality, Area 1. Scale bar is in centimeters. (See also Plate 14.)

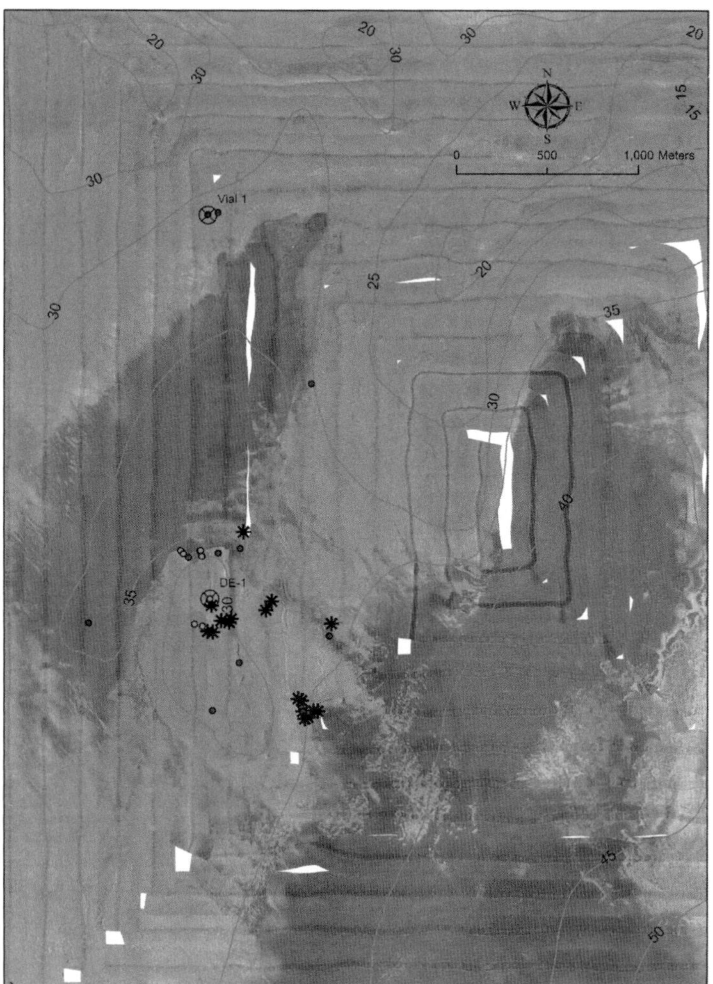

Figure 11.4. Map of the Crossing locality, Area 1. Background image is a sidescan sonar mosaic; crosshairs indicate lithic artifacts, stars indicate stone constructions, and small shaded circles are sample locations that did not produce cultural materials. (See also Plate 15.)

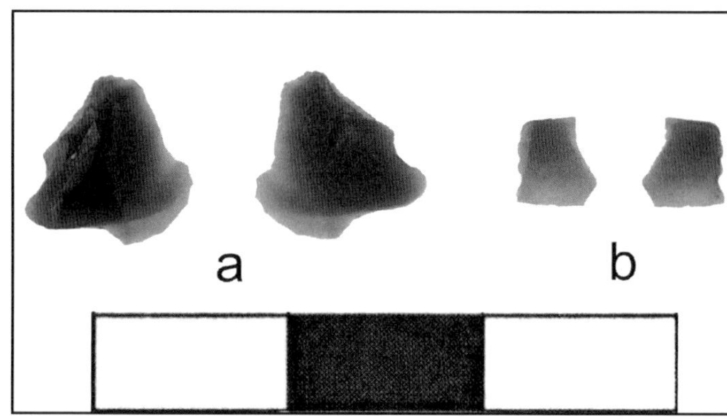

Figure 11.5. DA-1-1a and DA-1-1b lithic artifacts from the Gap locality, Area 3. Scale bar is in centimeters. (See also Plate 14.)

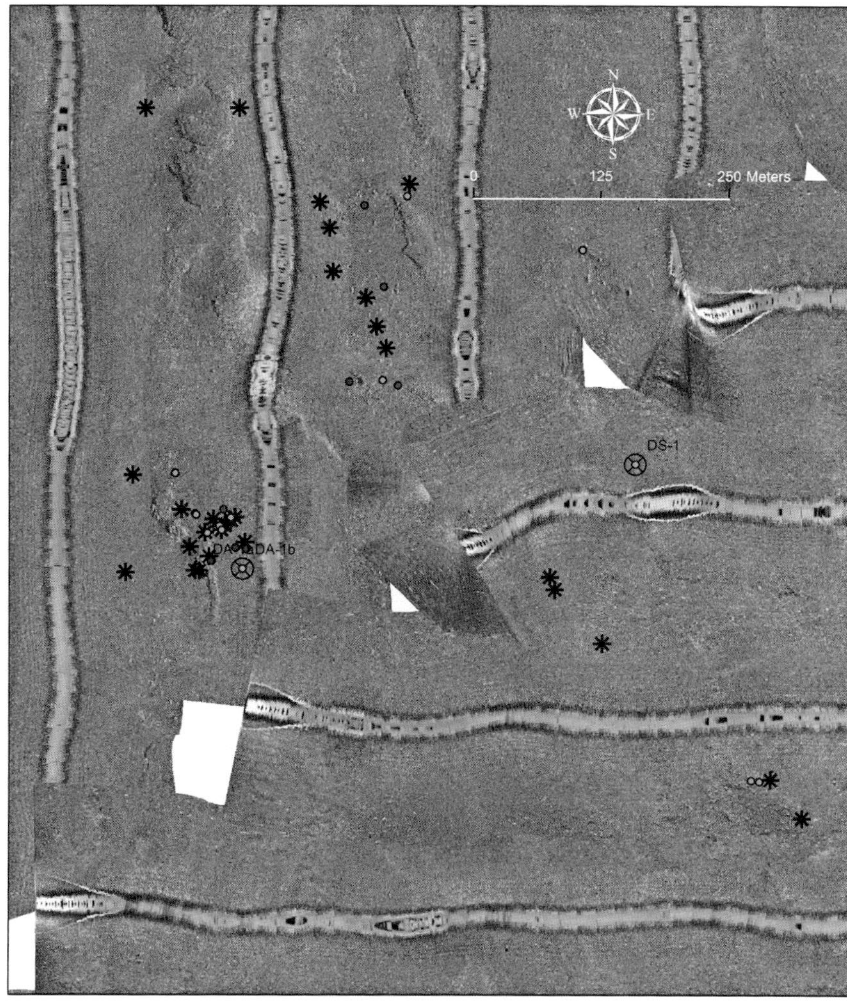

Figure 11.6. Map of Gap locality, Area 3. Background image is a sidescan sonar mosaic; crosshairs indicate lithic artifacts, stars indicate stone constructions, and small shaded circles are sample locations that did not produce cultural materials. DS-1 indicates a sample that contained microdebitage (lithic artifacts less than 1 mm). (See also Plate 16.)

The Vial 1 sample was located north of the smaller paleolake; the sample was taken in a 100 mL plastic vial in sediment underneath a scoured boulder at a depth of 95 feet. Vial 1a, which was recovered in this sample (Fig. 11.3, Plate 14), is a white-gray flake with an intact bulb of percussion. A spruce pole was also recovered from this locality and was radiocarbon dated to 8900 cal BP. An additional radiocarbon date—9020 cal BP (O'Shea et al. 2014: table S2; Chapter 10)—for the Crossing locality is provided from charcoal taken out of a stone ring hearth feature. Figure 11.4 (see also Plate 15) shows the Crossing locality with major cultural features and the location of lithic artifacts.

Gap Locality, Area 3

In Area 3, the Gap locality is 29 ha and has two clusters of hunting structures ($n = 31$) built between long, linear glacial eskers. Two flakes, DA-1a and DA-1b, were recovered in a sample taken near a cluster of V-shaped hunting blinds at 104 feet (Fig. 11.5, Plate 14). These two artifacts are made on a high-quality semitranslucent black chert. The source of this chert has not yet been identified. Figure 11.6 (see also Plate 16) shows the Gap locality with major cultural features and the location of the DA-1 sample.

Drop 45 Site, Area 3

Drop 45 is located in Area 3, at the base of a steep slope in the middle of a narrow portion of the AAR. This site was discovered during a scanning sonar survey where two drive lanes were immediately identified. Three hunting blinds are associated with the drive lane. The drive lane runs a length of 30 m and caribou would have been channeled up the lane into a cul-de-sac area. It is hypothesized that the operation of this complex hunting feature would require the cooperation of several hunters and their families, and was most likely the location of seasonal aggregation on the AAR (O'Shea et al. 2014). Eleven chert flakes

Figure 11.7. Flakes and debitage from the Drop 45 site: *top row (left to right)*, DP-1-1a, EG-1-2b, EG-1-2a, EO-1-2a, FA-1-2a, FB-1-1a; *bottom row (left to right)*, DP-1-1b, Unit 1a, EZ-1a, EO-1-2b, FE-1-2b, FE-1-2a, Unit 8a. Scale bar is in centimeters. (See also Plate 15.)

Figure 11.8. Thumbnail scraper on Bayport chert from the Drop 45 site. Scale bar is in centimeters. (See also Plate 14.)

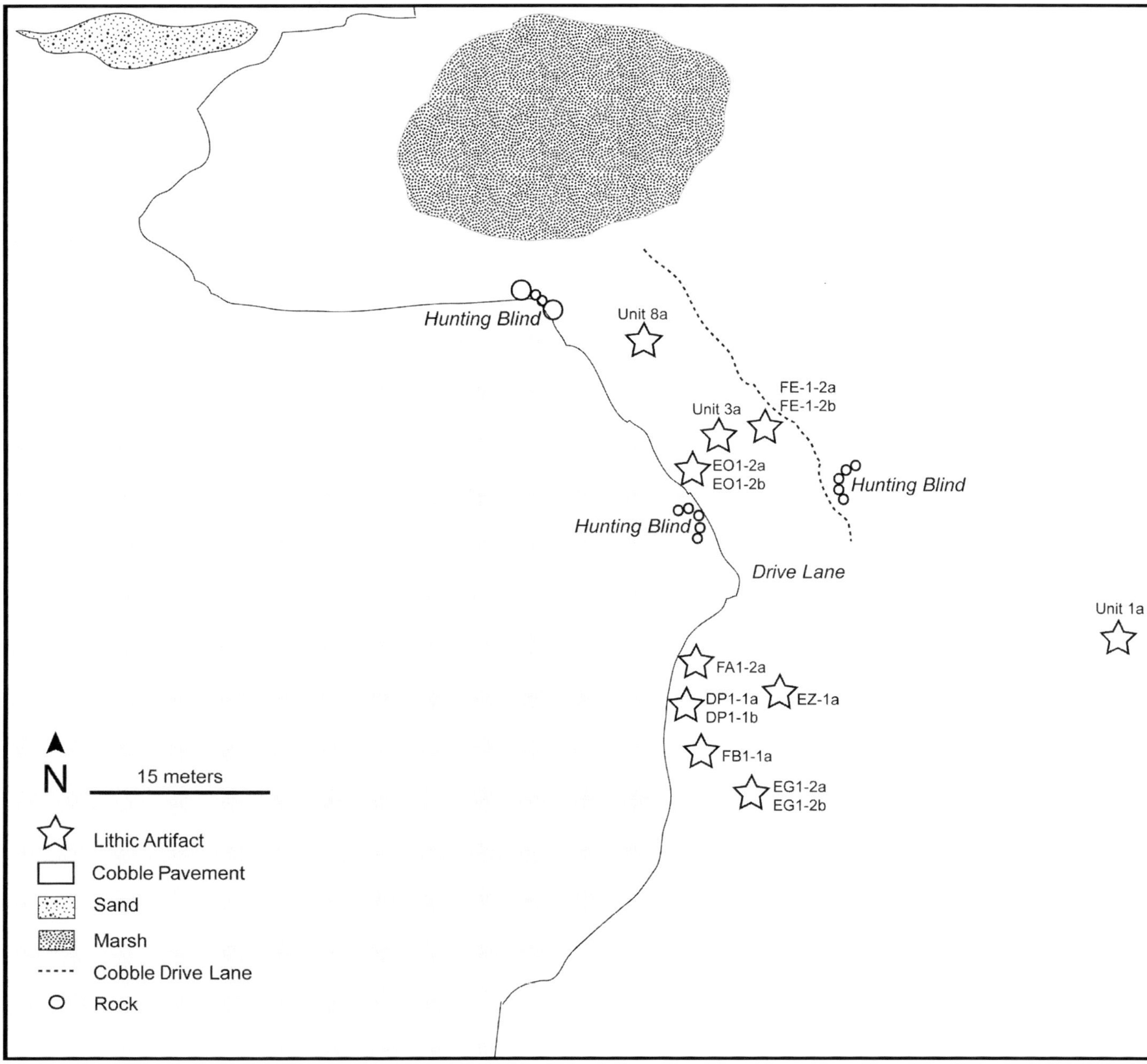

Figure 11.9. Plan map of the Drop 45 site with major cultural and geological features and lithic artifacts.

recovered from Drop 45 have been previously published as well as an extensive discussion of sampling procedures (O'Shea et al. 2014; Chapter 10). These 11 flakes were recovered during systematic hand sampling by SCUBA divers collecting sediment, which was screened on the bottom using one-quarter-inch (6.3 mm) scientific sieves. Two additional flakes (Unit 1a and Unit 8a; Fig. 11.7, Plate 15) and the scraper (Unit 3a; Fig. 11.8, Plate 14) were recovered during systematic excavation of 1 × 1 m squares using an airlift at 119 feet. The airlift is a 3-inch-diameter PVC tube that uses compressed air to lift sediments off the bottom into a 5-gallon plastic bucket. Sediments collected in the bucket were brought to the surface and screened on the boat through one-quarter-inch and one-eighth-inch mesh. All 3 lithic artifacts from airlift units were recovered in the one-quarter-inch screen. Figure 11.9 is a plan map of Drop 45 that indicates the location of these lithic artifacts and major cultural features.

The 11 chert flakes from Drop 45 are on two main raw materials: gray-brown cherts that are local, and an orange and black variety that has not yet been identified, although it has been suggested that it may fall within the range of Hudson Bay lowland cherts (William Fox, pers. comm., 2013) or Fossil Hill chert from Ontario (Patrick Julig, pers. comm., 2014). The scraper is a small thumbnail endscraper similar to those known from terrestrial Paleoindian sites. Referred to as thumbnails due to their small size, they are indicative of extensive resharpening throughout their use-life and are common in the archaeological record since they are often exhausted once they reach thumbnail size and are discarded. The scraper has multiple retouched flake scars on its working edge, and one ventral flake that may have been incidentally removed during use. Use-wear studies on endscrapers from the Paleoindian period in eastern North America indicate that these artifacts were used on hides, wood, antler, and bone (Loebel 2013).

Discussion

The lithic assemblage from submerged sites on the AAR is small with a total of 18 artifacts, fitting expectations for what may be found within built hunting features (see Chapter 7). Despite this low density, a wide variety of raw materials is represented and 1 formal artifact, a thumbnail scraper made on Bayport chert, has been recovered. Preliminary sampling has been done across different portions of the AAR, and two of these larger research localities have produced lithic flakes: the Crossing locality in Area 1 and the Gap locality in Area 3. Both of these localities will be targeted for more intensive sampling in the future. One archaeological site, Drop 45, represents a complex caribou hunting structure composed of multiple interrelated components, drive lanes and hunting blinds, and has been sampled extensively. From this site, 11 flakes and the thumbnail scraper were recovered. Given the extensive sampling regime at Drop 45, a discussion of the spatial distribution of the lithic artifacts is warranted.

As published previously, sampling at Drop 45 has been systematic along transects with only a portion of test units producing lithic artifacts (O'Shea et al. 2014). New excavations with an airlift have targeted 1 × 1 m squares on a grid system. The majority of these sampling locations have not produced lithic artifacts. Instead, lithic debris is nonrandomly distributed across the site and comes from four locations, including two primary clusters that produced more than one artifact. One flake (Unit 8a) was recovered from the northern portion of the central drive lane, and an additional flake (Unit 1a) was recovered far south and east of the primary site. One cluster of lithic debris is in the central portion of the drive lane, just north of two hunting blinds, and the other is located south of the drive lane in an open funnel area. The cluster in the central drive lane is composed of 4 flakes and the thumbnail scraper, and may indicate butchering and hide processing activities of animals killed by hunters placed in the adjacent hunting blinds. This spatial pattern is common in terrestrial game drives as well, as lithic artifacts are often recovered near or in hunting blinds (Chapter 7). The southern cluster may be indicative of a "gearing up" area where basic tool maintenance and resharpening were completed by hunters waiting along the funnel to drive animals into the lane.

The nature and size of the lithic assemblage recovered from submerged caribou hunting sites and structures on the AAR fit general expectations for what may be recovered from terrestrial hunting features and sites. In general, artifact densities tend to be low since hunting features are kept clean so they can be reused in future hunts. For this reason and others (e.g., caching or transport of meat to camp sites), faunal remains and butchering behaviors are often limited within hunting structures so the smell does not frighten off future animal targets (see Chapters 7, 14). The current absence of projectile points or fragments may be attributed to either limited sampling and/or the use of wood lance or bone and antler tipped spear hunting techniques, in which case, lithic projectiles would be absent (see O'Shea, Lemke, and Reynolds 2013).

Conclusion

The lithic artifacts recovered from submerged caribou hunting sites on the AAR fit general expectations for Late Paleoindian/Early Archaic hunter-gatherers in the Great Lakes region. Varied raw materials were used by these peoples, including immediately available local sources, those from other parts of Michigan, and perhaps others from farther afield. The forthcoming identification of the semitranslucent black, and the black and orange chert varieties, will further define the raw materials utilized by AAR foragers. The nonrandom distribution of lithic artifacts supports localized areas of prehistoric activities, and the formal character of the assemblage suggests hunting, butchering, and hide processing behaviors. Future investigations of submerged archaeological sites on the AAR will continue intensive sampling procedures and excavations that have proven successful at generating cultural artifacts 120 feet below Lake Huron.

12 Paleoenvironmental Reconstruction of the Alpena-Amberley Ridge Submerged Landscape during the Lake Stanley Lowstand (ca. 8.4–9 ka cal BP), Lake Huron

by Elizabeth Sonnenburg

Little is known about the paleogeography and environment of the Alpena-Amberley Ridge as there is limited sedimentation. Most lake-level and paleoenvironmental research in Lake Huron has focused on the more sediment loaded basins of the Georgian and Saginaw Bays. To gain a better understanding of the paleoenvironment of the ridge, between 2011 and 2013, a total of one hundred and seventy-one core, sediment, and rock samples were collected by divers and ponar sampler from a surface vessel. One hundred and two sediment grab samples and eleven short (10–25 cm) cores were obtained for analysis of microdebitage, microfossils, grain size, and organic content. Cores were subsampled at 2 cm intervals for analysis; lithofacies were logged in detail and photographed. Preliminary paleoenvironmental reconstructions based on results from these samples indicate that during the last Lake Stanley phase, the ridge was a relatively stable landscape with Subarctic vegetation, small shallow ponds, sphagnum bogs, wetlands, and rivers, and would have provided numerous potential resources for both caribou and prehistoric hunter-gatherers.

Introduction

Isostatic rebound and climate changes have dramatically altered the water levels and landscape of the Great Lakes watershed since deglaciation circa 13,000 years ago (Sonnenburg, Boyce, and Reinhardt 2013). In the case of Lake Huron, closing of the outlet at Sault Ste. Marie stopped inflow from Lake Superior and a drier climate reduced the amount of precipitation (Lewis and Anderson 2012). This combination of reduced inflow and precipitation accelerated evaporation, eventually causing Lake Huron to separate into at least three separate basins: Lake Hough (Georgian Bay) and two basins referred to as Lake Stanley (Fig. 12.1*A*; Chapter 3).

The Alpena-Amberley Ridge is a 200 km ridge of limestone that bisects Lake Huron (Fig. 12.1*A*), and was subaerially exposed during the Lake Stanley lowstand phase between eight and ten thousand years ago. The ridge has clear evidence of human occupation; in 2007 and 2008, a series of structures that resemble caribou drive lanes and hunting blinds were found in 40–60 m of water, approximately 90 km southeast of Alpena, Michigan (O'Shea and Meadows 2009). The discovery of these structures has given rise to numerous research questions. In this chapter, we investigate two important aspects of this landscape: (1) how the landscape may have looked during this period of exposure, and (2) the effects of rising water levels on the preservation potential of archaeological materials on the ridge.

Study Area

The Alpena-Amberley Ridge is a limestone and dolostone formation (Traverse and Onondaga groups) that bisects Lake Huron and stretches from Alpena, Michigan, to Amberley, Ontario (Fig. 12.1*A*). The ridge was referred to as "Six Fathom Shoal" on historic nautical maps, as sections of the ridge are only 11 m (1 fathom = 6 feet; 6 fathoms = 36 feet or 11 meters) below the current water level. Lake Huron is the second largest Great Lake by area, and has a maximum depth of 229 m. The lake is connected in the north to Lake Michigan by the Straits of Mackinac.

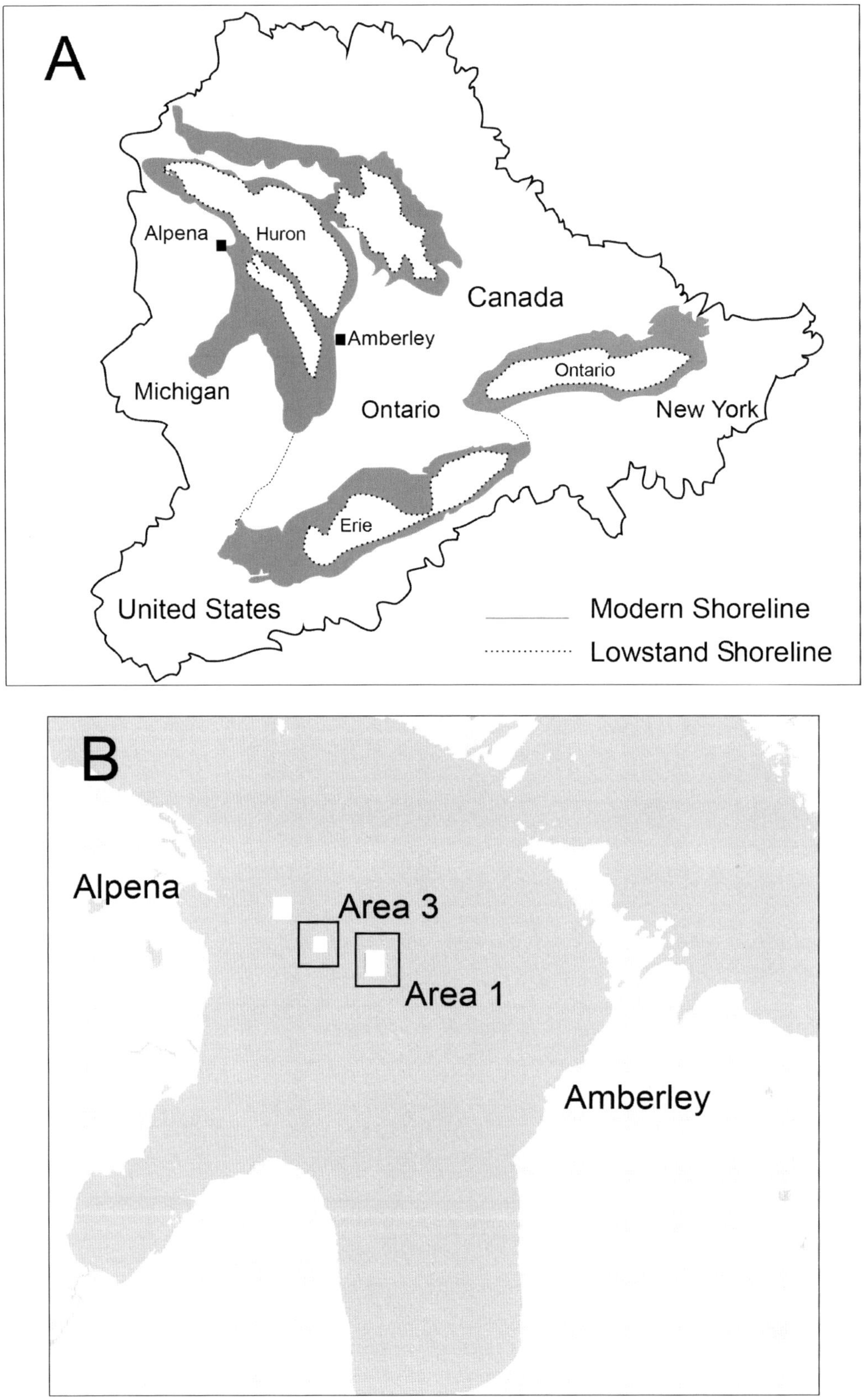

Figure 12.1. *A*, Great Lakes Huron, Erie, and Ontario showing lowstand shorelines between 10 and 8 ka BP (adapted from Croley and Lewis 2006); *B*, Lake Huron showing the Alpena-Amberley Ridge and study Areas 1 and 3.

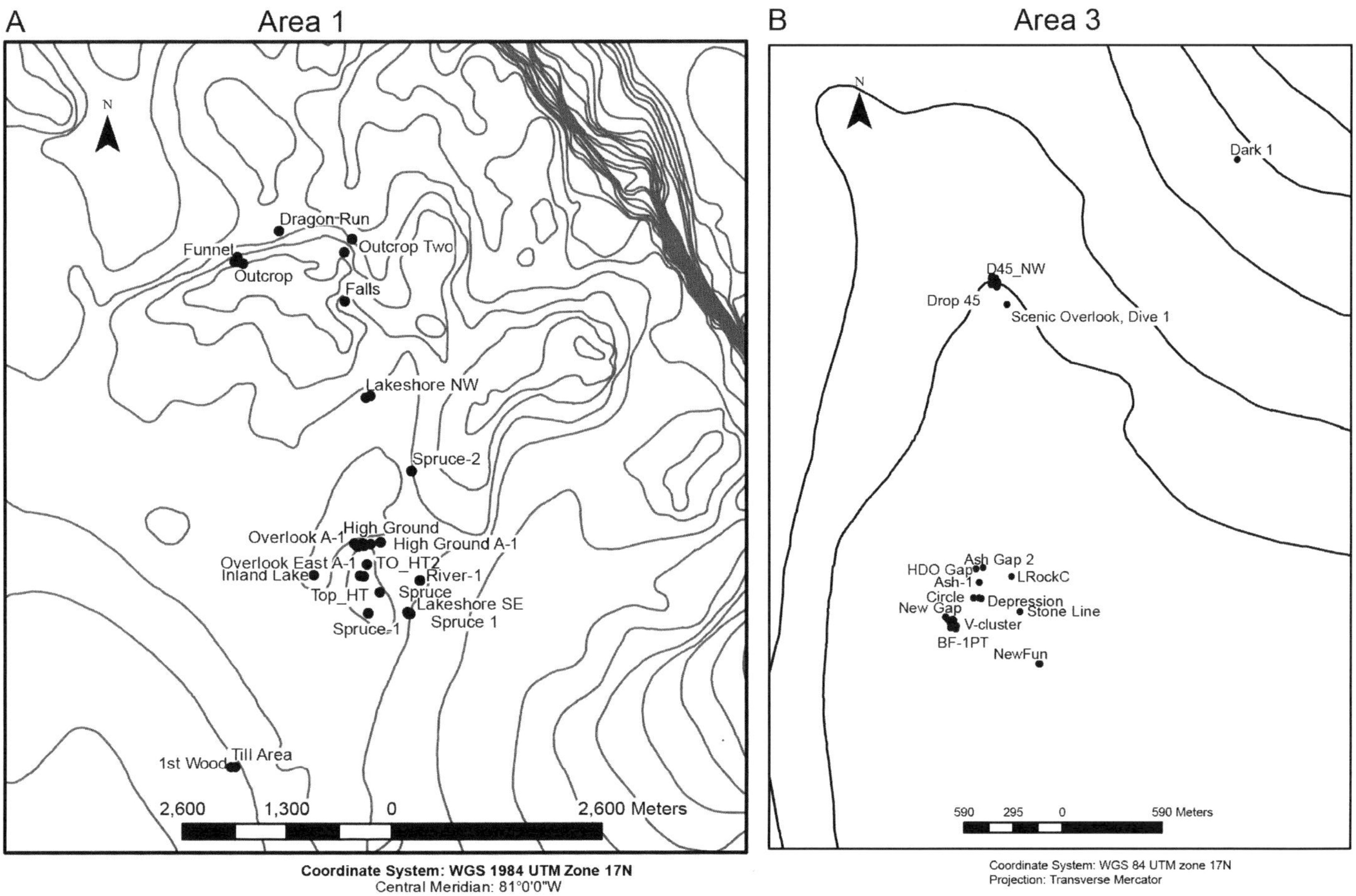

Figure 12.2. Detailed topography and sample locations of Area 1 (*A*) and Area 3 (*B*).

Water flows from Lake Superior via the St. Marys River at Sault Ste. Marie and to Lake Erie in the south by the St. Clair River (Croley and Lewis 2006). The two specific areas discussed in this study are approximately 4–6 km in diameter and are located between 50 and 90 km southeast of Alpena (Fig. 12.1*B*).

Isotopic studies of the lake show two distinct patterns between the northern and southern portions of the lake (Macdonald and Longstaffe 2008). During the Mattawa floods, pulses of glacial meltwater can be seen isotopically in the upper basin of Lake Stanley; the Saginaw basin, however, has evidence of hypersaline conditions (McCarthy et al. 2007; Chapter 3), and the isotopic signature seems to reflect input only from precipitation. Testate amoebae studies of the upper basin show brackish conditions as a reflection of a hydrologically closed basin (McCarthy et al. 2007). These drier conditions may have also been the trigger for dune formations on the western edge of Lake Huron and the eastern edge of Lake Michigan (Macdonald and Longstaffe 2008).

Methods

Between 2011 and 2013, a total of 171 samples were collected in Areas 1 and 3 on the ridge through diver survey and ponar sampler deployed from the survey vessel (Fig. 12.2). These samples consist of 102 sediment grab samples, 11 short cores, 51 lithic samples, and 7 wood samples (Fig. 12.3*A*, *B*). The sediment and core samples (subsampled at 2 cm increments) were wet sieved through 4 mm, 1 mm, 250 μm, 45 μm, and 10 μm sieves. The 4 mm and 1 mm samples were used to locate any large flakes, charcoal, and seeds (Fig. 12.3*C*, *D*). The 250 μm fraction was used for microdebitage analysis, the 43 μm for testate amoebae (Fig. 12.4), and the 10 μm for pollen (Fig. 12.3*E*, *F*). In most cases, an unsieved portion of the sample was retained for particle size and loss on ignition analysis. The cores were visually logged and photographed. Color was determined by using a Munsell soil color chart.

Figure 12.3. Organic materials recovered from the Alpena-Amberley Ridge. *A*, *B*, wood samples from Area 3; *C*, burnt plant material; *D*, charcoal; *E*, *Picea* (spruce) pollen; *F*, *Bryophyte* (moss) spore.

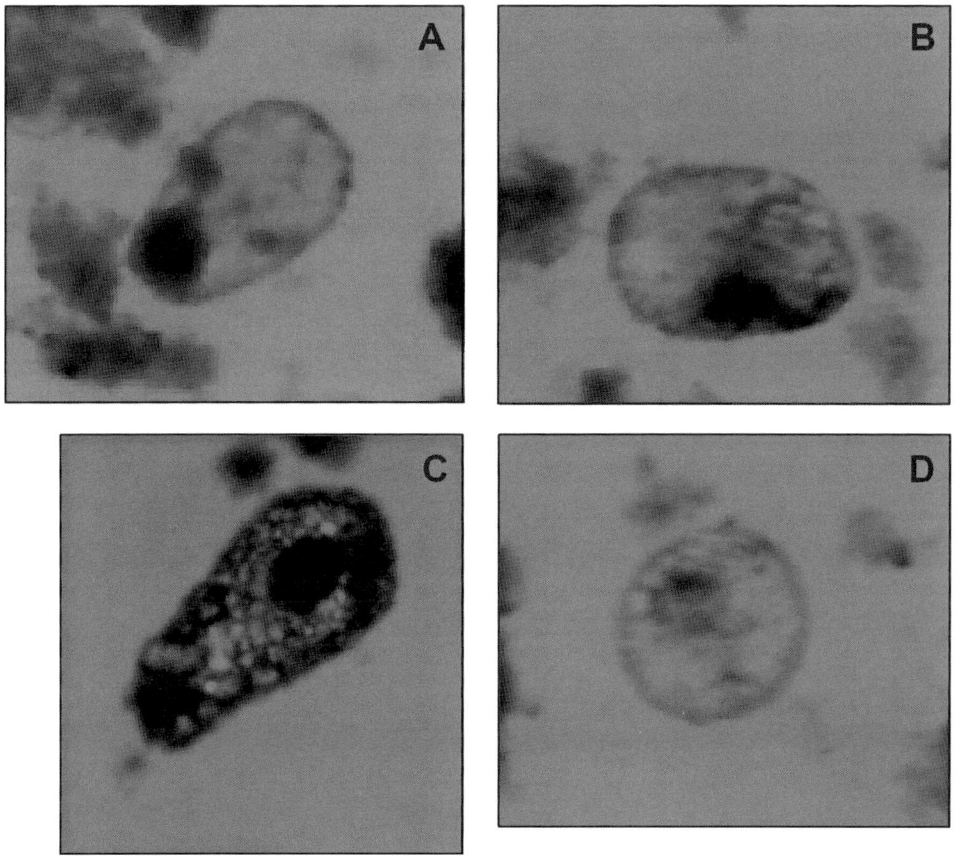

Figure 12.4. Light microscope images of testate amoebae recovered from ridge samples. *A*, *Hyalosphena papilio*; *B*, *Centropyxis constricta* 'aerophila'; *C*, *Difflugia oblonga*; *D*, *Difflugia globulus*.

Table 12.1a. Particle size averages.

Samples	Particle Size (μm)			
	mean	median	mode	SD
total average	494.9	449.45	573.7	297.5
Area 1 average	412.2	360.67	393.3	265.9
Area 3 average	728.4	700.11	1083	384.7

Table 12.1b. Distribution, skewness, and sorting.

Samples	Distribution (%)			Skewness		Sorting (%)				
	unimodal	bimodal	tri/polymodal	right	left	well sorted	moderately well sorted	moderately sorted	poorly sorted	very poorly sorted
total	66.15	23.08	10.77	93.80	6.20	1.54	21.54	26.15	35.38	15.38
Area 1	70.83	20.83	8.33	98.00	2.00	0.00	20.83	29.17	33.33	16.67
Area 3	52.94	29.41	17.65	82.40	17.60	5.88	23.53	17.65	41.18	11.76

Table 12.1c. Sediment classification.

Samples	Sediment Type (%)												
	medium sand	coarse sand	coarse silty very coarse sand	mud	medium silty medium sand	very coarse sand	coarse silty medium sand	very fine sand	fine silty medium sand	coarse silty coarse sand	very coarse silty very coarse sand	medium silt	fine sand
total	40.00	12.31	3.08	10.77	1.54	10.77	4.62	1.54	7.69	3.08	1.54	1.54	1.54
Area 1	50.00	8.33	0.00	12.50	2.08	6.25	6.25	2.08	10.42	0.00	0.00	0.00	2.08
Area 3	11.76	23.53	11.76	5.88	0.00	23.53	0.00	0.00	0.00	11.76	5.88	5.88	0.00

Based on Blott and Pye (2012).

Textural Analysis

The surface sediment samples were analyzed for particle size, shape and source, microdebitage, organic and carbonate content, and microfossils (testate amoebae and pollen). Particle size analysis was completed at McMaster University's Micropaleo Laboratory on a Coulter LS230 laser particle diffraction system. Any particles over 2 mm were removed to ensure the machine did not clog. The results were then analyzed statistically using the Gradistat program to determine sorting, and sediment type (Blott and Pye 2012; Table 12.1). The samples were not treated to remove organics and carbonates, as all the samples were over 80% silicates and contained few carbonates and organics (Table 12.2). Loss on ignition (organic and carbonate content) was completed using the steps outlined by Hieri, Lotter, and Lemcke (2001): drying at 105°C for 24 hours, followed by combustion of organics at 550°C for 4 hours, and 950°C for 2 hours for removal of carbonates.

Particle shape and source was completed by taking the 250 μm sieved portions and analyzing 1000 grains under light microscope at 20–40× magnification. Particles were assigned to shape categories following Powers (1953) and divided into classes based on angularity and sphericity. The particles were also characterized by lithic type (e.g., quartz, chert), and any samples with potential microdebitage (Fladmark 1982) were noted for future analysis by scanning electron microscopy. Comparisons among and between samples from Areas 1 and 3 were performed using averages and standard deviations (Fig. 12.5). An average of each sample type was completed along with the standard deviation. Samples that were outside the standard deviations were noted.

Table 12.2. Loss on ignition data.

Sample	Organic Content (%)	Carbonate Content (%)	Silicate Content (%)
CD-1	1.68	1.89	96.42
72212-2	0.60	2.27	97.13
62812E	0.08	0.14	99.78
CH-1	0.12	0.23	99.66
72212-3	0.32	2.22	97.46
CN-1	0.08	0.14	99.78
BW-1	**0.41**	**5.36**	**94.23**
62912A	0.20	0.46	99.34
81512F	0.37	0.77	98.86
BF-1	0.10	0.20	99.70
81512A	0.21	0.37	99.43
62912B	0.23	1.09	98.68
BD-1	0.22	1.09	98.69
62912C	0.11	0.20	99.68
BB-1	0.20	0.35	99.45
BY-1	0.10	0.23	99.67
52312	0.06	0.79	99.14
CM-1	0.25	1.12	98.63
72212-1	0.09	0.16	99.76
81412A	0.07	0.15	99.79
62812C	0.14	0.43	99.43
BP-1	0.36	1.65	97.99
62812G	0.04	0.08	99.88
62812F	0.09	0.17	99.73
81412C	0.10	0.23	99.67
62812B	0.09	0.21	99.69
CO-1	0.10	0.33	99.58
CQ-1	0.16	0.31	99.54
81512B	0.08	0.25	99.66
CC-1	0.21	0.51	99.28
62812D	0.12	0.23	99.65
62812A	0.43	1.56	98.01
62712A	0.12	0.27	99.61
72212-2	0.18	0.40	99.42
71512-2	0.11	0.21	99.68
inland lake	0.16	0.25	99.58
till area a	0.14	0.21	99.65
till area 2	0.17	0.27	99.56
CF-1	**0.98**	**9.91**	**89.10**
AAR-1 0-2	**1.53**	**7.33**	**91.14**
AAR-1 4-6	**1.00**	**5.61**	**93.39**
AAR-1 8-10	0.10	0.18	99.72
AAR-2	**0.70**	**7.79**	**91.51**
AAR-5 0-2	**1.26**	**6.41**	**92.33**
AAR-5 4-6	**0.95**	**3.74**	**95.31**
AAR-5 8-10	**1.27**	**4.80**	**93.92**
AAR-5 12-14	**1.33**	**6.78**	**91.89**
AAR-5 16-18	**1.16**	**6.66**	**92.19**
AAR-5 20-22	**1.29**	**6.63**	**92.08**
CM-1	0.30	1.43	98.27
71512-1	0.22	0.34	99.44
AAR-3 1-3	0.19	1.01	98.80
AAR-3 18-20	0.19	0.71	99.10
AAR-4	0.26	2.15	97.59
Core 1 0-2	0.09	0.18	99.73
Core 1 4-6	0.11	0.19	99.70
Core 1 8-10	0.19	0.31	99.50
Core 1 12-14	0.15	0.26	99.59
92912D	0.25	0.46	99.29
92912F	0.42	0.65	98.94
92912E 0-2	0.15	0.22	99.62
92912E 4-6	0.21	0.29	99.51
92912E 8-9	0.39	0.46	99.15
92912E 9-10	0.22	0.32	99.46
92912E 12-14	0.23	0.35	99.42
92912E 16-18	0.35	0.47	99.19
DA-1	0.36	0.61	99.03
DB-1	0.45	1.83	97.72
DC-1	**0.74**	**8.09**	**91.17**
DH-1	0.21	0.53	99.25
DI-1	0.36	0.85	98.78
DL-1	0.33	0.76	98.92
DO-1	0.72	1.83	97.45
BR-1	0.21	0.61	99.18
EN-1	0.26	0.38	99.36
EO-1-2	0.48	0.70	98.82
EQ-1	0.59	0.80	98.61
EI-1	0.16	0.25	99.59
FB-1	0.48	0.71	98.82
FE-1	0.53	1.58	97.90
DP-1	0.54	0.96	98.50
EB-1	0.18	0.39	99.43
EG-1	0.31	0.57	99.12
PONAR	0.25	0.36	99.39
DT-1	0.36	0.57	99.08
DS-1	0.35	0.96	98.68
EF-1	0.30	0.68	99.03
EE-1	0.38	0.68	98.94
DQ-1	0.17	0.49	99.34
BV-1	0.18	0.36	99.46
DR-1	0.26	0.42	99.32
DV-1	0.85	1.25	97.90
EO-1	0.02	0.19	99.79
DU-1	0.21	0.39	99.41
EK-1	0.22	0.41	99.36
EL-1	0.34	0.53	99.13
average	0.36	1.38	98.26
SD	0.34	2.19	2.48

Note: Data outside the normal distribution are in bold.

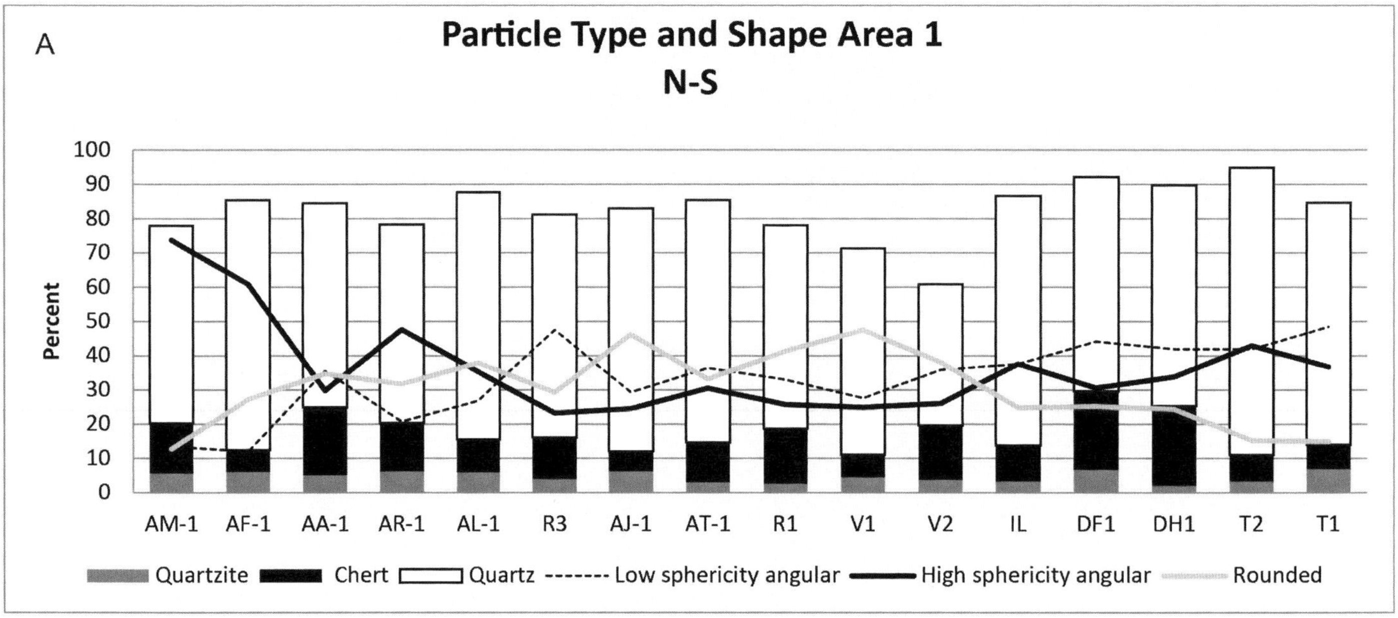

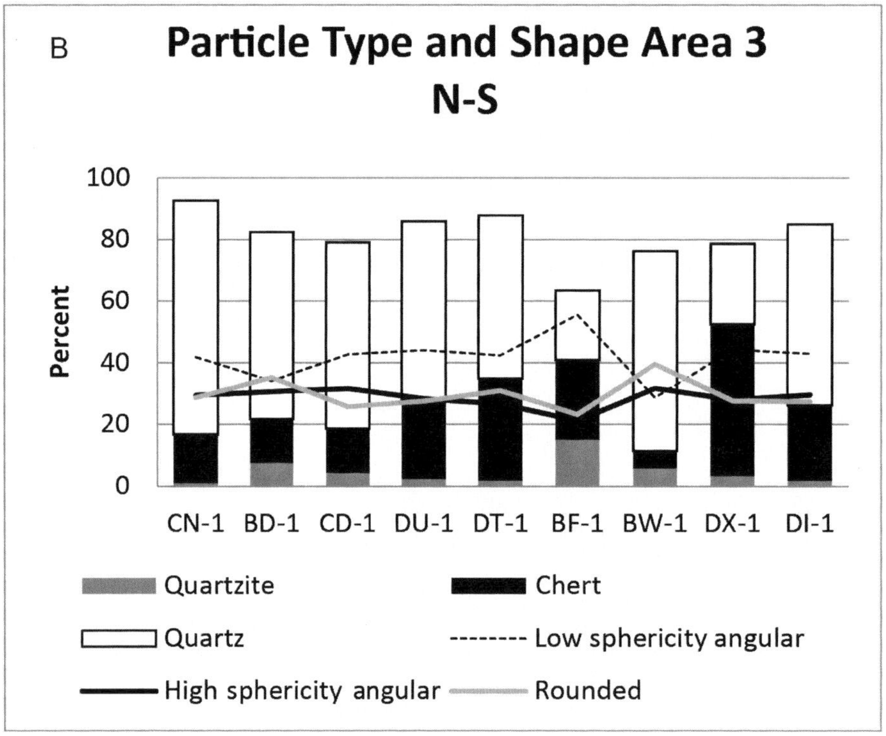

Figure 12.5. Characterizations of sediments from Areas 1 and 3 by material type (*A*) and particle shape (*B*). Note high abundances of chert and low sphericity angular particles in BF-1.

Microfossils

Testate amoebae were analyzed by splitting the 43 μm fraction into random 1/8 sections using a wet splitter (Scott and Hermelin 1993). Wet samples were then placed in a gridded Petri dish and analyzed under light microscope at 80× magnification until 150–200 specimens were identified (Patterson and Fishbein 1989). Identification of testate amoebae was completed using Kumar and Dalby (1998) and Scott, Medioli, and Schafer (2001). Pollen was also tentatively identified in some samples at the same time as the testate amoebae analysis. Pollen identification was based on McAndrews, Berti, and Norris (1973) and is noted simply as presence/absence for the purposes of this chapter. More detailed pollen analysis will be completed in a later phase of the project.

Testate amoebae assemblages were determined using R- and Q-mode cluster analysis in the Paleontological Statistics (PAST) program (Hammer, Harper, and Ryan 2001). Fractional abundances and standard error were calculated for each sample (Fishbein and Patterson 1993; Table 12.3). If a species had a standard error higher than the fractional abundance, it was not included in the cluster analysis. R-mode cluster analysis was used to determine similarities in species (Fig. 12.6). The resulting assemblages were determined by similarity using Euclidean distance (Fig. 12.7). In addition to cluster analysis, diversity was determined using the Shannon-Weaver diversity indices in the PAST program (Table 12.3).

Results

Textural Analysis and Microdebitage

Particle size analysis completed on 65 of the sediment samples from Area 1 (48 samples) and Area 3 (17 samples) shows a distinct difference between the sedimentary environments of the two areas. Area 1 had a wide range of particle sizes, from coarse sand to fine muds. The average particle size for Area 1 was 412 μm, with the dominant sediment type being medium sand (50%; Table 12.1a, c). Over 50% of the sediments were poorly to moderately sorted with a strongly unimodal, right-skewed distribution (Table 12.1b). Area 3 also had a wide range of particle sizes, but overall, the particles were coarser, with an average particle size of 728 μm, and the dominant sediment type was coarse to very coarse sand, with about 20% of the samples intermixed with coarse silt (Table 12.1a, c). Distribution was still strongly unimodal and right skewed; however, there was a much larger percentage of multimodal and left-skewed distributions (Table 12.1b).

A total of 96 samples were analyzed for organic, carbonate, and silicate content. Loss on ignition data did not show great differentiation between samples (Table 12.2). All samples contained at least 80% silicates. Organic content in all samples was less than 2%. Carbonate had the largest variation in samples—most samples contained less than 2%, but 10 had between 5%

Table 12.3. Microfossil assemblages based on Q-mode cluster analysis (Fig. 12.7). Most dominant species determined by R-mode cluster analysis (Fig. 12.6).

Assemblage	**Oligotrophic Pond**		**Kettle Hole**		**Fen**		**Forested Swamp/Bog**	
Sample	mean	SD	mean	SD	mean	SD	mean	SD
total counted	180.00	0.00	412.00	0.00	430.00	0.00	217.65	42.22
counts per cc	270.00	0.00	6592.00	0.00	1376.00	0.00	596.52	968.61
diversity	1.50	0.00	1.66	0.00	1.47	0.00	1.65	0.19
Centropyxis constricta 'aerophila'	36.11	0.00	27.43	0.00	13.26	0.00	39.19	8.44
Difflugia oblonga	32.78	0.00	0.97	0.00	5.35	0.00	5.60	5.36
D. globulus	0.00	0.00	4.37	0.00	0.93	0.00	14.95	8.43
C. constricta 'constricta'	0.56	0.00	34.71	0.00	1.16	0.00	5.77	3.63
C. aculeata 'discoides'	7.22	0.00	8.74	0.00	3.72	0.00	13.90	7.28
Cyphoderia ampulla	0.56	0.00	0.00	0.00	61.63	0.00	0.49	1.90
Hyalosphenia papilio	8.89	0.00	1.94	0.00	10.47	0.00	6.35	6.34

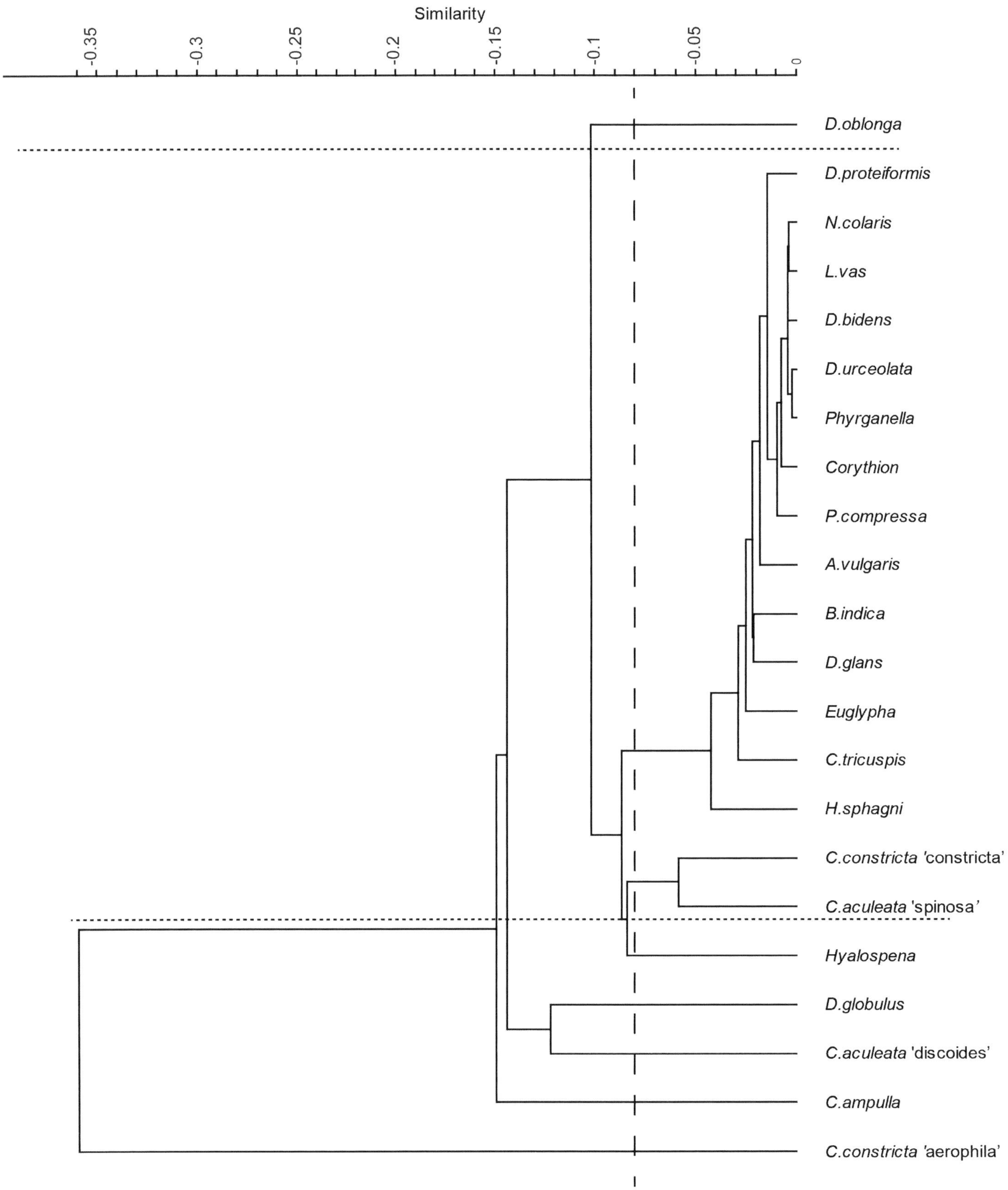

Figure 12.6. R-mode cluster analysis of testate amoebae from Areas 1 and 3. Species outside the dotted lines represent dominant species that have the most influence on assemblages.

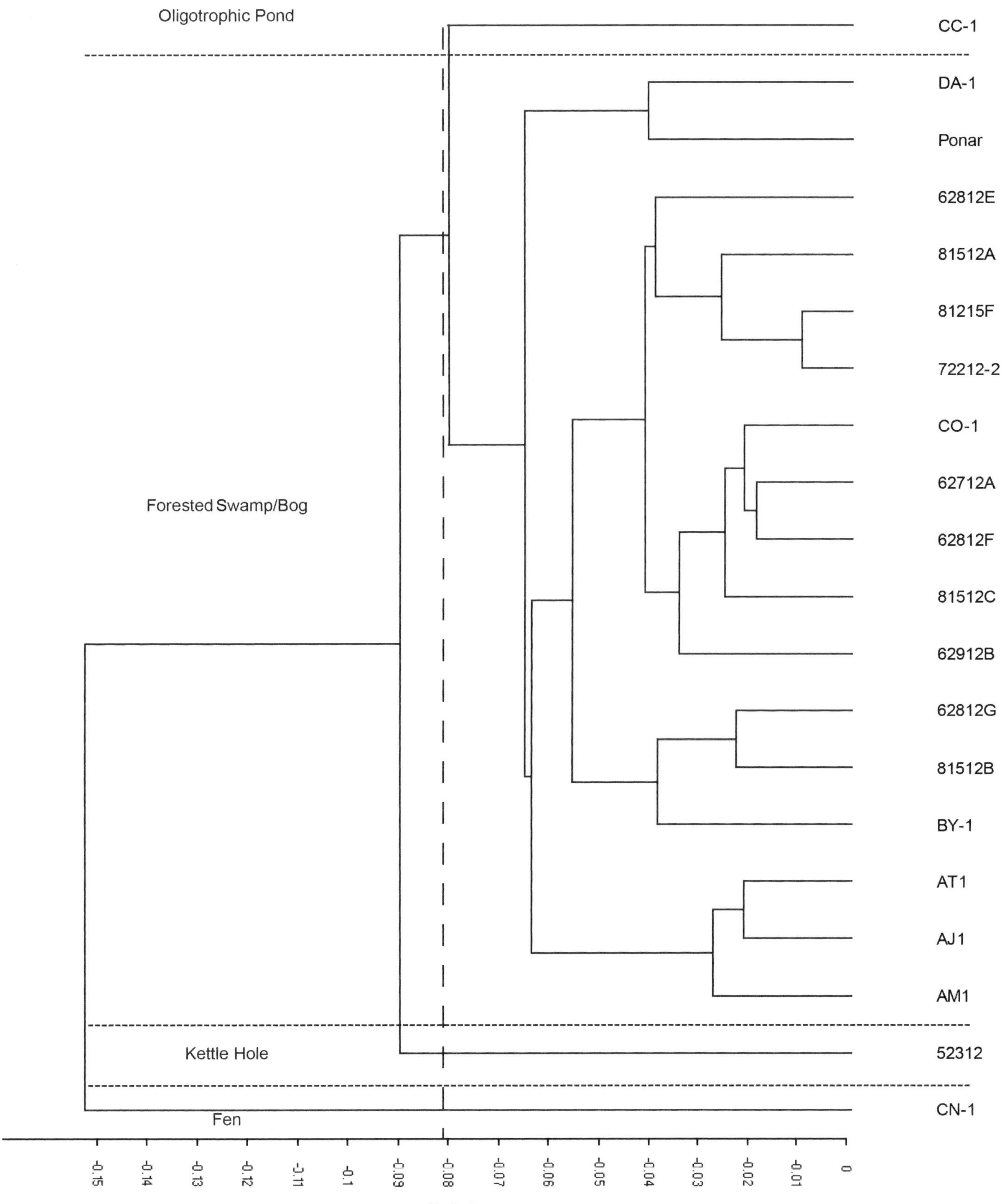

Figure 12.7. Q-mode cluster analysis of testate amoebae from Areas 1 and 3 showing assemblages (*dotted lines*).

and 10%, with a majority of these samples coming from core samples AAR1, 2, and 5 (7 total; Table 12.2).

Sixteen samples from Area 1 and 9 samples from Area 3 show that particle type was heavily dominated by quartz (60–80% in most samples), with lesser amounts of chert, limestone, sandstone, and quartzite (Fig. 12.5). Two notable exceptions are BF-1 and DX-1 in Area 3 (~25%) and Vial 2 (V2; ~40%) from Lakeshore Northwest in Area 1 (Figs. 12.2, 12.5). Particle shape was variable, but was mostly very angular to subangular (over 50%; Fig. 12.5) in Areas 1 and 3. None of the samples showed a dominant percentage of sub- to well-rounded particles. Of particular interest were samples that had a high percentage (over 40%) of angular and low sphericity particles, which can be indicative of microdebitage. The samples most likely to contain microdebitage are samples BF-1 and DX-1, which have the highest amounts of low sphericity angular particles, and cherts (Fig. 12.5*B*).

Testate Amoebae and Organic Materials

Statistically significant populations of testate amoebae were identified in 19 out of 41 samples analyzed. Dominant species in assemblages include *Centropyxid* species, *Difflugia oblonga*, *Hyalosphenia papilio*, and *Difflugia globulus*, which are found elsewhere in Lake Huron during the lowstand phase (McCarthy et al. 2012; Table 12.3). Not all samples have testate amoebae, indicating that the testate amoebae present are related to the last lowstand phase and not to present-day populations. The presence of distinct marsh and fen species (e.g., *H. papilio*, *C. ampulla*), and different assemblages in Areas 1 and 3, suggests unique microenvironments within the ridge (Figs. 12.6, 12.7).

Four distinct assemblages were identified based on Q-mode cluster analysis, sediment characteristics, and proximity to topographic features. These assemblages include the Oligotrophic Pond, Kettle Hole, Fen, and Forested Swamp/Bog (Table 12.3; Fig. 12.7). While there were similar assemblages on both Areas 1 and 3, there are distinct differences in assemblages between each area.

The Oligotrophic Pond assemblage consists of one sample (CC-1) that is located in a sandy topographic low known as the Depression in Area 3 (Fig. 12.2*B*) and which contains 17 cm high sand ripples. The dominant species are *C. constricta* 'aerophila' and *D. oblonga* (Table 12.3). The high percentage of *D. oblonga* is the unique factor in this assemblage, and is commonly associated with oligotrophic water bodies (Kihlman and Kauppila 2009).

The Kettle Hole assemblage is a single sample assemblage located next to a small topographic depression in Area 1 south of the High Ground/Overlook areas (Fig. 12.2*A*). This small depression is directly adjacent to the area where wood was recovered (see below). The assemblage contains the highest number of specimens (6592 per cc) and is approximately 70% *Centropyxids* (Table 12.3). Kettle hole mires develop due to blocks of ice melting in place during deglaciation; they are often surrounded by, or are part of, lakes and forests. These areas become shallow ponds and are often dominated by only one or two species of testate amoebae (Lamentowicz, Obremska, and Mitchell 2008; Lamentowicz and Obremska 2010).

The final single sample assemblage is the Fen, which consists of sample CN-1. The sample also has a high abundance of 1376 specimens per cc. The unique aspect of this assemblage is the dominance (over 60%) of *Cyphoderia ampulla*, which occurs only in very minute abundances in two other assemblages (Table 12.3). *Cyphoderia ampulla* has been found as a dominant species in a very shallow eutrophic lake during the autumn months (Davidova and Vasilev 2013). *Cyphoderia* is also found in minerotrophic and calcareous fens (Turner and Swindles 2012), but is generally associated most strongly with sphagnum mosses (Todorov et al. 2009). The lack of *Centropyxids* in this sample indicates that this area may be slightly elevated away from the water table, and is located on a topographic high (Scenic Overlook; Fig. 12.2*B*).

The majority of samples with statistically significant populations is represented by the Forested Swamp/Bog assemblage (Fig. 12.7; Table 12.3). This assemblage occurs in both Areas 1 and 3 and is dominated by *Centropyxids* (>50%) and *Difflugia globulus* (~15%), which is often seen in Arctic bogs and shallow ponds (Lamarre et al. 2013). In addition to the dominant species, this assemblage included a wide variety of wetland dwelling species associated with sphagnum mosses such as *Bullinaria indica* and *Heliopera sphagni* (Turner and Swindles 2012). The samples in this assemblage were located in lower lying elevations in Area 3 and adjacent to rivers and small lakes in Area 1, and near areas of recovered spruce and tamarack wood fragments (Figs. 12.2, 12.3*A*, *B*).

While testate amoebae data have formed the major part of the paleoenvironmental analysis, other microfossil and organic material has been recovered in a variety of samples that also provide clues to the environmental conditions on the Alpena-Amberley Ridge (Fig. 12.3). The most important of these are seven pieces of submerged wood that have been recovered (Fig. 12.3*A*, *B*). Two pieces more recently recovered from Area 3 have not yet been dated or identified, while five of the wood pieces from Area 1 have been identified and radiocarbon dated (Table 12.4). Two of these are pine and have anomalous dates of approximately 150 years before present, indicating that these pieces are not contemporaneous with exposure of the ridge. However, the other three wood specimens have been identified as spruce and tamarack, and provide dates between approximately 9000 and 8600 cal BP (Table 12.4). Recoveries of small pieces of charcoal (Fig. 12.3*C*, *D*) have yielded dates in this time period as well (Table 12.4). Pollen was also identified in samples that contained testate amoebae. While the pollen was not formally analyzed, initial identifications included *Picea* and *Tsuga* pollen and *Bryophyte* spores (Fig.12.3*E*, *F*), which support the testate amoebae data of forested swamps and mossy bogs.

Table 12.4. Radiocarbon ages from the Alpena-Amberley Ridge. All dates from the National Ocean Sciences Accelerator Mass Spectrometry Facility (NOSAMS) except where noted.

Sample #	BP	SDV	calBP	delta ^{13}C	Type
AA95226/Wood 1*	8038	46	8900	-25.5	spruce
Wood 4	7960	55	8829	-25.12	spruce
ATI Lake Huron	15300	120	18350	-24.7	charcoal
Wood 3	115	25	113	-25.55	pine
Wood 2	140	25	142	not measured	pine
Wood 5	7840	40	8640	-26.12	tamarack
92912E	105	20	150	-26.44	charcoal
92912F	8080	35	9020	-26.54	charcoal

*Date from the University of Arizona AMS laboratory.

Discussion

Paleogeographic Reconstructions

Paleogeographic maps utilizing sediment characteristics, microfossil abundances, and underwater topography allowed for a reconstruction of the landscape as it was prior to the end of the Lake Stanley lowstand (Fig. 12.8), providing a visualization of the environmental differences between Area 1 and Area 3 during the Lake Stanley lowstand phase. The cluster analysis of testate amoebae shows distinct assemblages that are unique to each area, as well as assemblages that are consistent in both areas. Area 3 is on average deeper (35–37 m below surface) than Area 1 (29–32 m below surface). The overall lack of sediment in Area 3 compared with Area 1 indicates that it may have experienced more scour as it would have been flooded prior to Area 1 and may have experienced more wave action than did Area 1.

Despite this potential scouring and damage to sediments through flooding, both Area 1 and Area 3 provided excellently preserved testate amoebae and wood samples, and the sediment shape from both areas indicates that sediment has not traveled extensively. This preserved environmental evidence allows us to create a reasonable reconstruction of the paleogeography and environment, while also identifying areas of high potential for the preservation of archaeological materials and artifacts.

Area 1

Area 1 is a landscape dotted with small kettle lakes or depressions, along with surrounding forested swamps and sphagnum bogs, similar to the kind of environments we see in northern Alberta (Fig. 12.8*A*). Paleoenvironmental interpretations based on pollen and macrofossil analysis of Georgian Bay indicate the area was prairie parkland (Chapter 3), but given the abundance of sphagnum moss, spruce, and tamarack, we believe that the ridge may have had an environment that was slightly cooler due to its location bisecting Lake Stanley, and is more closely related to a Subarctic environment (as described in Chapter 8).

Area 1 represents a patchwork of high-elevation areas of exposed bedrock, grass scrub, and wetland/bog areas (Fig. 12.8*A*). The high-elevation exposed bedrock has a thin drape of sand and does not have a high amount of dissolved and pitted limestone, indicating that these areas likely were not vegetated either with coniferous trees or sphagnum moss. These upland areas form natural constriction points where several of the stone structures are located. They also create uplands that overlook shallow inland lakes. The majority of the area was likely scrubby grassland, a premise derived from current Subarctic geography. Based on topographic features as well as on the presence of identified wood and testate amoebae assemblages that included very distinct marsh and sphagnum moss species, a patchwork

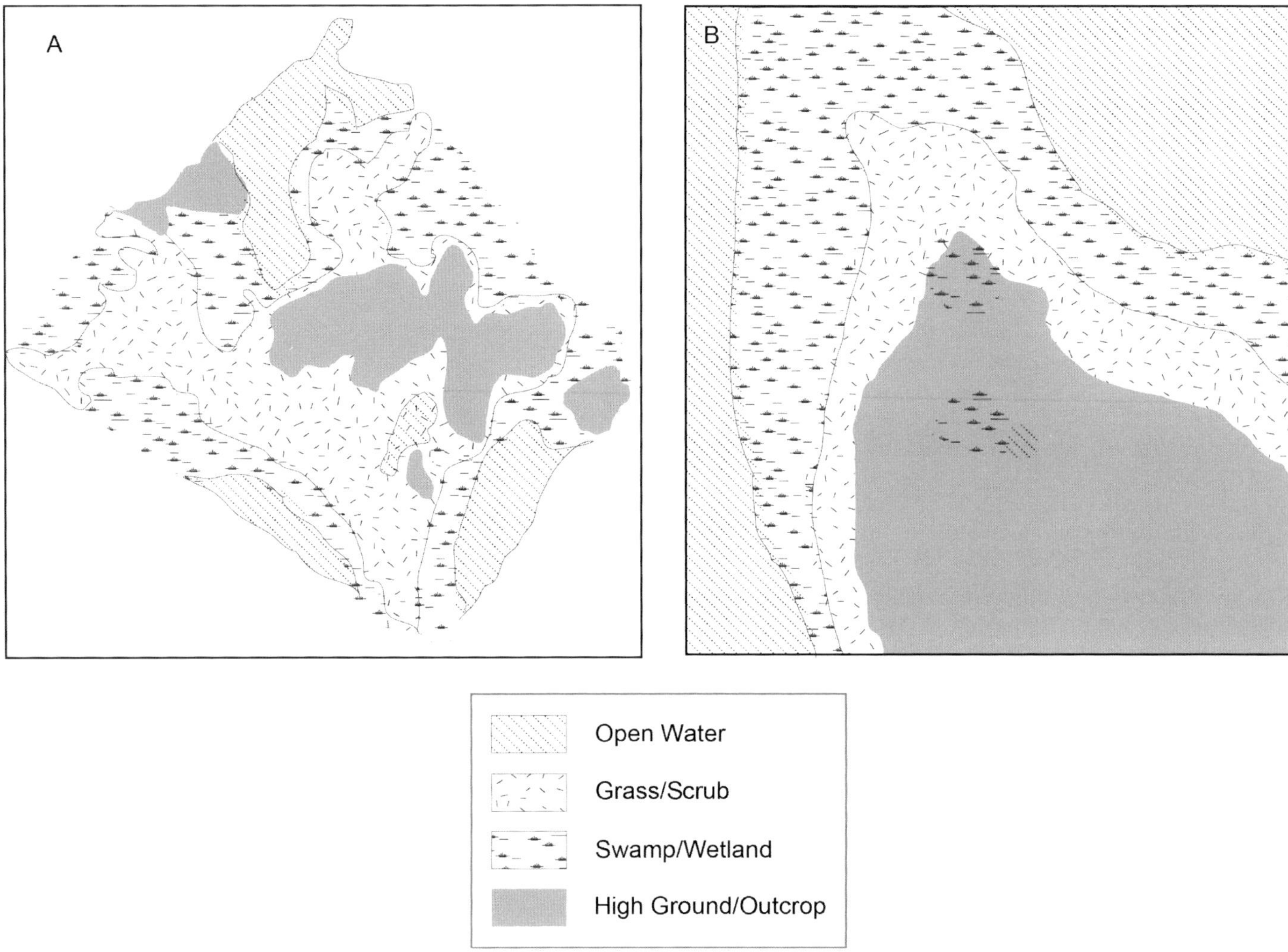

Figure 12.8. Paleogeographic reconstruction of Areas 1 (*A*) and 3 (*B*) based on testate amoebae assemblages, sediments, and topography.

of bogs, fens, and forested swamps fringed both the main lake and the inland water bodies. Watercourses and shallow lakes are identified primarily by topographic features and sediment type. The inland lake has a very uniform, well sorted sediment type, while the river has a typical poorly sorted, polymodal variety of sediments ranging from coarse sands to muds.

Area 3

One of the interesting aspects of these paleogeographic studies is the lack of sediment present in Area 3 as compared to Area 1. While the reason for this is not clear, it may be because Area 3 was affected by rising water levels sooner than Area 1 (there is an approximately 5–7 m difference in elevation; Fig. 12.2). And because Area 1 remained above water longer, Area 3 may have been subject to more shoreline erosion and sediment scour compared to Area 1. The preserved shoreline ridges in Area 3 are high (17 cm) and pronounced, and indicate strong shore action.

Area 3 is a less complex environment than Area 1, likely due to its less complicated elevation and smaller size (Fig. 12.8*B*). The landscape gradually increases in elevation northward until the peak of the "Overlook" area, where it drops off. The overlook area has some more complicated terrain, and is also the location of newly discovered stone features. There is a hummocky sphagnum-dominated area at the edge of the overlook, based on the presence of a unique testate amoebae assemblage heavily dominated by *Cyphoderia ampulla*. Further toward the center of the area, there is a small topographic depression containing well-sorted sands and a testate amoebae assemblage that indicates this was an oligotrophic pond, fringed by a forested swamp, where additional wood (species unknown) was recovered. Again, these sphagnum and forested swamp assemblages are located near V-shaped hunting structures (Chapter 10).

Archaeological Implications

The sedimentological information gained from grain size and morphological analysis, and the presence of testate amoebae and nonarboreal pollen, indicates that both Areas 1 and 3 have preserved sediments from the Lake Stanley lowstand. If the sediments had traveled great distances, or had been moved by water action, the sediments would be all well sorted and rounded. Very little of the sediment from all samples had rounded sediments, and the sediments ranged from moderately well sorted to very poorly sorted, indicating they were probably in situ from when they were laid down as post-glacial sediment.

Stone hunting structures are often located near natural topographic highs and pinch points. From a paleoenvironmental perspective, they also seem to be located near swampy and/or boggy areas, indicating that these areas may have been locales that attracted caribou and made them easier to exploit. Since caribou today live near swampy and/or boggy areas, we can reasonably assume that both caribou and people would have found the environment conducive to resource procurement (Chapter 10).

Conclusions

The Alpena-Amberley Ridge is a complex patchwork of multiple environments ranging from high rocky outcrops to swampy lowlands. Sediment and testate amoebae data strongly indicate that at least some of the sediments were preserved, and still record excellent paleoenvironmental information. The testate amoebae and recovered wood show the ridge to be less like the prairie parkland of the Upper Peninsula and southern Ontario, and closer to a Subarctic environment with spruce and tamarack trees and sphagnum-dominated bogs. Topographic data also reflect subtle changes in elevation within each area, showing depression and uplands with distinct microenvironments. These microenvironments provided natural pinch points for corralling caribou, in addition to fresh water and other resources such as plants, waterfowl and possible fish. The Alpena-Amberley Ridge provided all the resources necessary for both caribou and early prehistoric peoples to thrive in this unique landscape.

Acknowledgments

This paper has benefited from the contribution of many people and institutions. In particular we would like to thank Ashley Lemke, Elizabeth Callison, Drs. Francine McCarthy, Guy Meadows, Lee Newsom, and Eduard Reinhardt for their valued contributions to the research, and dive team members Tyler Schultz, Michael Courvoisier, and Annie Davidson. Institutionally, we would also acknowledge the support of the Museum of Anthropological Archaeology, University of Michigan; the Department of Computer Science, Wayne State University; and the Thunder Bay National Marine Sanctuary. This research was supported in part by grants from the National Science Foundation, award numbers BCS 0829324 and BCS0964424, and by NOAA's Ocean Exploration–Marine Archaeology program award number NA10OAR0110187.

PART IV

Conclusions

13 Paleoenvironments of the Upper Great Lakes

What We Know, and What We Need to Know

by Elizabeth Sonnenburg

The chapters in this monograph describe the environmental changes that have marked the early Holocene, particularly the influence of climate changes on the fluctuating water levels of the upper Great Lakes between 10,000 and 8000 years ago. Chapters 2 (Barnett) and 3 (McCarthy et al.) detail large-scale geological and environmental changes, while Chapter 12 (Sonnenburg) addresses how these changes affect smaller-scale processes on the ridge itself. By looking at the paleoenvironmental changes at different scales, we can more clearly see what large- and small-scale environmental processes may have influenced how prehistoric peoples viewed their landscapes and adapted to rapidly changing environmental and water level conditions over millennia. This chapter aims to summarize these multiscalar approaches—including how they can be used to understand environmental change on the ridge—and to propose how subsequent research can answer questions that our current knowledge cannot.

Modeling Paleoenvironments

Numerous water level and paleoenvironmental studies have investigated the pre- and post-glacial landscape of Lake Huron (e.g., Drzyzga, Shortridge, and Schaetzl 2012; Lewis and Anderson 2012; McCarthy et al. 2012; Janusas et al. 2004; Karrow 2004). The majority of these works focused on the more sediment rich areas of Saginaw and Georgian Bay and the eastern shore of Lake Michigan, and are primarily based on long sediment core records from the modern shoreline and climate records based on pollen transfer functions (McCarthy et al. 2012). Limited work has focused on the interior of Lake Huron (O'Shea and Meadows 2009) due to a lack of sedimentation (Thomas, Kemp, and Lewis 1973). However, recent studies have shown at least a thin drape of sediments, which is providing important new information about the pre- and post-depositional processes of the ridge (Sonnenburg and O'Shea, in review).

The knowledge of lowstands in the Great Lakes stems from the pioneering work of Stanley (1938b), who identified evidence of subaerial exposure in sediments of Lake Huron, and Hough (1962), who surmised that the lakes were isolated basins. Later work by McCarthy et al. (2007) and Lewis et al. (2007) demonstrated clear evidence and included a terminal date of 7900 BP as the time of the lowest level of Lake Stanley. While many archaeologists have surmised that the lowstand has inundated many archaeological sites from the Late Paleoindian/Early Archaic, the focus of archaeological site investigation has been on the more obvious and easier to locate glacial strandlines of glacial Lake Algonquin. The shift from the high water level of glacial Lake Algonquin to the low water levels of Lake Stanley provides an archaeological conundrum of sites that end up being submerged, deeply buried (Chapter 2), or both (Lovis et al. 1994).

The pollen record of Lake Huron identifies four phases of vegetation succession after deglaciation, and is summarized in Table 13.1 (McAndrews 1994). The time of the Lake Stanley lowstand covers the transition between Phases 1, 2a, and 2b. The change between phase 1 (spruce dominated) and 2 (pine dominated) represents the drying of the climate and the initial drop in lake levels. The change from phase 2a (jack/red pine) to 2b (white pine) is likely the result of increasing wet conditions and the rising of lake levels (McCarthy et al. 2012; Lewis and Anderson 2012). During the lowstand, large tracts of land were exposed, and the landscape resembled modern prairie parkland with spruce, tamarack, and cedar, along with scrubby brush and grasslands (McCarthy et al. 2012; Chapter 3).

While the pollen record provides an excellent record of vegetative changes, it does have limitations. Other techniques can complement the pollen record while also providing more fine-grained resolution. Testate amoebae in particular have been very successful in identifying more small-scale potential archaeological landscapes (e.g., Sonnenburg, Boyce, and Reinhardt 2009, 2013). As they are also more environmentally sensitive and live at the sediment-water interface, they react more quickly to shifts in water levels and climate than pollen (McCarthy et al. 1995).

Table 13.1. Summary of pollen zones, environment, and archaeological context for Lake Huron based on McAndrews, 1994.

Zones and Subzones	Dominant Species	Time Period	Environment	Archaeological Context
1	spruce	13–10 ka BP	tundra and boreal woodland	Paleoindian
1p	jack/red pine			
1a	high sedge			
1b	high spruce			
2	pine	10–8 ka BP	southern boreal forest	Paleoindian-Archaic
2a	jack/red pine			
2b	white pine			
3	beech	8 ka–200 BP	mixed and deciduous forest	Archaic, Woodland, Historic
3a	high hemlock	8–5 ka BP		
3b	low hemlock	5–3 ka BP		
3c	high hemlock	3–1 ka BP		
3d	white pine	1 ka–200 BP		
4	ragweed	200 BP	deforestation and farming	Historic/European settlement

The Alpena-Amberley Ridge

The unique record provided by the Alpena-Amberley Ridge allows a more detailed and site-specific look into the paleoenvironment of Lake Huron during the Lake Stanley lowstand. While much excellent work has provided records of the shoreline environments, particularly in the Georgian Bay region, the lack of data from within the lake—and the fact that the Lake Huron basin consisted of three separate and hydrologically closed basins—makes a large-scale environmental reconstruction of the entire basin impossible without these more detailed studies that are area specific.

The paleoenvironmental reconstruction thus far shows a complex landscape complete with multiple microenvironments that would have had an effect on the ability of ancient hunters to procure additional resources if necessary, but would also have impacted hunting blind placement, which is often topographically dependent (see Chapter 7). The ridge was a unique environment, and shows a different environmental picture than paleoenvironmental work done on the "mainland." The ridge itself was a feature that was both a link and a barrier. While it provided a transit corridor between groups in northern Michigan and southern Ontario, it also would have prevented sediment from entering the basins, and the Mattawa floods—which are seen as sudden pulses of glacial meltwater into the northern basin (Lewis and Anderson 2012)—would not have affected the southern basin in the same way because the ridge would have prevented these freshwater inputs from entering the southern basin. This explains why there is greater sedimentation in the northern basin, and why isotopic signatures differ greatly between the basins. The ridge may also have funneled wind and waves along it, creating a colder Subarctic corridor and allowing for an environment more familiar to relict populations of caribou to cross the ridge before they moved further north with the changing climate after 7000 BP.

The mainland shows a shift to pine from spruce and tamarack, looking closer to the modern boreal forest environment. Our data show that this boreal forest had not reached the ridge, and spruce and tamarack, based on wood recovered from the ridge, were likely still dominating the landscape. It is not surprising that the ethnographic analogies of Arctic caribou hunters work well for this environment—it would have closely resembled it from an environmental perspective. A boreal forest environment would also bring a different type of caribou hunting than the structures on the ridge attest to (Chapter 14).

Unanswered Questions and Future Directions

However, we are still unclear as to the landscape surrounding the ridge—parts of it would have been exposed, although inundated much earlier than the ridge as water levels recovered after the lowstand—and as to the effects of differential inundation of the landscape through time. This also begs the question about what happened to the ridge as an archaeological landscape as it became inundated. Presumably, parts of the ridge would have submerged more quickly than others, creating islands within the lake that may have still been utilized by Middle or even Late Archaic peoples. There are examples of other prehistoric populations in the Great Lakes returning to the same areas over and over despite major shifts in climate, vegetation, and water levels (Sonnenburg, Boyce, and Suttak 2012). If we are looking at 1000+ years of use of the ridge, would there be similar reasons that they would still return to the ridge even if they were using it in a different way (e.g., fishing instead of hunting caribou)? We have recovered stones that do resemble net sinkers, although it is unclear if they are in fact artifacts and not geofacts. However, it may point to continued use of the ridge as a resource hub even when the causeway had disappeared.

These questions require additional, long-term paleoenvironmental data through a more substantive coring program where there is more sediment. Transects of cores along the ridge and across the lake would help answer the questions of how the transition from a cold deep glacial lake to a series of hydrologically (and possibly hypersaline; Chapter 3) closed lakes manifested itself in shifts in sedimentation, vegetation, and trophic changes. We know a lot about the glacial Lake Algonquin and we know something about the Lake Stanley lowstand, but the actual timing and extent of the periods in between are still nebulous. This coring data would provide a much needed "middle-ground" between the large-scale environmental reconstructions of Lake Huron and the very small site-specific work currently being undertaken on the ridge. The combination of this multiscalar paleoenvironmental data may also elucidate how prehistoric peoples navigated a complex and ever-changing landscape over millennia.

14 Hunters and Hunting on the Alpena-Amberley Ridge during the Late Paleoindian and Early Archaic Periods

by Ashley K. Lemke and John M. O'Shea

Introduction

One aim of this monograph has been to understand the nature of the Alpena-Amberley Ridge (AAR) and the manner in which it was used by the ancient inhabitants of the Great Lakes. The task of this final chapter is to pull together the evidence relating to the human occupation of the ARR and to draw from it a plausible model of what these cultures were like.

In normal archaeological terms, the evidence for such modeling is extremely limited: a small handful of stone flakes, a fire ring, and a series of stones and boulders. But the AAR is not your normal archaeological setting. What it provides is unattainable elsewhere in Subarctic North America—it is an ancient landscape where the constructions and debris deriving from this early time period remain intact and accessible to archaeological investigation. The ability to record these hunting structures, to document their context in a thoroughly reconstructed environment, and to see how they were positioned relative to one another provides powerful insights into the way that human activities were structured. The tightly bounded chronology, imposed by the brief interval when the AAR was dry land, further enhances the ability to compare and understand how stone constructions figured in the landscape. In this final section, we use the strengths of the archaeological record of the AAR, and the insights drawn from the previous chapters, to provisionally model the AAR occupation.

Hunting Structures

The starting point for modeling is the structures themselves and their location on the landscape. It has previously been argued that the structures on the AAR—in their form, placement, and variety—bear strong similarities to caribou hunting features documented in more northerly regions (O'Shea, Lemke, and Reynolds 2013), and this assertion is further highlighted by Stewart's description of ethnographic examples (Chapter 8). Yet, the contrasts that exist are important and may, in the end, be more informative.

Looking to the stone constructions themselves, it is apparent that differing types of hunting structures were repeatedly built on the AAR, and that the distribution of different forms was not uniform across the landform. In Chapter 10, it was noted that open blinds, such as the V structures, are much more common in Area 3 compared to Area 1 (Table 14.1).

The possibility that differences in blind types represent a contrast between specific seasonal movement as opposed to a more generalized and opportunistic placement can be assessed by a closer examination of the different survey localities. A majority of the blinds in Area 3, which includes equal numbers of open and closed structures, are located on obvious seasonal routes of movement. The largest concentration of structures in Area 1 is in the Crossing locality. This would appear to be another

Table 14.1. Distribution of major structure types by research area.

Structure Type	Area 1	Area 3	Total
cluster	15	11	26
rectangle	1	3	4
V	3	14	17
total	19	28	47

predictable bottleneck, much like the Falls River region (Stewart et al. 2000). Yet here closed structures predominate and tend to be scattered back from the river margin. It is interesting to note that all the structures located to date in this locality are positioned south of the river, which presumably is indicative of an autumn movement of animals and tends to undermine the possibility that hunting here was not focused on specific seasonal migration. This result is consistent with the simulation model, which suggests that the preferred spring route of movement by caribou would have bypassed this river crossing. Taken together, these results indicate that the absence of open structures cannot be equated with the absence of a seasonal hunting focus.

While much of the discussion has been focused on hunting blinds and related features such as lines and cairns, they are not the only constructions that have been documented on the AAR. Three varieties of construction that may offer insight into the way that the AAR adaptation operated are caches, stone rings, and shelters.

The association of rectangular structures with caches is based entirely on ethnographic parallels and until some other kind of evidence can be identified, the link will always be uncertain. What we do know about the rectangular structures is that they are much less common than hunting blinds, and that they always occur in close proximity to clusters of simple blinds. The association with blinds could indicate that they are, indeed, storage structures or, alternatively, that they were simply another variety of hunting blind. The best argument against their being an alternative blind form is found at the AshGap V blind, where the rectangular structure is located just behind the open end of the V structure. In this position, the structure would seem ineffective as a blind. The association of these potential caches with the simple blinds is discussed further when the overall organization of hunting is considered.

Hollow stone rings used as hearths are unremarkable in terrestrial archaeology. The one confirmed fire ring (Chapter 10) from the AAR, in Area 1, is located in precisely the kind of setting where a hunter's camp site should be located: it is on the shore of a small lake and behind a hill, which separates and shields it from the hunting sites in the Crossing locality. It must be left to future research to determine whether there are additional rings or shelters in this location, but the find does provide confidence that other types of sites or uses of certain locations, such as camp sites, which have an inherently lower acoustic visibility, can be discovered on the AAR.

Like the discovery of a fire ring, the possibility that small shelters were being constructed in or adjacent to hunting blinds is important since they provide insight into aspects of the cultural adaptation beyond the simple capture of prey. Of the potential shelters observed to date, they all resemble temporary shelters that might have been used by hunters as they waited for the herds, rather than actual habitation structures. Going on Arctic archaeological examples, the stone foundations of habitation structures may resemble blinds and pose some difficulty for identification (see Chapter 8). In any event, habitation structures would more likely be in settings similar to the fire ring rather than in the hunting zones.

Considering all the different kinds of structures encountered, it is clear that the occupants of the AAR took advantage of the natural alignments and barriers that the post-glacial landscape offered, which were many, and that they used the readily available stone to create whatever additional features were needed to turn the natural settings into effective hunting sites. In some cases, this may have been as simple as moving cobbles out of the way to create an open lane; in others, it meant shifting a couple of boulders into a more desirable location. While these boulders are substantial, spruce poles of the type that have been recovered from the AAR would have provided ample leverage to move them (see Fig. 12.3*B*). While it is probably safe to assume that hunters attempted to minimize the effort involved in creating these structures, there are at least two instances where substantial amounts of effort and labor were expended in their construction.

One instance is found at the Dragon Blind, where two of the three large boulders forming the blind are red sandstone (Fig. 10.6, Plate 6; also see Chapter 8). Large specimens of this sandstone are not rare, but they are not particularly common either, which raises the possibility that they were specifically selected and transported for use, perhaps because of their red color. It is also noteworthy that at this same feature, several of the large boulders appear to have been partially lifted so that smaller stones could be wedged beneath them to increase the interior area of the blind.

A second instance is found at the Funnel Drive. While the Funnel complex is entirely composed of larger boulders, it appears to have been built at the site of a fortuitous natural concentration of rock (such concentrations appear to result from the breakup of limestone bedrock layers). This cannot be said, however, for the extended line of boulders that stretches out from the main structure. As evidenced in Figure 10.16 (see also Plate 9), these boulders have been placed in a spaced line on a level bedrock surface that is otherwise devoid of rock. In this instance, it was not simply shifting a couple of existing rocks into place. The boulders were moved a significant distance to the location, and then placed with some precision to form the discontinuous line.

The fact that ancient hunters were able and willing to undertake this kind of construction when necessary should not be surprising, as historical, ethnographic, and archaeological cases aptly illustrate this capability (see Chapters 7, 8). The more interesting question is how the process was realized and to what extent the final form of the feature was planned in advance.

Given the modular character of the simple structures, they could easily grow by aggregation without any specific initial plan. A key feature of the simple structures is that they are usable on their own when placed in suitable natural settings. If a particular location proved productive, more features could be added, either to increase the effectiveness of the location or to accommodate a greater number of hunters. The continued improvement of a desirable location may also have served to denote a particular individual's or group's continued claim to the use of the location. Both processes—growth by accretion, and the elaboration of a permanent facility to assert a claim to use—have ethnographic precedents.

Yet, it seems unlikely that the more complex features, such as the Funnel Drive or Drop 45, could have been constructed in such a progressive and unplanned manner. Even the Dragon Drive Lane contains a series of interlinked components that are needed for the structure to operate. In each of these cases, it is possible to envision a simpler, prior version of the complex form that might have occupied the same location; however, that simpler construction would have needed to be entirely reworked to create the complex hunting structures that resulted. It is probably no coincidence that the features that were the most complex to construct were also the hunting sites that implied the participation of a great number of people (see below).

Hunting Locations

The characterization of hunting structure placement has already been broached in the consideration of the distribution of differing kinds of hunting structures. In essence, four different kinds of location appear to have been selected for hunting features. These four—choke points, gaps, water crossings, and opportunistic—represent the range of hunting locations known from other ethnographic and archaeological examples (Chapter 7).

The Overlook locality in Area 3 represents a "choke point," where the landform dictated where the migrating animals would have to travel. These locations, which would have to be transited in both the spring and the autumn migrations, are highlighted in the simulation study (Chapter 4). Within the research zones studied so far, only two such locations are observed—the Overlook locality in Area 3, and in the southeast corner of Area 1, in a locality that has not yet been examined. As noted above, structures oriented toward both the spring and autumn migration have been identified in the Overlook locality, which supports its importance in both seasons, as does the unusually high density of structures in this area. Future research will show whether a similar pattern exists in the region's other choke point.

Hunting structures are also concentrated in gaps where natural features, such as glacial eskers, would tend to concentrate the moving herds into narrow channels. The Gap locality in Area 3 is the prime example of this setting. These locations served as local versions of the choke point kind of setting, and similarly contain a high density of structures that are oriented for spring as well as autumn hunting.

The third setting with major concentrations of structures is water crossings. Crossings of this kind, as in the Crossing locality in Area 1, provide a good match with ethnographic accounts of caribou hunting. While in the Falls River area (Stewart et al. 2000; see also discussion in Chapter 10) the river crossings were used in both seasons, the placement and orientation of structures in the Area 1 Crossing locality are overwhelmingly, if not exclusively, positioned to take animals during their southward autumn migration. While this distribution contrasts with the ethnographic case, it is consistent with the caribou simulation prediction that animals moving in the spring would probably bypass this crossing area (Chapter 4).

The fourth location type observed in the AAR is best thought of as opportunistic, near grazing areas and fresh water (this has parallels to the South American and Near Eastern drive lanes and blinds that are situated adjacent to browsing areas and freshwater drinking areas, or along day travel routes as opposed to migrations; see Chapter 7), and may not have any association with a seasonal migration. In Area 1, the locations of both the Funnel Drive and the Dragon Drive might be considered opportunistic given their setting between a large marsh and the high outcropping ridge of Six Fathom Scarp.

Each of these settings is reasonable and consistent with ethnographic data and archaeological expectations (see below). Of course, that is why each locality was selected for survey in the first place. Numerous other areas examined to date by the survey do not contain identifiable structures, and for this reason this categorization of preferred hunting settings is probably accurate, but until additional localities can be examined systematically, we will not know for certain.

The AAR in Global Perspective

When viewed from a global perspective, ungulate hunting strategies and structures reveal a surprising number of cross-cultural patterns in the exploitation of these animals. Specifically, hunting structures demonstrate a detailed knowledge and use of the regional landscapes and local topography, and an exploitation of specific aspects of ungulate behavior. The hunting structures beneath Lake Huron fit these general patterns. Similar to terrestrial sites, the AAR hunting structures can be used to infer the prey species, seasonality, weaponry, number of animals targeted, and size of corporate groups exploiting these animals. An examination of these hunting structures and sites reveals a detailed picture of prehistoric hunting strategies, even in the absence of robust faunal and lithic assemblages.

As shown in Chapter 7, ungulate hunting structures share common elements and common locations, and the AAR occurrences fit this same pattern. The AAR structures comprise the same fundamental components of other hunting structures, including stone drive lanes, cairns, and hunting blinds. In terms of hunting locations, the AAR cases exhibit the same use of local topography and knowledge of animal behavior. Similar to other geographic areas, the AAR structures are placed along migration routes and/or commonly used game trails, on natural bottlenecks, on elevated ridges, and perhaps near grazing areas (Bar-Oz and Nadel 2013; Nadel et al. 2013; Moreno 2012; Smith 2013; Chapter 4). The common elements and patterns that emerge from a global comparison can be used to generate archaeological expectations at both the regional and site level, and the AAR data can be viewed in light of these expectations.

First, terrestrial investigations reveal complex regional landscapes of many different types of hunting structures that are often reused and elaborated over time. The AAR data fit this expectation and reveal a complex, modified, reused, and multiseasonal (and most probably a multigenerational; see below) landscape. The AAR features also represent both ends of the spectrum of known hunting structures, consisting of both individual structures like the V blinds, and large-scale multicomponent and complex structures that incorporate more modular elements, such as Drop 45 and the Funnel Drive. While no specific data document how far camps tend to be from kill sites, they are often located some distance away (Bar-Oz and Nadel 2013; Brink 2005:15; Smith 2013; Stewart et al. 2000; Stewart, Keith, and Scottie 2004; Zeder et al. 2013:119), suggesting that the low number of campsites identified thus far on the AAR may be more attributable to a research focus on hunting localities as opposed to a real absence of campsites.

In terms of site-level expectations, the AAR data fit the expectations derived from known terrestrial cases as well. In general, artifact densities tend to be low at hunting structures due to extensive cleaning so that they may be used in future hunts. The limited lithic material from the AAR structures and the absence of faunal remains thus far agree with this expectation (Chapter 11). More specifically, the formal character of the lithic artifacts known from terrestrial game drives are commonly a small number of projectile points and bifacial tools, and many more small flakes from final stage biface reduction or tool rejuvenation (LaBelle and Pelton 2013). These expectations are consistent with the AAR data, in which flakes fitting these attributes, and of similar dimensions, have been recovered either in or adjacent to hunting blinds. The absence of definite projectile points or fragments from the AAR may be attributable to limited sampling or to wood lance hunting methods (O'Shea, Lemke, and Reynolds 2013), in which case, lithic projectiles would be absent. In addition, the thumbnail scraper on Baypoint chert is most likely indicative of hide processing behaviors.

For faunal remains, caribou represent a medium-sized animal when compared to the range of ungulates targeted by hunting structures, with bison on one end and gazelles on the other. In the global comparison, there seems to be a loose correlation between butchering patterns at hunting structures and body size of the prey species. The largest bodied animals are most often butchered at the hunting site, resulting in large bone beds and large-scale archaeological signatures. On the other end of the spectrum, smaller bodied ungulates such as gazelles are usually carried whole body to local camps or villages, with no butchering done at the hunting structure, resulting in the absence of faunal remains. Bighorn sheep, camelids, and caribou represent medium-size prey on this spectrum, and a different butchering pattern is apparent. Primary butchering is usually done at or very near the kill site, resulting in perhaps a few bones in the hunting structures (e.g., sheep remains from excavated hunting blinds at the Olson game drive in Colorado; LaBelle and Pelton 2013), but most often there is an absence of faunal remains (Brink 2005:14). For caribou specifically, the primary butchering done at the kill site typically is limited, and whole parts of the animal are either stored (depending on the season) or transported back to camp (Binford 1978b). These expectations for medium-sized animals suggest that faunal remains would be uncommon at the hunting structures, and rather tend to be found in caches and in camps. These expectations are at least partially met by the AAR data, where no faunal remains have been recovered thus far from the hunting structures; however, few confirmed campsites or caches have yet been identified.

Fortunately, despite the paucity of cultural materials—specifically, lithic and faunal remains, which may characterize hunting features—the formal attributes of the structures themselves, their placement on the landscape, and detailed regional analyses have been informative both for terrestrial studies and on the AAR. These formal attributes have been used to infer other information when direct evidence is lacking, such as the targeted prey species (Brink 2013; Nadel et al. 2013; O'Shea and Meadows 2009), the types of weaponry (Freisen 2013; O'Shea, Lemke, and Reynolds 2013), the season of use of hunting structures (Morrison 1981:182; O'Shea, Lemke, and Reynolds 2013), and the number of animals hunted. Combining all of these attributes allows for detailed model building of the AAR's social and economic use.

Modeling the Seasonal Use of the AAR

While season of use has already been described for each hunting locality, a second aspect to the seasonal organization of activity on the AAR may have substantial social significance. It has previously been noted that a majority of the simple hunting structures have orientations suggesting a focus on autumn hunting. This is consistent with global patterns of caribou hunting generally (Chapter 7; O'Shea, Lemke, and Reynolds 2013) since the animals are in their prime and their hides are in the best condition in autumn. Yet both of the complex structures identified to date are aligned to animals moving in the spring. Prior to the discovery of the Drop 45 Drive Lane, the orientation of the Funnel Drive was something of an anomaly, which was variously attributed to a later date when caribou had become scarce on the AAR (O'Shea, Lemke, and Reynolds 2013) or to the opportunistic hunting of grazing animals. With the discovery of Drop 45, the spring orientation of the Funnel Drive ceased to be an anomaly and, rather, began to take the shape of a pattern.

The implication of this association of complex drive structures with spring hunting is substantial since the structures not only require more labor to construct, but they require a greater number of people to operate. This implies that the hunters on the AAR were employing very different patterns of animal exploitation in the spring and in the autumn. In the fall, the simple blinds could be operated by very small, even family-sized, groups. By relying on natural features of the landscape, the hunters could simply hunker down in their blinds and wait to be surrounded by the migrating herds of caribou. In the spring, large numbers of hunters and helpers would have to aggregate at the complex hunting structures. This greater effort would presumably result in a larger take of animals, which would probably have been necessary to support the larger number of participants. Here again, the AAR adaptation has examples of the entire range of variability known about hunting structures (Chapter 7), including both large- and small-scale use.

A likely explanation for the differing seasonal patterns would relate to the relative importance of storage and sociability. The autumn hunt provides both a critical source of meat to be cached for the winter and an important source of hides, sinew, bone, antler, and other raw materials needed to equip and sustain the hunters over the winter. It would be quite plausible that this type of hunting would be conducted by smaller family or extended family groups prior to moving into winter camp. Over the winter, these small groups could be sustained on the cached meat and on the small mammals and fish that might be captured. By contrast, the spring hunt is primarily for fresh meat that will be consumed immediately to offset the lingering hunger of winter. The condition of the animals' flesh or hide was less important than the simple availability of food. The larger cooperative hunting structures would enable a large number of animals to be killed quickly and successfully (and thus feed a much larger number of people), and since storage would not be a strong imperative at this time of year, would facilitate the temporary aggregation of larger groups of people. This, in turn, would allow the sharing of information and mates among neighboring groups, the reaffirmation of important reciprocity and affiliation ties, and, perhaps, significant shuffling of members between neighboring groups. This pattern on the AAR fits with ethnographic accounts describing large-scale hunts in which hunting facilities serve as loci for family and band aggregations during cyclical nucleation (Carlson and Bement 2013; Smith 2013; Wilke 2013) and social and ceremonial activity is as important as subsistence (Sundstrom 2000).

Territoriality and Social Leadership

This model of differing seasonal postures among the AAR hunters is plausible, but it is incomplete without a consideration of leadership and territoriality among the AAR groups. While these factors are always difficult to approach archaeologically, the character of the stone structures on the AAR provides some initial insights.

While hunter-gatherers are notoriously acephalous and egalitarian in their life and organization, they often do recognize territorial rights and limited kinds of group leadership (e.g., Ames 1994; Flanagan 1989). As a resource, migrating caribou are similar to the great salmon runs of the Pacific Northwest in the sense that they present an almost limitless and predictable resource, but one that may be available for only a short time. As such, limiting access to the resource makes little sense. However, once an individual or group erects a permanent structure for harvesting the resource, rights to the facility, and by extension to its location, are generally recognized as belonging to the builder (or at least to the builder so long as he continues to utilize the facility).

In terms of usage and territorial claims, there are probably two models that would fit the pattern of simple structures on the AAR. The first would be analogous to modern ice fishermen on a frozen public lake. Each individual or group constructs their own facilities, augers their own ice holes, and drags out whatever kind of shelter they desire. No individual has the authority to deny access to any other fisherman. Rules of politeness and social norms keep fisherman from placing their camps too close to an already established site, but if a particular location begins producing fish, other fisherman will gravitate to that area.

The alternative model can be termed a homestead model. Under this scenario, a founding hunter or family will construct a simple hunting blind in a location they believe is advantageous. If it turns out to be a good spot, the hunter or descendants maintain and may elaborate the structure, or add entirely new ones to the location. Though increased in number, the structures are all still self-sufficient in terms of their use, but the increased quantity may permit descendants and affines to hunt together for mutual solidarity and support. Other groups would recognize the structures as permanent markers on the landscape indicating that the location was occupied or owned.

Either of these two models, or a combination of the two, could account for the construction and distribution of simple hunting structures and their gradual modification and elaboration, particularly in prime locations. On balance, however, the homestead model is probably the closer fit since the fishing analogy breaks down when the ice melts and no permanent marker or claim remains on the landscape. Among homesteaders, while the original soddie may have collapsed and decayed, family and neighbors alike know who built it and which 80 acres it was originally associated with. The linking of hunting structures and associated features with particular individuals, even if in the distant past, is a common feature in the accounts of Stewart's informants in the Falls River area (Stewart et al. 2000) and in Binford's accounts of Nunamiut groups living in the Brooks Range (1978b)—even among people that no longer used the stone alignments, blinds, or camps.

If we accept that something like the homestead model characterized the use of simple structures on the AAR, it would suggest that the discrete clusters of hunting features that are recognized archaeologically were gradually built up by relatively small related groups of individuals exercising some manner of land tenure in these particular locations. This could account not only for the proliferation of structures in desirable spots, but also for the distinct gaps that occur between the clusters, even though on the spatial scale of Paleoindians the distances are trivial (Chapter 8; Ellis, Carr, and Loebel 2011). It would also follow that associated facilities, such as potential caches and shelters, would represent elaborations that would similarly be with these core family groups. While the size and extensiveness of the local constructions must, in part, be a function of duration of use, they could also reflect the cumulative success and size of the owning group.

Under such a territorial system, even as successful families might monopolize highly desirable hunting locations, any hunter would still be capable of hunting somewhere, whether by constructing a very modest structure in an open location, or by using no structure at all, but simply the natural cover provided by large boulders. The difference would be the decreased certainty of hunting success in the less desirable spots, a lack of sharing resources with other groups, and the absence of a social network to fall back on in times of shortage.

The picture of social interaction on the AAR changes when the complex hunting structures are considered. Unlike the simple structures, the complex structures were a major undertaking requiring significant labor to construct and operate, and an underlying plan for how the component elements should fit together. Complex structures certainly could be modified and added to, but the core elements need to be in place before the structure can be successfully used. All this being said, they are not pharaonic in their scale or construction and probably could have been constructed to a usable form within a year or two, although they would certainly have required the cooperation of a larger group than was required to erect a simple structure. Yet would this entail the same kind of individual ownership attributed to the simpler structures?

Again, two models can be envisioned. The first might be analogous to boat ownership among the Inuit and Yupik (e.g., Grier 2000), where a successful family head is able to amass the social capitol necessary to construct a boat. As boat owner and acknowledged captain, other members of the community would cooperate as subordinate crewmembers to hunt in the boat. If this model were correct, we might expect complex structures to be located in prime hunting sites that already bore the marks of use and ownership in the form of multiple simple hunting structures and related facilities. The alternative would envision the construction of a complex structure as a collective enterprise performed under the direction of a particularly influential individual, such as a successful hunter or shaman (e.g., Binford 1991:51; Grier 2000). The structure would again be located in a prime location, but in this case, one that could not be individually claimed. The construction of this feature, and its use, would require some level of social/religious sanction to allow groups to cooperate and to share the meat produced by the hunt.

On balance, individual ownership of the structures seems unlikely. There is no inherent reason why individuals couldn't use simple blinds for spring hunting, and, indeed, several structures reflecting a spring orientation have been identified. So the most likely reason that groups converged on these complex structures in the spring was for social interaction. As noted above, since the animals are not prized for their hide or their meat for caching in the spring, meat produced from the kill would be primarily for immediate consumption, and the large number of animals that could be taken at one time in the complex structures would have permitted the temporary aggregation of a large number of people.

Coming at the end of a dark and isolated winter and with food stores running perilously low, it is easy to imagine the appeal of a collective spring hunt and jamboree. This model gains additional support from the simulation study, which predicts that the spring movement of animals would be relatively rapid and direct, meaning that the effective window for intercepting the herds would be narrow (Chapter 4). The more elaborate structures, located in prime intercept locations, would be the best guarantee that sufficient meat would be acquired to support all the people.

Taking the most plausible aspects of these models, along with their seasonal associations, we can envision small family groups or bands moving in the autumn to simple hunting structures within localities to which they claimed some manner of use rights. The fall hunting would be geared to acquiring sufficient meat, skins, and other raw materials to enable the group to survive the winter. After the hunt, meat would be cached and the groups would move to sheltered winter quarters. In the spring, these small groups would aggregate at the large spring hunting structures where they would prepare for the herd's arrival. Following the kill, the people would feast, socialize, and prepare for the coming summer.

What this narrative does not answer is where are the people during the rest of the year? Based on the environmental reconstruction, the AAR would have been an inhospitable place for much of the year and, as such, it is probably unlikely that any of the hunting groups maintained a permanent residence there (Chapter 12). More likely they traveled to the ridge in time to intercept the predictable movement of caribou during the spring and autumn migrations, and spent the rest of the year elsewhere. To the extent that meat from the autumn hunt was being cached, winter camps would need to be close enough to the caches to reach them during the winter, but the confines of the AAR fit well within the known territory of Arctic foragers who inhabitant some of the largest territories of any known hunter-gatherer group. While the actual wintering spots would clearly depend on the location of the AAR, a strong candidate for the inhabitants of the central AAR is probably the northern lower Michigan coast and further into the interior, such as the Foxie Otter Early Archaic site (Chapter 5). This area would have been sheltered with more tree cover and fuel than the AAR, and the shallow western basin lake would rapidly freeze over, providing a direct and efficient means to retrieve cached meat left on the AAR. In all probability, groups would remain at their fall encampments through the autumn, until this freeze-up of the

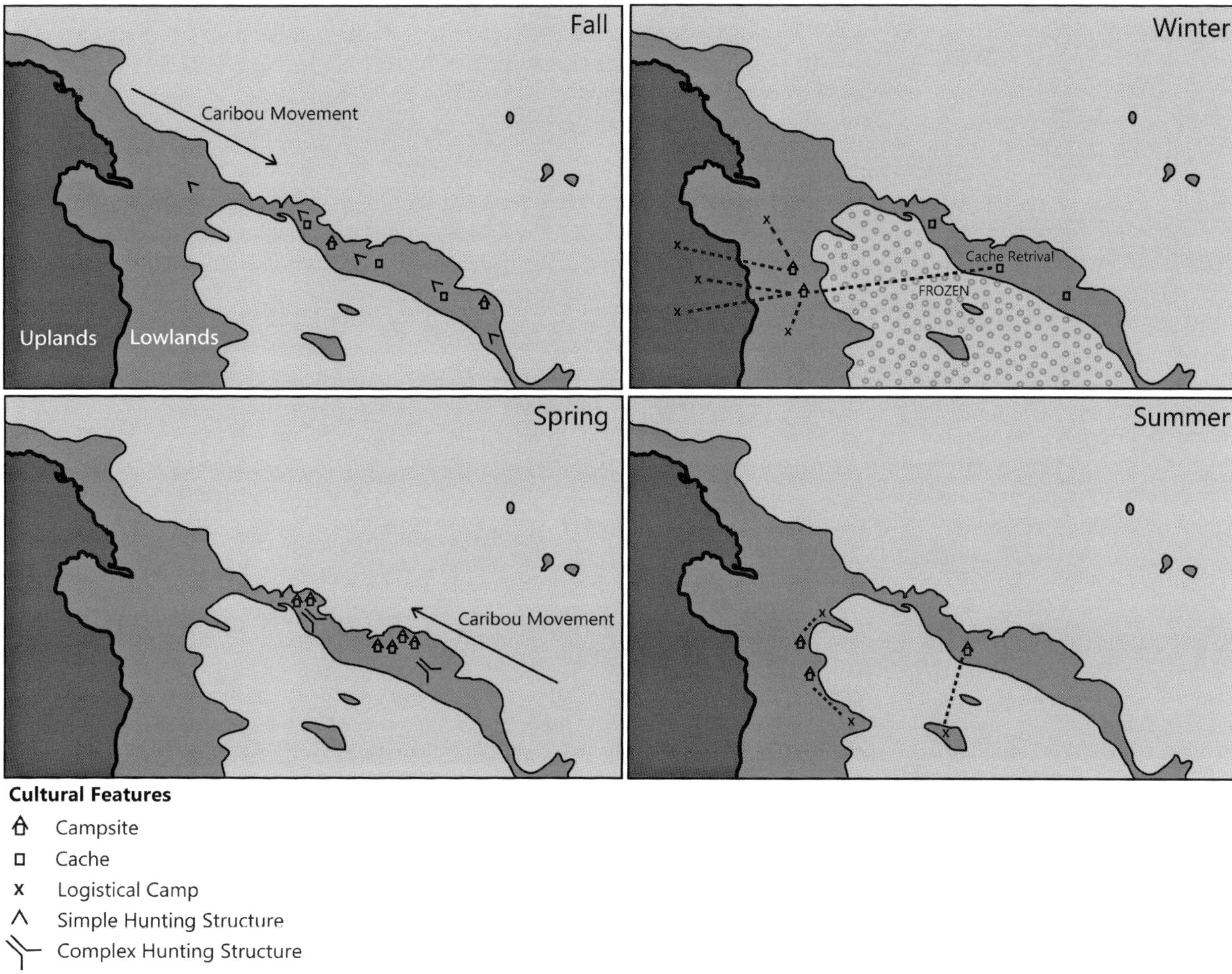

Figure 14.1. Seasonal occupations on the American portion of the Alpena-Amberley Ridge and predicted locations of major cultural features. Darkest gray indicates modern land surface, and lighter gray indicates additional land surfaces that would have been dry land during Lake Stanley. (See also Plate 16.)

western lake occurred. If this scenario is correct, we should expect the great majority of these winter camps to be buried beneath the coastal sediments of western Lake Huron (Chapter 2), although logistical hunting stations might be located further inland in what are now terrestrial settings (Fig. 14.1, Plate 16).

Logistically, the biggest problem for the hunters would be returning to the AAR in time for the spring migration, particularly if the western lake was also thawing. One approach would be to return to the AAR in the early spring before the thaw and maintain in place until the herds appear. The other would be to move north up the Michigan coast and then south along the AAR until the spring hunting sites were reached. Such movement would inevitably cross multiple autumn hunting territories, and would suggest that the perception of territorial rights was itself seasonal, a perception that would have been reinforced by the movement of multiple groups to the centrally located spring hunting sites. An advantage of this scenario is that even if the thaw came early, the hunters would still be in the path of the advancing herds.

Summer is a time when the population dispersed into smaller groups again. During the brief warming, the lakes, swamps, and marshes of the AAR would have provided for the kind of broad spectrum diet that has been suggested for other northern foragers during the Late Paleoindian period (see Chapters 5, 8). The exposed landscape would have experienced almost constant lake breezes, which would have served to disperse the biting insects and freshen the camps. Still, the AAR is narrow, and it would be

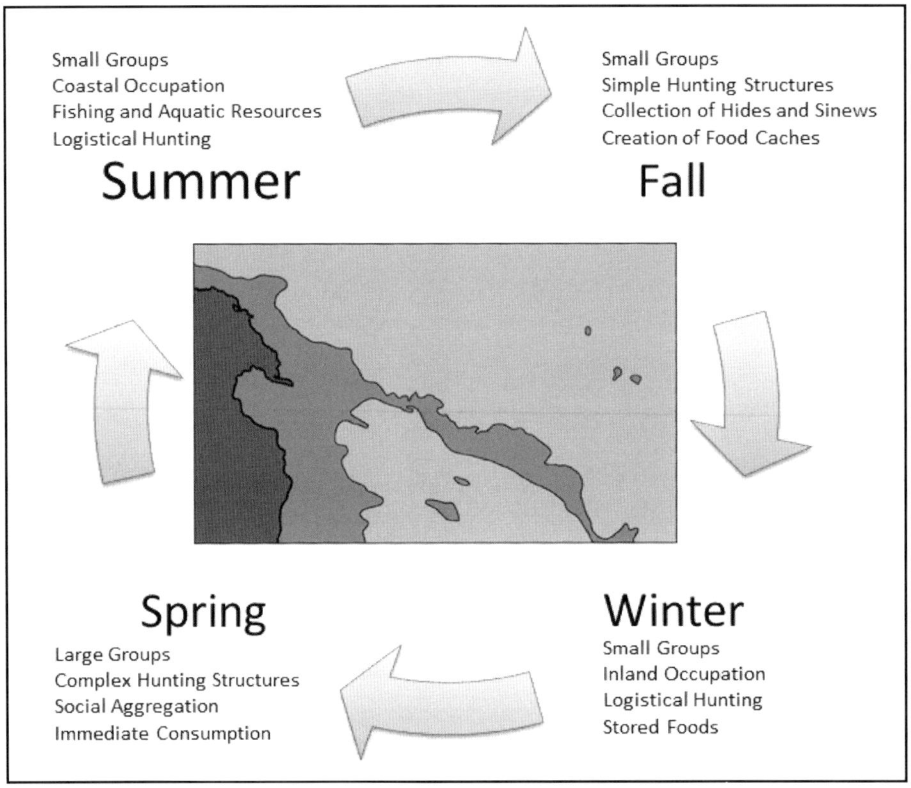

Figure 14.2. A proposed model of the seasonal round of Alpena-Amberley Ridge hunters and hunting, with diagnostic settlement pattern and subsistence attributes for each season.

difficult to occupy the area throughout the summer while avoiding the fall hunting sites that must be clean and clear before the animals' arrival. It is also possible that aquatic resources played an increasing role in group subsistence. Particularly on its westerly side, the shore of the AAR would have been well suited to fishing, and occupation on that portion of the ridge would have had little impact on the autumn movement of animals.

Clearly, certain aspects of this model are speculative, but it does narrow the range of possible adaptations that might have existed, and provides a means for future comparisons to other models of caribou hunters' mobility and sociality. As noted above, though, all of our current data come from a relatively limited area in the central portion of the AAR and it is possible—even likely—that the patterns of movement were quite different near the northern or southern ends of the AAR, or if the people made significant use of watercraft.

Conclusion

Overall, the picture that begins to emerge from the AAR is a Late Paleoindian/Early Archaic adaptation that is quite recognizable when viewed through the lens of northern caribou hunters, but one that is more alien to traditional reconstructions of Paleoindian lifeways (Fig. 14.2). A major difference is the investment in permanent hunting facilities, which tend to tie the hunters to defined places where they await their prey, rather than following their quarry as the Early Paleoindians are speculated to have done. This fundamental change in the relation to prey and land heralds future developments during the Archaic period in the Great Lakes region. The limited evidence of stone tool debris, despite the local availability of chert, may also suggest a very different kind of technological orientation, where untipped close-quarter thrusting spears would have been perfectly adequate to dispatch nearby animals, and tools fashioned on bone and antler accomplished many of the everyday tasks of life.

While the conduct of archaeological research on the AAR poses myriad problems for archaeological identification and recovery, these are the very factors that create its great potential. The preservation of these constructions and their existence within a preserved landscape provide a view of past cultural activity that is simply unavailable anywhere else in the Great Lakes region. In a very real sense, this is a new frontier that we have just begun to explore. The task for future interdisciplinary research is the sustained and systematic investigation of this unique and awe-inspiring land.

Bibliography

Abel, T.
1990 Thebes points. *Kewa Newsletter of the London Chapter, Ontario Archaeological Society* 90(8):16. London.

Agenbroad, L. D.
1978 Buffalo jump complexes in Owyhee County, Idaho. *Plains Anthropologist* 23(82):213–21.

Ali, M., and Robert G. Reynolds
2008 Embedding a social fabric component into cultural algorithms toolkit for an enhanced knowledge-drive engineering optimization. *International Journal of Intelligent Computing and Cybernetics* 1(4):563–97.

Ames, K. M.
1994 The Northwest coast: Complex hunter-gatherers, ecology, and social evolution. *Annual Review of Anthropology* 23:209–29.

Anderson, Tim W., and Christopher F. M. Lewis
2002 Upper Great Lakes climate and water-level changes 11 to 7 ka: Effect on the Sheguiandah archaeological site. In *The Sheguiandah Site: Archaeological, Geological and Paleobotanical Studies at a Paleoindian Site on Manitoulin Island, Ontario*, edited by Patrick J. Julig, pp. 195–234. Mercury Series, Archaeology Survey of Canada Paper 161. Canadian Museum of Civilization, Hull, Quebec.

Andrews, Thomas D., and John B. Zoe
1997 The Idaà trail: Archaeology and the Dogrib cultural landscape. In *At a Crossroads: Archaeology and First Peoples in Canada*, edited by George P. Nicholas and Thomas D. Andrews, pp. 160–77. Archaeology Press, Department of Archaeology, Simon Fraser University, Burnaby, British Columbia.

Arima, Eugene Y.
1984 Caribou Eskimo. In *Handbook of North American Indians. Vol. 5, Arctic*, edited by D. Damas, pp. 447–62. Smithsonian Institution, Washington, D.C.
1987 *Inuit Kayaks in Canada: A Review of Historical Records and Construction*. Mercury Series, Canadian Ethnology Service Paper 110. Canadian Museum of Civilization, Ottawa.

Aylsworth, J. M., C. M. Cunningham, and W. W. Shilts
1989 Surficial Geology, Thirty Mile Lake, District of Keewatin, Northwest Territories. Map 39-1989, scale 1:125,000. Geological Survey of Canada, Ottawa.

Bajc, A. F., Allen V. Morgan, and B. G. Warner
1997 Age and paleoecological significance of an early postglacial fossil assemblage near Marathon, Ontario, Canada. *Canadian Journal of Earth Sciences* 34:687–98.

Barnett, P. J.
1979 Glacial Lake Whittlesey: The probable ice frontal position in the eastern end of the Erie basin. *Canadian Journal of Earth Sciences* 16(3):568–74.
1985 Glacial retreat and lake levels, north central Lake Erie basin, Ontario. In *Quaternary Evolution of the Great Lakes*, edited by Paul F. Karrow and Parker E. Calkin, pp. 185–94. Geological Association of Canada, Special Paper 30.
1992 Quaternary geology of Ontario. In *Geology of Ontario*, pp. 1011–88. Ontario Geological Survey, Special Vol. 4, Pt. 2.

Barnett, P. J., and L. D. Delorme
2007 Record of late-glacial lake level fluctuations in the Lake Nipigon basin, northwestern Ontario, Canada. In *Yellowknife 2007: Abstracts*, p. 7. Annual Meeting of the Geological Association and the Mineralogical Association of Canada. Geological Association of Canada, Vol. 32.

Barnett, P. J., J. E. P. Dodge, M. K. McCrae, and A. Stuart
1999 Quaternary Geology, Newmarket Area, Ontario. Ontario Geological Survey, Map 2562.

Bar-Oz, G., and D. Nadel
2013 Worldwide large-scale trapping and hunting of ungulates in past societies. *Quaternary International* 297:1–7.

Bar-Oz, G., D. Nadel, U. Avner, and D. Malkinson
2011 Mass hunting game traps in the southern Levant: The Negev and Arava 'desert kites.' *Near Eastern Archaeology* 74:208–15.

Barth, Amy
2009 Top 100 Stories of 2009. *Discover*, Kalmbach Publishing. Accessed October 22, 2010, http://discovermagazine.com/2010/jan-feb/095.

Bartlein, P. J., and T. Webb III
1985 Mean July temperature at 6000 yr B.P. in eastern North America: Regression equations for estimates from fossil-pollen data. *Syllogeus* 55:301–42.

Bartlein, P. J., and C. Whitlock
1993 Paleoclimatic interpretation of the Elk Lake pollen record. In *Elk Lake, Minnesota: Evidence for Rapid Climate Change in the North-Central United States*, edited by J. P. Bradbury and W. E. Dean, pp. 275–93. Geological Society of America, Special Paper, Vol. 276. Boulder, Colorado.

Barton, Gary, R. J. Mandle, and M. A. Baltusis
1996 Predevelopment Freshwater Heads in the Glaciofluvial, Saginaw, and Marshall Aquifers in the Michigan Basin. U.S. Geological Survey Open-File Report 95-319.

Bechtel, S. K.
1988 The Thebes cluster: A new perspective from northwest Ohio. *Michigan Archaeologist* 34(4):114–26.

Bement, L. C., and B. J. Carter
2010 Jake Bluff: Clovis bison hunting on the southern plains of North America. *American Antiquity* 75(4):907–33.

Benedict, J. B.
2005 Tundra game drives: An arctic-alpine comparison. *Arctic, Antarctic, and Alpine Research* 37(4):425–34.

Bennett, John, and Susan Rowley (compilers and editors)
2004 *Uqalurait: An Oral History of Nunavut*. McGill-Queen's University Press, Montreal and Kingston.

Bergman, Carita M., J. A. Schaefer, and S. N. Luttich
2000 Caribou movement as a correlated random walk. *Oecologia* 123(3):364–74.

Best, C.
2009 Multi-objective Cultural Algorithms. Master's thesis, Wayne State University, Detroit, Michigan.

Betts, A. V. G., and V. Yagodin
2000 A new look at 'desert kites.' In *The Archaeology of Jordan and Beyond. Essays in Honor of James Sauer*, edited by L. E. Stager, J. A. Greene, and M. D. Cogan, pp. 31–44. Eisenbrauns, Winona Lake, Indiana.

Beverly and Qamanirjuaq Caribou Management Board
n.d. Beverly and Qamanirjuaq Caribou Range. Range Map. Accessed 2014, http://www.arctic-caribou.com/range_map.html.

Binford, Lewis R.
1978a Dimensional analysis of behavior and site structure: Learning from an Eskimo hunting stand. *American Antiquity* 43(3):330–61.
1978b *Nunamiut Ethnoarchaeology*. Academic Press, New York.
1980 Willow smoke and dog's tails: Hunter-gatherer settlement systems and archaeological site formation. *American Antiquity* 45:4–20.
1983 *In Pursuit of the Past: Decoding the Archaeological Record*. Thames and Hudson, New York.
1991 A corporate caribou hunt: Documenting the archaeology of past lifeways. *Expedition* 33(1):33–43.

Birket-Smith, Kaj
1929 *Report of the Fifth Thule Expedition 1921–24*. Vol. 5, Pt. 1, *The Caribou Eskimos: Material and Social Life and Their Cultural Position*. Gyldendalske Boghandel, Nordisk Forlag, Copenhagen.

Blasco, Steve M.
2000 Geological history of Fathom Five National Marine Park over the past 15,000 years. In *Ecology, Culture and Conservation of a Protected Area: Fathom Five Marine Park, Canada*, edited by S. Parker and M. Munawar, pp. 45–62. Ecovision Monograph Series. Brackhuys Publishers, Netherlands.

Blasco, Steve M., Christopher F. M. Lewis, Francine McCarthy, and Adam Sarvis
2001 Evidence for climate-driven low lake levels in the Georgian Bay basin at 7,600 B.P. In *Program and Abstracts*, pp. 6–7. International Association for Great Lakes Research, 44th Conference on Great Lakes Research. Green Bay, Wisconsin.

Blasco, Steve M., and Francine M. G. McCarthy
2004 Late Quaternary history of the Georgian Bay lake basin. In *St. Catharines 2004: Abstracts*, pp. 6–7. Annual Meeting of the Geological Association and the Mineralogical Association of Canada. Geological Association of Canada.

Blehr, O.
1990 Communal hunting as a prerequisite for caribou (wild reindeer) as a human resource. In *Hunters of the Recent Past*, edited by L. B. Davis and B. O. K. Reeves, pp. 304–26. Unwin Hyman, London.

Bliss, L. C., G. M. Courtin, D. L. Pattie, R. R. Riewe, D. W. A. Whitefield, and P. Widden
1973 Arctic tundra ecosystems. *Annual Review of Ecology and Systematics* 4:359–99.

Blott, Simon J., and Kenneth Pye
2012 Particle size scales and classification of sediment types based on particle size distributions: Review and recommended procedures. *Sedimentology* 59:2071–96.

Bowen, J. E.
1994 *Upper Mercer Flint Large Bifurcates of the Ohio Region*. Sandusky Valley Chapter, Archaeological Society of Ohio, Upper Sandusky.
1995 *Flint Ridge and Upper Mercer Dovetail Knife/Spearpoints of the Ohio Region: 7300 B.C.* Sandusky Valley Chapter, Archaeological Society of Ohio, Upper Sandusky.

Boyd, M., J. T. Teller, Z. Yang, L. Kingsmill, and C. Shultis
2010 An 8,900-year-old forest drowned by Lake Superior: Hydrological and paleoecological implications. *Journal of Paleolimnology* 47:339–55.

Bradshaw, R. H. W.
1981 Modern pollen-representation factors for woods in south-east England. *Journal of Ecology* 69(1):45–70.

Breckenridge, A.
2007 The Lake Superior varve stratigraphy and implications for eastern Lake Agassiz outflow from 10,700 to 8900 cal ybp (9.5–8.0 ^{14}C ka). *Palaeogeography, Palaeoclimatology, Palaeoecology* 246:45–61.

Breckenridge, A., and T. C. Johnson
2009 Paleohydrology of the upper Laurentian Great Lakes from the last glacial to early Holocene. *Quaternary Research* 71:397–408.

Breckenridge, A., T. C. Johnson, S. Beske-Diehl, and J. S. Mothersill
2004 The timing of regional late glacial events and post-glacial sedimentation rates from Lake Superior. *Quaternary Science Reviews* 23:2355–67.

Breckenridge, A., T. V. Lowell, T. G. Fisher, and S. Yu
2010 A late Lake Minong transgression in the Lake Superior basin as documented by sediments from Fenton Lake, Ontario. *Journal of Paleolimnology*. SpringerLink, July 18, 2010, DOI 10.1007/s10933-010-9447-z.

Brink, J.
2005 Inukshuk: Caribou drive lanes on southern Victoria Island, Nunvut, Canada. *Arctic Anthropology* 42(1):1–28.
2008 *Imagining Head-Smashed-In: Aboriginal Buffalo Hunting on the Northern Plains*. Athabasca University Press, Edmonton, Alberta.
2013 The Barnett site: A stone drive lane communal pronghorn trap on the Alberta Plains, Canada. *Quaternary International* 297:79–92.

Brink, J., and M. Rollans
1989 On the structure and function of drive lane systems at communal buffalo jumps. In *Hunters of the Recent Past*, edited by L. B. Davis and B. O. K. Reeves, pp. 152–67. Unwin Hyman, London.

Britton, K., V. Grimes, L. Niven, T. Steele, S. McPherron, M. Soressi, T. Kelly, J. Jaubert, J. J. Hublin, and M. Richards
2011 Strontium isotope evidence for migration in late Pleistocene *Rangifer*: Implications for Neanderthal hunting strategies at the Middle Palaeolithic site of Jonzac, France. *Journal of Human Evolution* 61:176–85.

Broeker, W. S., and William R. Farrand
1963 Radiocarbon age of Two Creeks forest bed, Wisconsin. *Geological Society of America Bulletin* 74:795–802.

Buckmaster, Marla M., and James R. Paquette
1988 The Gorto site: A preliminary report on a Late Paleo-Indian site in Marquette County, Michigan. *The Wisconsin Archeologist* 69(3):101–24.

Bupp, S. L.
2008 The Willow Springs Bison Pound: 48AB130. Master's thesis, University of Wyoming, Laramie.

Burch, Ernest S., Jr.
1986 The Caribou Inuit. In *Native Peoples, the Canadian Experience*, edited by R. Bruce Morrison and C. Roderick Wilson, pp. 106–33. McClelland and Stewart, Toronto.
1991 Herd following reconsidered. *Current Anthropology* 32(4):439–45.

Burch, Ernest S., Jr., and Yvon Csonka
1999 The Caribou Inuit. In *The Cambridge Encyclopedia of Hunters and Gatherers*, edited by R. B. Lee and R. Daly, pp. 56–60. Cambridge University Press, Cambridge.

Burnett, P., C. Bollong, J. Kennedy, C. Millinton, C. M. Berg, V. Zietz, A. Fife, K. Reed, and M. Seletstewa
2008 *Archaeological Data Recovery for the Rockies Express/Entrega Pipeline Project at the Joe Miller Site (48AB18), Albany County, Wyoming*. SWCA Environmental Consultants, Broomfield, Colorado.

Bursey, Jeffrey A.
2012 Early Archaic lithic technology: A case study from southern Ontario. *Archaeology of Eastern North America* 40:107–30.

Calvert, M. B., and Francine M. G. McCarthy
2010 When Nanabush wept: Paleodrought-forced early Holocene lowstands, and implications under projected climatic scenarios. *Abstract Book*, p. 43. IAGLR 2010, 53rd Annual Conference on Great Lakes Research, May 17–21. Toronto, Ontario.

Campbell, I. D., and John H. McAndrews
1992 CANPLOT: A FORTRAN-77 program for plotting stratigraphic data on a PostScript device. *Computers in Geoscience* 18:309–35.

Carlson, K.
2011 Prehistoric Bison Procurement: Human Agency and Drive Lane Topography on the Northwestern Plains. Master's thesis, Department of Anthropology, Northern Arizona University.

Carlson, K., and L. Bement
2013 Organization of bison hunting at the Pleistocene/Holocene transition on the plains of North America. *Quaternary International* 297:93–99.

Chernysh, A. P.
1989 O mustyerskikh zhilishchakh i poseleniyakh. In *Kamennyvek Pamyatniki, Metodika, Problemy*, edited by S. N. Bibikov, pp. 72–81. Naukova dumka, Kiev.

Chowns, T. J.
2003 State of the Knowledge of Woodland Caribou in Ontario. Report prepared for Forestry Research Partnership. http://www.forestresearch.ca/product_catalogue/reports.htm.

Chung, C. J., and Robert G. Reynolds
1996 A testbed for solving optimization problems using cultural algorithms. In *Evolutionary Programming V*, edited by L. J. Fogel, P. J. Angeline, and T. Bäck, pp. 225–36. MIT Press, Cambridge, Massachusetts.

Clark, Donald W.
1987 *Archaeological Reconnaissance at Great Bear Lake*. Mercury Series, Archaeological Survey of Canada Paper 136. Canadian Museum of Civilization, Ottawa.

Cleland, C. E.
1965 Barren ground caribou (*Rangifer arcticus*) from an early man site in southeastern Michigan. *American Antiquity* 30:350–51.

Coe, Joffre L.
1960 Prehistoric Cultural Change and Stability in the Carolina Piedmont Area. PhD thesis, Department of Anthropology, University of Michigan, Ann Arbor.
1964 *The Formative Cultures of the Carolina Piedmont*. The American Philosophical Society, Philadelphia, Pennsylvania.

Cook, R. A., and William A. Lovis
2014 Lake levels, mobility and lithic raw material selection and reduction strategies: A Great Lakes case study. *Environmental Archaeology* 19(1):55–71.

Cowling, S. A., M. T. Sykes, and R. H. W. Bradshaw
2001 Palaeovegetation-model comparisons, climate change and tree succession in Scandinavia over the past 1500 years. *Journal of Ecology* 89(2):227–36.

Croley, Thomas E., II, and Christopher F. M. Lewis
2006 Warmer and drier climates that make terminal Great Lakes. *Journal of Great Lakes Research* 32:852–69.

Dalton, K.
2011 A Geospatial Analysis of Prehistoric Hunting Blinds and Forager Group Size at Cowhead Slough, Modoc County, California. Master's thesis, California State University–Chico, Chico.

Damas, David
1988 The contact-traditional horizon of the central Arctic: Reassessment of a concept and reexamination of an era. *Arctic Anthropology* 25:101–38.

Davidova, Rosita, and Victor Vasilev
2013 Seasonal dynamics of the testate amoeba fauna (protoza: Arcellinida and Euglyphida) in Durankulak Lake (northeastern Bulgaria). *Acta Zoologica Bulgarica* 65(1):27–36.

Davidson-Hunt, Ian J., Phyllis Jack, Edward Mandamin, and Brennan Wapioke
2005 Iska Tewizaagegan (Shoal Lake) plant knowledge: An Anishinaabe (Ojibway) ethnobotany of northwestern Ontario. *Journal of Ethnobiology* 25(2):189–227.

Dawson, K. C. A.
1983 Cummins site: A Late Paleo-Indian (Plano) site at Thunder Bay, Ontario. *Ontario Archaeology* 39:3–31.

Deane, R. E.
1950 *Pleistocene Geology of the Lake Simcoe District, Ontario*. Geological Survey of Canada, Memoir 256. Cloutier, Ottawa.

Delcourt, P. A., H. R. Delcourt, and T. Webb III
1984 *Atlas of Mapped Distributions of Dominance and Modern Pollen Percentages for Important Tree Taxa of Eastern North America*. AASP Contributions Series, No. 14. American Association of Stratigraphic Palynologists Foundation, Dallas, Texas.

Deller, D. Brian
1976 The Heaman site: A preliminary report on a Paleo-Indian site in Middlesex County, Ontario. *Ontario Archaeology* 27:13–28. Toronto.
1979 Paleo-Indian reconnaissance in the counties of Lambton and Middlesex, Ontario. *Ontario Archaeology* 32:3–20. Peterborough.
1989 Interpretation of chert type variation in Paleoindian industries, southwestern Ontario. In *Eastern Paleoindian Lithic Resource Use,* edited by C. Ellis and J. Lothrop, pp. 191–220. Westview Press, Boulder, Colorado.

Deller, D. Brian, and Christopher J. Ellis
1984 Crowfield: A preliminary report on a probable Paleo-Indian cremation in southwestern Ontario. *Archaeology of Eastern North America* 12:41–71. Buffalo.
1992 *Thedford II: A Paleo-Indian Site in the Ausable River Watershed of Southwestern Ontario*. Memoirs, No. 24. Museum of Anthropology, University of Michigan, Ann Arbor.
2011 *Crowfield (AfHj-31): A Unique Paleoindian Fluted Point Site from Southwestern Ontario*. Memoirs, No. 49. Museum of Anthropology, University of Michigan, Ann Arbor.

DeLoura, Mark (editor)
2001 *Game Programming Gems 2*. Charles River Media, Hingham, Massachusetts.

Dibb, Gordon C.
2004 The Madina phase: Late Pleistocene and Early Holocene occupation along the margins of the Simcoe Lowlands in

south-central Ontario. In *The Late Palaeo-Indian Great Lakes: Geological and Archaeological Investigations of Late Pleistocene and Early Holocene Environments,* edited by Lawrence J. Jackson and Andrew Hinshelwood, pp. 117–61. Mercury Series, Archaeology Paper 165. Canadian Museum of Civilization, Gatineau, Quebec.

Dobosi, V. T.
1991 Upper Paleolithic excavations in Hungary between 1986–1990. In *Precirculated Papers of the UISPP*, pp. 79–86. Bratislava.

Dobson, D. M., Theodore C. Moore, and David K. Rea
1995 The sedimentation history of Lake Huron and Georgian Bay: Results from analysis of seismic reflection profiles. *Journal of Paleolimnology* 13:231–49.

Dredge, L. A., and W. R. Cowan
1989 Quaternary geology of the southwestern Canadian Shield. In *Quaternary Geology of Canada and Greenland*, pp. 214–49. Geological Survey of Canada, Geology of Canada, No. 1.

Drzyzga, Scott A., Ashton M. Shortridge, and Randall J. Schaetzl
2012 Mapping the phases of glacial Lake Algonquin in the upper Great Lakes region, Canada and USA, using a geostatistical isostatic rebound model. *Journal of Paleolimnology* 47:357–71.

Dustin, F.
1935 A study of the Bayport chert. *Papers of the Michigan Academy of Science, Arts and Letters* 20(1934):465–75. Ann Arbor.

Dyke, A. S., and V. K. Prest
1987 Paleogeography of Northern North America, 18,000–5,000 Years Ago. Map 1703A, scale 1:12,500,000. Geological Survey of Canada, Ottawa.

Earwood, Caroline
1997 Bog butter: A two thousand year history. *The Journal of Irish Archaeology* 8:25–42.

Eastman, John
1995 *The Book of Swamp and Bog Trees, Shrubs, and Wildflowers of Eastern Freshwater Wetlands*, illustrated by Amelia Hansen. Stackpole Books, Mechanicsville, Pennsylvania.

Edwards, T. W. D., B. B. Wolfe, and G. M. MacDonald
1996 Influence of changing atmospheric circulation on precipitation $\delta^{18}O$-temperature relations in Canada during the Holocene. *Quaternary Research* 46:211–18.

Eisenberg-Degen, D.
2010 A hunting scene from the Negev: The depiction of a desert kite and throwing weapon. *Israel Exploration Journal* 60:146–65.

Eley, B. E., and Peter H. von Bitter
1989 *Cherts of Southern Ontario*. Royal Ontario Museum, Toronto.

Ellis, Christopher J.
1981 Investigations of a Transitional Paleo-Indian to Early Archaic Lithic Industry in Southwestern Ontario. Report on file, Ontario Ministry of Culture, Heritage Branch, Toronto.
1989 The explanation of northeastern Paleoindian lithic procurement patterns. In *Eastern Paleoindian Lithic Resource Use*, edited by C. Ellis and J. Lothrop, pp. 139–64. Westview Press, Boulder, Colorado.
2004a Hi-Lo: An early lithic complex in southern Ontario. In *The Late Palaeo-Indian Great Lakes: Geoarchaeological and Archaeological Studies of Late Pleistocene and Early Holocene Environments*, edited by Lawrence J. Jackson and Andrew Hinshelwood, pp. 57–83. Mercury Series, Archaeology Paper 165. Canadian Museum of Civilization, Gatineau, Quebec.
2004b The Hi-Lo component at the Welke-Tonkonoh site, area C. *Kewa Newsletter of the London Chapter, Ontario Archaeological Society* 4(5):1–19. London.
2011 Measuring paleoindian range mobility and land-use in the Great Lakes/Northeast. *Journal of Anthropological Archaeology* 30:385–401.

Ellis, Christopher J., Dillon H. Carr, and Thomas J. Loebel
2011 The Younger Dryas and Late Pleistocene peoples of the Great Lakes region. *Quaternary International* 242:534–45.

Ellis, Christopher J., and D. Brian Deller
1982 Hi-Lo materials from southwestern Ontario. *Ontario Archaeology* 38:3–22.
1986 Post-glacial Lake Nipissing waterworn assemblages from the southeastern Huron basin area. *Ontario Archaeology* 45:39–60. Peterborough.
1991 A small (but informative) Early Archaic component at the Culloden Acres site, area B. *Kewa Newsletter of the London Chapter, Ontario Archaeological Society* 91(8):2–17. London.
2013 Hi-Lo point life histories. *Kewa Newsletter of the London Chapter, Ontario Archaeological Society* 13(2–4):1–39. London.

Ellis, Christopher J., Albert C. Goodyear, Dan F. Morse, and Kenneth B. Tankersley
1998 Archaeology of the Pleistocene-Holocene transition in eastern North America. *Quaternary International* 49/50:151–66.

Ellis, Christopher J., I. Kenyon, and M. Spence
1990 The Archaic. In *The Archaeology of Southern Ontario to A.D. 1650*, edited by C. J. Ellis and C. Ferris, pp. 65–124. Occasional Publications 5. London Chapter, Ontario Archaeological Society.

Ellis, Christopher J., Peter A. Timmins, and Holly Martelle
2009 At the crossroads and periphery: The Archaic archaeological record of southern Ontario. In *Archaic Societies: Diversity and Complexity across the Midcontinent*, edited by Thomas E. Emerson, Dale L. McElrath, and Andrew C. Fortier, pp. 787–837. Suny Press, Albany, New York.

Ellis, Christopher J., Stanley Wortner, and William A. Fox
1991 Nettling: An overview of an Early Archaic "Kirk corner-notched cluster" site in southwestern Ontario. *Canadian Journal of Archaeology* 15:1–34.

Ellis, Clifford, M. J. Nemiroff, L. H. Somers, and K. S. Luttrell
1979 *State of Michigan Skin, Scuba, and Surface-Supply Diving Fatality Statistics, 1965–1978*. Michigan Sea Grant Program Publications Office, University of Michigan, Ann Arbor.

Enloe, J. G.
2003 Acquisition and processing of reindeer in the Paris basin. In *Zooarchaeological Insights into Magdalenian Lifeways*, edited by S. Costamagno and V. Laroulandie, pp. 23–31. British Archaeological Reports, International Series No. 1144, Oxford.

Enloe, J. G., and F. David
1997 *Rangifer* herd behavior: Seasonality of hunting in the Magdalenian of the Paris basin. In *Caribou and Reindeer Hunters of the Northern Hemisphere*, edited by Lawrence J. Jackson and Paul T. Thacker, pp. 52–68. Avebury, Brookfield, Vermont.

Eschman, D. F., and Paul F. Karrow
1985 Huron basin glacial lakes: A review. In *Quaternary Evolution of the Great Lakes*, edited by Paul F. Karrow and Parker E. Calkin, pp. 79–93. Geological Association of Canada, Special Paper 30.

Evenson E. B., and A. Dreimanis
1976 Late glacial (14,000–10,000 years B.P.) history of the Great Lakes region and possible correlations. In *Quaternary Glaciations in the Northern Hemisphere*, pp. 217–39. UNESCO International Geological Correlation Programme, Report No. 3 on the session in Bellingham, Washington.

Farrand, William R.
1988 *The Glacial Lakes around Michigan*. Geological Survey Division, Michigan Department of Environmental Quality, Bulletin 4. Lansing.

Finamore, P. F.
1985 Glacial Lake Algonquin and the Fenelon Falls outlet. In *Quaternary Evolution of the Great Lakes*, edited by Paul F. Karrow and Parker E. Calkin, pp. 125–32. Geological Association of Canada, Special Paper 30.

Fish, J., and H. Carr
1990 *Sound Underwater Images: A Guide to the Generation and Interpretation of Side Scan Sonar Data*. Lower Cape Publishing, Orleans, Massachusetts.

Fishbein, Evan, and R. Timothy Patterson
1993 Error-weighted maximum likelihood (EWML): A new statistically based method to cluster quantitative micropaleontological data. *Journal of Paleontology* 67(3):475–86.

Fisher, Daniel C.
1995 Experiments in subaqueous meat caching. *Current Research in the Pleistocene* 12:77–80.
2009 Paleobiology and extinction of proboscideans in the Great Lakes region of North America. In *American Megafaunal Extinctions at the End of the Pleistocene*, edited by Gary Haynes, pp. 55–76. Vertebrate Paleobiology and Paleoanthropology series, edited by Eric Delson and Eric J. Sargis. Springer Science + Business Media, New York.

Fisher, T. G.
2003 Chronology of glacial Lake Agassiz meltwater routed to the Gulf of Mexico. *Quaternary Research* 59:271–76.

Fisher, T. G., and D. G. Smith
1994 Glacial Lake Agassiz: Its northwest maximum extent and outlet in Saskatchewan (Emerson phase). *Quaternary Science Reviews* 13:845–58.

Fitting, James E.
1963a The Hi-Lo site: A Late Paleo-Indian site in Michigan. *Wisconsin Archeologist* 44(2):87–96.
1963b An early post fluted point tradition in Michigan: A distributional analysis. *Michigan Archaeologist* 9:21–25.
1970 *The Archaeology of Michigan*. Natural History Press, Garden City, New Jersey.

Fitting, James E., Jerry DeVisscher, and Edward J. Wahla
1966 *The Paleo-Indian Occupation of the Holcombe Beach*. Anthropological Papers, No. 27. Museum of Anthropology, University of Michigan, Ann Arbor.

Fladmark, Knut
1982 Microdebitage analysis: Initial considerations. *Journal of Archaeological Science* 9:205–20.

Flanagan, J. G.
1989 Hierarchy in simple "egalitarian" societies. *Annual Review of Anthropology* 18:245–66.

Fox, W. A.
1977 The Lakehead complex: New insights. In *Collected Archaeological Papers*, edited by D. S. Melvin, pp. 127–54. Archaeological Research Report 13. Ontario Ministry of Culture and Recreation, Toronto.
2009 Ontario cherts revisited. In *Painting the Past with a Broad Brush: Papers in Honour of James Valliere Wright*, edited by David L. Keenlyside and Jean-Luc Pilon, pp. 339–54. Mercury Series, Archaeology Paper 170. Canadian Museum of Civilization, Gatineau, Quebec.
2013 Stories in stone and metal. In *Before Ontario: The Archaeology of a Province*, pp. 134–41. McGill-Queens University Press, Montreal.
2014 Lithic source research in northeastern Ontario–A brief history. *Arch Notes, Newsletter of the Ontario Archaeological Society* 19(1):5–7. Toronto.

Friesen, T. Max
2002 Analogues at Iqaluktuuq: The social context of archaeological inferences in Nunavut, Arctic Canada. *World Archaeology* 34(2):330–45.
2004a Kitigaaryuit: A portrait of the Mackenzie Inuit in the 1890s, based on the journals of Isaac O. Stringer. *Arctic Anthropology* 41:222–37.
2004b A tale of two settlement patterns: Environmental and cultural determinants of Inuit and Dene site distributions. In *Hunters and Gatherers in Theory and Archaeology*, edited by George M. Crothers, pp. 299–315. Occasional Paper 31. Center for Archaeological Investigations, Southern Illinois University, Carbondale.
2013 The impact of weapon technology on caribou drive system variability in the prehistoric Canadian Arctic. *Quaternary International* 297:13–23.

Friesen, T. Max, and Andrew M. Stewart
1994 Protohistoric settlement patterns in the interior district of Keewatin: Implications for Caribou Inuit social organization.

In *Threads of Arctic Prehistory: Papers in Honour of William E. Taylor Jr.*, edited by David Morrison and Jean-Luc Pilon, pp. 341–60. Mercury Series, Archaeological Survey of Canada Paper 149. Canadian Museum of Civilization, Hull, Quebec.
2004 Variation in subsistence among Inland Inuit: Zooarchaeology of two sites on the Kazan River, Nunavut. *Canadian Journal of Archaeology* 28:32–50.
2013 To freeze or to dry: Seasonal variability in caribou processing and storage in the barrenlands of northern Canada. *Anthropozoologica* 48(1):89–109.

Frison, G. C.
1968 Site 48SH312: An Early Middle period bison kill in the Powder River basin of Wyoming. *Plains Anthropologist* 13(39):31–39.
1970 The Glenrock Buffalo Jump, 48CO304: Late prehistoric period buffalo procurement and butchering. *Plains Anthropologist* 15(50):1–45.
1971 The buffalo pound in north-western plains prehistory: Site 48CA302, Wyoming. *American Antiquity* 36(1):77–91.
2004 *Survival by Hunting: Prehistoric Human Predation and Animal Prey*. University of California Press, Berkeley.

Frison, G. C., M. Wilson, and D. J. Wilson
1976 Fossil bison and artifacts from an Early Altithermal period arroyo trap in Wyoming. *American Antiquity* 41(1):28–57.

Fulton, R. J.
1989 *Quaternary Geology of Canada and Greenland*. Geological Survey of Canada, Geology of Canada, No. 1.

Fulton, R. J., and J. T. Andrews (editors)
1987 The Laurentide Ice Sheet. *Géographie Physique et Quaternaire* 41:179–318.

Gao, C.
2005 Ice-wedge casts in Late Wisconsin glaciofluvial deposits, southern Ontario, Canada. *Canadian Journal of Earth Sciences* 42:2117–26.

Gates, C.
1989 Kaminuriak herd. In *People and Caribou in the Northwest Territories*, edited by E. Hall, pp. 123–29. Department of Renewable Resources, Government of the Northwest Territories, Yellowknife.

Geertz, C.
1973 *The Interpretation of Cultures: Selected Essays*. Basic Books, New York.

Gordon, Bryan C.
1996 *People of Sunlight, People of Starlight: Barrenland Archaeology in the Northwest Territories of Canada*. Mercury Series, Paper 154. Canadian Museum of Civilization, Gatineau, Quebec.

Government of Yukon
2013 Ta'an Kwach'an—People of the Lake. Department of Tourism and Culture. Accessed November 13, 2013, http://www.tc.gov.yk.ca/people_of_the_lake.html.

Gramly, R. M.
1982 *The Vail Site: A Palaeo-Indian Encampment in Maine*. Bulletin of the Buffalo Society of Natural Sciences, Vol. 30. Buffalo, New York.
1988 *The Adkins Site: A Palaeo-Indian Habitation and Associated Stone Structure*. Persimmon Press, Buffalo, New York.

Greenman, Emerson F.
1940 A geologically dated camp site, Georgian Bay, Ontario. *American Antiquity* 5(3):194–99.
1943 An early industry on a raised beach near Killarney, Ontario. *American Antiquity* 8(3):260–65.

Greenman, Emerson F., and George M. Stanley
1941 Two post-Nipissing sites near Killarney, Ontario. *American Antiquity* 6(4):305–13.

Grier, C.
2000 Labor organization and social hierarchies in North American Arctic whaling societies. In *Hierarchies in Action: Cui Bono?*, edited by M. W. Diehl. Center for Archaeological Investigations, Occasional Paper No. 27. Southern Illinois University.

Griffin, L. D.
2000 Mean, median and mode filtering of images. *Proceedings: The Mathematical, Physical and Engineering Sciences* 456:2995–3004.

Hallendy, N.
2001 *Inuksuit: Silent Messengers of the Arctic*. Douglas and McIntyre, Vancouver.

Halsey, John R., and Wayne R. Lusardi
2008 *Beneath the Inland Seas: Michigan's Underwater Archaeological Heritage*. Michigan Department of History, Arts and Libraries, Lansing.

Hamilton, Scott
2004 Early Holocene human burials at Wapekeka (FlJj-1), northern Ontario. In *The Late Palaeo-Indian Great Lakes: Geological and Archaeological Investigations of Late Pleistocene and Early Holocene Environments*, edited by Lawrence J. Jackson and Andrew Hinshelwood, pp. 337–68. Mercury Series, Archaeology Paper 165. Canadian Museum of Civilization, Gatineau, Quebec.
2013 A world apart? Ontario's Canadian Shield. In *Before Ontario: The Archaeology of a Province*, edited by Marit K. Munson and Susan M. Jamieson. McGill-Queen's University Press, Kingston, Ontario.

Hammer, Øyvind, David A. T. Harper, and Paul D. Ryan
2001 PAST: Paleontological statistics software package for education and data analysis. *Palaeontologica Electronica* 4:1–9. http://palaeo-electronica.org/2001_1/past/issue1_01.htm.

Hanks, Christopher C.
1988 *The Foxie Otter Site: A Multicomponent Occupation North of Lake Huron*. Anthropological Papers, No. 79. Museum of Anthropology, University of Michigan, Ann Arbor.

Hansel, A. K., D. M. Mickelson, A. F. Scheider, and C. E. Larsen
1985 Late Wisconsinan and Holocene history of the Lake Michigan basin. In *Quaternary Evolution of the Great Lakes*, edited by

Paul F. Karrow and Parker E. Calkin, pp. 39–53. Geological Association of Canada, Special Paper 30.

Harding, L.
1953 The cairn of Hani. *Annual of the Department of Antiquities of Jordan* 2:8–56.

Harvaqtuurmiut Elders, Darren Keith, Joan Scottie, and Ruby Mautara'inaaq
1994 Harvaqtuuq: Place Names of the Lower Kazan River. Report on file, Federal Archaeology Office, Parks Canada, Canadian Heritage, Ottawa.

Haupt, Randy L., and Sue Ellen Haupt
1998 *Practical Genetic Algorithms*, 2nd ed. Wiley-Interscience, New York.

Heard, Douglas C.
1997 Causes of barren-ground caribou migrations and implications to hunters. In *Caribou and Reindeer Hunters of the Northern Hemisphere*, edited by Lawrence J. Jackson and Paul T. Thacker, pp. 27–31. Avebury, Brookfield, Vermont.

Heiri, Oliver, André F. Lotter, and Gerry Lemcke
2001 Loss on ignition as a method for estimating organic and carbonate content in sediments: Reproducibility and comparability of results. *Journal of Paleolimnology* 25:101–10.

Helms, S., and A. V. G. Betts
1987 The desert "kites" of the Badiyat Esh-Sham and north Arabia. *Paléorient* 13(1):41–67.

Hershkovitz, I., Y. Ben-David, B. Arensburg, A. Gorebn, and A. Pinchasov
1987 Rock engravings in southern Sinai. In *Sinai: Part 2—Human Geography*, edited by G. Gvirtzman, A. Shmueli, Y. Gradus, and I. Beit-Arieh, pp. 605–16. Tel Aviv University, Tel Aviv.

Hinshelwood, Andrew
2004 Archaic reoccupation of Late Palaeo-Indian sites in northwestern Ontario. In *The Late Palaeo-Indian Great Lakes: Geological and Archaeological Investigations of the Late Pleistocene and Early Holocene Environments*, edited by Lawrence J. Jackson and Andrew Hinshelwood, pp. 225–49. Mercury Series, Archaeology Paper 165. Canadian Museum of Civilization, Gatineau, Quebec.

Hoaglund, J. R., III, G. C. Huffman, and N. G. Grannemann
2002 Michigan basin regional groundwater flow discharge to three Great Lakes. *Ground Water* 40(4):390–405.

Hockett, B., C. Creger, B. Smith, C. Young, J. Carter, E. Dillingham, R. Crews, and E. Pellegrini
2013 Large-scale trapping features from the Great Basin, USA: The significance of leadership and communal gatherings in ancient foraging. *Quaternary International* 297:64–78.

Hoffecker, J. F.
2002 *Desolate Landscapes: Ice-Age Settlement in Eastern Europe*. Rutgers University Press, New Brunswick.

Hough, Jack L.
1955 Lake Chippewa, a low stage of Lake Michigan indicated by bottom sediments. *Geological Society of America Bulletin* 66(8):957–68.
1958 *Geology of the Great Lakes*. University of Illinois Press, Urbana.
1962 Lake Stanley, a low stage of Lake Huron indicated by bottom sediments. *Geological Society of America Bulletin* 73(5):613–20.
1963 The prehistoric Great Lakes of North America. *American Scientist* 51(1):84–109.

Hunter, R. Douglas, Irina P. Panyushkina, Steven W. Leavitt, Alex C. Wiedenhoeft, and John Zawiskie
2006 A multiproxy environmental investigation of Holocene wood from a submerged conifer forest in Lake Huron, USA. *Quaternary Research* 66:67–77.

Irving, W. N.
1968 The barren grounds. In *Science, History and Hudson Bay,* Vol. 1, edited by C. S. Beals, pp. 26–54. Department of Energy, Mines and Resources, Government of Canada, Ottawa.

Jackson, Lawrence J.
1990 Interior Paleoindian settlement strategies: A first approximation for the lower Great Lakes. In *Early Paleoindian Economies of Eastern North America*, edited by K. B. Tankersley and B. L. Isaac, pp. 95–142. Research in Economic Anthropology Supplement, Vol. 5. JAI Press, Greenwich, Connecticut.
1997 Caribou range and Early Paleo-Indian settlement disposition in southern Ontario, Canada. In *Caribou and Reindeer Hunters of the Northern Hemisphere*, edited by Lawrence J. Jackson and Paul T. Thacker, pp. 132–64. Avebury, Brookfield, Vermont.
1998 *The Sandy Ridge and Halstead Paleo-Indian Sites: Unifacial Tool Use and Gainey Phase Definition in South-Central Ontario*. Memoirs, No. 32. Museum of Anthropology, University of Michigan, Ann Arbor.
2004 Changing our views of Late Palaeo-Indian in southern Ontario. In *The Late Palaeo-Indian Great Lakes: Geological and Archaeological Investigations of Late Pleistocene and Early Holocene Environments*, edited by Lawrence J. Jackson and Andrew Hinshelwood, pp. 25–56. Mercury Series, Archaeology Paper 165. Canadian Museum of Civilization, Gatineau, Quebec.

Jackson, Lawrence J., Chris Ellis, Allen V. Morgan, and John H. McAndrews
2000 Glacial lake levels and eastern Great Lakes Palaeo-Indians. *Geoarchaeology* 15:415–40.

Jackson, Lawrence J., and Andrew Hinshelwood (editors)
2004 *The Late Palaeo-Indian Great Lakes: Geological and Archaeological Investigations of Late Pleistocene and Early Holocene Environments*. Mercury Series, Archaeology Paper 165. Canadian Museum of Civilization, Gatineau, Quebec.

Jackson, Marion, and Judith Nasby
1987 *Contemporary Inuit Drawings*. Macdonald Stewart Art Centre, Guelph, Ontario.

Jain, Anil K.
1986 *Fundamentals of Digital Image Processing*. Prentice-Hall, Englewood Cliffs, New Jersey.

Janes, R. R.
1983 *Archaeological Ethnography among the Mackenzie Basin Dene, Canada*. Technical Paper 28. Arctic Institute of North America, Calgary.

Janusas, Scarlett E.
1984 *A Petrological Analysis of Kettle Point Chert and Its Spatial and Temporal Distribution in Regional Prehistory*. Mercury Series, Archaeology Paper 128. National Museum of Man, Ottawa.

Janusas, Scarlett E., Steve Blasco, Stan McClellan, and Jessica Lusted
2004 Prehistoric drainage and archaeological implications across the submerged Niagara escarpment north of Tobermory, Ontario. In *The Late Palaeo-Indian Great Lakes: Geological and Archaeological Investigations of Late Pleistocene and Early Holocene Environments*, edited by Lawrence J. Jackson and Andrew Hinshelwood, pp. 303–14. Mercury Series, Archaeology Paper 165. Canadian Museum of Civilization, Gatineau, Quebec.

Jenness, Diamond
1922 *Report of the Canadian Arctic Expedition 1913–18*. Vol. 12, *Life of the Copper Eskimos*. F. A. Acland, Ottawa.

Jin, J.
2011 Path Planning in Reality Games Using Cultural Algorithm: The Land Bridge Example. Master's thesis, Wayne State University, Detroit, Michigan.

Jin, X., and Robert G. Reynolds
1999 Using knowledge-based evolutionary computation to solve nonlinear constraint optimization problems: A cultural algorithm approach. In *Proceedings of the 1999 Congress on Evolutionary Computation*, pp. 1672–78. Washington, D.C.

Johnson, M. F.
1996 Paleoindians near the edge: A Virginia perspective. In *The Paleoindian and Early Archaic Southeast*, edited by D. G. Anderson and K. E. Sassaman, pp. 187–212. University of Alabama Press, Tuscaloosa.

Julig, Patrick J.
1980 The Nipissing transgression around southern Lake Huron. *Canadian Journal of Earth Sciences* 17:1271–74.
1993 Report on reconnaissance archaeological survey conducted in the Norra Storfjället region of the Vindelfjällen Nature Reserve, Västerbottens Län, Sweden, 1993. In *Tärna-Okstindan Glacial History Project 1990–1993*, pp. 9–17. Center for Arctic Research, Umeå University.
1994 *The Cummins Site Complex and Paleoindian Occupations in the Northwestern Lake Superior Region*. Ontario Archaeological Reports 2. Ontario Heritage Foundation, Toronto.
2002 Archaeological conclusions from the Sheguiandah site research. In *The Sheguiandah Site: Archaeological, Geological and Paleobotanical Studies at a Paleoindian Site on Manitoulin Island, Ontario*, edited by Patrick J. Julig. Mercury Series, Archaeological Survey of Canada Paper 161. Canadian Museum of Civilization, Hull, Quebec.

Julig, Patrick J. (editor)
2002 *The Sheguiandah Site: Archaeological, Geological and Paleobotanical Studies at a Paleoindian Site on Manitoulin Island, Ontario*. Mercury Series, Archaeological Survey of Canada Paper 161. Canadian Museum of Civilization, Hull, Quebec.

Julig, Patrick J., and Darrel Long
2010 Why did Paleo-Indians select the Sheguiandah site? An evaluation of quarrying and quartzite material selection based on petrographic analysis of core artifacts. In *Ancient Mines and Quarries: A Trans-Atlantic Perspective*, edited by Margaret Brewer-LaPorta, Adrian Burke, and David Field. Oxbow Books, Oxford.

Julig, Patrick J., and William C. Mahaney
2002 Geoarchaeological studies of the Sheguiandah site and analysis of museum collections. In *The Sheguiandah Site: Archaeological, Geological and Paleobotanical Studies at a Paleoindian Site on Manitoulin Island, Ontario,* edited by Patrick J. Julig. Mercury Series, Archaeological Survey of Canada Paper 161. Canadian Museum of Civilization, Hull, Quebec.

Julig, Patrick J., John H. McAndrews, and William C. Mahaney
1990 Geoarchaeology of the Cummins site on the beach of proglacial Lake Minong, Lake Superior Basin, Canada. In *Archaeological Geology of North America*, edited by N. P. Lasca and J. Donahue, pp. 21–49. Geological Society of America, Boulder, Colorado.

Julig, Patrick J., L. A. Pavlish, and R. G. V. Hancock
1987 INAA of archaeological quartzite from Cummins site, Thunder Bay, Ontario: Determination of source. In *Current Research in the Pleistocene*, Vol. 4, edited by J. I. Mead, pp. 59–61. Center for the Study of Early Man, University of Maine, Orono.

Justice, N. D.
1995 *Stone Age Spear and Arrow Points of the Midcontinental and Eastern United States. A Modern Survey and Reference*. Indiana University Press, Bloomington.

Karrow, Paul F.
2004 Ontario geological events and environmental change in the time of the Late Palaeo-Indian and Early Archaic cultures (10,500 to 8,500 B.P.). In *The Late Palaeo-Indian Great Lakes: Geological and Archaeological Investigations of Late Pleistocene and Early Holocene Environments*, edited by Lawrence J. Jackson and Andrew Hinshelwood, pp. 1–23. Mercury Series, Archaeology Paper 165. Canadian Museum of Civilization, Gatineau, Quebec.

Karrow, Paul F., E. C. Appleyard, and A. L. Endres
2007 Geological and geophysical evidence for pre-Nipissing (>5,000 years BP) transgression infilled valleys in the Lake Huron basin, Ontario. *Journal of Paleolimnology* 37:419–34.

Karrow, Paul F., and B. G. Warner
1990 The geological and biological environment for human occupation in southern Ontario. In *The Archaeology of Southern Ontario to A.D. 1650*, edited by C. J. Ellis and N. Ferris, pp. 5–35. Occasional Publications 5. London Chapter, Ontario Archaeological Society.

Kaszycki, C. A.
1985 History of glacial Lake Algonquin in the Haliburton area, south central Ontario. In *Quaternary Evolution of the Great Lakes*, edited by Paul F. Karrow and Parker E. Calkin, pp. 110–23. Geological Association of Canada, Special Paper 30.

Keith, Darren
2004 Caribou, river and ocean: Harvaqtuurmiut landscape organization and orientation. *Etudes/Inuit/Studies* 28(2):39–56.

Keith, Darren, and T. Max Friesen
n.d. Iqaluktuurmiutat: Life at Iqaluktuuq. Kitikmeot Heritage Society, Cambridge Bay, Nunavut. http://www.kitikmeotheritage.ca/research/Iqaluktuurmiutat.pdf.

Kempe, S., and A. Al-Malabeh
2013 Desert kites in Jordan and Saudi Arabia: Structure, statistics and function, a Google Earth study. *Quaternary International* 297:126–46.

Kennedy, D. L.
2011 The "works of the old men" in Arabia: Remote sensing in interior Arabia. *Journal of Archaeological Science* 38:3185–203.
2012 Kites—New discoveries and a new type. *Arabian Archaeology and Epigraphy* 23:145–55.

Kenyon, W.
1959 *The Inverhuron Site. Bruce County–Ontario 1957.* Occasional Paper 1. Art and Archaeology Division, Royal Ontario Museum, Toronto.

Kihlman, Susanna M., and Tommi Kauppila
2009 Mine water-induced gradients in sediment metals and arcellacean assemblages in a boreal freshwater bay (Petkellahti, Finland). *Journal of Paleolimnology* 42:533–50.

Klein, R. G.
1999 *The Human Career. Human Biological and Cultural Origins*, 2nd ed. University of Chicago Press, Chicago and London.

Kolen, J.
1999 Hominids without homes: On the nature of Middle Paleolithic settlement in Europe. In *The Middle Paleolithic Occupation of Europe*, edited by W. Roebroeks and C. Gamble, pp. 139–75. University of Leiden Press, Leiden.

Kornfeld, M., G. C. Frison, and M. L. Larson
2010 *Prehistoric Hunter-Gatherers of the High Plains and Rocky Mountains.* Left Coast Press, Walnut Creek, California.

Krist, Frank, and Daniel Brown
1994 GIS modeling of Paleo-Indian period caribou migrations and viewsheds in northeastern lower Michigan. *Photogrammetric Engineering and Remote Sensing* 60(9):1129–37.

Kuehn, Stephen R.
1998 New evidence for Late Paleoindian-Early Archaic subsistence behavior in the western Great Lakes. *American Antiquity* 63(3):457–76.
2007 Late Paleoindian subsistence strategies in the western Great Lakes region: Evidence for generalized foraging from northern Wisconsin. In *Foragers of the Terminal Pleistocene in North America*, edited by R. B. Walker and B. N. Driskell, pp. 88–98. University of Nebraska Press, Lincoln.

Kuehn, Stephen R., and J. A. Clark
2012 Analysis of faunal remains from three Late Paleoindian (Lake Poygan phase) sites in east-central Wisconsin. *Illinois Archaeology* 24:123–58.

Kumar, Arun, and Andrew P. Dalby
1998 Identification key for Holocene lacustrine arcellacean (thecamoebian) taxa. *Palaeontologica Electronica* 1:1–39. http://palaeoelectronica.org/1998_1/dalby/issue1.htm.

LaBelle, J., and S. R. Pelton
2013 Communal hunting along the Continental Divide of northern Colorado: Results from the Olson game drive (5BL147), USA. *Quaternary International* 297:45–63.

Lamarre, A., G. Magnan, M. Garneau, and É. Boucher
2013 A testate amoebae-based transfer function for paleohydrological reconstruction from boreal and subarctic peatlands in northeastern Canada. *Quaternary International* 306(3):88–96.

Lamentowicz, Mariusz, and Milena Obremska
2010 A rapid response of testate amoebae and vegetation to inundation of a kettle-hole mire. *Journal of Paleolimnology* 4:499–511.

Lamentowicz, Mariusz, Milena Obremska, and Edward A. D. Mitchell
2008 Autogenic succession, land-use change, and climatic influences on the Holocene development of a kettle-hole mire in northern Poland. *Review of Palaeobotany and Palynology* 151:21–40.

Larsen, Curtis E.
1987 *Geological History of Glacial Lake Algonquin and the Upper Great Lakes.* U.S. Geological Survey Bulletin 1801. U.S. Government Printing Office.
1999 A century of Great Lakes levels research: Finished or just the beginning. In *Retrieving Michigan's Buried Past: The Archaeology of the Great Lakes State*, edited by John R. Halsey and M. Stafford, pp. 1–30. Bulletin 64. Cranbrook Institute of Science, Bloomfield Hills, Michigan.

Larson, G. J., T. V. Lowell, and N. E. Ostrom
1994 Evidence for the Two Creeks interstade in the Lake Huron basin. *Canadian Journal of Earth Sciences* 31:793–97.

Lartet, E., and H. Christy
1875 *Reliquae Aquitanicae: Being Contributions to the Archaeology of Périgord and Adjoining Provinces of Southern France.* Williams and Norgate, London.

Leavitt, Steven W., Irina P. Panyushkina, T. Lange, Alex Wiedenhoeft, L. Cheng, R. Douglas Hunter, J. Hughes, F. Pranschke, A. F. Schneider, J. Moran, and R. Stieglitz
2006 Climate in the Great Lakes region between 14,000 and 4,000 years ago from isotopic composition of conifer wood. *Radiocarbon* 48:205–17.

Lee, T. E.
1952 A preliminary report on an archaeological survey of southwestern Ontario for 1950. *National Museum of Canada Bulletin* 126:64–75.
1953 A preliminary report on the Sheguiandah site, Manitoulin Island. *National Museum of Canada Bulletin* 128:58–67.
1954a The Giant site. *National Museum of Canada Bulletin* 132:66–69.
1954b The first Sheguiandah expedition, Manitoulin Island, Ontario. *American Antiquity* 20(2):101–11.
1955 The second Sheguiandah expedition, Manitoulin Island, Ontario. *American Antiquity* 21(1):63–71.
1956 Position and meaning of a radiocarbon sample from the Sheguiandah site, Ontario. *American Antiquity* 22(1):79.
1957 The antiquity of the Sheguiandah site. *Canadian Field Naturalist* 71(3):117–37.
1963 A Point Peninsula site, Manitoulin Island, Lake Huron. *Bulletin of the Massachusetts Archaeological Society* 26(2):19–30.

Legge, A. J., and P. A. Rowley-Conwy
1987 Gazelle killing in Stone Age Syria. *Scientific American* 257:76–83.

Lemaître, S., and P. L. van Berg
2008 The engraved rock sites of Hemma (Syria). *International Newsletter on Rock Art* 52:5–12.

Lemke, Ashley K., John O'Shea, and Elizabeth Sonnenburg
2013 Late Paleoindian and Early Archaic Caribou Hunters underneath Lake Huron. Poster presented at the Paleoamerican Odyssey Conference, Sante Fe, New Mexico.

Lennox, P. A.
1993 The Kassel and Blue Dart sites: Two components of the Early Archaic, bifurcate base projectile point tradition, Waterloo County, Ontario. *Ontario Archaeology* 56:1–31. Toronto.
2000 The Rentner and McKean sites: 10,000 years of settlement on the shores of Lake Huron, Simcoe County, Ontario. *Ontario Archaeology* 70:16–65. Toronto.

Lester, P.
2005 A* Pathfinding for Beginners. Gamedev.net. archive.gamedev.net/archive/reference/articles/article2003.html.

Levine, Mary Ann
1997 The tyranny continues: Ethnographic analogy and eastern Paleo-Indians. In *Caribou and Reindeer Hunters of the Northern Hemisphere*, edited by Lawrence J. Jackson and Paul T. Thacker, pp. 221–44. Avebury, Brookfield, Vermont.

Lewis, Christopher F. M., and Tim W. Anderson
1989 Oscillations of levels and cool phases of the Laurentian Great Lakes caused by inflows from glacial Lake Agassiz and Barlow-Ojibway. *Journal of Paleolimnology* 2:99–146.
2012 The sedimentary and palynological records of Serpent River Bog, and revised early Holocene lake-level changes in the Lake Huron and Georgian Bay region. *Journal of Paleolimnology* 47:391–410.

Lewis, Christopher F. M., and Steve M. Blasco
2001 Evidence for late Wisconsin high velocity glaciofluvial flushing followed by early Holocene low lake levels and closed basin conditions in the lower Great Lakes. In *Program and Abstracts*, pp. 74–75. International Association for Great Lakes Research, 44th Conference on Great Lakes Research. Green Bay, Wisconsin.
2002 Early to middle Holocene hydrologic lake closure: Dry climate impact on the Great Lakes of North America. In *Abstracts with Programs*, Vol. 34, p. A7. Geological Society of America.

Lewis, Christopher F. Michael, Steve M. Blasco, and Pierre L. Gareau
2005 Glacial isostatic adjustment of the Laurentian Great Lakes basin: Using the empirical record of strandline deformation for reconstruction of early Holocene Paleo-lakes and discovery of a hydrologically closed phase. *Géographie physique et Quaternaire* 59(2–3):187–210.

Lewis, Christopher F. M., Clifford W. Heil Jr., J. Brad Hubeny, John W. King, Theodore C. Moore Jr., and David K. Rea
2007 The Stanley unconformity in Lake Huron basin: Evidence for a climate-driven closed lowstand about 7900 ^{14}C BP, with similar implications for the Chippewa lowstand in Lake Michigan basin. *Journal of Paleolimnology* 37(3):435–52.

Lewis, Christopher F. M., Paul F. Karrow, Steve M. Blasco, Francine M. G. McCarthy, John W. King, Theodore C. Moore Jr., and David K. Rea
2008 Evolution of lakes in the Huron basin: Deglaciation to present. *Aquatic Ecosystem Health & Management* 11(2):127–36.

Lewis, Christopher F. Michael, John W. King, Stefan M. Blasco, Gregory R. Brooks, John P. Coakley, Thomas E. Croley II, David L. Dettman, Thomas W. D. Edwards, Clifford W. Heil Jr., J. Bradford Hubeny, Kathleen R. Laird, John H. McAndrews, Francine M. G. McCarthy, Barbara E. Medioli, Theodore C. Moore Jr., David K. Rea, and Alison J. Smith
2008 Dry climate disconnected the Laurentian Great Lakes. *EOS* 89:541–42.

Lewis, Christopher F. M., Theodore C. Moore Jr., David K. Rea, David L. Dettman, A. M. Smith, and L. A. Mayer
1994 Lakes of the Huron basin: Their record of runoff from the Laurentide Ice Sheet. *Quaternary Science Reviews* 13:891–922.

Liljeblad, S.
1986 Oral tradition: Content and style of verbal arts. In *Handbook of North American Indians*. Vol. 11, *Great Basin*, edited by W. L. D'Azevedo, pp. 641–59. Smithsonian Institution, Washington, D.C.

Linacre, E. T.
1977 A simple formula for estimating evaporation rates in various climates, using temperature data alone. *Agricultural Meteorology* 18:409–24.

Liu, D.
2011 Multi-objective Cultural Algorithms. PhD thesis, Wayne State University, Detroit, Michigan.

Loebel, Thomas
2013 Endscrapers, use-wear, and Early Paleoindians in eastern North America. In *The Eastern Fluted Point Tradition*, edited by J. Gingerich, pp. 315–30, University of Utah Press, Salt Lake City.

Loiacono, D., J. Togelius, P. L. Lanzi, L. Kinnaird-Heether, S. M. Lucas, M. Simmerson, D. Perez, Robert G. Reynolds, and Y. Saez
2008 The WCCI 2008 Simulated Car Racing Competition. Computational Intelligence and Games, 2008, IEEE Symposium.

Long, D. F. G., Patrick J. Julig, and R. G. V. Hancock
2002 Characterization of Sheguiandah quartzite and other potential sources of quartzarenite artifacts in the Great Lakes region. In *The Sheguiandah Site: Archaeological, Geological and Paleobotanical Studies at a Paleoindian Site on Manitoulin Island, Ontario*, edited by Patrick J. Julig, pp. 265–95. Mercury Series, Archaeological Survey of Canada Paper 161. Canadian Museum of Civilization, Hull, Quebec.

Loope, H. M.
2006 Deglacial Chronology and Glacial Stratigraphy of the Western Thunder Bay Lowland, Northwest Ontario, Canada. Master's thesis, University of Toledo, Ohio.

Lovis, William A.
2009 Hunter-gatherer adaptations and alternative perspectives on the Michigan Archaic: Research problems in context. In *Archaic Societies: Diversity and Complexity across the Midcontinent*, edited by Thomas E. Emerson, Dale L. McElrath, and Andrew C. Fortier, pp. 725–54. Suny Press, Albany, New York.

Lovis, William A., M. B. Holman, G. William Monaghan, and R. K. Skowronek
1994 Archaeological, geological and paleoecological perspectives on regional research design in the Saginaw Bay region of Michigan. In *Great Lakes Archaeology and Paleoecology: Exploring Interdisciplinary Initiatives for the Nineties*, edited by R. I. MacDonald and B. Warner, pp. 81–94. Quaternary Sciences Institute, University of Waterloo, Ontario.

Lowell, T. V., T. G. Fisher, G. C. Comer, I. Hajdas, N. Waterson, K. Glover, H. M. Loope, J. M. Schaefer, V. Rinterknecht, W. Broecker, G. Denton, and J. T. Teller
2005 Testing the Lake Agassiz meltwater trigger for the Younger Dryas. *EOS* 86:365–73.

Lubinski, P. M.
1999 The communal pronghorn hunt: A review of the ethnographic and archaeological evidence. *Journal of California and Great Basin Anthropology* 21:158–81.

Luedtke, B. E.
1978 Chert sources and trace-element analysis. *American Antiquity* 43(3):413–23.
1979 The identification of sources of chert artifacts. *American Antiquity* 44(4):744–56.

Lyons, Natasha, Peter Dawson, Matthew Walls, Donald Uluadluak, Louis Angalik, Mark Kalluak, Philip Kigusuituak, Luke Kiniski, and Luke Suluk
2010 Person, place, memory, thing: How Inuit elders are informing archaeological practice in the Canadian north. *Canadian Journal of Archaeology* 34:1–31.

Macdonald, Rebecca A., and Fred J. Longstaffe
2008 The Late Quaternary oxygen-isotope composition of southern Lake Huron. *Aquatic Ecosystem Health and Management* 11(2):137–43.

MacNeish, R. S.
1952 A possible early site in the Thunder Bay District, Ontario. *National Museum of Canada Bulletin* 126:23–47.

Manker, E.
1960 *Fångstgropar och stalotomter*. Acta Lapponica XV. Uppsala.

Mannik, H. (interviewer and editor)
1998 *Inuit Nunamiut: Inland Inuit*. Inuit Heritage Centre, Baker Lake, Nunavut.

Markham, Samantha
2012 An introduction to the Paleoindian projectile point assemblage recovered from the Mackenzie I site near Thunder Bay, Ontario. *Minnesota Archaeologist* 71:60–73.

Martin, Susan R. (editor)
1993 20KE20: Excavations at a prehistoric copper workshop. *Michigan Archaeologist* 39:127–93.

Mason, Ronald J.
1981 *Great Lakes Archaeology*. Academic Press, New York.

Mason, Ronald J., and Carol Irwin
1960 An Eden-Scottsbluff burial in northeastern Wisconsin. *American Antiquity* 26:43–57.

McAndrews, John H.
1994 Pollen diagrams for southern Ontario applied to archaeology. In *Great Lakes Archeology and Paleoecology: Exploring Interdisciplinary Initiatives for the Nineties*, edited by R. MacDonald and B. Warner, pp. 179–95. Quaternary Sciences Institute, University of Waterloo, Ontario.

McAndrews, John H., Albert A. Berti, and Geoffrey Norris
1973 *Key to the Quaternary Pollen and Spores of the Great Lakes*. Royal Ontario Museum, Toronto.

McCabe, R. E., B. O'Gara, W. O'Gara, and H. M. Reeves
2004 *Prairie Ghost: Pronghorn and Human Interaction in Early America*. University Press of Colorado, Boulder.

McCarthy, Francine M. G., Steve M. Blasco, Christopher F. M. Lewis, and P. H. Harrison
2011 The submerged early postglacial beach off Flowerpot Island—Implications for major climate-driven changes in water level and water quality in the recent geologic past. Conference Proceedings, *Leading Edge*, St. Catharines. http://escarpment.org/education/conference/eleven/index.php.

McCarthy, Francine M. G., E. S. Collins, John H. McAndrews, H. A. Kerr, D. B. Scott, and F. S. Medioli
1995 A comparison of postglacial arcellacean ("thecamoebian") and pollen succession in Atlantic Canada, illustrating the potential of arcellaceans for paleoclimatic reconstruction. *Journal of Paleontology* 69:980–93.

McCarthy, Francine M. G., and John H. McAndrews
2012 Early Holocene drought in the Laurentian Great Lakes basin caused hydrologic closure of Georgian Bay. *Journal of Paleolimnology* 47:411–28. DOI 10.1007/s10933-010-9410-z.

McCarthy, Francine, John McAndrews, Steve Blasco, and Sarah Tiffin
2007 Spatially discontinuous modern sedimentation in Georgian Bay, Huron basin, Great Lakes. *Journal of Paleolimnology* 37:453–70.

McCarthy, Francine M. G., Sarah H. Tiffin, Adam P. Sarvis, John H. McAndrews, and Steven M. Blasco
2012 Early Holocene brackish closed basin conditions in Georgian Bay, Ontario, Canada: Microfossil (thecamoebian and pollen) evidence. *Journal of Paleolimnology* 47:429–45. DOI 10.1007/s10933-010-9415-7.

McInnes, C. R.
2003 Velocity field path-planning for single and multiple unmanned aerial vehicles. *The Aeronautical Journal* 107:419–26.

Microsoft Corporation
2010 Microsoft XNA Education Catalogue. Accessed June 30, 2010, http://creators.xna.com/en-US/education/.

Moerschfelder, F.
1985 Locating the Sources of Haldimand Chert and Related Workshop Sites along Rogers Creek: An Ongoing Survey. License report on file with the Ontario Ministry of Tourism, Culture and Sport, Archaeology office, London.

Monaghan, G. William, and William A. Lovis
2005 *Modeling Archaeological Site Burial in Southern Michigan: A Geoarchaeological Synthesis*. Michigan State University Press, East Lansing.

Moore, Theodore C., David K. Rea, L. A. Mayer, Christopher F. M. Lewis, and D. M. Dobson
1994 Seismic stratigraphy of Lake Huron-Georgian Bay and postglacial lake level history. *Canadian Journal of Earth Sciences* 31(11):1606–17.

Moreno, E.
2012 The construction of hunting sceneries: Interactions between humans, animals and landscape in the Antofalla Valley, Catamarca, Argentina. *Journal of Anthropological Archaeology* 31(1):104–77.

Morgan, Allen V.
1972 Late Wisconsinan ice-wedge polygons near Kitchener, Ontario, Canada. *Canadian Journal of Earth Sciences* 9:607–17.

Morrison, D.
1981 Chipewyan drift fences and shooting-blinds in the central barren grounds. In *Megaliths to Medicine Wheels: Boulder Structures in Archaeology*, edited by M. Wilson, K. L. Road, and K. J. Hardy, pp. 171–87. Proceedings of the Eleventh Annual Chacmool Conference. University of Calgary Archaeological Association, Calgary.

Murray, Malcolm R.
2002 Is laser particle size determination possible for carbonate-rich lake sediments? *Journal of Paleolimnology* 27:173–83.

Nadel, D., G. Bar-Oz, U. Avner, E. Boaretto, and D. Malkinson
2010 Walls, ramps and pits: The construction of the Samar desert kites, southern Negev, Israel. *Antiquity* 84:976–92.

Nadel, D., G. Bar-Oz, U. Avner, D. Malkinson, and E. Boaretto
2013 Ramparts and walls: Building techniques of kites in the Negev highland. *Quaternary International* 297:147–54.

Neff, B. P., and J. R. Killian
2003 The Great Lakes Water Balance: Data Availability and Annotated Bibliography of Selected References. Water-Resources Investigations Report 02-4296.

Newby, P., J. Bradley, A. Spiess, B. Shuman, and P. Leduc
2005 A Paleoindian response to Younger Dryas climate change. *Quaternary Science Reviews* 24:141–54.

Newby, P. E., P. Killoran, M. R. Waldorf, B. N. Shuman, R. S. Webb, and T. Webb III
2000 14,000 years of sediment, vegetation, and water-level changes at the Makepeace Cedar Swamp, southeastern Massachusetts. *Quaternary Research* 53:352–68.

Newman, M., and Patrick Julig
1989 The identification of protein residues on lithic artifacts from a stratified boreal forest site. *Canadian Journal of Archaeology* 13:119–32.

Niven, L., T. Steele, W. Rendu, J. B. Mallye, S. McPherron, M. Soressi, J. Jaubert, and J. J. Hublin
2012 Neandertal mobility and large-game hunting: The exploitation of reindeer during the Quina Mousterian at Chez-Pinaud Jonzac (Charente-Maritime, France). *Journal of Human Evolution* 63:624–35.

Noble, W. C.
1968 Vision pits, cairns and petroglyphs at Rock Lake, Algonquin Provincial Park, Ontario. *Ontario Archaeology* 11:47–64.

Norris, Dave
2012 Current archaeological investigations in Ontario: The discovery of and preliminary information regarding several Paleoindian sites east of Thunder Bay. *The Minnesota Archaeologist* 71:45–59.

Ochoa, A., A. Padilla, S. Gonzalez, A. Castro, and S. Hal
2008 Improve a game board based on cultural algorithms. *The International Journal of Virtual Reality* 7(2):41–46.

O'Gara, B. W.
2004 Physical characteristics. In *Pronghorn Ecology and Management*, edited by B. O'Gara and J. D. Yoakum, pp. 109–43. University Press of Colorado, Boulder.

Ontario Woodland Caribou Recovery Team
2008 Woodland Caribou (*Rangifer tarandus* caribou) (Forest-dwelling, Boreal Population) in Ontario. Prepared for the Ontario Ministry of Natural Resources, Peterborough, Ontario.

O'Shea, John M.
2004 *Ships and Shipwrecks of the Au Sable Shores Region of Western Lake Huron*. Memoirs, No. 39. Museum of Anthropology, University of Michigan, Ann Arbor.
2008 Ancient Hunters and the Lake Stanley Causeway: A Pilot Study. NSF High-Risk Grant #BCS-0829324, University of Michigan, Ann Arbor.

O'Shea, John M., Ashley K. Lemke, and Robert G. Reynolds
2013 "Nobody knows the way of the caribou": *Rangifer* hunting at 45° north latitude. *Quaternary International* 297:36–44.

O'Shea, John M., Ashley Lemke, Robert Reynolds, Elizabeth Sonnenburg, and Guy Meadows
2013 Approaches to the archaeology of submerged landscapes: Research on the Alpena-Amberley Ridge, Lake Huron. *Proceedings of the 2013 AAUS/ESDP Curaçao Joint International Scientific Diving Symposium*, pp. 211–15. American Academy of Underwater Sciences and European Scientific Diving Panel Joint International Scientific Diving Symposium, October 24–27, 2013, Curaçao. American Academy of Underwater Sciences, Dauphin Island, Alabama.

O'Shea, John M., Ashley K. Lemke, Elizabeth P. Sonnenburg, Robert G. Reynolds, and Brian D. Abbott
2014 A 9,000-year-old caribou hunting structure beneath Lake Huron. *Proceedings of the National Academy of Sciences* 111(19):6911–15.

O'Shea, John M., and Guy A. Meadows
2009 Evidence for early hunters beneath the Great Lakes. *Proceedings of the National Academy of Sciences* 106(25):10120–23.

Panyushkina, Irina P., and Steven W. Leavitt
2007 Insights into Late Pleistocene/Early Holocene paleoecology from fossil wood around the Great Lakes region. In *Late-Glacial History of East-Central Wisconsin*, edited by T. S. Hooyer, pp. 47–57. Guide Book for the 53rd Midwest Friends of the Pleistocene Field Conference. Wisconsin Geological and Natural History Survey, Madison.

Parker, L. R.
1986a Haldimand chert: A preferred raw material in southwestern Ontario during the early Holocene period. *Kewa Newsletter of the London Chapter, Ontario Archaeological Society* 86(4):4–21. London.
1986b Haldimand Chert and Its Utilization during the Early Holocene Period in Southwestern Ontario. Master's thesis, Department of Anthropology, Trent University, Peterborough, Ontario.

Patterson, R. Timothy, and Evan Fishbein
1989 Re-examination of the statistical methods used to determine the number of point counts needed for micropaleontological quantitative research. *Journal of Paleontology* 6:245–48.

Pengelly, James W., and Keith J. Tinkler
2004 Lake level changes and aboriginal cultural manifestations in areas adjacent to and including Niagara Peninsula. In *The Late Palaeo-Indian Great Lakes: Geological and Archaeological Investigations of Late Pleistocene and Early Holocene Environments*, edited by Lawrence J. Jackson and Andrew Hinshelwood, pp. 201–24. Mercury Series, Archaeology Paper 165. Canadian Museum of Civilization, Gatineau, Quebec.

Pereira Evangelista, Bruno, Alexandre Santos Lobao, Riemer Grootjans, and Antonio Leal de Farias
2009 *Beginning XNA 3.0 Game Programming: From Novice to Professional*, 1st ed. Apress, Berkeley, California.

Pettit, C. J., F. Sheth, W. Harvey, and M. Cox
2009 Building a 3D Object Library for Visualizing Landscape Futures. 18th World IMACS/MODSIM Congress, July 13–17. Cairns, Australia.

Phillips, Brian A. M., and Christopher L. Hill
2004 Deglaciation history and geomorphological character of the region between the Agassiz and Superior basins, associated with the 'interlakes composite' of Minnesota and Ontario. In *The Late Palaeo-Indian Great Lakes: Geological and Archaeological Investigations of Late Pleistocene and Early Holocene Environments*, edited by Lawrence J. Jackson and Andrew Hinshelwood, pp. 275–301. Mercury Series, Archaeology Paper 165. Canadian Museum of Civilization, Gatineau, Quebec.

Pilon, Jean-Luc, and Luke Dalla Bona
2004 Insights into the early peopling of northwestern Ontario as documented at the Allen site (EcJs-1), Sioux Lookout District, Ontario. In *The Late Palaeo-Indian Great Lakes: Geological and Archaeological Investigations of Late Pleistocene and Early Holocene Environments*, edited by Lawrence Jackson and Andrew Hinshelwood, pp. 315–35. Mercury Series, Archaeology Paper 165. Canadian Museum of Civilization, Gatineau, Quebec.

Pleger, Thomas C., and James B. Stoltman
2009 The Archaic tradition in Wisconsin. In *Archaic Societies: Diversity and Complexity across the Midcontinent*, edited by Thomas E. Emerson, Dale L. McElrath, and Andrew C. Fortier, pp. 697–723. Suny Press, Albany, New York.

Powers, M. C.
1953 A new roundness scale for sedimentary particles. *Journal of Sedimentary Research* 23:117–19.

Prest, V. K.
1970 Quaternary geology of Canada. In *Geology and Economic Minerals of Canada*, pp. 675–764. Geological Survey of Canada, Economic Geology Report No. 1, 5th ed.

Price, D. T., D. H. Halliwell, M. J. Apps, and C. H. Peng
1999 Adapting a path model to simulate the sensitivity of central-Canadian boreal ecosystems to climate variability. *Journal of Biogeography* 26(5):1101–13.

Quimby, George I.
1959 Lanceolate points and Fossil Beach ridges in the upper Great Lakes region. *American Antiquity* 24(4):424–26.
1963 A new look at geochronology in the upper Great Lakes region. *American Antiquity* 28(4):558–59.

Rasmussen, Knud
1930 *Report of the Fifth Thule Expedition 1921–24*. Vol. 7, No. 2, *Observations on the Intellectual Culture of the Caribou Eskimos*, translated by W. E. Calvert. Gyldendalske Boghandel, Nordisk Forlag, Copenhagen.
1931 *Report of the Fifth Thule Expedition 1921–24*. Vol. 8, No. 1–2, *The Netsilik Eskimos, Social Life and Spiritual Culture*, translated by W. E. Calvert. Gyldendalske Boghandel, Nordisk Forlag, Copenhagen.

Rea, David K., Theodore C. Moore, Christopher F. M. Lewis, L. A. Mayer, David L. Dettman, A. J. Smith, and D. M. Dobson
1994 Stratigraphy and paleolimnologic record of lower Holocene sediments in northern Lake Huron and Georgian Bay. *Canadian Journal of Earth Sciences* 31:1586–605.

Reeves, B. O. K.
1978 Head-Smashed-In: 5500 years of bison jumping in the Alberta plains. *Plains Anthropologist* 23(82):151–74.

Reher, C. A., and G. C. Frison
1980 *The Vore Site, 48CK302, a Stratified Buffalo Jump in the Wyoming Black Hills*. Plains Anthropologist, Memoir 16.

Reimer, P. J., M. G. L. Baille, E. Bard, A. Bayliss, J. W. Beck, C. Bertrand, P. G. Blackwell, C. E. Buck, G. Burr, K. B. Cutler, P. E. Damon, R. L. Edwards, R. G. Fairbanks, M. Friedrich, T. P. Guilderson, K. A. Hughen, B. Kromer, F. G. McCormac, S. Manning, C. Bronk Ramsey, R. W. Reimer, S. Remmele, J. R. Southon, M. Stuiver, S. Talamo, F. W. Taylor, J. van der Plicht, and C. E. Weyhenmeyer
2004 IntCal04 terrestrial radiocarbon age calibration, 0–26 cal kyr BP. *Radiocarbon* 46:1029–58.

Reimers, E., and T. Ringberg
1983 Seasonal changes in body weight of Svalbard reindeer from birth to maturity. *Acta Zoologica Fennica* 175:69–72.

Reynolds, Craig W.
1987 Flocks, herds, and schools: A distributed behavioral model. *Computer Graphics* 21(4):25–34.

Reynolds, Robert G.
1986 An adaptive computer model for the evolution of plant collecting and early agriculture in the eastern valley of Oaxaca. In *Guilá Naquitz: Archaic Foraging and Early Agriculture in Oaxaca, Mexico*, edited by Kent V. Flannery, pp. 439–500. Academic Press, Orlando.
1994 An introduction to cultural algorithms. In *Proceedings of the Third Annual Conference on Evolutionary Programming*, edited by A. V. Sebald and L. J. Fogel, pp. 131–39. World Scientific Press, Singapore.

Reynolds, Robert G., M. Ali, and T. Jayyousi
2008 Mining the social fabric of archaic urban centers with cultural algorithms. *Computer* 41(1):64–72.

Reynolds, Robert G., and B. Peng
2005 Knowledge learning and social swarms in cultural algorithms. *Journal of Mathematical Sociology* 29:1–18.

Reynolds, Robert G., B. Peng, and R. Whallon
2005 Emergent Social Structures in Cultural Algorithms. Proceedings of the NAACSOS Conference 2005, Notre Dame.

Robinson, B. S., J. C. Ort, W. A. Eldridge, A. L. Burke, and B. G. Pelletier
2009 Paleoindian aggregation and social context at Bull Brook. *American Antiquity* 74:423–47.

Roosa, W. B.
1977 Great Lakes Paleoindian: The Parkhill site, Ontario. In *Amerinds and Their Paleoenvironments in Northeastern North America*, edited by W. S. Newman and B. Salwen, pp. 349–54. Annals of the New York Academy of Sciences, Vol. 288. New York Academy of Sciences, New York.

Ross, William
1997 The Interlakes composite: A redefinition of the initial settlement of the Agassiz-Minong Peninsula. *Wisconsin Archaeologist* 76(3–4):244–68.

Rowe, J. S.
1972 *Forest Regions of Canada*. Canadian Forestry Service Publication No. 1300. Department of the Environment, Ottawa.

Ruberg, S. A., D. F. Coleman, T. H. Johengen, G. A. Meadows, H. W. Van Sumeren, G. A. Lang, and B. A. Biddanda
2005 Groundwater plume mapping in a submerged sinkhole in Lake Huron. *Marine Technology Society Journal* 39:65–69.

Saleem S., and Robert G. Reynolds
2000 Cultural algorithms in dynamic environments. In *Proceedings of the 2000 Congress on Evolutionary Computation*, pp. 1513–20. San Diego, California.

Sanders, Karen
2009 *Bodies in the Bog and the Archaeological Imagination*. University of Chicago Press, Chicago.

Saranoha, D. A.
1985 Mathematical models of tundra communities and populations. *Annual Review in Automatic Programming* 12:377–79.

Sarvis, Adam P., Francine M. G. McCarthy, and Steve M. Blasco
1999 Explaining the lowstand in Georgian Bay approximately 7,200 years ago: A paleolimnological approach using microfossil evidence. In *Leading Edge'99*. Niagara Escarpment Commission, Burlington, Ontario.

Sassaman, Kenneth
2010 *The Eastern Archaic, Historicized*. Alta Mira Press, Toronto.

Schaefer, J. A.
2003 Long-term range recession and the persistence of caribou in the taiga. *Conservation Biology* 17:1435–39.

Scott, Geoffrey A. J.
1995 *Canada's Vegetation: A World Perspective*. McGill-Queen's University Press, Montreal and Kingston.

Scott, David B., and J. Otto R. Hermelin
1993 A device for precision splitting of micropaleontological samples in liquid suspension. *Journal of Paleontology* 67:151–54.

Scott, David B., Franco S. Medioli, and Charles T. Schafer
2001 *Monitoring in Coastal Environments Using Foraminifera and Thecamoebian Indicators*. Cambridge University Press, Cambridge.

Sharp, Henry S.
1977 The Caribou Eater Chipewyan: Bilaterality, strategies of caribou hunting and the fur trade. *Arctic Anthropology* 14(2):35–40.

Shilts, W. W., J. M. Aylsworth, C. A. Kaszycki, and R. A. Klassen
1987 Canadian Shield. In *Geomorphic Systems of North America*, pp. 119–61. Centennial Special Vol. 2. Geological Society of America, Boulder, Colorado.

Shott, Michael J.
1999 The Early Archaic: Life after the glaciers. In *Retrieving Michigan's Buried Past: The Archaeology of the Great Lakes State*, edited by John R. Halsey and M. Stafford, pp. 71–82. Bulletin 64. Cranbrook Institute of Science, Bloomfield Hills, Michigan.

Shott, Michael J., and P. D. Welch
1984 Archaeological resources of the Thumb area of Michigan. *Michigan Archaeologist* 30(1):1–79.

Shott, Michael J., and Henry T. Wright
1999 The Paleo-Indians: Michigan's first people. In *Retrieving Michigan's Buried Past: The Archaeology of the Great Lakes State*, edited by John R. Halsey and M. Stafford, pp. 59–70. Bulletin 64. Cranbrook Institute of Science, Bloomfield Hills, Michigan.

Shuman, B., P. Bartlein, N. Logar, P. Newby, and T. Webb III
2002 Parallel climate and vegetation responses to the early Holocene collapse of the Laurentide Ice Sheet. *Quaternary Science Reviews* 21:1793–805.

Shuman, B., T. Webb III, P. Bartlein, and J. W. Williams
2002 The anatomy of a climatic oscillation: Vegetation change in eastern North American during the Younger Dryas chronozone. *Quaternary Science Reviews* 21:1777–91.

Simons, Donald B.
1997 The Gainey and Butler sites as focal points for caribou and people. In *Caribou and Reindeer Hunters of the Northern Hemisphere*, edited by Lawrence J. Jackson and Paul T. Thacker, pp. 105–31. Avebury, Brookfield, Vermont.

Simons, Donald B., Michael J. Shott, and Henry T. Wright
1984 The Gainey site: Variability in a Great Lakes Paleo-Indian assemblage. *Archaeology of Eastern North America* 12:266–79. Buffalo.

Sirois, L., G. B. Bonan, and H. H. Shugart
1994 Development of a simulation model of the forest-tundra transition zone of northeastern Canada. *Canadian Journal of Forest Research* 24(4):697–706.

Smith, B. D.
2013 Modifying landscapes and mass kills: Human niche construction and communal ungulate harvests. *Quaternary International* 297:8–12.

Smith, James G. E.
1978 Economic uncertainty in an "original affluent society": Caribou and Caribou Eater Chipewyan adaptive strategies. *Arctic Anthropology* 15:68–88.

Smith, James G. E., and Ernest S. Burch
1979 Chipewyan and Inuit in the central Canadian subarctic, 1613–1977. *Arctic Anthropology* 16:76–101.

Somers, Lee H., Clifford Tetzloff, and Robert F. Anderson
1968 Operation submich. In *Proceedings of the 11th Conference on Great Lakes Research*, pp. 658–53. Great Lakes Research Institute, University of Michigan, Ann Arbor.

Sonnenburg, Elizabeth P., Joseph I. Boyce, and Eduard G. Reinhardt
2009 Multi-proxy paleoenvironmental record of Colonial land-use change in the lower Rideau canal system (Colonel By Lake), Ontario, Canada. *Journal of Paleolimnology* 42(4):515–32.
2013 Multi-proxy lake sediment record of prehistoric (Paleoindian-Archaic) archaeological paleoenvironments at Rice Lake, Ontario, Canada. *Quaternary Science Reviews* 73:77–92.

Sonnenburg, Elizabeth P., Joseph I. Boyce, and Philip Suttak
2012 Holocene paleoshorelines, water levels and submerged prehistoric site archaeological potential of Rice Lake (Ontario, Canada). *Journal of Archaeological Science* 39(12):3552–67.

Sonnenburg, Elizabeth, and John O'Shea
in review Preservation potential of in-situ sediments, microfossils and archaeological materials on the Alpena-Amberley Ridge, Lake Huron. *Geoarchaeology*.

Spiess, A. E.
1979 *Reindeer and Caribou Hunters: An Archaeological Study*. Academic Press, New York.

Spiess, A. E., D. Wilson, and J. W. Bradley
1998 Paleoindian occupation in the New England-Maritimes region: Beyond cultural ecology. *Archaeology of Eastern North America* 26:201–64.

Srinivasan, S., and S. Ramakrishnan
2012 Cultural algorithm toolkit for multi-objective rule mining. *International Journal on Computational Sciences & Applications (IJCSA)* 2(4):9–23.

Stanley, George M.
1936 Lower Algonquin beaches of Penetanguishene peninsula. *Geological Society of America Bulletin* 47(12):1933–60.
1937 Lower Algonquin beaches of Cape Rich, Georgian Bay. *Geological Society of America Bulletin* 48(11):1665–86.
1938a Impounded early Algonquin beaches at Sucker Creek, Grey County, Ontario. *Papers of the Michigan Academy of Science, Arts and Letters* 23:477–95.
1938b The submerged valley through Mackinac Straits. *Journal of Geology* 46:966–74.

Stefansson, V.
1951 *My Life with the Eskimo*. Macmillan Company, New York.

Steinhauser, F.
1979 *Climatic Atlas of North and Central America: Maps of Mean Temperature and Precipitation*. WMO. UNESCO Cartographia, Hungary.

Steward, Julian H.
1941 *Culture Element Distributions: XIII, Nevada Shoshoni*, pp. 209–359. University of California Anthropological Records Vol. 4, No. 2. University of California Press, Berkeley.

Stewart, Andrew
2014 Viewing Cultural Landscapes in the Long and Short Term: Inland Inuit Settlement Patterning on the Lower Kazen River, Nunavut, Canada. Paper presented at the 79th Annual Meeting of the Society of American Archaeology, Austin, Texas.

Stewart, Andrew, and T. Max Friesen
1998 Report on Archaeological Surveys of the Fall Caribou Crossing National Historic Site; Report on Faunal Remains. Report on file, Ms 4100. Canadian Museum of Civilization, Gatineau.

Stewart, Andrew M., T. Max Friesen, Darren Keith, and L. Henderson
2000 Archaeology and oral history of Inuit land use on the Kazan River, Nunavut: A feature-based approach. *Arctic* 53:260–78.

Stewart, Andrew M., Darren Keith, and J. Scottie
2004 Caribou crossings and cultural meanings: Placing traditional knowledge and archaeology in context in a Inuit landscape. *Journal of Archaeological Method and Theory* 11:83–112.

Stopp, M. P.
1994 Cultural utility of the cobble beach formation in coastal Newfoundland and Labrador. *Northeast Anthropology* 48:69–89.
2002 Ethnohistoric analogues for storage as an adaptive strategy in northeastern subarctic prehistory. *Journal of Anthropological Archaeology* 21:301–28.

Storck, Peter L.
1974 Two probable Shield Archaic sites in Killarney Provincial Park, Ontario. *Ontario Archaeology* 21:3–36. Toronto.
1976 Preliminary Report of Work Done under Licence Number 76-B-0082: Kincardine Area Survey; Fisher Site Excavation. Report on file at the Ontario Ministry of Tourism, Culture and Sport, Archaeology office, London.
1978 The Coates Creek site: A possible Late Paleo-Indian-Early Archaic site in Simcoe County, Ontario. *Ontario Archaeology* 30:25–46. Toronto.
1997 *The Fisher Site: Archaeological, Geological and Paleobotanical Studies at an Early Paleo-Indian Site in Southern Ontario, Canada*. Memoirs, No. 30. Museum of Anthropology, University of Michigan, Ann Arbor.
2002 Projectile points from the Sheguiandah site. In *The Sheguiandah Site: Archaeological, Geological and Paleobotanical Studies at a Paleoindian Site on Manitoulin Island, Ontario*, edited by Patrick J. Julig, pp. 139–54. Mercury Series, Archaeological Survey of Canada Paper 161. Canadian Museum of Civilization, Hull, Quebec.
2004 *Journey to the Ice Age: Discovering an Ancient World*. University of British Columbia Press in association with the Royal Ontario Museum, Vancouver and Toronto.

Storck, Peter L., and Arthur E. Spiess
1994 The significance of new faunal identifications attributed to an Early Paleoindian (Gainey complex) occupation at the Udora site, Ontario, Canada. *American Antiquity* 59(1):121–42.

Storck, P. L., and Peter H. von Bitter
1989 The geological age and occurrence of Fossil Hill formation chert: Implications for Early Paleoindian settlement patterns. In *Eastern Paleoindian Lithic Resource Use*, edited by C. Ellis and J. Lothrop, pp. 165–89. Westview Press, Boulder, Colorado.

Stout, B.
1996 Smart moves: Intelligent pathfinding. *Game Developer* October/November 1996:28–35.

Stringer, C., and C. Gamble
1993 *Search of the Neanderthals: Solving the Puzzle of Human Origins*. Thames and Hudson, New York.

Sundstrom, L.
2000 Cheyenne pronghorn procurement and ceremony. In *Pronghorn Past and Present: Archaeology, Ethnography, and Biology*, edited by J. V. Pastor and P. M. Lubinski, pp. 119–32. Plains Anthropologist Memoir, Vol. 32. Plains Anthropological Society, Lincoln, Nebraska.

Svoboda, J., S. Péan, and P. Wojtal
2005 Mammoth bone deposits and subsistence practices during mid-upper Palaeolithic in central Europe: Three cases from Moravia and Poland. *Quaternary International* 126–128:209–21.

Taylor, E.
1920 *Primitive Culture*, Vol. 1, p. 1. J. P. Putnam's Sons, New York.

Taylor, J. G., and William Turner
1969 William Turner's journey to the caribou country with the Labrador Eskimos in 1780. *Ethnohistory* 16(2):141–64.

Teller, J. T., and D. W. Leverington
2004 Glacial Lake Agassiz: A 5000 year history of change and its relationship to the $\delta^{18}O$ record of Greenland. *Geological Society of America Bulletin* 116:729–42.

Teller, J. T., D. W. Leverington, and J. D. Mann
2002 Freshwater outbursts to the oceans from glacial Lake Agassiz and their role in climatic change during the last deglaciation. *Quaternary Science Reviews* 21:879–87.

Thacker, Paul
1997 The significance of *Rangifer* as a human prey species during the central European upper Paleolithic. In *Caribou and Reindeer Hunters of the Northern Hemisphere*, edited by Lawrence J. Jackson and Paul T. Thacker, pp. 82–104. Avebury, Brookfield, Vermont.

Thomas, Richard L., A. L. W. Kemp, and Christopher F. M. Lewis
1973 The surficial sediments of Lake Huron. *Canadian Journal of Earth Sciences* 10:226–71.

Thorleifson, L. H., and F. J. Kristjansson
1993 *Quaternary Geology and Drift Prospecting, Beardmore-Geraldton Area, Ontario*. Geological Survey of Canada, Memoir 435. Ottawa.

Timmermans, S.
1999 The Southwinds site: A Late Paleo-Indian 'Hi-Ho' encampment in Middlesex County. *Kewa Newsletter of the London Chapter, Ontario Archaeological Society* 99(8):4–14. London.

Timmins, P.
1995 Stelco 1: A Late Paleo-Indian Hi-Lo site in the region of Haldimand-Norfolk. *Kewa Newsletter of the London Chapter, Ontario Archaeological Society* 95(5):2–22. London.

Todd, L. C., D. C. Jones, R. S. Walker, P. C. Burnett, and J. Eighmy
2001 Late Archaic bison hunters in northern Colorado. *Plains Anthropologist* 46(176):125–47.

Todorov, Milcho, Vassil Golemansky, Edward A. D. Mitchell, and Thierry J. Heger
2009 Morphology, biometry, and taxonomy of freshwater and marine interstitial *Cyphoderia* (Cercozoa: Euglyphida). *The Journal of Eukaryotic Microbiology* 56(3):279–89.

Tulurialik, Ruth Annaqtuusi, and David F. Pelly
1986 *Qikaaluktut, Images of Inuit Life*. Oxford University Press, Toronto.

Turner, T. Edward, and Graeme T. Swindles
2012 Ecology of testate amoebae in moorland with a complex fire history: Implications for ecosystem monitoring and sustainable land management. *Protist* 163:844–55.

Vallee, Frank G., Derek G. Smith, and Joseph D. Cooper
1984 Contemporary Canadian Inuit. In *Handbook of North American Indians*. Vol. 5, *Arctic*, edited by D. Damas, pp. 662–75. Smithsonian Institution, Washington, D.C.

Van Berg, P. L., M. Vander Linden, S. Lemaître, N. Cauwe, and V. Picalause
2004 Desert-kites of the Hemma plateau (Hassake, Syria). *Paléorient* 30(1):89–99.

Vitale, K.
2009 Learning Group Behavior in Games Using Cultural Algorithms and the Land Bridge Simulation Example. Master's thesis, Wayne State University, Detroit, Michigan.

Von Bitter, Peter
2002 The geological history of an important Palaeoindian manufacturing site: Sheguiandah, Manitoulin Island. In *The Sheguiandah Site: Archaeological, Geological and Paleobotanical Studies at a Paleoindian Site on Manitoulin Island, Ontario*, edited by Patrick J. Julig. Mercury Series, Archaeological Survey of Canada Paper 161. Canadian Museum of Civilization, Hull, Quebec.

Walls, Matthew
2009 *Caribou Inuit Traders of the Kivalliq, Nunavut, Canada*. BAR International Series 1895. Archaeopress, Oxford.

Walters, Carl J., R. Hilborn, and R. Peterman
1975 Computer simulation of barren-ground caribou dynamics. *Ecological Modeling* 1:303–15.

Webb, T., III, B. Shuman, and J. W. Williams
2004 Climatically forced vegetation dynamics in eastern North America during the late Quaternary period. In *The Quaternary Period in the United States*, edited by A. R. Gillespie, S. C. Porter, and B. F. Atwater, pp. 459–78. Developments in Quaternary Science, I. Elsevier, New York.

White, R.
1989 Husbandry and herd control in the upper Paleolithic: A critical review of the evidence. *Current Anthropology* 30(5):609–32.

Wilke, P. J.
2013 The Whiskey Flat pronghorn trap complex, Mineral County, Nevada, western United States: Preliminary report. *Quaternary International* 297:79–92.

Wilson, Aaron K., and Jeffery T. Rasic
2008 Northern Archaic settlement and subsistence patterns at Agiak Lake, Brooks Range, Alaska. *Arctic Anthropology* 45(2):128–45.

Wobst, H. Martin
2011 Epilogue. In *Hunter Gatherer Archaeology as Historic Process*, edited by K. E. Sassaman and D. H. Holly Jr., pp. 248–57. University of Arizona Press, Tucson.

Woodley, P. J.
1996 The Early Archaic occupation of the Laphroaig site, Brant County, Ontario. *Ontario Archaeology* 62:39–62. Toronto.
1997 The Witz and Koeppe II sites, Ancaster, and the Hi-Lo occupation of southern Ontario. In *Preceramic Southern Ontario*, edited by P. Woodley and P. Ramsden, pp. 149–71. Occasional Papers in Northeastern Archaeology, No. 9. Copetown Press, NL.

Yansa, C. H., and T. G. Fisher
2007 Absence of a Younger Dryas signal along the southern shoreline of glacial Lake Agassiz in North Dakota during the Moorhead phase (12,600–11,200 CALYBP). *Current Research in the Pleistocene* 24:24–28.

Zeder, Z., G. Bar-Oz, S. Rufolo, and F. Hole
2013 New perspectives on the use of kites in mass-kills of Levantine gazelle: A view from northeastern Syria. *Quaternary International* 297:110–25.

Zobrist, A.
1969 A model of visual organization for the game of GO. In *Proceedings of the May 14–16, 1969, Spring Joint Computer Conference*, pp. 103–12. New York, New York.

Plate 1. Serious Game Modeling of Caribou Behavior *(see Chapter 4)*

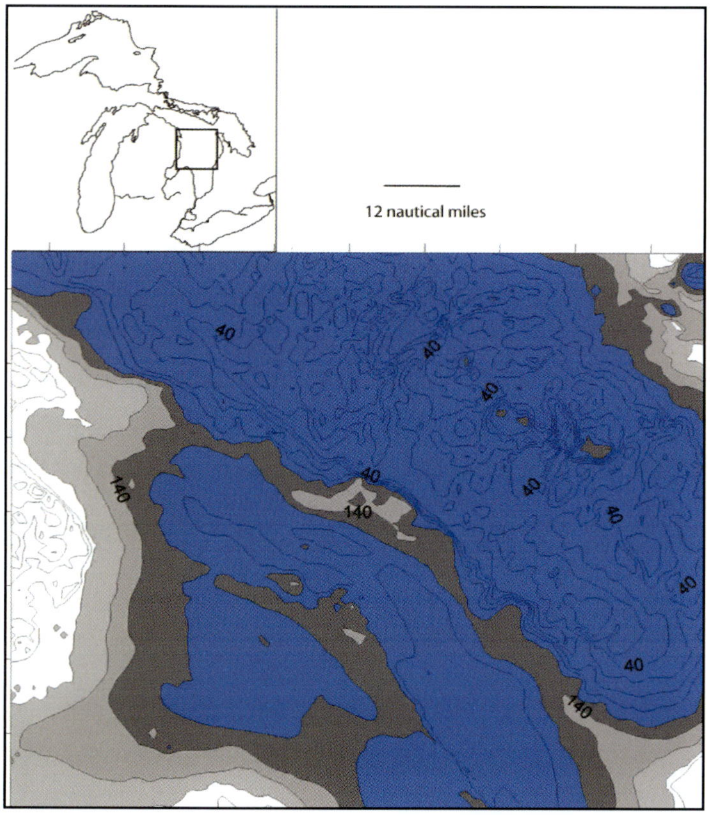

(above) Caribou herd movement through the virtual landscape. The herd in the lead is clearly emphasizing movement to the goal location while others are moving closer to the edge of the dense vegetation to facilitate foraging and are moving slower.

(left) Alpena-Amberley land bridge across Lake Huron as represented in the virtual world here. The lighter the color, the higher the elevation above the lake floor.

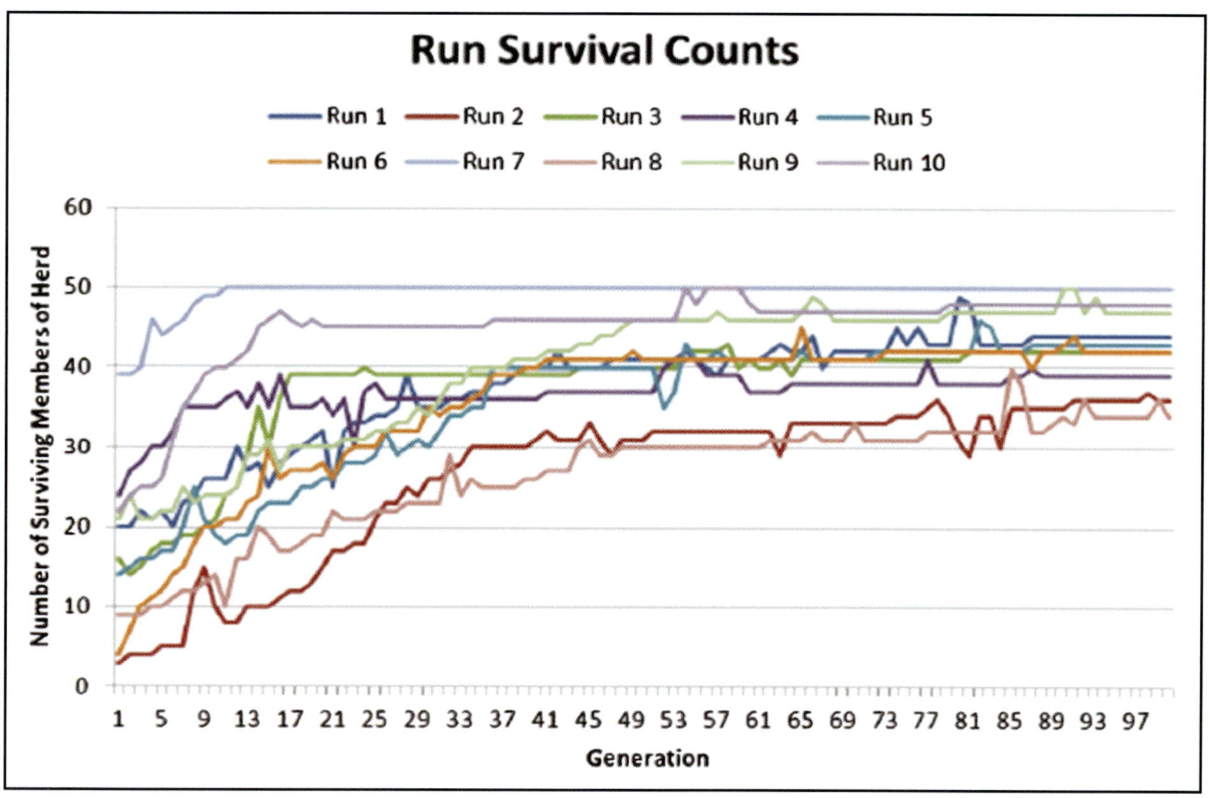

The comparison between the learning curves for each of the 10 runs. Those runs that are able to produce herds that minimize herd loss during the traversal process, such as 7 and 10, emphasize goal direction over browsing. Those that are more likely to be depleted, such as run 2, conversely emphasize browsing over final location goal.

Plate 2. Sheguiandah Site *(see Chapter 5)*

(left) View of test pit location from Swamp 4 of the Sheguiandah site (taken in 2013). Although described as Swamp 4 by Lee (1955), this is actually a small flat shallow depression in the quartzite bedrock ridge of the site, protected by knobs.

(below) Quartzite scrapers showing staining from overlying peat deposits.

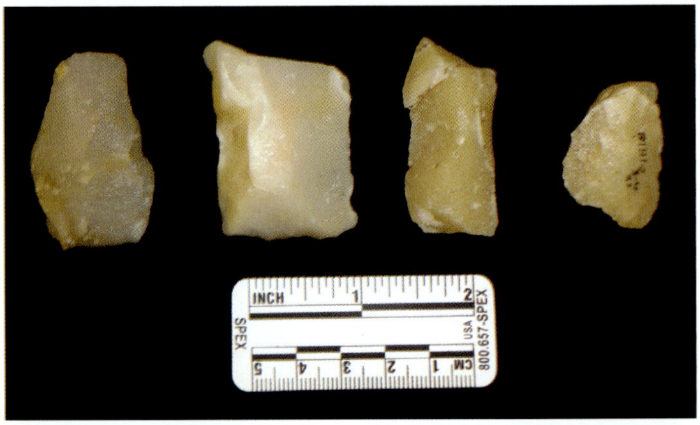

Sheguiandah quartzite. *top row (left to right)*, blade, backed blade, and backed side scraper; *bottom row*, backed side scrapers.

Sheguiandah quartzite. *top row*, blades; *bottom row*, large flake cutting tools with burins.

Plate 3. Southern Huron Basin *(see Chapter 6)*

Southern Huron basin chert sources.

Collingwood chert Archaic period bifaces from southwestern Ontario.

Deavitt lanceolates from the Heaman site and vicinity.

Plate 4. Lower Kazan River Boulder Features *(see Chapter 8)*

Continuous rock ring or arc feature: heavy tent ring of large boulders.

Twinned boulder lines. Brian Ookowt is at the far end of a double line of rocks.

Cobble clusters: white quartzite toolstone caches (right foreground and where Roy Avaala is pointing).

Plate 5. Constructed Features on the Alpena-Amberley Ridge *(see Chapters 9 and 10)*

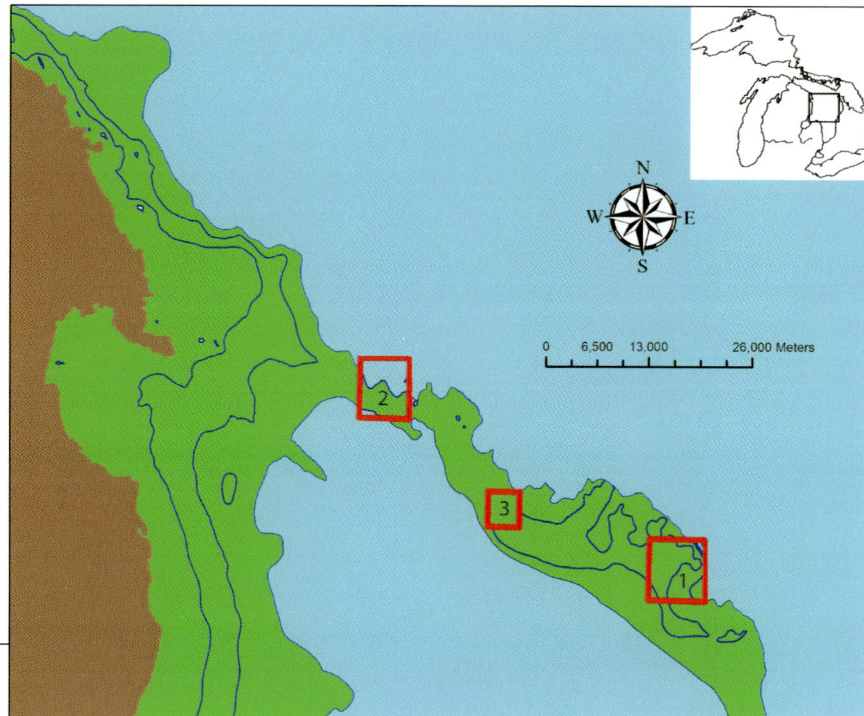

Location of principal research areas overlain on the exposed landform of the American portion of the Alpena-Amberley Ridge. Dark brown area is the modern land surface, while the blue areas were underwater during the Lake Stanley stage (less than 140 m amsl). Contour interval is 10 m.

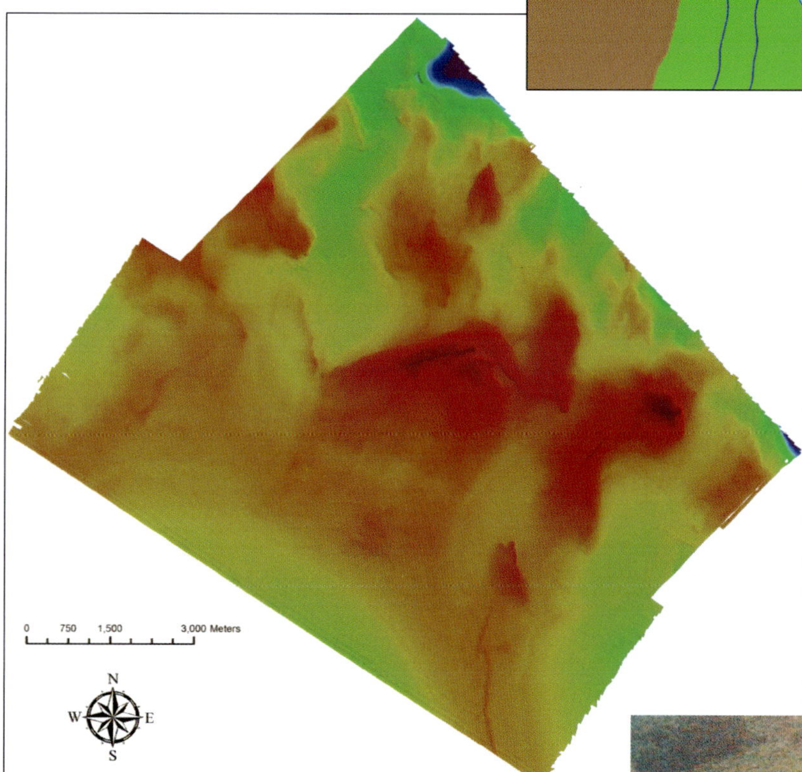

Multibeam sonar image of Area 1 and adjacent bottom areas. Redder colors denote shallower depths. The central limestone ridge creating Six Fathom Shoal is prominent in the center of the image.

A V structure from the Gap locality in Area 3. The "V" is oriented to the north and is located at a depth of 32 m. The orange object in the center of the "V" marks the location of a bottom sample.

Plate 6. Constructed Features on the Alpena-Amberley Ridge *(see Chapter 10)*

The Dragon Blind in Area 1 is associated with a long drive lane. This photograph shows these stones, along with a series of small rocks around the perimeter. The upward tilt of the main stones is visible in this photo.

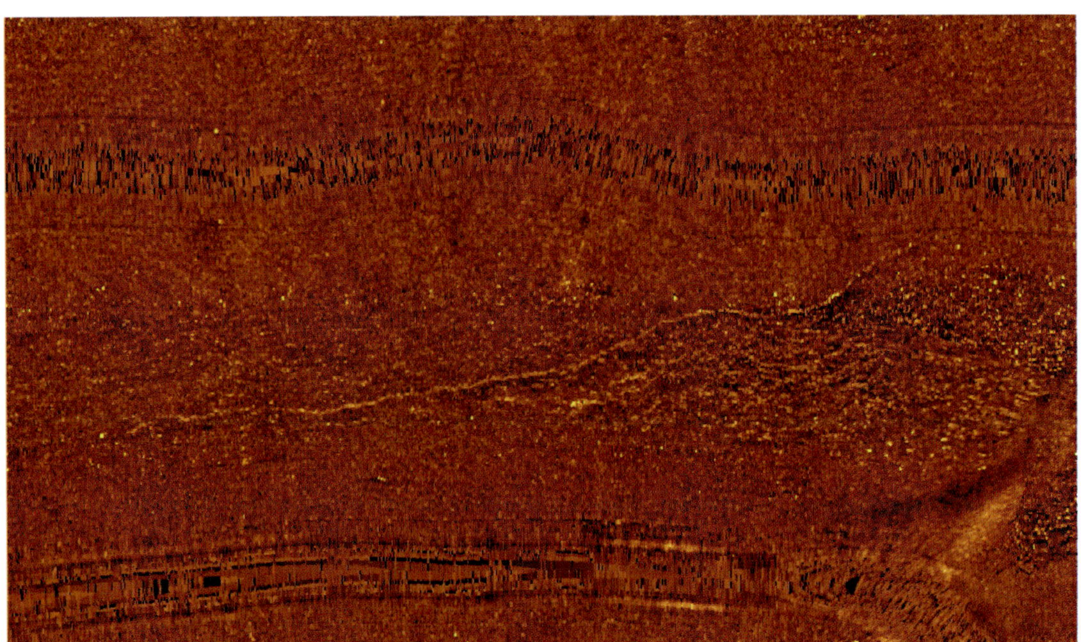

A sonar mosaic of the Dragon Drive Lane. This feature in Area 1 consists of a long linear stone feature, with several associated stone cairns, and at least one hunting blind (the Dragon Blind).

Plate 7. Constructed Features on the Alpena-Amberley Ridge *(see Chapter 10)*

A view of the linear rock line of the Dragon Drive Lane as viewed from the Dragon Blind. It should be noted that the compass rose on the image is inverted and the actual view is to the south.

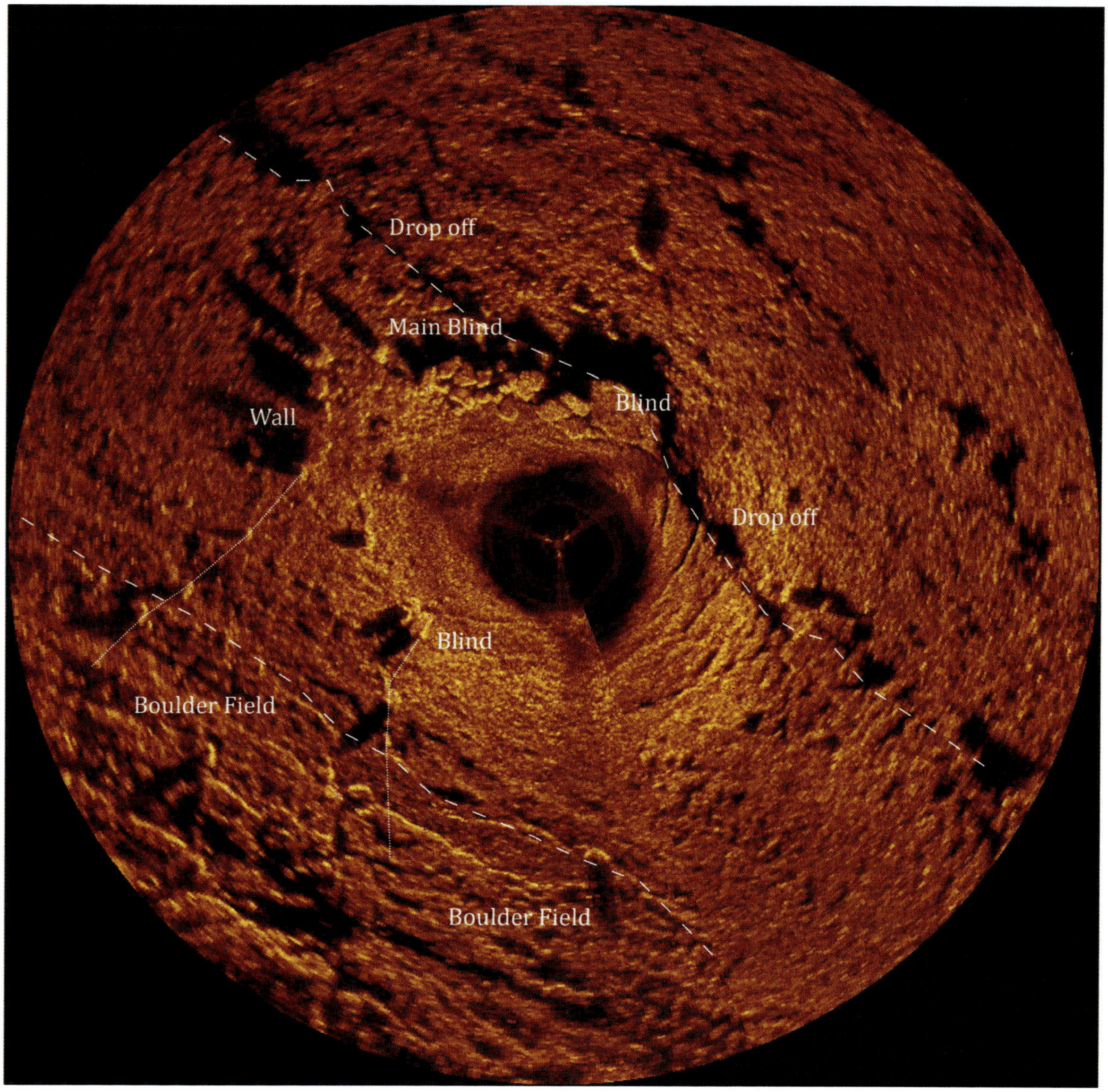

Scanning sonar image of the Funnel Drive in Area 1. The dark circular area in the center of the image is the location of the tripod suspending the scanning sonar head.

Plate 8. Constructed Features on the Alpena-Amberley Ridge *(see Chapter 10)*

The main blind of the Funnel Drive looking north.

The gap produced by the convergence of the main blind and stone line at the Funnel Drive. Note that a large stone has been placed in the center of the opening. Divers in the center of the photo are collecting bottom samples. Photo courtesy of Tane Casserley of the Thunder Bay National Marine Sanctuary.

Plate 9. Constructed Features on the Alpena-Amberley Ridge *(see Chapter 10)*

Photograph of line of spaced boulders extending out from main wall of Funnel Drive.

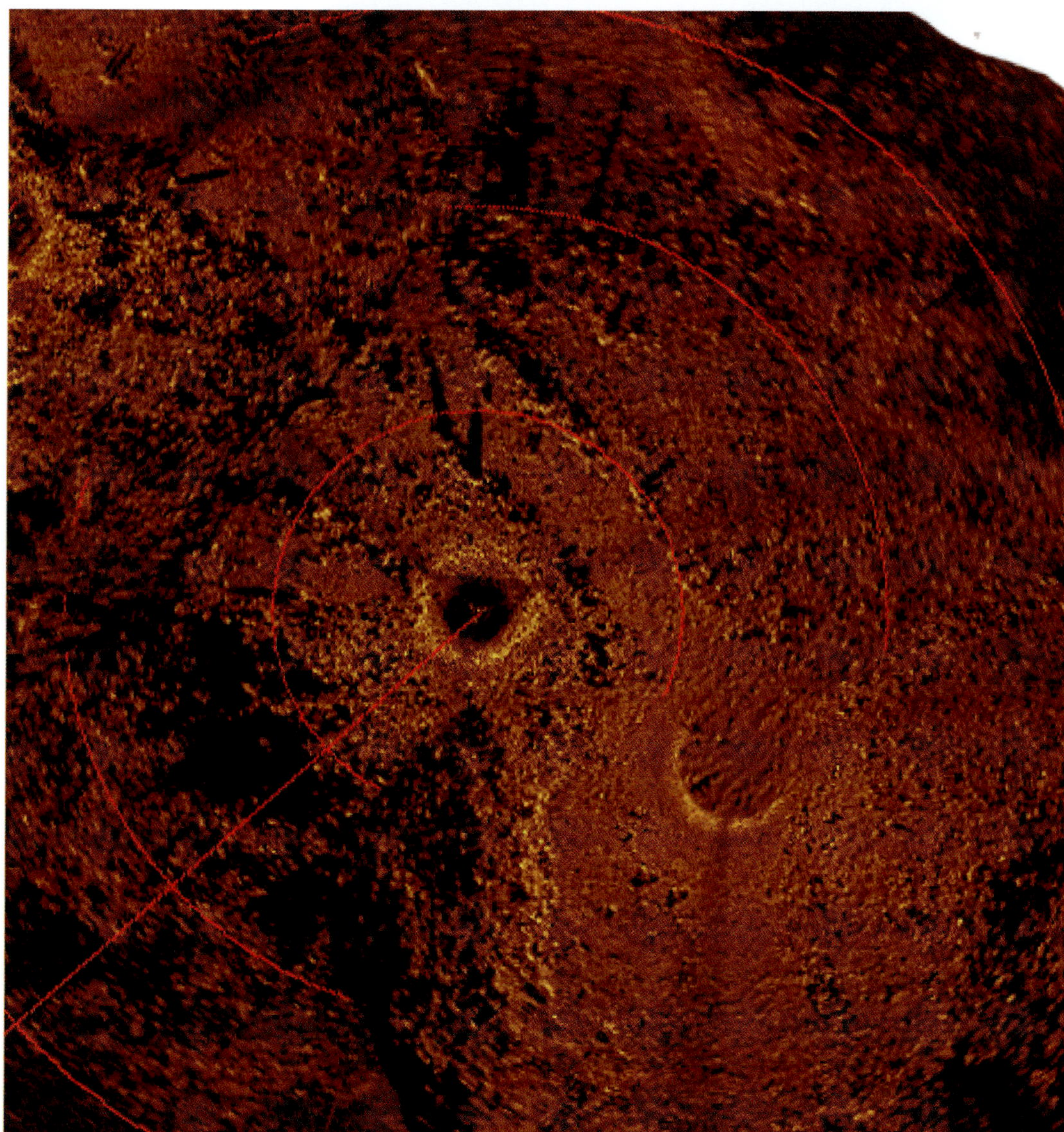

Drop 45 Drive Lane in Overlook locality of Area 3: a mosaic of two scanning sonar images. Red arcs in scan image are spaced at 15 m intervals out from the central scan location.

Plate 10. Constructed Features on the Alpena-Amberley Ridge *(see Chapter 10)*

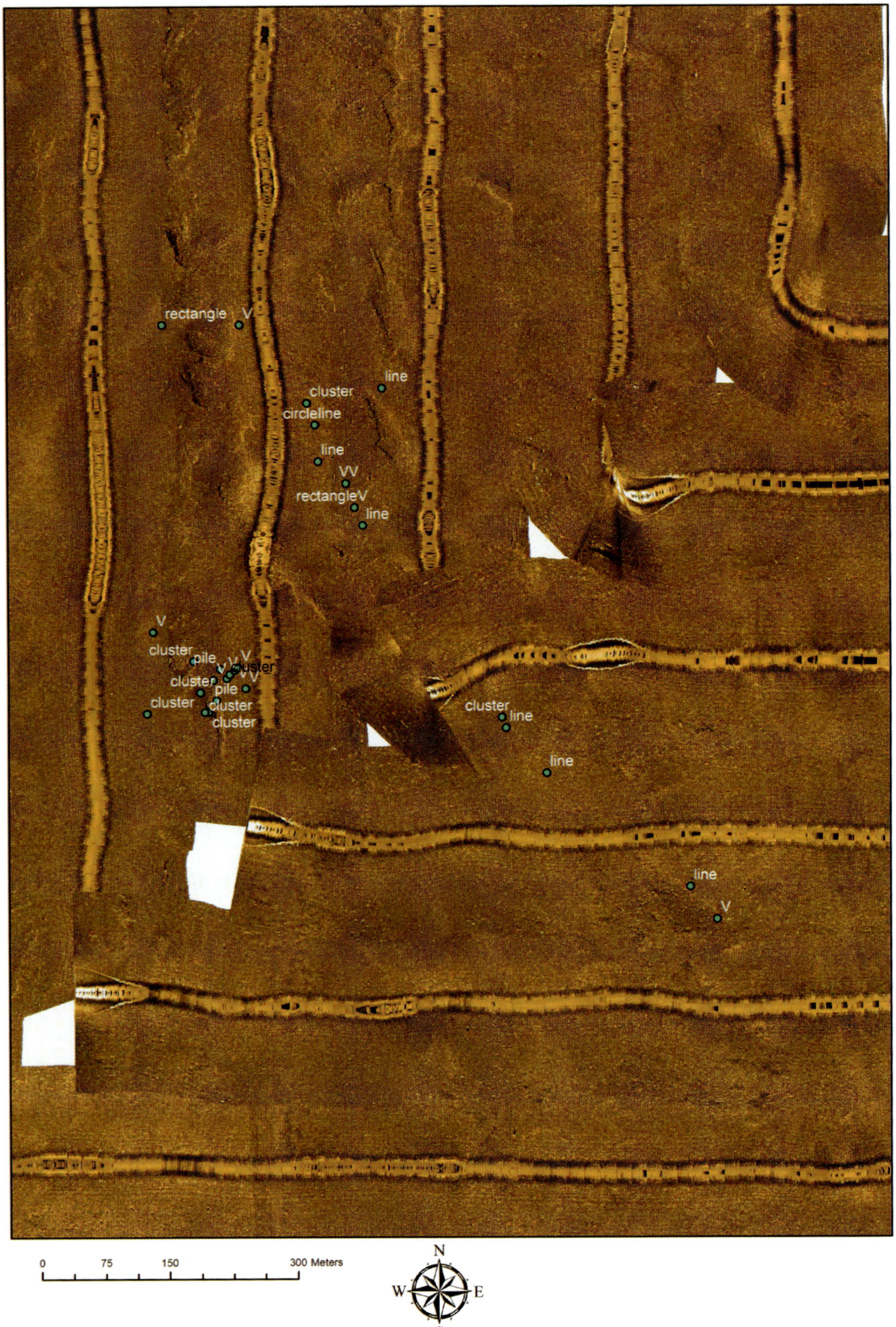

The Gap locality in Area 3, showing the main concentrations of features identified. Distribution is overlain on a side scan sonar mosaic of the locality. Channeling glacial deposits are in clear evidence in the areas of main feature concentration.

Plate 11. Constructed Features on the Alpena-Amberley Ridge *(see Chapter 10)*

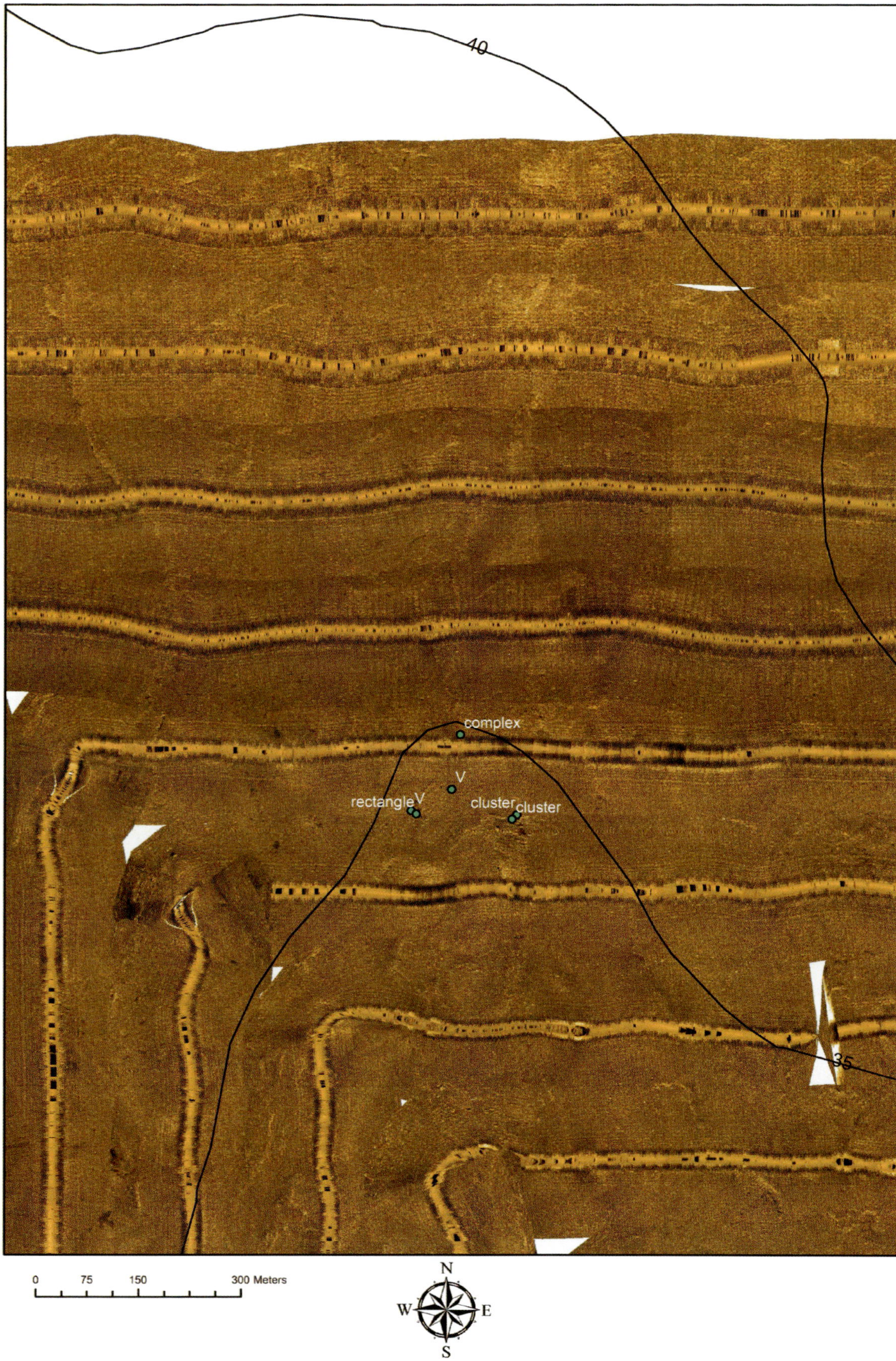

The Overlook locality in Area 3 showing the locations of structures near the top of the ridge. The distribution is overlain on a side scan sonar mosaic of the locality. Contour interval is 5 m reported in depth below surface.

Plate 12. Constructed Features on the Alpena-Amberley Ridge *(see Chapter 10)*

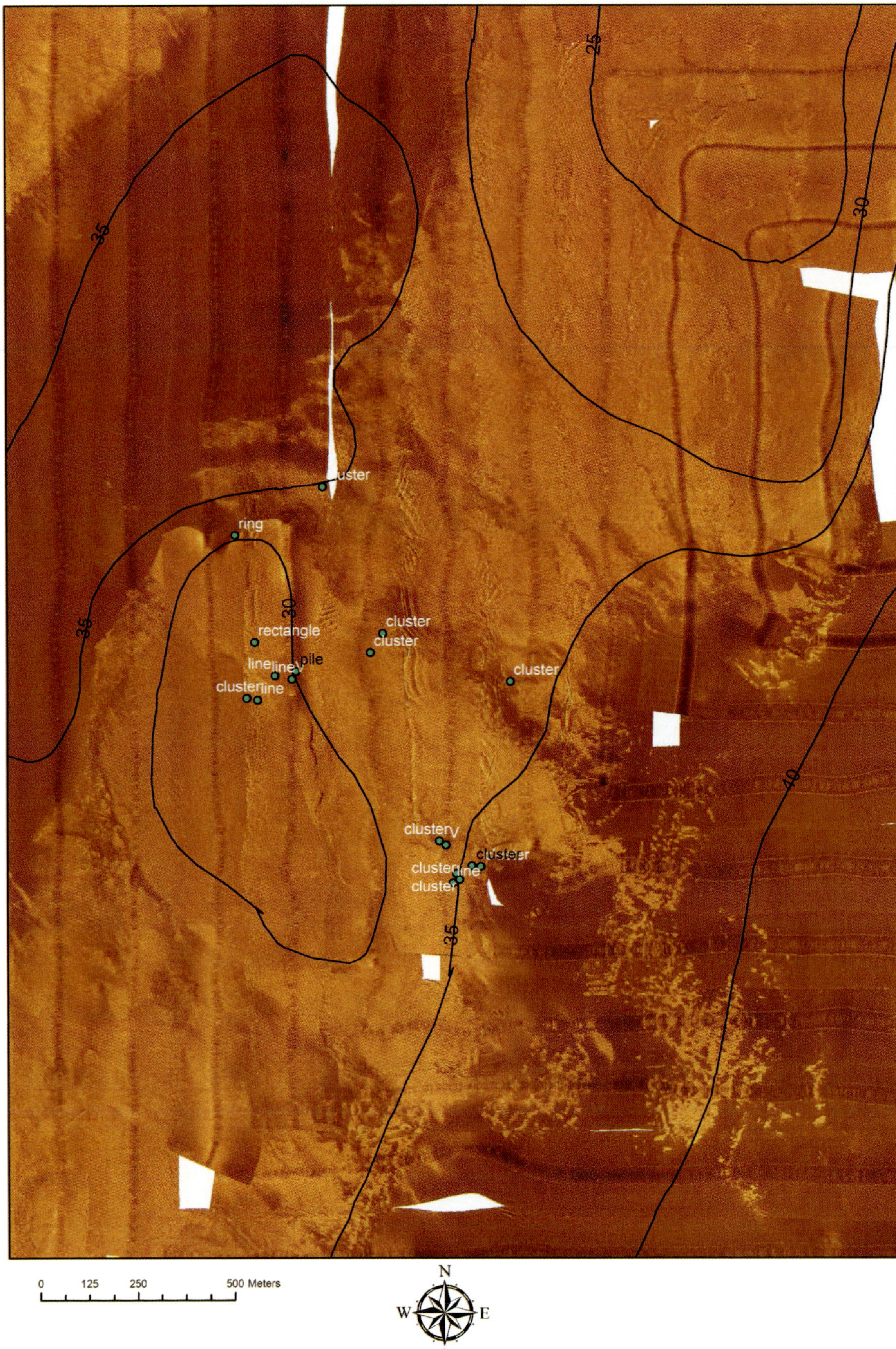

The Crossing locality in Area 1 showing the location of identified features. The distribution is overlain on a side scan sonar mosaic of the locality. Dark areas in the side scan image are areas of sand that would have been underwater during the occupation of the AAR. Contour interval is 5 m reported in depth below surface.

Plate 13. Constructed Features on the Alpena-Amberley Ridge *(see Chapter 10)*

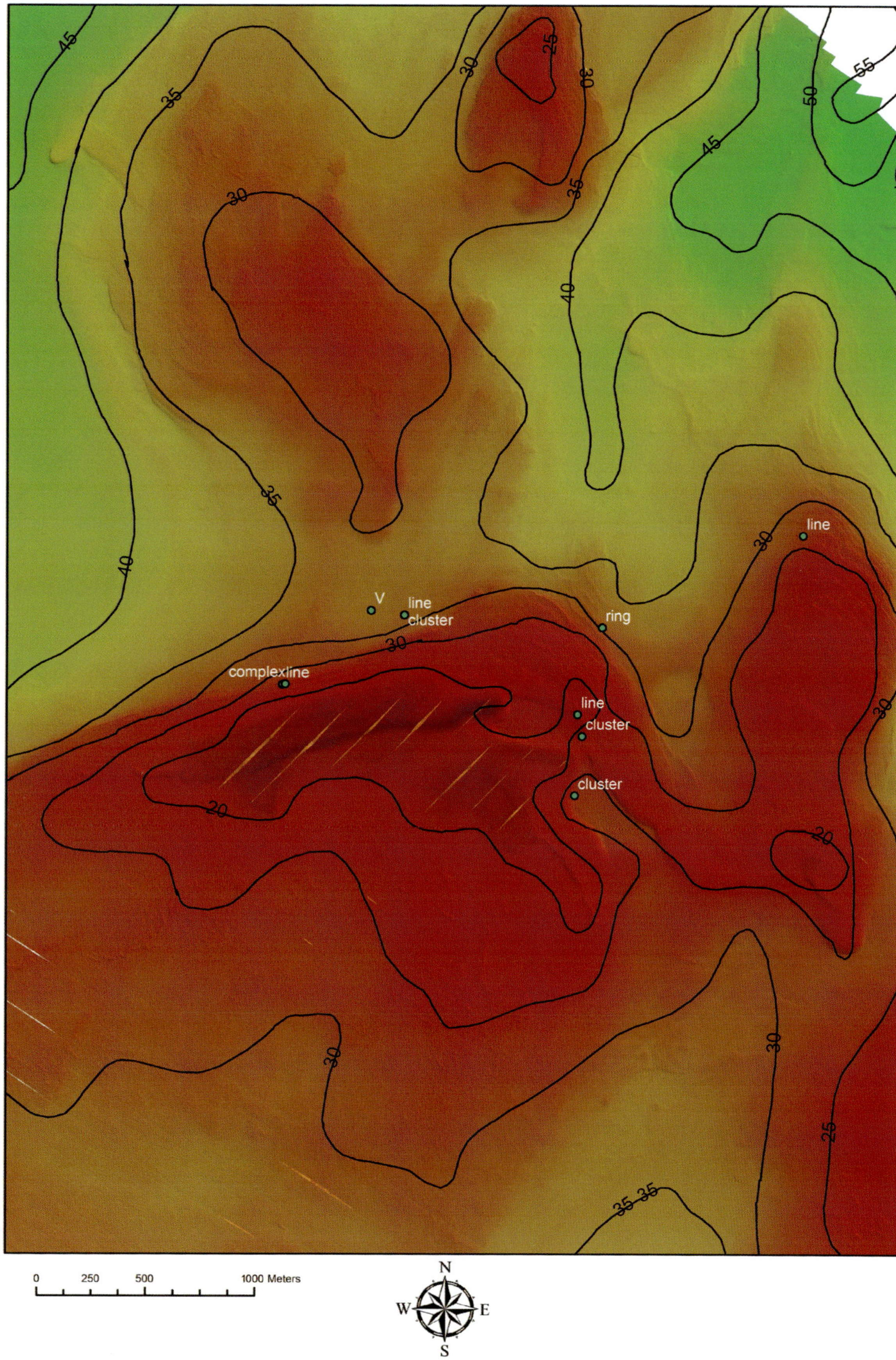

The Dragon locality in Area 1 showing the location of identified features. The distribution is overlain on a multibeam sonar mosaic of depth. The contour interval is 5 m reported in depth below surface. The location labeled "complex line" is the Funnel Drive.

Plate 14. Lithic Artifacts from the Alpena-Amberley Ridge *(see Chapter 11)*

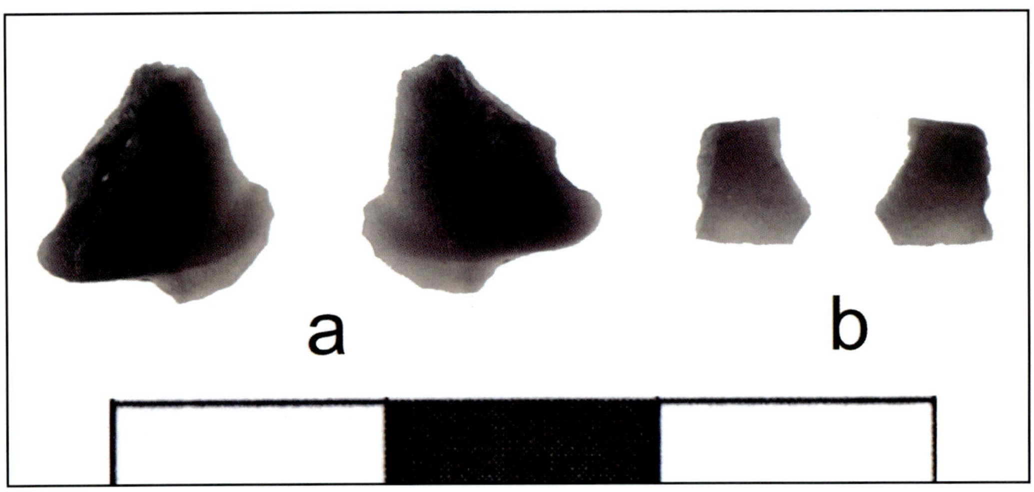

(top left) DE-1a flake from the Crossing locality, Area 1.

(top right) Vial 1a flake from the Crossing locality, Area 1.

(above left) DA-1-1a and DA-1-1b lithic artifacts from the Gap locality, Area 3.

(left) Thumbnail scraper on Bayport chert from the Drop 45 site.

Scale bar is in centimeters.

Plate 15. Lithic Artifacts from the Alpena-Amberley Ridge *(see Chapter 11)*

Flakes and debitage from the Drop 45 site.

top row (left to right), specimen numbers DP-1-1a, EG-1-2b, EG-1-2a, EO-1-2a, FA-1-2a, FB-1-1a

bottom row (left to right), specimen numbers DP-1-1b, Unit 1a, EZ-1a, EO-1-2b, FE-1-2b, FE-1-2a, Unit 8a

Scale bar is in centimeters.

Map of the Crossing locality, Area 1. Background image is a sidescan sonar mosaic; crosshairs indicate lithic artifacts, stars indicate stone constructions, and small shaded circles are sample locations that did not produce cultural materials.

Plate 16. Lithic Artifacts (*see Chapter 11*); Hunters and Hunting on the Ridge (*see Chapter 14*)

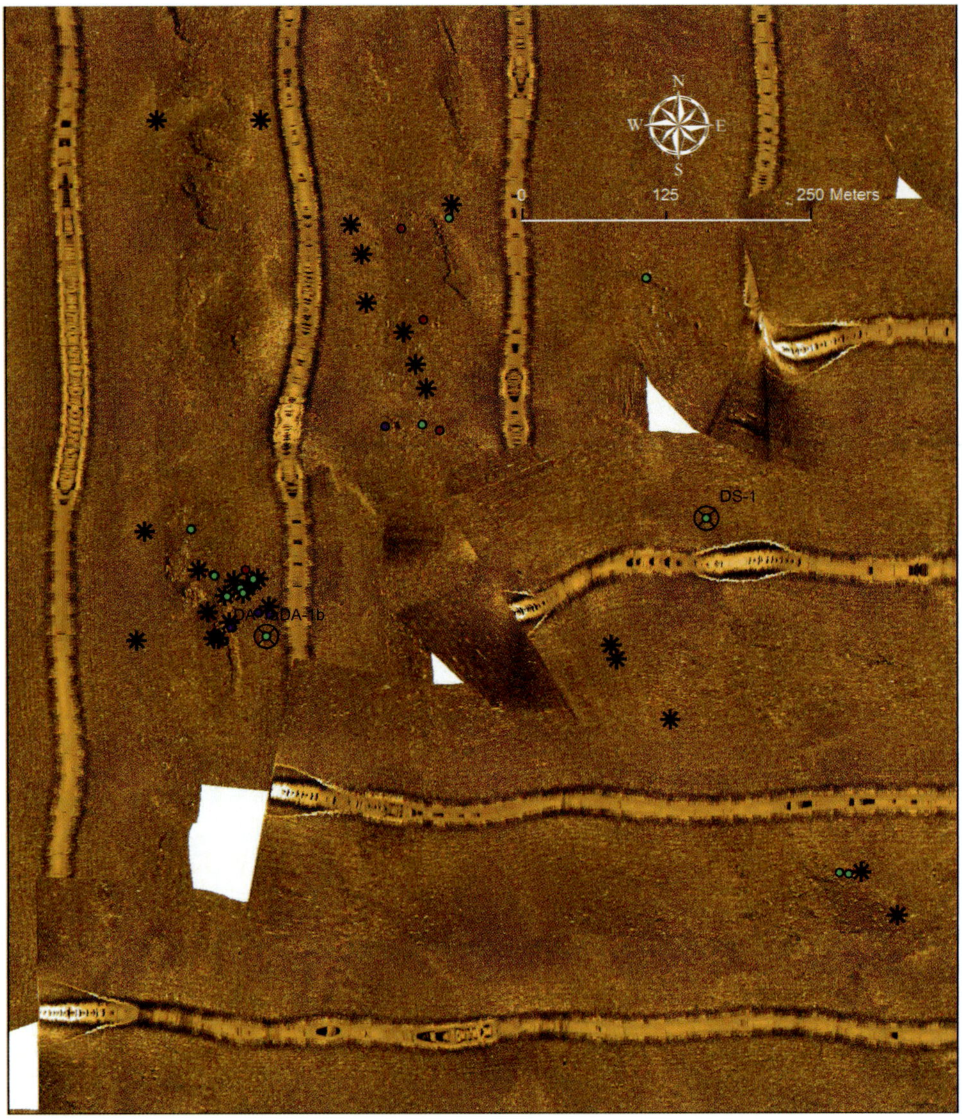

(*left*) Map of Gap locality, Area 3. Background image is a sidescan sonar mosaic; crosshairs indicate lithic artifacts, stars indicate stone constructions, and small shaded circles are sample locations that did not produce cultural materials. DS-1 indicates a sample that contained microdebitage (lithic artifacts less than 1 mm).

(*below left*) Seasonal occupations on the American portion of the Alpena-Amberley Ridge and predicted locations of major cultural features. Darkest brown areas indicate current land surfaces; lighter brown indicates areas that would have been dry land during Lake Stanley.

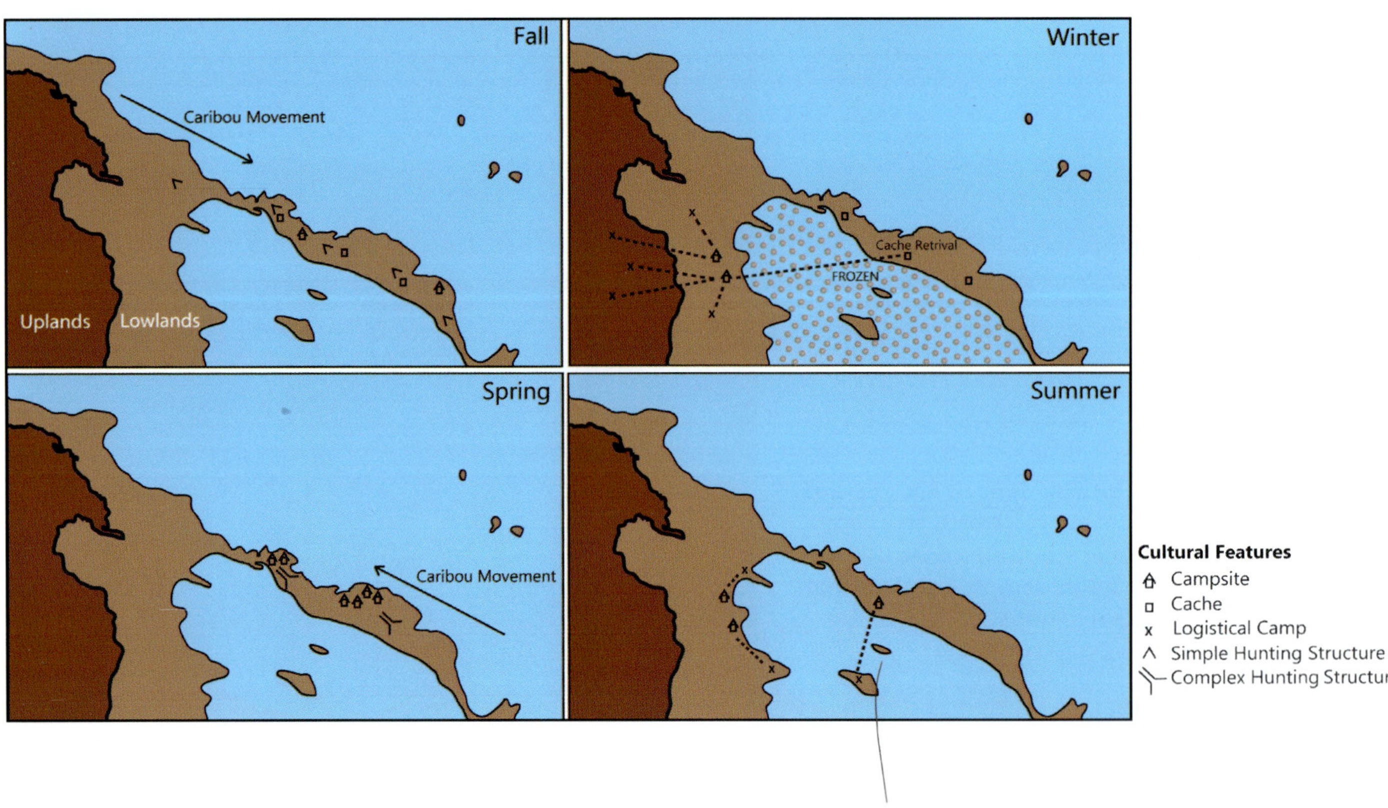